Social Scienc
Research Design
and Statistics

A Practitioner's Guide to Research
Methods and SPSS Analysis

Alfred P. Rovai, Ph.D.
Regent University
Virginia Beach, VA 23464

Jason D. Baker, Ph.D.
Regent University
Virginia Beach, VA 23464

Michael K. Ponton, Ed.D.
Regent University
Virginia Beach, VA 23464

WATERTREE PRESS

Social Science Research Design and Statistics
A Practitioner's Guide to Research Methods and SPSS Analysis

First Edition (Paperback)

Copyright ©2013 by Alfred P. Rovai, Jason D. Baker, and Michael K. Ponton

Published by Watertree Press LLC
PO Box 16763, Chesapeake, VA 23328
http://www.watertreepress.com

ISBN: 978-0-9787186-7-1 (paperback)

Library of Congress Control Number: 2012943871

Publisher's Cataloging-in-Publication Data

Rovai, Alfred P.
   Social science research design and statistics: a practitioner's guide to research methods and SPSS analysis / Alfred P. Rovai, Jason D. Baker, Michael K. Ponton — First Edition
      p. cm.
   Includes bibliographical references, glossary, and index.
   Contents: Social science research methods and statistical analysis using SPSS software
      — Research designs, threats to validity, descriptive and inferential statistics, evaluation
      of test assumptions, and interpretation of statistical results.
   ISBN: 978-0-9787186-7-1 (pbk.)
   1. Social science—Statistical methods—Computer programs. 2. Social science—
Research—Methodology.   I. Baker, Jason D.   II. Ponton, Michael K.   III. Title.
   HA32.R68 2013
   300.285'555—dc22

                                    2012943871

Printed in the United States of America

Contents

Preface

"A judicious man uses statistics, not to get knowledge, but to save himself from having ignorance foisted upon him."

Thomas Carlyle, Scottish historian and essayist, 1795-1881

Purpose

This book was developed to serve multiple purposes.

- As a planning guide for professionals engaged in active research involving the design and execution of quantitative, qualitative, and mixed methods research in the social sciences.

- As a reference book for university courses in social science research methods and statistics.

- As a study guide for undergraduate and graduate students to assist in preparing for research and statistics examinations.

- As a manual to assist in the preparation of scholarly journal articles, research proposals, and reports, to include dissertations and theses, and to assist SPSS users in the selection of statistical tests, evaluation of test assumptions, and interpretation of SPSS outputs.

- As an aid for decision makers requiring background information in order to evaluate social science research reports and program evaluations.

This book integrates social science research methods and the descriptions of 46 univariate, bivariate, and multivariate tests to include a description of the purpose, assumptions, example research question and hypothesis, SPSS procedure, and interpretation of SPSS output for each test. Included throughout the book are various sidebars highlighting key points, images and SPSS screenshots to assist understanding the material presented, self-test reviews at the end of each chapter, a decision tree to facilitate identification of the proper statistical test, examples of SPSS output with accompanying analysis and interpretations, links to relevant web sites, and a comprehensive glossary. Underpinning all these features is a concise, easy to understand explanation of the material.

This book does not focus on mathematical underpinnings nor does it present a tutorial on basic SPSS software usage. Rather, it assumes the reader has a working knowledge of research design, statistics, and SPSS software as it presents a pragmatic treatment of social science research methods, including evaluation research, and describes how to interpret SPSS outputs. It assumes the reader has background knowledge of research methods, statistics, and SPSS and has access to SPSS statistical software.

IBM SPSS version 20 was used to produce the SPSS output presented in this book. This version includes newer menu items but allows users to access menu items of earlier SPSS versions by way of SPSS legacy dialogs. For example, the legacy dialogs under SPSS > Graphs > Legacy Dialogs allow one to select the limited charts within the IBM SPSS that were available in earlier versions of SPSS. However, SPSS version 20 includes Chart Builder as a graphics engine that offers SPSS users more flexibility in graphing.

In addition to this paperback version, searchable electronic versions of this book incorporating various elements of interactivity to include hyperlinks are available from e-book stores for use with various electronic devices. Users of any version are encouraged to provide the authors with feedback to include recommendations regarding possible changes and additions for future editions.

Outline of Chapters

Chapter 1 – Introduction

- Purpose of research

- Research Traditions to include new trends in research

- Research ethics to include the importance of ethical research, characteristics of ethical research, and institutional review boards

Chapter 2 – Qualitative Research

- Basic concepts to include assumptions, sampling, qualitative designs, and central questions
- Qualitative research tools to include data collection, question construction, data analysis, and reporting the findings
- Threats to validity

Chapter 3 – Quantitative Research

- Basic concepts to include assumptions, constructs, sampling, scaling, scales of measurement, and measurement validity
- The normal distribution and normal curve transformations
- Item and test analysis
- Statistical abbreviations and symbols
- Quantitative research design to include descriptive designs, correlational designs, experimental designs, quasi-experimental designs, pre-experimental designs, single case designs, and mixed methods designs
- Quantitative research proposals and reports
- Threats to validity

Chapter 4 – Evaluation Research

- Evaluation types, formative evaluations, summative evaluations, and evaluation strategies
- Evaluation framework and evaluations questions
- Outline of an evaluability assessment

Chapter 5 – Descriptive Statistics

- Data with missing values and data preparation
- Measures of central tendency
- Measures of dispersion
- Measures of relative position

- Graphs and charts

Chapter 6 – Inferential Statistics

- Basic concepts to include types of variables, estimation, central limit theorem, confidence intervals, hypothesis testing, and probability theory

- Evaluating test assumptions to include dealing with deviations

- Interactive test decision tree

Chapter 7 – Goodness of Fit Tests

- Overview

- Explanations of when and how to use six goodness of fit tests and how to interpret the results of each test: chi-square goodness of fit test, binomial test, one-sample Kolmogorov-Smirnov test, one-sample Shapiro-Wilk test, Wald-Wolfowitz runs test, and one-sample *t*-test

Chapter 8 – Difference Tests

- Overview to include multivariate tests, factorial designs, post hoc multiple comparison tests, contrasts, and controlling Type I error

- Explanations of when and how to use 15 difference tests and how to interpret the results of each test: McNemar test, related samples sign test, Wilcoxon signed ranks test, Cochran's *Q* test, Mann-Whitney *U* test, median test, Kruskal-Wallis *H* test, Friedman test, Levene's test of equality of variances, independent *t*-test, dependent *t*-test, between subjects analysis of variance, within subjects analysis of variance, multivariate analysis of variance, and analysis of covariance

Chapter 9 – Correlation and Prediction Tests

- Overview to include correlation, reliability, regression, and cross-validation

- Explanations of when and how to use 25 correlation and regression tests and how to interpret the results of each test: Pearson chi-square contingency table analysis, relative risk, phi, Cramer's *V*, lambda, contingency coefficient, eta correlation coefficient, Spearman rank order correlation coefficient, gamma, Somers' *d*, Kendall's tau-*b*, Kendall's tau-*c*, intraclass correlation coefficient, binomial logistic regression, Cohen's kappa measure of agreement, Pearson product-moment correlation coefficient (Pearson's *r*), internal consistency reliability analysis (Cronbach's alpha, split-half, Guttman, parallel, strict parallel), point-biserial correlation coefficient, partial correlation, bivariate regression, multiple regression and correlation, discriminant analysis, principal components and factor analysis, canonical correlation analysis, and two-step cluster analysis

Alfred P. Rovai, Ph.D.
Jason D. Baker, Ph.D.
Michael K. Ponton, Ed.D.

Chapter 1: Introduction

Social research is, by definition, research that is focused on people. Such research is used within the social sciences to increase our understanding of human behavior, improve professional practice and policies, and generally enhance our knowledge of people.

1.1: Social Research

Introduction

Humans are inquisitive creatures. From our youngest days, we engage with the world around us and attempt to make meaning out of our sensory experiences. As we grow, we realize that there are a variety of sources of knowledge from which we can learn. As children, we learn much simply by listening to authority figures, whether parents, teachers, or other adults. While authoritative statements are enough at first, a natural curiosity begs for more clarification beyond indicative and imperative statements. Stories, folk tales, traditions, and other resources passed through the generations enhance our knowledge base. Mastering literacy opens up realms of knowledge beyond the immediate and enable us to learn from thinkers and writers from a wide array of backgrounds, cultures, and time periods, and significantly advances our understanding of the world around us. In the midst, we process these new channels of information through our personal experiences and continually build our understanding.

In addition to these meaning-making activities that we engage in as humans, often on a subconscious or unconscious level, there are structured, deliberate approaches to gathering and weighing information that we call research. Creswell (2012) defines research as "a process of steps used to collect and analyze information to increase our understanding of a topic or issue" (p. 3). Research is conducted across a diverse array of disciplines – from biology and chemistry, to psychology and education, and even in literature and film – and each tradition includes its own perspectives, designs, and methods.

Since this book is about social science research design and analysis, with a primary focus on quantitative research methods, this chapter will consider the nature of social research. In particular, it will review the purpose of social research, discuss the perspectives associated with dominant social research traditions (including qualitative, quantitative, mixed methods, and evaluation), and highlight some new trends in research that are emerging in a digital world. Additionally, the chapter will present an overview of research ethics. In addition to highlighting the importance of ethical research, this chapter will present characteristics of ethical research and discuss the role of institutional review boards (IRBs) for the protection of human subjects in research.

Purpose of Research

How do we know what we know? Epistemology, or the study of knowledge, is the field that attempts to answer this question and in the process poses additional ones. What are our sources of beliefs and information? We may come to know something through a variety of sources. For example, a child may learn about the dangers of touching a hot stove through the instruction or testimony of parents warning the child not to touch the burner or simply by reaching out and touching the stove directly. Both are potential sources of information that are processed and interpreted differently, yet contribute to the overall knowledge of the child. Audi (2011) identifies a number of basic sources of belief including "perceptual, memorial, introspective, *a priori*, inductive, and testimony-based beliefs" (p. 6).

More than just knowledge, however, epistemology is also concerned about the justification of belief. How do we know that these beliefs are trustworthy? What's the difference between beliefs and true knowledge and how can the former be used to develop the latter? How are we sure that what we think we know is justifiable? In other words, for a belief (regardless of the source) to be actual knowledge rather than mere speculation or fantasy, it must come from reliable sources and be weighed appropriately. This is where research comes in.

Research is a systematic gathering and analyzing of information. Creswell (2012) identifies three steps that describe the general research process: "1. Pose a question. 2. Collect data to answer a question. 3. Present an answer to a question." (p. 3). In the current era of data-driven and evidence-based approaches, recommendations based on research often carry more weight than anecdotes, personal experiences, or tradition. Learning how to effectively design research and analyze data are skills that are becoming increasingly important and in demand far beyond universities and think tanks.

Research Traditions

Despite this common purpose and overarching approach, there are a variety of research traditions that beget various research designs and methods.

The first type of research to which students are often exposed is the scientific method. The scientific method is typically taught as the standard approach to natural science research and is outlined with the steps of

observe, develop a question, develop a hypothesis, conduct an experiment, analyze data, state conclusions, generate new questions. (Windschitl, Thompson, & Braatens, 2008, p. 942)

At the heart of the scientific method is an approach to research that involves inquiry and hypothesis testing by means of experimental testing. Such a framework is not without its critics, ranging from Bauer's (1992) assertion that science does not actually progress by way of the scientific method to Windschitl et al. (2008) who argue that the scientific method is weak pedagogically and should be replaced by model-based inquiry.

Beyond the realm of the natural sciences, there are a variety of research traditions that are found within the social sciences and humanities. Some of these, such as quantitative designs including experimental, quasi-experimental, and correlational, bear a loose resemblance to their natural science counterparts as largely deductive research approaches. Others, such as qualitative methods including critical-theory, narrative analysis, and ethnography, are further away from the scientific method and are more inductive in nature.

There are two broad approaches to logical reasoning: deductive and inductive. Deductive reasoning moves from general principles to specific conclusions. Inductive reasoning, in contrast, begins with specifics and then works toward broader generalizations.

The classic deductive argument is the syllogism, which begins with a major premise, moves through a minor premise, and then deduces a conclusion. A famous example of a syllogism is:

- All men are mortal
- Socrates is a man
- Therefore, Socrates is mortal

Within the realm of social science research, deductive reasoning can be seen in methods that begin with theory, propose hypotheses, engage in observations, and then draw conclusions. Typically, deductive reasoning begets quantitative research methods. Trochim (2006a) describes this approach:

> We might begin with thinking up a theory about our topic of interest. We then narrow that down into more specific hypotheses that we can test. We narrow down even further when we collect observations to address the hypotheses. This ultimately leads us to be able to test the hypotheses with specific data – a confirmation (or not) of our original theories. (para. 2)

In contrast, inductive reasoning is evident in methods that begin without such a theory but instead start with the observations, assemble them into patterns, and ultimately derive a theory or generalization as a result. Typically, inductive reasoning begets qualitative research methods. Trochim (2006a) presents a typical sequence,

> In inductive reasoning, we begin with specific observations and measures, begin to detect patterns and regularities, formulate some tentative hypotheses that we can explore, and finally end up developing some general conclusions or theories. (para. 3)

It's actually quite common, and not terribly surprising, to find that many social science researchers pursue a combination of deductive and inductive approaches. Mixed-methods research, as it is called, combines quantitative and qualitative methods to investigate a problem. As Newman and Benz (1998) advise:

If we accept the premise that scientific knowledge is based on verification methods, the contributions of information derived from a qualitative (inductive) or quantitative (deductive) perspective can be assessed. It then becomes clear how each approach adds to our body of knowledge by building on the information derived from the other approach. (p. 20)

Such a triangulation of methodologies often produces results that are richer and more insightful than either approach alone.

Qualitative Research

Qualitative research is an inductive research approach. To the qualitative researcher, research cannot be seen as an activity independent of the researcher. As Denzin (2008) declares,

In the social sciences today there is no longer a God's-eye view that guarantees methodological certainty. All inquiry reflects the standpoint of the inquirer. (p. 153)

Qualitative researchers do not accept a clean break between epistemology and ontology; knowledge is not independent of being. Although there is no single ordered sequence in qualitative research, Creswell (2007) outlines a number of broad steps in the process: acknowledge the broad assumptions that provoked the qualitative study, bring a topic and review the literature, ask open-ended research questions, collect a variety of sources of data, analyze the qualitative data inductively, experiment with varied forms of narrative to represent the data, and finally discuss the findings (pp. 51-52). Qualitative research values individuality, culture, and social justice.

Quantitative Research

Quantitative research is a deductive research approach. To the quantitative researcher, the world is external to the researcher and there's an objective reality independent of any observations. This reality can be understood in the whole by dividing it up into smaller pieces and studying the parts. Within these smaller environments, observations can be taken and the relationships among variables can be hypothesized, tested, and reproduced. In the quantitative approach, the researcher begins with theory, generates hypotheses, tests those hypotheses through observation and analysis, and then draws conclusions.

Generalizability is a central benefit of, and purpose for, quantitative research. By drawing representative samples from larger populations and testing hypothesized relationships among variables, quantitative researchers aim to find results that can be generalized beyond the scope of their studies.

Mixed Methods Research

> ### Key Point
> Combining quantitative and qualitative research designs, often called mixed methods research, is an increasingly popular approach in the social sciences.

Mixed methods research is a pragmatic research approach. To the mixed methods researcher, a combination of qualitative and quantitative methods provides a better research approach than either in isolation. There is no single model of mixed methods research because a mixed methods study incorporates aspects of both qualitative and quantitative research. The mixed methods researcher, however, needs to carefully plan and justify the use of both qualitative and quantitative data and not attempt to combine them in a haphazard manner. As Bryman (2007) cautions,

> Mixed methods research is not necessarily just an exercise in testing findings against each other. Instead, it is about forging an overall or negotiated account of the findings that brings together both components of the conversation or debate. (p. 21)

Whether the qualitative and quantitative aspects are conducted sequentially or concurrently, they need to be purposefully selected, implemented, evaluated, and documented.

Evaluation Research

Evaluation research is an applied research approach. To the evaluation researcher, programs can and should be systematically assessed to determine their worth or value.

The generic goal of most evaluations is to provide 'useful feedback' to a variety of audiences including sponsors, donors, client-groups, administrators, staff, and other relevant constituencies. (Trochim, 2006b, para. 3)

Such evaluation research may be formative (i.e., designed to strengthen the program) or summative (i.e., examining the effects or outcomes of the program), which often takes the form of commentary concerning the quality and effectiveness of a program.

New Trends in Research

The growth of the Internet and cloud computing has brought with it voluminous amounts of digital information combined with high-performance, low-cost computing power. While the majority of social science research is still conducted using sampling techniques and quantitative, qualitative, or mixed-methods designs, there is a growing interest in conducting large-scale research initiatives using census or near-census data that has been collected and stored digitally by a variety of companies, organizations, and government agencies. Additionally, the emergence of social networking and mobile computing means that consumers are voluntarily producing and sharing enormous quantities of personal information that could be used for analysis.

A May 2011 report by the *McKinsey Global Institute* estimated that companies and individuals are producing and storing the equivalent of over 60,000 U.S. Libraries of Congress every year (Manyika et al., 2011, p.15). This has resulted in the emergence of so-called big data, which are "datasets whose size is beyond the ability of typical database software tools to capture, store, manage, and analyze" (Manyika et al., 2011, p. 1). Corporations and organizations are analyzing big data for a variety of purposes ranging from human genome research and US census data to advertising and global development.

The emergence of digital data (big and otherwise) that can be stored and analyzed online has led to the emergence of new approaches to research including data mining, network analysis, predictive modeling, and information visualization. While these approaches can be used for a variety of types of research (not merely social research), they hold the potential for large-scale social science research studies.

Data Mining

Data mining is an approach designed to analyze large datasets and find meaningful patterns through computer-based analysis. Data mining often involves the use of classification, cluster analysis (grouping related data based on statistical algorithms rather than a priori classification), anomaly detection, and association rule learning (testing and discovering relationships among variations) in order to derive human-readable patterns in the midst of otherwise overwhelming datasets.

Network analysis

Network analysis is "A set of techniques used to characterize relationships among discrete nodes in a graph or a network" (Manyika et al., 2011, p.29). In social research, network analysis can be used to find connections between individuals, communities, or organizations. For example, Stanley Milgram's "small world problem" study resulted in the now-commonplace "six degrees of separation" framework. While Milgram mailed out letters to 296 people, which were then passed around and ultimately, mailed back, with network analysis, a computer algorithm could determine the degrees of separation using data from hundreds of millions of Facebook users.

Predictive Analytics

Predictive analytics use statistical and mathematical techniques to relate a variety of variables and create models used to predict future behavior or outcomes. Well-known examples of predictive analytics are FICO® credit scores to predict financial risk, IRS analysis of tax returns to predict misrepresentation and prompt audits, and police departments analyzing data to produce crime hotspots in order to better allocate personnel and resources.

Information Visualization

Information visualization refers to

techniques used for creating images, diagrams, or animations to communicate, understand, and improve the results of big data analyses. (Manyika et al., 2011, p.31)

Visualization of results from large datasets make it possible to communicate large amounts of information in graphical form more quickly and efficiently than the same information presented in other formats. According to Ware (2012),

Visual displays provide the highest bandwidth channel from the computer to the human. Indeed, we acquire more information through vision than though all of the other senses combined. (p. 2)

1.2: Research Ethics

Importance of Ethical Research

A common way of viewing ethics is as norms for conduct that distinguish between acceptable and unacceptable behavior. Although social research is designed to be about and for the benefit of humans, not all such research has been conducted in an ethical manner. Neuman (2011) describes three cases of ethical controversy: Stanley Milgram's obedience study, Laud Humphreys's tearoom trade study, and the Zimbardo prison experiment (p. 93).

In the most famous of these three, the Milgram experiment, research participants were assigned as "teachers" and applied what they thought were electric shocks to "pupils" who made mistakes in a memory test. The experiment investigated the power of authority by observing how far the "teachers" would go in applying increasingly high levels of (simulated) voltage, with approximately two-thirds of the "teachers" applying the maximum 450 volts. This study raised ethical concerns "over the use of deception and the extreme emotional stress experienced by subjects" (Neuman, 2011, p. 93). It also highlights power and trust relationships that exist between researchers and research participants and how those dynamics can cause real harm, even in a simulated scenario.

A failure to conduct research ethically has multiple negative consequences. Centrally, unethical research often causes harm to one or more human subjects. They may suffer physical or psychological harm, stress, anxiety, discomfort, or even legal harm. They could be negatively affected by deception, coercion, or loss of privacy. Unethical research can also undermine the study itself and result in incorrect observations, analyses, or conclusions. Additionally, unethical research harms the field, in general, by sowing distrust of research and researchers, which could curtail future opportunities for important study.

Characteristics of Ethical Research

Flinders (1992) proposes four ethical perspectives with which to evaluate the protection of human subjects in qualitative research – utilitarian, deontological, relational, and ecological –

which could also serve as a broad philosophical framework for research ethics generally. The utilitarian perspective views actions as ethical if they are likely to result in more benefit than harm, have consequences that are positive, and provide the greatest good for the greatest number of individuals. The deontological approach emphasizes strict adherence to universal rules of moral behavior (e.g., "do not tell a lie") regardless of the consequences of actions. The relational perspective considers whether decisions and actions reflect a caring attitude toward others. Finally, the ecological perspective considers actions in terms of the participants' culture and their larger social systems. Each of these perspectives have value for the researcher, but to promote ethical research among a diverse population, some practical standards for ethical research have been adopted.

> ### Key Point
> At the most fundamental level, ethical research is characterized by informed consent, voluntary participation, avoidance of harm, confidentiality, and protection of vulnerable populations.

Informed Consent

Informed consent means that research participants need to know what they are being asked to participate in before deciding whether to engage in the study. The researcher is obligated to informed the potential subject about the purpose of the research, the voluntary nature of participation, the duration of the study, the procedures and activities that will be conducted, any potential benefits, risks, or discomforts to participants, what records will be maintained, how privacy (or confidentiality or anonymity) will be maintained, how the collected information will be used, how to discontinue participation in the study, and any other relevant information. Informed consent is often obtained by way of a signed written consent form; however, even when such a form is not used (e.g., anonymous survey research), the researcher is still obligated to communicate the relevant information to the potential subject and receive their assent to participate. Although U.S. federal guidelines permit omission or altering of informed consent standards under certain conditions if necessary to conduct the research, such situations are considered to be exceptions under the supervision of an Institutional Review Board.

Voluntary Participation

Once the potential subject has been informed about the details of the study through the informed consent process, ethical research requires that participation be voluntary. Participation in research is to be voluntary and failure to participate should not cause subjects to incur a penalty or lose any benefits to which they are otherwise entitled. Similarly, subjects should be permitted to withdrawal or terminate their participation at any point without penalty or loss of benefits. Coercion is not to be used to recruit, employ, or maintain subject participation in research studies.

Avoidance of Harm

Ethical research should not harm subjects. In general, research should pose no more than a minimal risk to participants. According to the Code of Federal Regulations, minimal risk is defined as

> the probability and magnitude of harm or discomfort anticipated in the research are not greater in and of themselves than those ordinarily encountered in daily life or during the performance of routine physical or psychological examinations or tests. (Protection of Human Subjects, 2009)

Research that involves greater than minimal risk (but still not harm) is generally weighed against the benefit that it would offer the possibility of direct benefit to the participants, yield generalizable knowledge about the subject's disorder or condition, or present an opportunity to understand, prevent, or alleviate a serious problem.

Confidentiality

Researchers are obligated to protect the confidentiality of study participants. Subjects have the right to expect that any personally identifying information will be limited to the authorized researchers and not be revealed externally (unless the subjects themselves authorize such exposure). Anonymity, where the identities of the participants are unknown even to the researchers, is not required for ethical research but certainly guarantees confidentiality. Additionally, researchers should take steps to ensure that all study-related data (e.g., papers, electronic files, etc.) is stored in a secure manner (e.g., locked cabinet, password-protected files) to preserve participant confidentiality.

Protection of Vulnerable Populations

For a variety of reasons, certain populations are considered especially vulnerable and subject to additional levels of protection. Children, for example, lack both the intellectual ability and legal standing to give their consent to participate in research. Accordingly, while children are still required to assent to participate in research, their parents or legal guardians must also grant permission. Vulnerable populations include children, prisoners, pregnant women, handicapped or mentally disabled persons, and economically or educationally disadvantaged individuals. In such cases, it is required that the Institutional Review Board focus particularly on the protection of these vulnerable populations and ensure that there are additional safeguards in place to protect their rights and well being.

Institutional Review Boards

Federal regulations concerning the protection of human subjects in research (The Code of Federal Regulations, 45 CFR 46) require an Institutional Review Board (IRB) to ensure compliance for any research conducted or supported by any federal department or agency. Accordingly, nearly every college, university, institute, or other research agency has an IRB comprised of researchers and community members who review all research proposals prior to data collection. IRBs serve to provide an institutional and governmental required evaluation of certain proposed projects and investigations to ensure their compliance with ethical standards for the protection of human research subjects by treating them humanely, maintaining their dignity, and preserving their rights.

For the purpose of IRB review, research is defined as a systematic investigation, including research development, testing and evaluation, designed to develop or contribute to generalizable knowledge. Human subjects are living individuals about whom an investigator (whether professional or student) conducting research obtains (1) Data through intervention or interaction with the individual, or (2) Identifiable private information. (Protection of Human Subjects, 2009)

Academic assignments which are part of normal, typical coursework that are not intended for dissemination are not required to undergo IRB review. Additionally, surveys or other data collection efforts for the purpose of program or institutional improvement and are not intended for dissemination are not required to undergo review. Such efforts are still required to be conducted in an ethical manner that includes appropriate participant protections. Human subjects data collected in such activities may not be used in future publications or presentations; there is no ex post facto IRB approval of such activities to legitimize turning these studies into approved human research.

The IRB review process typically begins with the principal investigator who is required to complete a research review application. In addition to a detailed description of the proposed study, researchers are required to submit relevant documentary evidence (e.g., grant proposals, consent forms, questionnaires, test instruments, advertisements, debriefing statements, contact letters, etc.) in order for the IRB to conduct its review. For students working under the guidance of a faculty member, the faculty member typically must "sign off" on the application as well.

When an IRB receives an application, it will examine the proposal to determine whether it warrants exempt, expedited, or full board review. The depth of the review process, the required documentation, and the time to complete the review often varies based on this classification. The IRB reviews the proposed purpose, procedures, and subject populations to be used and determines whether the proposed study is consistent with the characteristics of ethical research and whether the benefits of the activity outweigh the risks to subjects and that the subjects' rights are not violated. Issues considered in this analysis include ensuring that risks to the subjects are reasonable in relation to anticipated benefits, selection of subjects is equitable, informed consent is properly sought and documented, adequate preparation is taken to protect the privacy and confidentiality of subjects, and adequate provisions are made for the ongoing monitoring of the subjects' welfare.

Submission of an application to an IRB is no guarantee of approval. Review boards may require additional information, clarification of points, or even substantive changes to a proposal prior to approval. Some studies require approval from multiple IRBs, depending on the nature of the population being studied. Additionally, studies can be rejected by IRBs. This might occur if the study risks appear to outweigh the benefits, the proposal does not sufficiently provide the information necessary for the IRB to make a decision, or the proposed research raises serious ethical questions.

Researchers may not begin data collection until the proposed study has been approved by the appropriate IRB. Studies with data collection that extends beyond a year past the initial approval are subject to continuing review. In addition, the IRB itself is required to prepare and maintain adequate documentation of activities including copies of all proposals, minutes of IRB meetings, copies of correspondence, written procedures, and lists of members. All such records are required to be retained for at least three years while records relating to approved research are to be retained for at least three years after completion of the research (Protection of Human Subjects, 2009).

1.3: Chapter 1 Review

The answer key is at the end of this section.

1. The study of knowledge is called:

    A. Ontology

    B. Epistemology

    C. Axiology

    D. Metaphysics

2. Which is not a step in the general research process?

    A. Pose a question

    B. Collect data to answer a question

    C. Analyze data to answer a question

    D. Present an answer to a question

3. Recommendations based on which of the following has the greatest influence on policy?

    A. Anecdotes

    B. Personal experiences

    C. Tradition

    D. Research

4. Which of the following is NOT part of the scientific method?

    A. Create a theory

    B. Develop a hypothesis

    C. Conduct an experiment

    D. State conclusions

5. Which type of reasoning moves from general principles to specific conclusions?

    A. Inductive

    B. Deductive

    C. Positivist

D. Metaphysical

6. Which research method applies inductive reasoning?

    A. Quantitative

    B. Correlational

    C. Qualitative

    D. Quasi-Experimental

7. Which of the following is a pragmatic research approach?

    A. Qualitative

    B. Quantitative

    C. Mixed methods

    D. Evaluation

8. Which of the following is a deductive research approach?

    A. Qualitative

    B. Quantitative

    C. Mixed methods

    D. Evaluation

9. Which of the following uses computer-based analysis to find patterns in large datasets?

    A. Data mining

    B. Network analysis

    C. Predictive analytics

    D. Information visualization

10. Which of the following can best be used to replicate the small world experiment using online data?

    A. Data mining

    B. Network analysis

    C. Predictive analytics

    D. Information visualization

11. Why did the Milgram experiment cause ethical controversy?

    A.   Participants were bribed

    B.   Participants were not volunteers

    C.   Participants were deceived

    D.   Participants were subjected to physical pain

12. Which of the following ethical perspectives emphasizes universal rules of morality?

    A.   Utilitarian

    B.   Deontological

    C.   Relational

    D.   Ecological

13. Which of the following ethical perspectives values the needs of society over those of the individual?

    A.   Utilitarian

    B.   Deontological

    C.   Relational

    D.   Ecological

14. Which is NOT a core characteristic of ethical research?

    A.   Voluntary participation

    B.   Confidentiality

    C.   Avoidance of harm

    D.   Compensation for participation

15. When is a written consent form typically omitted?

    A.   Drug testing

    B.   Psychological testing

    C.   Anonymous survey

    D.   Children's research

16. Which is NOT required for ethical research?

    A.   Informed consent

    B.   Anonymity

C. Protection of vulnerable populations

D. Confidentiality

17. Who must grant assent and consent for research on children?

A. Children must assent and consent

B. Children must assent and parents must consent

C. Parents must assent and consent

D. Parents must assent and children must consent

18. What does IRB stand for?

A. Institutional Review Board

B. Internal Review Board

C. Institutional Research Board

D. Internal Research Board

19. Which of the following is NOT required to undergo IRB review?

A. Class assignments

B. Program improvement surveys

C. All of the above

D. None of the above

20. When may researchers begin collecting data?

A. Before IRB review

B. During IRB review

C. After IRB approval

D. After IRB rejection

Chapter 1 Answers

1B, 2C, 3D, 4A, 5B, 6C, 7C, 8B, 9A, 10B, 11C, 12B, 13A, 14D, 15C, 16B, 17B, 18A, 19C, 20C

Chapter 2: Qualitative Research

Qualitative research is the investigation of social phenomena in order to gather an in-depth understanding of human behavior and the reasons that govern such behavior. It seeks out the "why" and not the "how" of specific phenomena through the analysis of unstructured information.

2.1: Basic Concepts

Introduction

Strauss and Corbin (1998) defined qualitative research as

any type of research that produces findings not arrived at by statistical procedures or other means of quantification... [Q]ualitative analysis [is] a nonmathematical process of interpretation. (pp. 10-11)

Creswell (2012) and Denzin and Lincoln (2000) identify the following qualitative research assumptions:

- Qualitative researchers are concerned primarily with process, rather than outcomes or products.

- Qualitative researchers are interested in meaning, -how people make sense of their lives, experiences, and their structures of the world.

- The qualitative researcher is the primary instrument for data collection and analysis.

- Qualitative research involves fieldwork. The researcher physically goes to the people, setting, site, or institution to observe or record behavior in its natural setting; emic (insider's point of view)

- Qualitative research is descriptive in that the researcher is interested in process, meaning, and understanding gained through words or pictures.

- The process of qualitative research is inductive in that the researcher builds abstractions, concepts, hypotheses, and theories from details.

- Reality is socially constructed.

- Primacy of subject matter.

- Variables are complex, interwoven, and difficult to measure.

Qualitative data are acquired via observations, extant documents, interviews, questionnaires, and audiovisual materials (Creswell, 2012) thereby producing data unconstrained by the researcher; that is, the researcher can uncover anything unlike quantitative instruments that restrict the measurement in some manner (e.g., closed-ended questions with fixed response choices). The typical characteristics of qualitative research are (Creswell, 2012, p. 16):

- The study is exploratory in an attempt to generate an in-depth understanding of a targeted "central phenomenon" (i.e., "the key concept, idea, or process studied") with little, if any, knowledge of relevant variables;

- The literature is used to support the importance of the research problem (i.e., the dilemma that the research addresses) but initially has a lesser role than in quantitative research because of the study's exploratory nature;

- The research question(s) and purpose statement are broad to reflect exploration thereby enabling the researcher to be open to the emerging data;

- A small number of participants are studied and chosen based on the research purpose;

- The data produced are typically text-based (e.g., the participants' responses in their own words);

- The data are transformed into findings via analyzing the text for common themes;

- Report writing reflects the exploratory nature of the study by revealing the emergence of the findings with subsequent discussion that includes how the researcher's background creates a subjective lens for interpretation.

Although this book is primarily focused on quantitative research and analysis, nevertheless it is common in many research designs to incorporate both quantitative and qualitative methods thereby producing a mixed methods design. Mixing methods can often produce richer findings and a deeper understanding of the research problem via several designs (cf. Creswell, 2012, pp. 539-547):

- Convergent (simultaneous) design – collecting quantitative and qualitative data simultaneously. For example, administering a survey with both closed-ended (i.e., fixed responses) and open-ended (i.e., no response options) questions.

- Explanatory (sequential) design – first collecting quantitative data but then collecting qualitative data in an attempt to explain, clarify, expand, or elaborate the quantitative findings.

- Exploratory (sequential) design – first collecting qualitative data but then collecting quantitative data that can focus on constructs revealed in the qualitative findings.

- Embedded (simultaneous or sequential) design – collecting one type of data to support the other. Creswell (2012) stated that "most examples in the literature support adding qualitative data into a quantitative design" (p. 544).

It is the embedded design that uses qualitative data to support what is primarily a quantitative design that is relevant to this book rather than a complete discussion of how to design, conduct, and analyze every possible variation of qualitative research. The various sampling procedures as well as a description of some of the many qualitative designs used are provided to introduce the vast spectrum of research tools for engaging in qualitative research.

Sampling

In qualitative research, "purposeful sampling" (Patton, 2002, p. 230) is used. Unlike quantitative research in which a sample is often chosen to represent a population and the sample size is based upon statistical considerations, in qualitative research samples are chosen based on the purpose of the study. With respect to sample size, Patton (2002) stated the following:

> Sample size depends on what you want to know, the purpose of the inquiry, what's at stake, what will be useful, what will have credibility, and what can be done with available time and resources. (p. 244)

Thus, qualitative researchers select a sample guided by what they hope to acquire with respect to the data. Patton (2002, pp. 230-246) and Creswell (2012, pp. 206-209) described several qualitative sampling methods and their associated purpose:

Before data collection, the following sampling strategies may be invoked:

- *Extreme or deviant case sampling* – To learn from extreme manifestations of the central phenomenon under study. An example of this would be studying students who scored a perfect score on a standardized test in which the central phenomenon is high academic achievement.

- *Intensity sampling* – To learn from intense but not extreme manifestations of the central phenomenon under study. An example would be studying students who scored above the 75th percentile on a standardized test, which is still high academic achievement but not extreme.

- *Maximum variation sampling* – To uncover commonality among diverse samples. An example would be studying the characteristics of leaders from disparate fields (e.g., military, business, volunteer agencies, etc.) in an attempt to uncover common leadership practices.

- *Homogeneous sampling* – To create an in-depth description of a particular group with similar backgrounds or common experiences. An example would be interviewing a focus group of shoppers at a given department store in an attempt to describe their satisfaction with the store's check out procedure.

- *Typical case sampling* – To describe what is average, normal, or typical for a specified group—which can involve studying only a single person or site—particularly to someone unfamiliar with normative information. For example, the member of a given tribe may be selected because others in the tribe do not recognize the member as being remarkable in any given way and, thus, represents a typical member.

- *Critical case sampling* – To make a logical generalization to other cases that are less extreme on a relevant dimension. For example, a local municipality might want to know if a given ordinance is written in a manner that is understandable by the entire community; thus, it might conduct a study using a sample of less-educated citizens with the notion that if this group can understand the ordinance, everyone else should be able to as well.

- *Criterion sampling* – To study cases associated with some predetermined criterion of importance to the study's purpose. An example would be a study of the triage procedure in an emergency room whereby cases are selected for study based upon a criterion that defines an excessive wait time.

- *Theory-based sampling* – To help understand a theory by studying samples that manifest a construct associated with the theory. For example, a researcher might want to develop a theory regarding the how a social worker copes with infant abuse; thus, a sample of social workers who have been involved with this situation is studied.

After data collection has begun, the following sampling strategies may be invoked:

- *Snowball sampling* – To locate information rich sources using knowledgeable others (i.e., as more sources are identified, the sample grows like a snowball). For example, in studying employee satisfaction with an inventory system, a few employees could be selected for the study that work with the system; after collecting data from them, they could be asked to identify others that work with the system who can then be studied thereby increasing the sample.

- *Confirming/disconfirming sampling* – To help verify the accuracy of preliminary findings. Confirming samples are similar to the original samples that have been used to develop the preliminary findings and, thus, should themselves produce similar findings; disconfirming samples are dissimilar to the original samples and should provide contrary findings. Of course, if either of these results do not occur, then the preliminary findings should be questioned.

- *Opportunistic sampling* – To gather additional information when opportunities arise. For example in the theory-based sample of social workers described above, the researcher may come across a social worker who has no experience with infant abuse but with teenager abuse; therefore, the researcher takes advantage of the opportunity to study this social worker in an attempt to inform the resultant theory (e.g., to see if preliminary findings should be limited to infant abuse).

> Key Point
> The sampling strategy used in qualitative research depends upon the study's purpose.

Qualitative Designs

There are a variety of research methods subsumed under the broad category of qualitative designs. A particular method is often referred to as a

tradition... [that refers to] a group of scholars who agree among themselves on the nature of the universe they are examining, on legitimate questions and problems to study, and on legitimate techniques to seek solutions. (Jacob, 1987, pp. 1-2)

Gall, Gall, and Borg (2007) categorize qualitative research traditions into a triumvirate of methods used to understand "the nature of lived experience," "cultural and social phenomena," and "language and communication phenomena" (p. 490) into the following three investigations.

Investigations of the Nature of Lived Experience

Cognitive psychology

> the study of the structures and processes involved in mental activity, and of how these structures and processes are learned or how they develop with maturation. (p. 492)

Phenomenology

> the study of the world as it appears to individuals when they lay aside the prevailing understandings of those phenomena and revisit their immediate experience of the phenomena....[i.e.,] how individuals construct reality. (p. 495)

Phenomenographic research

> a specialized method for describing the different ways in which people conceptualize the world around them. (p. 497)

Life history research

> the study of the life experience of individuals from the perspective of how these individuals interpret and understand the world around them... [and] might be called a biography, a life story, an oral history, a case study, a testimonial, or a portrait.... [or if the researcher writes about him or herself might be called] an autobiography or a memoir. (p. 498)

Investigations of the Nature of Cultural and Social Phenomena

Symbolic interactionism

> the study of how individuals engage in social transactions and how these transactions contribute to the creation and maintenance of social structures and the individual's self-identity. (p. 500)

Action research

a type of self-reflective investigation that professional practitioners undertake for the purpose of improving the rationality and justice of their work. (p. 500)

Ethnography

intensive study of the features of a given culture and the patterns in those features. (p. 500)

Cultural studies and critical-theory research

[the study of] contestation of oppressive power relationships in a culture. (p. 491)

Ethnomethodology

the study of the techniques that individuals use to make sense of everyday social environments and to accomplish the tasks of communicating, making decisions, and reasoning within them. (p. 518)

Investigations of Language and Communication Phenomena

Narrative analysis.

[the study of] organized representations and explanations of human experience. (p. 491)

Ethnographic content analysis

the examination of the content of documents found in field settings as reflections of social interactions in the culture. (p. 520)

Ethnography of communication

the study of how members of a cultural group use speech in their social life. (p. 520)

Hermeneutics

the study of the process by which individuals arrive at the meaning of any text. (p. 520)

Semiotics

the study of sign systems, in particular, the study of how objects (e.g., letters of the alphabet) come to convey

meaning and how sign systems relate to human behavior.
(p. 522)

Structuralism and poststructuralism

structuralism…focuses on the systemic properties of
phenomena, including relationships among elements of a
system... [whereas] poststructuralism is a postmodern
approach to the study of systems, especially language as
a system, that denies the possibility of finding any inherent
meaning in them (pp. 523-524).

Central Questions

In order to help choose an appropriate qualitative tradition,
Patton (2002) provided central questions for numerous traditions
(note: not all overlap those already mentioned). Researchers
should review these questions in light of their research interests
to facilitate choosing an appropriate research design, which
includes choosing proper measurement tools directed at seeking
insights into these questions. The traditions and questions are
(Patton, 2002, pp. 132-133):

- *Ethnography* – "What is the culture of this group of
  people?"

- *Autoethnography* – "How does my own experience of this
  culture connect with and offer insights about this culture,
  situation, event, and/or way of life?"

- *Reality testing: Positivist and realist approaches* – "What's
  really going on in the real world? What can we establish
  with some degree of certainty? What are plausible
  explanations for verifiable patterns? What's the truth
  insofar as we can get at it? How can we study a
  phenomenon so that our findings correspond, as much as
  possible, to the real world?"

- *Constructionism/constructivism* – "How have the people in
  this setting constructed reality? What are their reported
  perceptions, 'truths,' explanations, beliefs, and worldview?
  What are the consequences of their constructions for their
  behaviors and for those with whom they interact?"

- *Phenomenology* – "What is the meaning, structure, and essence of the lived experience of this phenomenon for this person or group of people?"

- *Heuristic inquiry* – "What is my experience of this phenomenon and the essential experience of others who also experience this phenomenon intensely?"

- *Ethnomethodology* – "How do people make sense of their everyday activities so as to behave in socially acceptable ways?"

- *Symbolic interaction* – "What common set of symbols and understandings has emerged to give meaning to people's interactions?"

- *Semiotics* – "How do signs (words, symbols) carry and convey meaning in particular contexts?"

- *Hermeneutics* – "What are the conditions under which a human act took place or a product was produced that makes it possible to interpret its meanings?"

- *Narratology/narrative analysis* – "What does this narrative or story reveal about the person and world from which it came? How can this narrative be interpreted to understand and illuminate the life and culture that created it?"

- *Ecological psychology* – "How do individuals attempt to accomplish their goals through specific behaviors in specific environments?"

- *Systems theory* –"How and why does this system as a whole function as it does?"

- *Chaos theory: Nonlinear dynamics* – "What is the underlying order, if any, of disorderly phenomenon?"

- *Grounded theory* – "What theory emerges from systematic comparative analysis and is grounded in fieldwork so as to explain what has been and is observed?"

- *Orientational: Feminist inquiry, critical theory, queer theory, among others* – "How is X perspective manifest in this phenomenon?"

2.2: Research Tools

Data Collection

Qualitative data collection is primarily obtained through observations and interviews, with additional artifacts, that are guided by questions. Data may consist of written documents, the researcher's field notes, and recordings.

Question Construction

As mentioned previously, the inclusion of a discussion regarding qualitative research is in support of the embedded mixed methods design that uses qualitative data to support a quantitative design. A very common application of this is the inclusion of a few open-ended questions among many closed-ended items. To this end, the quality of the response is related to the quality of the question; therefore, when constructing questions consider the following (cf. Creswell, 2012, p. 389):

- Make sure the language is clear (devoid of jargon and technical language) and the reading level is appropriate for the intended participants. What might be understandable to the researcher who is likely well-educated may not be universally understood; therefore, consider the sample's linguistic characteristics, knowledge, and abilities.

- Do not confuse the participant by a question that is actually multiple questions; instead, create separate, focused questions. The phrases "double-barreled" and "triple-barreled" are used to describe a question that is actually two or three questions, respectively.

- Do not make a question too long as this will reduce the focus of the question and, consequentially, the focus of the response. When reviewing a potential question, the researcher should question the inclusion of each word, phrase, and, perhaps, sentence.

- Avoid negatively worded phrases as such phrases may make a question both wordy and unclear.

- Avoid leading words or phrases so that the data are the result of the participants' positions rather than the researcher's interests. Note: There is a distinction between

creating questions that support the research purpose
(admirable!) versus creating questions that influence a
response and, thus, does not accurately represent a
participant's views (not admirable!); work toward the
former while avoiding the latter.

- Make sure the question is appropriate for all participants.
When open-ended questions are part of a survey, it will go
to all participants; therefore, make sure that each question
is applicable to every respondent.

Interviews

Data can also be acquired by directly asking one or more
participants questions in real time such as in face-to-face
settings or electronically (e.g., via telephone or computer). When
several participants are interviewed, they are referred to as a
focus group that consists of participants with some common
experience or knowledge relevant to the research purpose. The
interview can be structured, meaning that the questions and their
order are fixed, or unstructured, meaning that the researcher
asks any questions that come to mind. In either case, however,
qualitative researchers often ask probes that are follow-up
questions used "for clarification or elaboration when a response
is incomplete or ambiguous" (Nardi, 2006, p. 70). In addition to
notes, researchers often audiotape the interview for subsequent
transcription.

Observations

By observing others in their natural settings, qualitative
researchers are able to gather authentic information with respect
to the participants' actual behaviors. There are disadvantages to
this method such as access imitations to targeted sites as well
as participant behavior modification due to being watched;
however, this method of data collection provides firsthand
information in contrast to recollections gathered via
questionnaires as well as an opportunity to gather data on
participants who might not be able to articulate their thoughts
well (e.g., preschoolers, mentally impaired persons). The
qualitative researcher can take on the role of a participant
observer, meaning that he or she actively engages in the
participants' activities, or a nonparticipant observer, meaning that
there is no engagement in activities; however, based upon the

emerging nature of qualitative research, roles can be changed during the observation process. In either case, field notes should be acquired that are both descriptive of the situation (i.e., a description of the events and people) as well as reflective (i.e., the researcher's interpretation of the observations).

Artifacts

Qualitative information can be found in documents—public or private—as well as audiovisual material. Documents include e-mails, diaries, informal personal notes, official letters, and corporate literature and provide the qualitative researcher with text ready for analysis. In contrast, audiovisual material, which includes video recordings, audio recordings, and photographs, require reduction to text before data analysis can occur.

Data Analysis

After all qualitative data are in text form, data analysis can occur. Such analysis may include crafting a description of the events and people involved in the study, but will always involve generating a list of themes that are categories of the major ideas or concepts in the data. Creswell (2012, pp. 236-253) described a systematic way for conducting a thematic analysis by hand. Although there are software tools available for analyzing qualitative data, nevertheless it is good for a researcher to understand the rudiments of "hand" analyzing such data as a primer to what might be done electronically. In addition, with a small amount of textual data it is more efficient to analyze text data in this manner.

1. Read all of the text. In order to get a general sense of the data, the initial step is to read the textual data in its entirety, which should be done several times. The goal is to get fully engaged in all of the data thereby developing both a big and little mental pictures of what is going on in the research situation. As the data are read, the researcher should insert brief notes reflecting any meanings ideated during the reading.

2. Develop a list of codes. The "little pictures" are the codes, or categories of minor ideas or concepts, that emerged during the reading. After Step 1, create a numerical list of codes—perhaps 15 or 20—that will be used in the coding process. A

coding category can be any concept that helps divide the text segments into common categories. Note that one code may be for "description of events/people" rather than for a particular idea or concept.

3. Code the data. Start the coding process by reading the text, marking various text segments (i.e., one or more sentences) in some manner—e.g., underlining, circling, or parenthesizing—and insert the numerical code generated in Step 2. Note that as data are coded, the researcher might want to refine the description of the code or even add new codes to the coding list; both actions typically occur. Although "in vivo codes" (codes using a participant's own words; Creswell, 2012, p. 244) can be used, it is typical to have codes written in the researcher's words. Note that not all text segments must be coded as the point is to ultimately generate a big picture of the data; that is, to move from individual words, phrases, and sentences to a few important themes. During the coding process if a particularly dramatic or supportive text segment is uncovered, it should be marked as a candidate for insertion in the subsequent report in order to lend support to the findings (see "emic data"; Creswell, 2012, p. 471).

4. Review the codes and coding process. After Step 3, the coding list may have grown to 40 or more codes. In this step, the researcher should attempt to remove any redundancy in the codes and simplify the list. If a code was generated with very few associated text segments, the researcher should consider eliminating the code entirely.

5. Recode the data. With this reduced coding list, recode the data. Note that there is no limit to the number of iterations involved in the coding process; it continues until the researcher is satisfied with the results.

6. Develop themes. Themes are categories of major ideas or concepts into which the codes are subsumed. The number of themes of course will vary (as will the number of codes) but should be around 5 to 7 (Creswell, 2012, p. 244).

7. Develop thematic relationships. While not always done in data analysis, some qualitative researchers take thematic analysis a step further by "layering the analysis" or

"interconnecting themes" (Creswell, 2012, pp. 251-252). Layering builds on the notion that some themes may support other themes; that is, themes can be major or minor and presented in a report as a layer of themes (i.e., major above minor) to highlight this supportive relationship. Interconnectivity builds on the notion that themes may be related sequentially due either to causal relationships or to time; a reporting of this would illustrate such a sequential path.

Additional Data

During data analysis, the researcher may decide that more data are needed. This might be due to missing pieces of information or questions generated during analysis; however, regardless of the reason, the exploratory nature of qualitative research allows the researcher to go back to the field and acquire more data until he or she deems that saturation ("new data will not provide any new information or insights for the developing categories"; Creswell, 2012, p. 433) has occurred. The additional data should be coded using the coding scheme developed.

Effect Size

Onwuegbuzie (2000) argues that effect size should be analyzed and reported in qualitative research — even though it is often more thought of as important in quantitative research as an indicant of practical significance — to add richness to the thematic analysis. To this end, a matrix can be created (i.e., participant by theme) that highlights those participants who provided "a significant statement or observation" (Onwuegbuzie, 2000, p. 8) in support of each theme. In addition, a table can be created for each participant that indicates the number of words or statements made in support of each theme; this measure of effect size may be normalized by all words, statements, or even interview time for a given participant thereby producing an adjusted effect size.

Reporting the Findings

Descriptions should be detailed thereby enabling the reader to fully understand salient aspects of the events and people involved; presenting a map of the scene may also be useful in this regard. Coding, themes, effect sizes, and thematic relationships should represented by tables and/or lists as well as figures that highlight any thematic sequencing generated by a interconnectivity analysis or hierarchical relationships between themes such as uncovered by a layering analysis. Emic data should be inserted in the discussion judiciously to add support and, at times, drama to the findings; usually pseudonames are used to preserve participant anonymity.

2.3: Threats to Validity

Introduction

When discussing research, the term validity is used to describe how well a study is designed and conducted to produce accurate conclusions; that is, accurate insights in response to the research question(s). From this perspective, validity is just as much a concern in qualitative research as it is in quantitative research even though the latter is typically associated with discussions concerning threats to validity. Johnson (1997) provides a rich discussion of descriptive, interpretive, and theoretical validity as well as addressed internal and external validity that are more closely allied to quantitative methods. This section is based extensively on Johnson's 1997 article.

Researcher Bias

An overarching concern in qualitative research—and, truth be told, in quantitative research as well!—is that of a researcher's preconceived notions interfering with an objective interpretation of the data. In this regard, because qualitative research typically uses methods that provide less structured responses from participants (e.g., via open-ended questions or observations) when compared to quantitative research, the opportunity for a researcher to interject his or her own cognitive filters in selecting particular facets of the data for focused discussion is greater. In both quantitative and qualitative designs, however, researcher bias can be present as the data or findings (i.e., processed data) can and often are discussed based upon the researcher's own knowledge of the research topic.

Thus, bias can be viewed from either an ethical or unethical perspective. The ethical perspective is merely recognition that one's knowledge and attitudes create a lens that influences how data are collected and findings are interpreted. This does not suggest any nefarious ulterior motive but rather recognition that different people often see and interpret similar things differently. A researcher should strive toward an objective collection of data and interpretation of resultant findings by engaging in "reflexivity, which means that the researcher actively engages in critical self-reflection about his or her potential biases and predispositions" (Johnson, 1997, p. 284). Often in qualitative research, researchers will discuss in their reports their background and experiences that might influence the research as well as any methods employed to reduce the possibility of researcher bias. The unethical perspective of bias is a purposeful misrepresentation of the design, data, findings, or interpretations to suit individual objectives, which should always be avoided.

> **Key Point**
> Researcher bias can be viewed from either an ethical or unethical perspective.

Descriptive Validity

This type of validity refers to the degree to which a researcher has accurately described and reported aspects of the study (e.g., setting, participants, behaviors, interactions). As the purpose of a qualitative study does not typically include generalizing to other settings but rather involves an in-depth investigation of a particular phenomenon, accurately describing the characteristics of the study that make it separable from other settings is of paramount importance. One way to promote this type of validity is via "investigator triangulation" (Johnson, 1997, p. 285) that involves multiple researchers working separately to record the study's context but later working together to craft an accurate description.

Interpretive Validity

Whereas descriptive validity refers to accuracy in reporting the more factual aspects of a study, interpretive validity refers to the degree to which a researcher has accurately presented the cognitive aspects of the study's participants; that is, the portrayal of their beliefs, attitudes, and intentions. To facilitate interpretative validity, a researcher must work diligently to understand what a participant believes, feels, and wants as well as why; that is, the researcher must attempt to see and understand things from the participant's perspective. To better accomplish this type of validity, a researcher can engage in "participant feedback" (Johnson, 1997, p. 285), also referred to as "member checking" (Creswell, 2012, p. 259), in which a participant is provided an opportunity to review and correct the researcher's interpretations. (Note: As per Creswell, member checking can also be used to improve descriptive validity.) In addition, the researcher can reduce threats to interpretive validity by providing the exact words of the participant thereby eliminating or reducing any interpretation on the researcher's part. These exact words are referred to as "verbatims" (Johnson, 1997, p. 285) or "emic data" (Creswell, 2012, p. 471); Creswell differentiated "etic data" as the researcher's "interpretation of the participants' perspectives" (p. 471) using the researcher's language.

Theoretical Validity

A theory explains relationships between constructs; constructs are abstract expressions (e.g., happiness) that are typically represented by measured variables (e.g., minutes spent laughing). Thus, theoretical validity refers to the degree to which a theory generated from the study is consistent with the relationships observed in the data (i.e., "fits the data"; Johnson, 1997, p. 286). "Extended fieldwork" (Johnson, 1997, p. 286) promotes theoretical validity because it provides the researcher with an increased opportunity to interact with the people and events under study thereby enabling a theory to be created that aligns with a deep understanding of the research situation. "Theory triangulation" in which multiple theories are considered in explaining relationships can also improve theoretical validity as such a process promotes convergence toward "a more cogent explanation" (Johnson, 1997, p. 286) by discounting rival explanations. "Investigator triangulation" (Johnson, 1997, p. 287) can also support this form of validity as multiple researchers discuss relationships and develop a theory collaboratively.

Johnson (1997) discussed other methods to promote theoretical validity: (a) "Pattern matching" (p. 287) involves making predictions based upon the theory generated; as predictions are observed to occur, the theory is better supported;

(b) "Negative case sampling" (p. 284) involves identifying cases that may not support the theory generated; in this manner, the researcher is attempting to remain open-minded about the possibility that the theory may be incorrect and is looking for disconfirming evidence—when none or little is found, the theory is supported; and (c) "Peer review" (p. 287) involves discussing with colleagues the proposed theory in light of the methods used and data generated so that they can provide critical feedback that not only may inform the resultant explanation but also suggest further investigation.

Internal Validity

Internal validity refers to the degree to which a theory that expresses causal relationships is accurate. When qualitative methods are being used to generate a theory explaining a phenomenon's process (cf. grounded theory; Creswell, 2012, p. 423), cause and effect relationships are sought. In this regard, the methods already discussed to promote theoretical validity are salient in promoting internal validity as "rival hypotheses" (i.e., explanations contrary to the theory generated; Johnson, 1997, p. 288) are discounted. In addition, "methods triangulation" (Johnson, 1997, p. 288) and "data triangulation" (Johnson, 1997, p. 289) should also be used. Methods triangulation involves using multiple research methods —qualitative or quantitative—whereas data triangulation involves using multiple sources of data (i.e., using the same research method applied to multiple people, settings, or times) to generate evidence that informs the explanation of causal relationships.

External Validity

External validity refers to the degree to which a study's findings "can be applied to individuals and settings beyond those that were studied" (Gall et al., 2007, p. 388), which is referred to as generalizability. Generalizability is not usually associated with qualitative research because this form of research typically focuses on unique settings or people rather than settings or people representative of a larger population. However, Stake used the term "naturalistic generalization" (Johnson, 1997, p. 290) and Campbell the term "proximal similarity" (Johnson, 1997, p. 291) to support the notion that the findings from a qualitative study can be roughly generalized to similar settings and people.

Thus, promoting external validity requires a detailed and accurate reporting of the study's methods, setting, participants, etc. thereby allowing a reader of the findings to determine similitude to other contexts.

2.4: Chapter 2 Review

The answer key is at the end of this section.

1. Which of the following might support a description of the scene in a report?

    A. Coding list

    B. Map

    C. A description of the researcher's background

    D. A figure outlining thematic sequencing

2. Which of the following is used to describe how well a study is designed and conducted to produce accurate conclusions?

    A. Reflexivity

    B. Opportunistic

    C. Reliability

    D. Validity

3. Which of the following represents poor practice in qualitative research?

    A. Asking open-ended questions

    B. Asking a question that supports the research purpose

    C. Gathering additional data after data analysis has begun

    D. Asking a question that influences a response which does not accurately represent a participant's view

4. Which of the following mixed methods designs would use qualitative research to support a primarily quantitative design?

    A. Action research

    B. Embedded design

    C. Exploratory design

    D. Ethnomethodology

5. A researcher should generate approximately how many themes?

A. 1

B. 6

C. 20

D. 40

6. Which of the following qualitative designs would be used to study the culture of an African tribe?

   A. Hermeneutics

   B. Semiotics

   C. Phenomenology

   D. Ethnography

7. Typically what form are the data produced via qualitative research?

   A. Textual

   B. Numeric

   C. Theoretical

   D. Opportunistic

8. Which of the following is used to describe the situation when new data no longer provide additional insights?

   A. Saturation

   B. Triangulation

   C. Reflexivity

   D. Validity

9. Which of the following might be used to support interpretive validity?

   A. An accurate description of the research situation

   B. Proximal similarity

   C. Naturalistic generalization

   D. Participant feedback

10. Which of the following describes a question on a survey that actually consists of two questions?

A. Single-barreled

B. Double-barreled

C. Triple-barreled

D. Probe

11. Which of the following might describe researcher bias?

A. Ethical

B. Unethical

C. All of the above

D. None of the above

12. An in vivo code refers to which of the following?

A. Data generated from a narratology design

B. Interconnected themes

C. A code in the researcher's own words

D. A code in the participant's own words

13. Which of the following qualitative sampling strategies may occur after data collection has begun?

A. Intensity sampling

B. Critical case sampling

C. Opportunistic sampling

D. Criterion sampling

14. Coding and recoding should occur how many times?

A. Once

B. Twice

C. Three times

D. As many times as the researcher feels it is necessary

15. Which of the following refers to a researcher who actively engages in the participants' activities?

A. Participant observer

B. Nonparticipant observer

C. Phenomenologist

D. Ethnographer

16. Which of the following refers to an aspect of thematic analysis in which the supportive relationships of themes are analyzed?

A. Path analysis

B. Causal analysis

C. Interconnectivity analysis

D. Layering analysis

17. Which of the following describes an interview in which the questions are fixed and ordered?

A. Structured

B. Unstructured

C. Reflexive

D. Thematic

18. Which of the following describes multiple researchers working at first separately but later collectively to craft an accurate description of the aspects of the study?

A. Investigator triangulation

B. Member checking

C. Peer review

D. Data triangulation

19. Which of the following qualitative designs would address the following question: "How do words carry/convey meaning?"

A. Orientational

B. Grounded theory

C. Systems theory

D. Semiotics

20. An autobiography is one form of which of the following qualitative designs?

A.   Symbolic interactionism

B.   Cultural study

C.   Life history research

D.   Cognitive psychology

Chapter 2 Answers

1B, 2D, 3D, 4B, 5B, 6D, 7A, 8A, 9D, 10B, 11C, 12D, 13C, 14D, 15A, 16D, 17A, 18A, 19D, 20C

Chapter 3: Quantitative Research

Quantitative research is the systematic investigation of social phenomena using statistical techniques. This chapter first reviews the basic quantitative concepts and then describes the major quantitative research designs and threats to validity.

3.1: Basic Concepts

Introduction

Quantitative research is a type of research in which the investigator uses scientific inquiry. The assumptions of quantitative research include (Creswell, 2003):

- The world is external and objective.
- Reality is seen as one and therefore by dividing and studying its parts the whole can be understood.
- Phenomena are observable facts or events and everything occurring in nature can be predicted according to reproducible laws.
- Variables can be identified and relationships measured.
- Theoretically derived relationships between variables are tested using hypotheses.
- The researcher and the components of the problem under study are perceived as independent and separate (i.e., etic, an outsider's point of view).

Quantitative research starts with the statement of a problem. It can be something to be explained, to be further understood, etc. The problem should address a gap in the professional literature and, when answered, should improve professional practice. It may address a present problem or one that is anticipated.

The problem statement produces one or more research questions. A good research question should be specific, testable using empirical methods, feasible, and imply a statistical procedure. Good research questions build on previous research. Therefore, it is essential that the researcher conduct a thorough literature review prior to formulating any problem statement or research question.

Quantitative research involves the analysis of numerical data using statistical procedures in order to test a hypothesis. The field of statistics is divided into descriptive statistics and inferential statistics (there are further subdivisions under each subdivision that will be discussed in subsequent chapters).

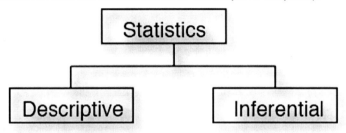

Below is a brief summary of the basic concepts of quantitative research starting with the concept of a construct.

Constructs

A construct is a concept for a set of related behaviors or characteristics of an individual that cannot be directly observed or measured (Gall, Gall, & Borg, 2007). Its name recognizes its social construction. Sense of classroom community, intelligence, and computer anxiety are examples of constructs. They cannot be directly measured. Consequently, the researcher must first operationalize the construct in order to collect valid data. This operationalization is the development or identification of specific research procedures that result in empirical measurements of the construct. Operationalization defines the measuring method used and permits other researchers to replicate the measurements.

- The *constitutive definition* of a construct is a dictionary-like definition using terms commonly understood within the discipline (Gall, Gall, & Borg, 2007). It provides a general understanding of the characteristics or concepts that will be studied, but must be complemented with an operational definition before the construct can be measured.

- An *operational definition* of a construct describes a measurement procedure that must be identified before actual measurement can take place; i.e., it operationalizes the construct by describing how it will be measured. For example, an operational definition for student sense of classroom community could be sense of classroom community as measured by the Classroom Community Scale (CCS; Rovai, 2002) at http://www.sciencedirect.com/science/article/pii/S1096751602001021.

Operationalizing constructs is not limited to the use of test instruments. For example, American psychologist Edward C. Tolman operationalized hunger in a study that he conducted as the time since last feeding.

It is important in measurement planning and operationalizing constructs to avoid selecting instruments that result in range effects. Range effects are typically a consequence of using a measure that is inappropriate for a specific group (i.e., it is too easy, too difficult, not age appropriate, etc.). There are two types of range effects:

1. A ceiling effect is the clustering of scores at the high end of a measurement scale.

2. A floor effect is the clustering of scores at the low end of a measurement scale.

Looking for a test instrument to operationalize a construct? Check out ERIC/AE Test Locator at http://ericae.net/testcol.htm. Once a construct of interest for a study has been operationalized, it's time to formulate a data collection plan. Sampling is a key component of this plan.

Sampling

Sampling involves the collection, analysis, and interpretation of data gathered from random samples of a population under study. The target population is the population to which the researcher wants to generalize study results; the experimentally accessible population is the subset of the target population to which the researcher has experimental access; and the sample is the group of participants from the experimentally accessible population who will participate in the research study and will be measured. To foster external validity of study findings, it is important that both the experimentally accessible population and the sample be representative of the target population. These terms are depicted graphically in the following figure.

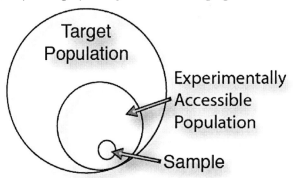

There are two types of sampling, probability sampling and non-probability sampling.

1.   *Probability sampling* uses some form of random selection of research participants from the experimentally accessible population. Only random samples permit true statistical inference and foster external validity. Probability sampling includes several subcategories.

    •   A *simple random sample* is a sample selected from a population in such a manner that all members of the population have an equal and independent chance of being selected.

    •   A *stratified random sample* is one in which the accessible population is first divided into subsets or strata; e.g., a population of college students is first divided into freshmen, sophomores, juniors, and seniors, and then individuals are selected at random from each stratum. This method ensures that all groups are represented in the correct proportions and the method retains the benefits of simple random sampling for each stratum.

    •   A *cluster random sample* is a sample in which existing clusters or groups are randomly selected and then each member of the cluster is used in the research. For example, if classes of students are selected at random as the clusters, then the students in each selected class become participants in the research study. External validity is likely to be an issue if a sufficient number of sampling units, classes in this example, are not selected.

2. Non-probability sampling (purposeful or theoretical sampling) does not involve the use of randomization to select research participants. Consequently, research participants are selected because of convenience or access. External validity is an issue.

- A *convenience sample* is one in which the researcher relies on available participants. While this is the most convenient method, a major risk is to generalize the results to a known target population because the convenience sample may not be representative of the target population.

- A *purposive sample* is selected on the basis of the researcher's knowledge of the target population. The researcher chooses research participants who are similar to this population in attributes of interest.

- A *quota sample* is a stratified convenience sampling strategy. The sample is formed by selecting research participants who reflect the proportions of the target population on key demographic attributes such as gender, race, socioeconomic status, education level, etc. Research participants are recruited as they become available and the researcher assigns them to demographic groups based on their attributes. When the quota for a given demographic group is filled, the researcher stops recruiting participants from that particular group.

Sampling Frame

The sampling frame is the list of sampling units, which may be individuals, organizations, or other units of analysis from the experimentally accessible population. Randomly selecting study participants from a suitable sampling frame is an example of probability sampling. A list of registered students may be the sampling frame for a survey of the student body at a university. However, problems arise if sampling frame bias exists.

Telephone directories are often used as sampling frames, for example, but tend to under-represent the poor (who have no phones) and the wealthy (who may have unlisted numbers). If the researcher does not have a sampling frame, then he or she is restricted to less satisfactory samples that cannot be randomly selected because not all individuals within the population will have the same probability of being selected.

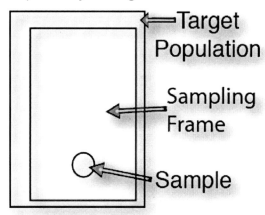

The above figure depicts a sampling frame that does not include the entire target population. Consequently, the sampling frame as well as the sample are biased, creating an external validity issue for the research findings.

Sampling Error

Sampling error occurs when the researcher is working with sample data rather than population data. When one takes a sample from a population, as opposed to collecting information from the entire population by way of a census, there is a probability that one's sample will not reflect the characteristics of the population because of chance error.

The formula for sampling error is:

$$SE = \sqrt{\frac{\sigma^2}{N}}$$

Increasing sample size reduces sampling error. In most quantitative studies, a 5% sampling error is acceptable.

Non-Sampling Error

Non-sampling error is caused by human error and can result in bias. Biemer and Lyberg (2003) identify five potential sources of non-sampling error:

- *Specification error* occurs when the measurement instrument is not properly aligned with the construct that is measured. In other words, the construct validity of the instrument is weak.

- *Coverage or frame error* occurs when the sampling frame is a biased representation of the target population.

- *Nonresponse error* occurs when some members of the sample don't respond. A high response rate is essential to reliable statistical inference.

- *Measurement error* occurs when data collection is not reliable. Instrument reliability as well as inter- and intra-rater reliability are ways to help protect against measurement error.

- *Processing error* occurs as a result of editing mistakes, coding errors, data entry errors, programming errors, etc. during data analysis.

Measurement

Once the researcher has collected a sample and operationalized relevant constructs, measurement can take place. Measurement is the process of representing the construct with numbers in order to depict the amount of a phenomenon that is present at a given point in time. The purpose of this process is to differentiate between people, objects, or events that possess varying degrees of the phenomenon of interest. A measured phenomenon is referred to as a variable.

There are three basic types of measurement:

- *Self-report measurement* – One can measure a variable by asking participants to describe their behavior, to express their opinions, or to engage in interviews or focus groups in order to express their views. Alternatively, study participants can be asked to complete a survey, either face-to-face or online using the Internet. The self-report is the least accurate and most unreliable of the three types of measurements. Moreover, the least accurate type of self-report measurement is the retrospective self-report in which a person is asked to look back in time and remember details of a behavior or experience. Nonetheless, self-report measurements remain the most common type of measurement in social science research.

• *Physiological measurement* – Physiological measurement deals with measurements pertaining to the body. An apparatus can be used to take measurements; e.g., a scale to measure weight, a tape measure to measure height, a device to measure heart rate, or a galvanic skin response sensor to measure anxiety.

• *Behavioral measurement* – Behaviors can be measured through observation; e.g. recording reaction times, reading speed, disruptive behavior, etc. For example, the researcher defines key behaviors and trained observers then employ a count coding system to count the number of instances and/or duration of each key behavior. The employment of such a systematic approach to observation is important for the research study because, among its benefits, it promotes external validity by enhancing the replicability of the study. Measurement can be live or sessions can be recorded for later coding. Alternatively, the observer can view behavior and afterwards complete a Likert scale questionnaire or checklist providing his or her judgment regarding the observed behaviors.

Social scientists can better measure a construct if he or she looks at it from two (or more) different perspectives. For example, behavioral measures of the construct of interest can be used to confirm self-report measures and vice-versa. This procedure is referred to as triangulation.

Triangulation is the use of more than one measurement technique to measure a single construct in order to enhance the confidence in and reliability of research findings. This concept can be extended to encompass the use of quantitative and qualitative methodologies in a single mixed methods research study to determine the degree to which findings converge and are mutually confirming. Additionally, triangulation can be used for behavioral measurement by using more than one observer to record the same session. In this way inter-observer agreement can be checked periodically throughout the data collection phase of the study.

A distribution is a list of the individual scores related to some measured construct; e.g., sense of classroom community scores. When one examines the interrelationships among these scores – in particular, how they cluster together and how they spread out – then one is examining this distribution. To help visualize interrelationships among the scores of any distribution one uses measures of central tendency, measures of dispersion, measures of relative position, and graphs and charts. These measures are discussed in the next chapter.

An asymptotic distribution is a sample distribution that approximates the true distribution of a random variable for large samples, but not necessarily for small samples. Common distributions include the following:

- *Normal* or Gaussian distributions model continuous random variables that form a bell shaped curve.

- *Binomial distributions* model discrete random variables. A binomial random variable represents the number of successes in a series of trials in which the outcome is either success or failure.

- *Poisson distributions* model discrete random variables. A Poisson random variable typically is the count of the number of events that occur in a given time period when the events occur at a constant average rate.

- *Geometric distributions* also model discrete random variables. A geometric random variable typically represents the number of trials required to obtain the first failure.

- *Uniform distributions* model both continuous random variables and discrete random variables. The values of a uniform random variable are uniformly distributed over an interval.

Scaling is the branch of measurement that involves the construction of an instrument. Three unidimensional scaling methods frequently used in social science measurement are Likert, Guttman, and Thurstone scalings.

Likert Scaling

The Likert scale (pronounced Lick-ert) is a unidimensional, summative design approach to scaling named after its originator, psychologist Rensis Likert (Hopkins, 1998). It consists of a fixed-choice response format to a series of equal-weight statements regarding attitudes, opinions, and/or experiences. The set of statements act together to provide a coherent measurement of some construct. When responding to Likert items, respondents identify their level of agreement or disagreement to the statements. Likert scales are typically expressed in terms of a five- or seven-point scale and assume that the intensity of the reactions to the statements is linear. For example, the choices of a five-point scale might be strongly disagree, somewhat disagree, neither agree nor disagree, somewhat agree, and strongly agree. Individual statements that use this format are known as Likert items.

Alternatively, a semantic differential scale (a type of Likert scale) asks a person to rate a statement based upon a rating scale anchored at each end by opposites. For example,

Semantic Differential Scale

All murders should receive the death penalty.						
Strongly Agree					Strongly Disagree	
|	|	|	|	|	|	|
1	2	3	4	4	6	7

(circle level that applies)

In summary,

- A Likert scale is a multi-item, summative scale, in which a score for the measured construct is obtained by adding scores across all Likert items.

- The range of responses should be based on the nature of the statements presented. For example, if the statements relate to estimates of time frequency, the responses may range from never to very frequently.

- Likert scale items with less than five items are generally considered too coarse for useful measurement while items with more than seven items are considered too fine.

Odd-numbered Likert scales have a middle value that reflects a neutral or undecided response. It is possible to use an even number of responses. The respondent is forced to decide whether he or she leans more towards either end of the scale for each item. Forced-choice scales are those missing the middle or neutral option and forcing the participant to take a position. However, there are risks with this approach. Forcing a response may reduce the accuracy of the response. Individuals who truly do not agree or disagree will not like being forced to take a position, thereby reducing their likelihood to answer other items accurately. Additionally, forced-choice scales cannot be meaningfully intercorrelated or factor-analyzed (Johnson, Wood & Blinkhorn, 1988).

Likert scales can be assumed to produce interval scale data when the format clearly implies to the respondent that rating levels are evenly-spaced. However, researchers are not consistent on this point, as some researchers view Likert data as ordinal scale and others view the same data as interval scale. In particular, educational researchers tend to view this data as interval scale and health science researchers tend to view this data as ordinal scale. When in doubt, one should check the manual that accompanies the test instrument or check to see how other researchers in one's field use data generated by the test instrument in published research reports.

Guttman Scaling

The Guttman scale is a cumulative design approach to scaling. Its purpose is to establish a one-dimensional continuum for the concept one wishes to measure. Essentially, the items are ordered so that if a respondent agrees with any specific statement in the list, he or she will also agree with all previous statements. For example, take the following five-point Guttman scale. If the respondent selects item 3, it means that he or she agrees with the first 3 items but does not agree with items 4 and 5.

Guttman Scale

Please check the highest numbered statement with which you agree:

1. One should not murder.

2. Murders should be punished.

3. Sentences for murder should be severe.

4. More murders should receive the death penalty.

5. All murders should receive the death penalty.

Thurstone Scaling

The Thurstone scale also consists of a series of items. Respondents rate each item on a 1-11 scale in terms of how much each statement elicits a favorable attitude representing the entire range of attitudes from extremely favorable to extremely unfavorable. A middle rating is for items in which participants hold neither a favorable nor unfavorable opinion. The scale attempts to approximate an interval level of measurement. For example, take the following Thurstone scale.

Thurstone Scale

Please check all those statements with which you agree:

_____   1. All killers should be punished. (6.0)

_____   2. Killing a person is OK in self-defense. (9.0)

_____   3. Killing someone is never OK. (4.5)

_____   4. All killers should receive the death penalty. (1.0)

_____   5. Many killings are justified. (10.0)

_____   6. Killing someone is rarely OK. (5.5)

_____   7. Sentences for killers should be harsh. (2.0)

This technique attempts to compensate for the limitation of the Likert scale in that the strength of the individual items is taken into account in computing the score for each item. The weights for the checked statements are added and divided by the number of statements answered. For example, a respondent who selected choices 1, 3, and 7 above would have a score of

6.0 + 4.5 + 5.5 = 16/3 = 5.3. Dividing by the number of statements checked (3) puts the total score on the 1-11 scale.

Variables

A variable is any characteristic or quality that varies. For example, if a group of people consists of both men and women, then group members vary by gender, so gender is a variable. If students in a class achieve different scores on a test, then test score is a variable.

Once a construct has been operationalized and measured, the resultant measurements represent one or more variables depending on the number of subscales generated by the instrument. For example, the Classroom Community Scale (Rovai, 2002), which uses a Likert scale, produces a total classroom community score as well as subscale scores representing classroom social community and classroom learning community. Each set of scores is considered a variable.

When the value of a variable is determined by chance, that variable is called a random variable. For example, if a coin is tossed 30 times, the random variable X is the number of tails that come up. There are two types of random variables: discrete and continuous.

If a variable can take on any value between two specified values, it is called a continuous variable; otherwise, it is called a discrete variable. A discrete variable is one that cannot take on all values within the limits of the variable. For example, consider responses to a three-point rating scale that measures socioeconomic status (low, medium, high). The scale cannot generate the value of 2.5. Therefore, data generated by this rating scale represent a discrete variable.

Discrete variables are also called categorical variables or qualitative variables. Quantitative (or numeric) variables are continuous variables that have values that differ from each other by amount or quantity (e.g., test scores).

Scales of Measurement

An important factor that determines the amount of information that is provided by a variable is its measurement scale. Measurement scales are used to define and categorize variables. Specifically, variables are categorized as ratio, interval, ordinal, and nominal. Each has a decreasing level of measurement (from ratio to nominal) and each has a different mathematical attribute. These scales influence the statistical procedure one can use to analyze the data as well as the statistics used to describe the data. In general, one should use the highest level of measurement possible.

The four scales are described below in order of the level of information conveyed, from highest (ratio) to lowest (nominal).

Ratio scale variables allow one to quantify and compare the sizes of differences between them. They also feature an absolute zero, thus they allow for statements such as x is two times more than y. Examples of ratio scales are measures such as weight (in pounds), height (in inches), distance (in miles), and speed (in miles per hour).

> **Key Point**
> Counting, greater than or less than operations, addition and subtraction of scale values, and multiplication and division of scale values are permissible with ratio scale data.

Interval scale units, like ratio scale units, are equal to each other. That is, interval scale variables have equal intervals. However, unlike ratio scale variables, interval scales have an arbitrary zero. Consequently, negative values are permissible. For example, temperature, as measured in degrees Fahrenheit or Celsius, represents an interval scale. The difference between a temperature of 100 degrees and 90 degrees is the same difference as between 90 degrees and 80 degrees. One can also say that a temperature of 100 degrees is higher than a temperature of 90 degrees, and that an increase from 20 to 40 degrees is twice as much as an increase from 30 to 40 degrees. However, ordinal scales do not allow for statements such as 100 degrees is two times more than 50 degrees because the scale contains an arbitrary zero.

> **Key Point**
> Counting, greater than or less than operations, and addition and subtraction of scale values are permissible with interval scale data.

Ordinal scale variables allow one to rank order the items one measures in terms of which has less and which has more of the quality represented by the variable, but they do not provide information regarding much more. In other words, the values simply express an order of magnitude with no constant intervals between units. For example, one might ask study participants to estimate the amount of satisfaction on a scale of 1 to 10. Resultant data are often considered ordinal scale data because the interval between rankings is not necessarily constant. That is, the difference between rankings of 9 and 10 may not be the same as the difference between rankings of 1 and 2. This is most evident in the case of rankings in a horse race. The distance between ranks is not constant as the horse that come in second may have lost by a nose but the separation between other horses may have been greater. Many researchers consider IQ as an ordinal scale variable because the differences between IQ scores are not constant. Some researchers also consider Likert scale data to be ordinal.

Ordinal data can often appear similar to nominal data (in categories) or interval data (ranked from 1 to *N*). Ordinal data in categories are often referred to as collapsed ordinal data. An example of a collapsed ordinal variable is socioeconomic status (low, medium, high).

> **Key Point**
> Counting and greater than or less than operations are permissible with ordinal scale data.

Nominal scale variables are unordered categories. Also called categorical or discrete variables, they allow for only qualitative classification. That is, they can be measured only in terms of whether individual units of analysis belong to some distinctively different categories, but one cannot rank order the categories. In other words, numbers are assigned to categories as names. Which number is assigned to which category is arbitrary. All one can say is that two individuals are different in terms of a categorical variable, but one cannot say which category has more of the quality represented by the variable. Gender (male, female) is an example of a nominal scale variable. The researcher could code male as 1 and female as 2 in SPSS, or vice versa. Either way, the results will be the same.

> **Key Point**
> Counting operations are permissible with nominal scale data.

Measurement Validity

Validity as discussed in this section refers to the validity of measurements. It does not refer to research design validity, which is addressed separately in section 3 (Threats to Validity) of this chapter. Validity as described here refers the relative correctness of a measurement. In other words, it evaluates how well an instrument measures a construct and refers to the degree to which evidence and theory support the interpretations of test scores. The major types of measurement validity are summarized below (Gall, Gall, & Borg, 2007):

Face validity is an evaluation of the degree to which an instrument appears to measure what it purports to measure. It is the simplest and least scientific form of validity. It addresses the question: Does the instrument seem like a reasonable way to gain the information the researchers are attempting to obtain? It is often evaluated by the researcher.

> It [face validity] refers, not to what the test actually measures, but to what it appears superficially to measure. Face validity pertains to whether the test "looks valid" to the examinees who take it, the administrative personnel who decide on its use, and other technically untrained observers. (Anastasi, 1988, p. 144)

Unlike content validity, face validity does not depend on established theories for support (Fink, 1995).

Content validity is based on the extent to which a measurement reflects the specific intended domain of content based on the professional expertise of experts in the field (Anastasi, 1988). Unlike face validity, it depends on established theories for support. It is frequently assessed using a panel of experts that evaluate the degree to which the items on an instrument address the intended domain, nothing less and nothing more.

Construct validity refers to whether an instrument actually reflects the true theoretical meaning of a construct, to include the instrument's dimensionality; i.e., existence of subscales (Fink, 1995). Construct validity also refers to the degree to which inferences can be made from the operationalizations in a study to the theoretical constructs on which those operationalizations are based. Consequently, construct validity is related to external validity and encompasses both the appropriateness and adequacy of interpretations. Construct validity includes convergent and discriminant validity.

- *Convergent validity* is the degree to which scores on one test correlate with scores on other tests that are designed to measure the same construct.

- *Discriminant validity* is the degree to which scores on one test do not correlate with scores on other tests that are not designed to assess the same construct. For example, one would not expect scores on a trait anxiety test to correlate with scores on a state anxiety test.

Criterion validity relates to how adequately a test score can be used to infer an individual's most probable standing on an accepted criterion (Hopkins, 1998). It is used to show the accuracy of a measure by comparing it with another measure that has been demonstrated to be valid. Criterion validity includes predictive validity and concurrent validity.

- *Predictive validity* is the effectiveness of an instrument to predict the outcome of future behavior. Examples of predictor measures related to academic success in college include SAT scores and high school grade point average.

- *Concurrent validity* is the effectiveness of an instrument to predict present behavior by comparing it to the results of a different instrument that has been shown to predict that behavior. The relationship between the two tests reflects concurrent validity if the two measures were administered at about the same time, the outcomes of both measures predict the same present behavior, and one of the two tests is known to predict this behavior.

Normal Distribution

A smooth curve is referred to as a density curve (rather than a frequency curve as one sees in the histogram of a small sample). The area under any density curve sums to 1. Since the density curve represents the entire distribution, the area under the curve on any interval represents the proportion of observations in that interval.

The normal distribution is an example of a density curve (see figure 3.1). Therefore, for a normal distribution:

- 34.1% of the scores will fall between μ and 1σ
- 13.6% of the scores will fall between 1σ & 2σ
- 2.15% of the scores will fall between 2σ & 3σ

Therefore, 49.85% of the scores (34.1% + 13.6% + 2.15%) of a normally distributed variable fall between the mean and either +3σ or -3σ. In other words, 99.7% of the scores fall between -3σ and +3σ; that is, 0.3% fall outside this range. One encounters the concept of "Six Sigma" in business quality programs. Such programs attempt to reduce error to outside the range of 6σ (approximately three scores in a million).

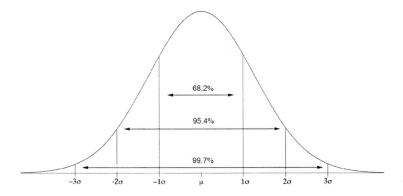

Figure 3.1. Normal curve

The normal distribution has the appearance of a bell-shaped curve. Other normal curve characteristics:

- Normal curves are unimodal and symmetric about the mean.

- For a perfectly normal distribution, mean = median = mode = Q_2 (second quartile) = P_{50} (fiftieth percentile). If the mean is not equal to the median, the distribution is skewed, with the mean being closer than the median to the skewed end of the distribution.

- Normal curves are asymptotic to the abscissa (refers to a curve that continually approaches the x-axis but does not actually reach it until x equals infinity; the axis so approached is the asymptote).

- Normal curves involve a large number of cases.

The normal or Gaussian distribution is the statistical distribution used in parametric statistics. The notation for a normal distribution is $N(\mu, \sigma)$. Its importance flows from the fact that any sums of normally distributed variables are normally distributed. Sums of variables that individually are not normally distributed also tend to be normally distributed.

There are infinitely many normal distributions that differ by the value of their means and standard deviations. One of these distributions is designated the standard normal distribution, which has a mean of 0 and a standard deviation of 1. (See the discussion on z-scores in the next section.)

One reason the normal distribution is important is that many social science variables are distributed approximately normally. Although the distributions are only approximately normal, they are usually quite close. A second reason the normal distribution is so important is that it is easy for statisticians to work with it. Many types of statistical tests can be used for normal distributions. Additionally, if the mean and standard deviation of a normal distribution are known, it is easy to convert back and forth from raw scores to percentiles.

Normal Curve Transformations

Transforming raw scores into standardized scores serves two purposes:

- It facilitates interpretation of raw scores.
- It allows comparison of two scores on two different scales.

A standard score is a general term referring to a score that has been transformed for reasons of convenience, comparability, etc. The basic type of standard score, known as a z-score, is an expression of the deviation of a score from the mean score of the group in relation to the standard deviation of the scores of the group. Most other standard scores are linear transformations of z-scores, with different means and standard deviations.

Z-Score, N(0,1)

A *z-score* distribution is the standard normal distribution, $N(0,1)$, with mean = 0 and standard deviation = 1. A z-score is a way of standardizing the scales of two or more distributions.

Z-scores permit one to describe a particular score in terms of where it fits into the overall group of scores in a normal distribution. A positive z-score indicates the number of standard deviations a score is above the mean of its own distribution, whereas a negative z-score indicates the number of standard deviations a score is below the mean of its own distribution.

Examples:

- A z-score of 1.0 is one standard deviation above the mean.
- A z-score of -1.5 is one-and-a-half standard deviations below the mean.
- A z-score of 0 is equal to the mean.

The formulas for calculating z-scores from raw scores and for converting z-scores back to raw scores are given below.

$$Z = \frac{(X - M)}{SD}$$

$$X = (Z)(SD) + M$$

T-Score, N(50,10)

A *T-score* is a normalized standard score with a mean of 50 and a standard deviation of 10. Thus a *T*-score of 60 represents a score one standard deviation above the mean. In a great number of testing situations, especially in education and psychology, scores are reported in terms of *T*-scores. Since *T*-scores do not contain decimal points or negative signs they are used more frequently than z-scores.

T-scores are calculated from z-scores as follows

$$T = 10Z + 50$$

Normal Curve Equivalent (NCE) Score, N(50, 21.06)

Another increasingly popular standardized score is the *NCE-score*. NCE-scores are normalized standard scores with a mean of 50 and a standard deviation of 21.06. The standard deviation of 21.06 was chosen so that NCE scores of 1 and 99 are equivalent to the 1st (P_1) and 99th (P_{99}) percentiles.

NCE scores are computed from z-scores as follows

$$NCE = 21.06Z + 50$$

Stanine Score

Stanine scores are groups of percentile ranks consisting of nine specific bands, with the 5th stanine centered on the mean, the first stanine being the lowest, and the ninth stanine being the highest. Each stanine is one-half standard deviation wide. Stanines are most often used to describe achievement test results as follows:

9th stanine, very superior, top 4% of scores.
8th stanine, superior, next 7% of scores.
7th stanine, considerably above average, next 12% of
    scores.
6th stanine, slightly above average, next 17% of scores.
5th stanine, average, middle 50% of scores.
4th stanine, slightly below average, next 17% of scores.
3rd stanine, considerably below average, next 12% of
    scores.
2nd stanine, poor, next 7% of scores.
1st stanine, very poor, bottom 4% of scores.

Standardized Norm-Referenced Testing

A norm-referenced test defines the performance of test-takers in relation to one another. In contrast, a criterion-referenced test defines the performance of each test taker without regard to the performance of others. The success is being able to perform a specific task or set of competencies at a certain predetermined level or criterion.

A standardized norm-referenced test is a norm-referenced test that assumes human traits and characteristics, such as academic achievement and intelligence, are normally distributed. The test compares a student's test performance with that of a sample of similar students. The normal curve represents the norm or average performance of a population and the scores that are above and below the mean within that population. Common standardized norm-referenced tests include the following:

ACT (formerly American College Testing Program or
    American College Test), $N(20,5)$
Graduate Record Examination (GRE), $N(500,100)$

SAT (formerly Scholastic Aptitude Test, Scholastic
Assessment Test), $N(500,100)$
Law School Admission Test (LSAT), $N(500,100)$
Graduate Management Admission Test (GMAT), $N(500,100)$
Minnesota Multiphasic Personality Inventory (MMPI), uses T-
scores, $N(5010)$
Wechsler Adult Intelligence Scale, $N(100,15)$
Stanford–Binet Intelligence Scales, $N(100,16)$
Otis–Lennon School Ability Test (OLSAT), $N(100, 16)$

Item and Test Analysis

Item analysis is the process used to evaluate the
effectiveness of items in a test by exploring the examinees'
responses to each item. Test analysis, on the other hand,
examines how the test items perform as a set.

Depending on the specific purpose of testing, the
effectiveness of items can be demonstrated many different ways.
In the context of classical test theory (e.g., Gulliksen, 1987), item
analysis is performed for tests with multiple-choice items. The
item analysis procedure provides such useful information as the
difficulty of each item, the discrimination power of the item, and
other properties of choices or distractors (Henrysson, 1971).

Item analysis has two major applications: psychometric tests
and achievement tests. Item analysis of psychometric tests
addresses issues such as the dimensionality of the test
instrument and internal consistency reliability analysis. However,
for achievement tests, item analysis is related to issues of item
difficulty and of the value of each item in discriminating between
high and low achievers.

The first step in performing an item analysis of an
achievement test is the tabulation of the responses that have
been made to each item of the test, that is, how many individuals
got each item correct, how many chose each of the possible
incorrect answers, and how many skipped the item. One must
have this information for the upper and lower portions of the
group, based on the total test score. From this type of tabulation,
one will be able to answer the following questions about each
item:

- How difficult is the item?

- Does the item distinguish between the higher and lower scoring examinees?
- Do some examinees select all the options? Or are there some options that no examinees choose?

Thompson and Levitov (1985) maintain that

items tend to improve test reliability when the percentage of students who correctly answer the item is halfway between the percentage expected to correctly answer if pure guessing governed responses and the percentage (100%) who would correctly answer if everyone knew the answer. (pp. 164-165)

Difficulty Index

The difficulty index is used to determine the difficulty level of test items. For items with one correct answer worth a single point, the item difficulty index is the number of correct answers divided by the number of respondents. The higher the difficulty factor, the easier the question is. A value of 1 means all test takers answered the question correctly.

When an item is worth other than a single point, or when there is more than one correct choice per item, the item difficulty is the average score on that item divided by the highest number of points for any one alternative.

Ebel and Frisbie (1986) suggest the following interpretations for this index:

- Very Easy: 0.91 and above
- Easy: 0.76 to 0.90
- Optimum Difficulty: 0.26 to 0.75
- Difficult: 0.11 to 0.25
- Very Difficult: 0.10 and below

Discrimination Index

The discrimination index is used to determine if each item on a test adequately discriminates between upper and lower achieving examinees. For technical reasons, this type of analysis is usually carried out on the top and bottom 27% of examinees (that is, the extreme 54%). When the number of examinees is small, the upper and lower groups can be defined as above and below the median (Wiersma & Jurs, 1990).

The discrimination index (D) is computed as follows

$$D = \frac{(N_U - N_L)}{n}$$

where N_L is the number of examinees from the lower group who correctly answered the item, N_U is the number of examinees from the upper group who correctly answered the item, and n is the number of examinees in one group.

The simplest way to use the discrimination index for test development/evaluation is to retain the items with the highest values (e.g., over .40), to eliminate the ones with the lowest (e.g., below .20), and to consider for modification those items between these two points (Ebel & Frisbie, 1986).

Additionally, the point-biserial correlation can be used to correlate the test takers performance on a single test item with their total score on the test. The point-biserial correlation (rpb) is the special case of the Pearson product moment correlation applied to a dichotomous and a continuous variable. The dichotomous variable is coded as 1 = correct, 0 = not correct. Items that discriminate well are those which have point-biserial correlations between .3 and .7.

A positive coefficient means that test-takers who correctly answered the item generally did well on the test as a whole, while those who did poorly on the item did poorly on the test.

A negative coefficient means that test-takers who did well on the test as a whole missed the item while those who did poorly on the test correctly answered the item.

Statistical Abbreviations and Symbols

Abbreviations using Latin letters should be italicized while abbreviations using Greek letters should not be italicized.

| $\neq$ | not equal |
| > | greater than |

$\geq$	greater than or equal
$<$	less than
$\leq$	less than or equal
$\pm$	plus and minus
$*$	asterisk; multiplication, interaction
ANCOVA	analysis of covariance
ANOVA	analysis of variance
b	y-intercept of a line
C	contingency coefficient
d	Cohen's measure of effect size
D	decile, discrimination index
D_i	Cook's distance
D^2	Mahalanobis distance
df	degrees of freedom
E	event
f	frequency
F	Fisher's F-ratio
h^2	communality
H_0	null hypothesis
H_1 or H_A	alternative or research hypothesis

ICC	intraclass correlation coefficient
M	mean, arithmetic average
m	slope of a line
MANCOVA	multivariate analysis of covariance
MANOVA	multivariate analysis of variance
Md	median
Mo	mode
MS	mean square
MSE	mean square error
n	subsample size
N	sample size
$N(\mu, \sigma)$	normal distribution
ns	not significant
$p(E)$	probability of event E
P	percentage, percentile
pr	partial correlation
Q	quartile
r	Pearson correlation coefficient
r_{pb}	point-biserial correlation coefficient
r^2	Pearson coefficient of determination

R	multiple correlation coefficient
R_c	canonical correlation coefficient
R^2	multiple coefficient of determination
s	sample standard deviation
s^2	sample variance
SEM	standard error of measurement
SS	sum of squares
t	t-test statistic
U	Mann-Witney U statistic
V	Cramér's V
z	standard score
α	alpha, Type I error
β	beta, Type II error, regression coefficient
χ^2	chi-square test statistic
η	eta, correlation coefficient
η^2	eta square, effect size
η_p^2	partial eta square, effect size
ε	epsilon, measure of sphericity departure

γ	gamma, measure of ordinal association
κ	kappa, inter-rater agreement
μ	mu, population mean
Φ	phi correlation coefficient
Σ	sigma (capitalized), summation
σ	sigma, population standard deviation
σ^2	sigma square, population variance
τ_b	tau-b, measure of ordinal association
τ_c	tau-c, measure of ordinal association

3.2: Quantitative Research Designs

Introduction

A research design is a blueprint for research that focuses on the logical structure of the research and identifies how research participants are grouped and when data are to be collected. Yin (1989) emphasizes that a good research design deals with a logical problem and not a logistical problem.

Quantitative research designs are most often used for explanation or theory testing. There are two major types of social science quantitative research designs (Gall, Gall, & Borg, 2007):

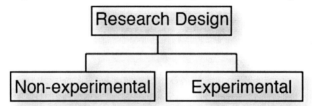

Non-experimental designs identify the characteristics of a phenomenon and describe the variable(s) under study. The researcher tests relationships between variables without controlling or manipulating research participants and/or conditions. In other words, the researcher studies what naturally occurs or has already occurred.

Although the professional literature is not in agreement with a non-experimental topology, the following three classifications of non-experimental designs encompass the major types of non-experimental research:

- Descriptive designs, to include survey research
- Correlational designs
- Causal-comparative or ex post facto designs

Experimental designs involve research in which the researcher tests relationships between variables by controlling or manipulating research participants and/or conditions. There are four types of experimental designs:

- True experimental designs
- Quasi-experimental designs
- Pre-experimental designs

- Single-case designs

Some textbooks combine quasi-experimental and pre-experimental designs into a single quasi-experimental category.

Non-Experimental Designs

Descriptive Designs

A descriptive research design or study (sometimes called observational study or survey research) is meant to generate an accurate record of what is happening in a specific situation with a given population. The researcher does not attempt to exert control over the phenomena of interest. Instead, phenomena are observed (measured) as they occur in a situation or at a given point or points in time. Findings of such studies may identify the defining characteristics (attributes or behavior) of a specific phenomenon or group, and/or determine the prevalence of a phenomenon (i.e., how frequently it occurs). Moreover, descriptive studies describe characteristics without investigating relationships between variables. They may be used to develop theory, identify problems, make judgments, inform policy, etc. Because there is no attempt to explore causality, there are no independent and dependent variables.

There are two basic types of descriptive studies (Campbell & Stanley, 1963; Gall, Gall, & Borg, 2007):

1. A *cross-sectional design* is used to collect data that reflect current attitudes, opinions, or beliefs. The defining feature of a cross-sectional study is that it collects data on and compares different population groups at a single snapshot in time. Surveys (questionnaires) and interviews are frequently used to collect data.

2. A *longitudinal or time series design* is used to study individuals over time. The defining feature of a longitudinal design is that researchers conduct several observations of the same research participants over a period of time, sometimes lasting years. Longitudinal designs are subclassified as follows:

   - A *trend study design* involves identifying a population and examining changes within that population repeatedly over time; e.g., university faculty. Typically, trend studies are not composed of the same people at different time periods.

- A *cohort study design* follows a specific subpopulation repeatedly over time, but not the same people. Different samples are drawn over time of the same population of interest; e.g., university alumni who graduated in 1998.

- A *panel study design* examines the same people from a specific population repeatedly over time. The sample is called a panel. Panel studies can involve replacement of panel members as they leave the study because they no longer meet certain criteria, such as age or informed consent.

Use of surveys is a very popular means for collecting data in descriptive studies. Surveys can be deployed:

- face-to-face in group settings and completed at a set time using pencil and paper or respondents can be asked to return the completed survey at a later time

- the mail can be used for distributing and returning surveys

- the telephone can be used

- e-mail surveys can also be used

Electronic surveys sent by e-mail is a popular survey delivery method. E-mail provides an easier, less expensive, and more immediate means of response over regular mail (Flaherty et al., 1998). Survey Monkey at http://www.surveymonkey.com/ is a popular resource used for managing electronic surveys. A minimum of two weeks should be allowed for collecting electronic surveys. The best time to initiate an electronic survey is early in the morning of a business day. Periodic follow-up contacts have positive effects on response rates to mail as well as to e-mail surveys.

Relatively large sample sizes with reasonable response rates are required in order to minimize nonresponse error. Common criteria for volunteer or survey response rates are cited by Mangione (1995):

- higher than 85%: excellent rate
- 70% to 85%: very good rate
- 60% to 70%: acceptable

- 50% to 60%: barely acceptable
- below 50%: not scientifically acceptable

However, response rates are declining for all types of surveys, possibly attributable to the large amount of surveying that takes place. As a consequence, survey response rates are frequently below 50%, severely limiting their scientific value.

Dillman (1978) developed the *total design method* (*TDM*) to obtain high response rates from surveys. He explains his method as follows:

> The appeal of the *TDM* is based on convincing people first that a problem exists that is of importance to a group with which they identify, and second, that their help is needed to find a solution. The researcher is portrayed as a reasonable person who, in light of the complexity of the problem, is making a reasonable request for help, and, if forthcoming, such help will contribute to the solution of that problem. The exchange the researcher seeks to establish is broader than that between him or herself and the questionnaire recipient, that is, if you do something for me, I'll do something for you. Rather, the researcher is identified as an intermediary between the person asked to contribute to the solution of an important problem and certain steps that might help solve it. Thus the reward to the respondents derives from the feeling that they have done something important to help solve a problem faced by them, their friends, or members of a group including community, state, or nation, whose activities are important to them. (pp. 162-163)

Gall, Gall, and Borg (2007) recommend the following actions to increase survey response rates:

- Having sponsorship or endorsement for the survey by someone who is highly-respected in the population being surveyed.

- Having a good, short justification of the survey that addresses the importance of the study.

- Notifying individuals in advance that a survey is coming.

- Keeping the survey short.

- Assuring confidentiality or anonymity. Maintaining confidentiality means that only the investigator(s) or individuals of the research team can identify the responses of individual research participants. Providing anonymity means that either the study does not collect identifying information of individual research participants (e.g., name, e-mail address, etc.), or the study cannot link individual responses with participants' identities.

- Make call-backs where needed for telephone surveys. In mail and e-mail surveys, provide periodic reminders to complete the survey. Provide a new copy of the survey at each opportunity along with a personalized notice.

- Offer to provide feedback regarding the study.

- Offer nominal remuneration. Linking the return of the survey to entrance into a drawing for a prize can increase response rates.

- Use certified or express mail for mail surveys.

Interviews, although primarily used as a data gathering technique by qualitative researchers, can also be used in descriptive studies and especially in mixed-methods studies. Typically, interviews are conducted one-on-one, in contrast to focus groups, which are group interviews. There are three types of interviews:

- *Structured interviews* use pre-formulated questions and regulation regarding the order of the questions and time available.

- *Semi-structured interviews* use some pre-formulated questions, but there is no strict adherence to them. New questions might emerge during the interview process.

- *Unstructured interviews* have few, if any, pre-formulated questions. The interviewees are free to say whatever they desire.

> **Key Point**
> Large sample sizes are required for descriptive studies, on the order of 100 participants or more in each major group.

A *meta analysis* is often also characterized as a type of descriptive study in which the units of analysis are individual studies rather than people. It incorporates a systematic review of the research literature to determine treatment effect or effect size by combining data from multiple studies. The aim of the meta-analysis is to determine the magnitude of an effect with adequate precision based on numerous research studies that address the phenomenon of interest. More weight is given to studies with more precise estimates (Glass, 1976). This type of analysis is especially useful when there are multiple studies with conflicting results. Meta-analyses are important because decisions about an intervention or the validity of a hypothesis should not be based on the results of a single study as results typically vary among studies.

A meta-analysis starts with a systematic process of identifying similar studies during a comprehensive literature review. After identifying the studies, the researcher defines the ones to retain for the meta-analysis. Then structured formats are used to key-in information taken from the selected studies. Finally, the researcher combines the data to arrive at a summary estimate of the effect, its 95% confidence interval, and conducts a test of the homogeneity of the studies.

Correlational Designs

A correlational design produces studies that examine relationships (i.e., correlation, association, co-variation) between two or more existing, non-manipulated variables drawing from a single group of research participants. For example, correlation studies seek to determine relationships between variables, such as sense of classroom community and grade point average.

Scatterplots are graphic representations of correlations between two variables.

Correlational studies are also used to make predictions using regression analysis. In regression analysis, one designates one variable as the dependent variable or DV (also called the response variable or criterion variable) and the other variable(s) as the independent variable(s) or IV(s) (also called predictor variables or explanatory variables). IVs are potential causes or influences on the DV. There are also situations when one is not exploring cause and effect relationships. In these situations it is customary not to designate variables as DV or IV.

There is no attempt to manipulate variables or to establish causal relationships in correlation studies, although such studies are often used to explore possible causal relationships. A common error is to confuse correlation and causation. Correlation is a necessary but not a sufficient condition for determining causality. Correlations describe a relationship between two variables, but do not explain why the variables are related. One cannot verify cause and effect relationships using correlation only. All that correlation shows is that the two variables are related. There may be one or more other variables – e.g., confounding variables – that influence or explain this relationship. For example, drowning rate and rate of ice cream sales are positively correlated, but no one would claim that this relationship is causal. A confounding variable is temperature, related to both ice cream consumption and deaths by drowning. Statistics alone can never prove causality, but it can show one where to look.

One must address several factors to obtain evidence of a cause and effect relationship:

- Temporal precedence of the cause over the effect – one must show that the cause happened before the effect. For example, let's say that one discovers that computer anxiety and computer experience are inversely related (i.e., as one goes up the other goes down). Does that mean low computer experience causes computer anxiety? Or does computer anxiety cause low experience with the computer?

- Covariation of the cause and effect – one must show that the effect covaries with the hypothesized cause.

- No plausible alternative explanations for the effect – it's possible that there is some unknown extraneous variable that is the real cause.

- Theoretical basis for the cause and effect relationship – there should be a theory-based causal mechanism that can explain the relationship.

> **Key Point**
> Large sample sizes of 30 participants or more are required for correlation studies.

A causal-comparative study explores the possible causes or consequences of differences that already exist between or among groups of individuals (Gall, Gall, & Borg, 2007). The IVs are not manipulated by the researcher but occur naturally or were manipulated prior to the research; e.g., dropouts versus non-dropouts and females versus males. Causal-comparative studies are also called ex post facto studies because both the effect and the presumed cause have already occurred and must be studied after the fact. Causal-comparative studies typically involve two or more groups (depending on the number of levels of the IV). Individuals are selected because they belong to a specific population.

These studies differ from correlational studies in that correlational studies explore relationships between variables, not group differences, and involve only one group. Although the outcomes of causal-comparative research might suggest that changes in one variable cause changes in other variables, this cannot be verified without further research.

There is no random assignment of participants to groups in causal-comparative studies. They are assigned based on their status; e.g., dropouts or non-dropouts and males or females.

Therefore, alternative explanations for causality pose threats to internal validity in the form of rival hypotheses. Some things to look out for with causal-comparative studies:

- Correlation-causation fallacy (e.g., an extraneous variable like anxiety could be the cause of lung disease rather than smoking if anxiety is related to both smoking and lung disease).

- Direction of causality (i.e., which variable is the cause and which variable is the effect?). For example does lack of experience using computers contribute to computer anxiety or does computer anxiety contribute to lack of computer experience?

- Post hoc fallacy (when an effect is observed, and a plausible event preceding it is claimed to be cause); e.g., stock market fluctuations explained by various current world events that appear plausible but are only guesses.

The researcher typically employs one or more of the following procedures to control extraneous variables in causal-comparative studies:

- Use a matched pairs design.

- Hold potential extraneous variables constant across groups. In other words, make the groups as homogeneous as possible, except for the IV.

- Use statistical control; i.e., conduct *ANCOVA*.

Although causal-comparative designs are similar to the pre-experimental non-equivalent group posttest only design, they are treated as more credible because of the effort that is made to control extraneous variables.

> Key Point
> Large sample sizes on the order of 30 participants or more per group are required for causal-comparative studies.

Experimental Designs

An experimental study involves designs in which the researcher controls the manipulation of the IV (i.e., the treatment or condition). There are three types of experimental studies:

- True experiments
- Quasi-experiments
- Pre-experiments

Experimental studies can incorporate one or both of the following designs:

Between-subjects designs in which the researcher is comparing different groups of research participants who experience different interventions.

Within-subjects or repeated measures designs in which the researcher is comparing the same participants repeatedly over time.

Studies that include both designs are called mixed between and within designs. This design requires at least one between-subjects IV and one within-subjects IV in the same hypothesis test. In the simplest 2 x 2 design one would have participants randomly assigned to one of two groups and each group would be measured twice.

> **Key Point**
> A minimum of 15 participants are required per group (some researchers claim a minimum of 20-25 participants for each group).

True Experiments

True experiments are the models for research conducted in the natural and social sciences. The three characteristics of true experimental designs:

1. *Manipulation* – The experimenter introduces an experimental intervention in the study as the independent variable (IV). The researcher manipulates this IV by administering it to some research participants and withholding it from other participants. In other words, the researcher varies the IV and observes the effect that the manipulation has on the dependent variable (DV).

2. *Control* – Campbell and Stanley (1963) observed that obtaining scientific evidence requires at least one comparison. Control groups are used for this purpose. The term *control group* refers to the participants that do not receive the experimental intervention and their performance on the DV serves as a basis for evaluating the performance of the experimental group (the group that received the experimental intervention).

3. *Randomization* – Randomization is the random assignment or allocation of research participants to groups from the sample. The term random means every participant has an independent and equal chance of being assigned to any group. Random assignment is not to be confused with random selection. Random selection, associated with external validity, means that research participants are randomly selected from some target population to participate in the study.

The purpose of true experimental studies is to investigate possible cause-and-effect relationships by exposing one or more experimental groups to one or more treatment conditions and comparing the results to one or more control groups not receiving the treatment.

True experiments are ideally suited to studying cause and effect relationships because they incorporate procedures to minimize the influence of extraneous variables that could produce the effect presumed to be attributed to the experimental intervention. An extraneous variable is a variable that may compete with the IV in explaining the outcome and presents a rival hypothesis to explain the research results.

In the designs below, X reflects exposure to an experimental intervention of some type and O represents an observation (i.e., measurement). Multiple rows reflect multiple groups. For example, two rows indicate the study consists of two groups. R designates the group or groups that are formed by a random assignment (as opposed to random selection) procedure. N can be used to indicate nonequivalent groups and C is used to denote assignment to groups by cutoff scores. Time moves from left to right.

Equivalent Pretest-Posttest Control Group Design

The *equivalent pretest-posttest control group design* is very common (Campbell & Stanley, 1963). Additional groups are often introduced in this design. The design is used when it is necessary to measure groups on pretest measures, despite the fact that the groups are equivalent. Random assignment does not guarantee equivalency, particularly with small sample sizes.

Equivalent Pretest-Posttest Control Group			
R	O_1	X	O_2
R	O_3		O_4

Time ⟶

Major sources of internal invalidity: testing, instrumentation, and experimental mortality.

Recommended hypothesis test: between subjects *ANCOVA*, DV = posttest scores, IV = group, and covariate = pretest scores.

Solomon Four-Group Design

The *Solomon four-group design* is meant to deal with a potential testing threat (Campbell & Stanley, 1963). A testing threat to internal validity occurs when the act of taking a pretest affects how people score on a posttest. Note that two of the four groups receive the treatment and two do not. Furthermore, two of the groups receive a pretest and two do not.

Solomon Four Group			
R	O_1	X	O_2
R	O_3		O_4
R		X	O_5
R			O_6

Time ————➤

Major sources of internal invalidity: instrumentation and experimental mortality.

Recommended hypothesis test: 2 x 2 *ANOVA*, DV = posttest scores and IV = group. If the main and interactive effects of pretesting are negligible, conduct an *ANCOVA* of O_4 versus O_2, with pretest scores = covariate.

Equivalent Posttest-Only Control Group Design

The *equivalent posttest-only control group design* is the most powerful true experiment when properly executed with random assignment (Campbell & Stanley, 1963). When the groups are not equivalent, the study becomes a very weak pre-experiment.

Equivalent Posttest-Only Control Group		
R	X	O_1
R		O_2

Time ————➤

Major sources of internal invalidity: instrumentation and experimental mortality.

Recommended hypothesis test: independent *t*-test, DV = posttest scores and IV = group.

Quasi-Experiments

Quasi-experimental research designs lack one or more of the three characteristics of a true experiment. Frequently, quasi-experimental studies employ in-tact, naturally occurring groups and consequently do not employ random assignment of research participants to groups (Campbell & Stanley, 1963; Gall, Gall, & Borg, 2007).

Quasi-experimental designs were developed to explore causality in situations where one cannot use a true experiment. The distinctive feature of quasi-experiments is the use nonequivalent groups.

- Assignment is nonrandom.
- Groups may be different.
- Group differences may affect outcomes.

The purpose of quasi-experimental designs is to approximate the conditions of the true experiment in a setting that does not allow for random assignment of participants to treatment and control conditions. Because quasi-experimental studies use existing groups, this design is often more convenient and less disruptive to the participants and the researcher.

Shadish, Cook, and Campbell (2002) argue for three principles when working with quasi-experimental designs:

- Identification and evaluation of plausible threats to internal validity.

- Use of multiple control groups, multiple baselines. Use of statistical control as a last resort.

- Use of coherent pattern matching. This principle involves making a complex prediction about a particular causal hypothesis that would leave few viable alternative explanations. The logic behind this principle is that the more complex the prediction, the less likely that a given alternative could generate the same results.

Nonequivalent Pretest-Posttest Control Group Design

The *nonequivalent pretest-posttest control group design* is a very popular quasi experimental design. It is very similar to the true experimental version of this design with the exception that nonequivalent groups are used. Like the true experiment, this design can also include more than two groups.

Nonequivalent Pretest-Posttest Control Group			
N	O_1	X	O_2
N	O_3		O_4
	Time $\longrightarrow$		

Major sources of internal invalidity: testing, instrumentation, selection, interactions with selection, and experimental mortality.

Recommended hypothesis test: between subjects *ANCOVA*, DV = posttest scores, IV = group, and covariate = pretest scores.

Time Series Design

The *time series design* involves repeated measurements (i.e., observations) of the same group, both before and after treatment (Campbell & Stanley, 1963). The interval between observations is held constant throughout the entire range of observations, to include the interval between the last pretest and the first posttest. The number of pretest and posttest observations can vary.

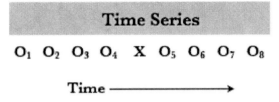

$$O_1 \quad O_2 \quad O_3 \quad O_4 \quad X \quad O_5 \quad O_6 \quad O_7 \quad O_8$$

Time ⟶

Major sources of internal invalidity: history, testing, and instrumentation.

Recommended hypothesis test: within-subjects one-way *ANOVA*, DV = scores and IV = observation.

Multiple Time Series Design

The *multiple time series design* adds a control group to the design.

Multiple Time Series

$$O_1 \quad O_2 \quad O_3 \quad O_4 \quad X \quad O_5 \quad O_6 \quad O_7 \quad O_8$$

$$O_9 \quad O_{10} \quad O_{11} \quad O_{12} \qquad O_{13} \quad O_{14} \quad O_{15} \quad O_{16}$$

Time ⟶

Major sources of internal invalidity: testing instrumentation, and experimental mortality.

Recommended hypothesis test: mixed subjects two-way *ANOVA*, DV = scores and IVs = observation and group.

Counterbalanced Design

In a *counterbalanced design* (also known as a *Latin square*), all groups are exposed to all treatments, but in a different order. In the design outlined below there are only posttests, but variations of this design to include pretests are possible.

Counterbalanced			
X_1O_1	X_2O_2	X_3O_3	X_4O_4
X_2O_5	X_4O_6	X_1O_7	X_3O_8
X_3O_9	X_1O_{10}	X_4O_{11}	X_2O_{12}
X_4O_{13}	X_3O_{14}	X_2O_{15}	X_1O_{16}

Time ⟶

Major sources of internal invalidity: testing, instrumentation, selection, interactions with selection, and experimental mortality.

Recommended hypothesis test: mixed three-way *ANOVA*, DV = scores and IVs = group, treatment, and observation.

Pre-Experiments

A pre-experimental study is a study that utilizes one of three designs that are universally regarded as very weak and crude. Campbell and Stanley (1963) describe pre-experiments as having such a total absence of control as to be of almost no scientific value. Consequently they are of very limited value.

The purpose of such studies is to obtain preliminary research data to determine the effectiveness of an intervention. They may be used for a pilot test preceding a more systematic study. Some researchers do not consider a pre-experimental study as a separate type of study; e.g., Gall, Gall, and Borg (2007). These researchers typically include the pre-experimental study into the quasi-experimental category, while recognizing its inherent weakness.

The three research designs that are typically associated with pre-experimental studies, as displayed below.

One-Shot Case Study Design

The first and weakest design is the *one-shot case study*.

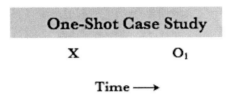

X O_1

Time ⟶

Major sources of internal invalidity: history, and maturation.

Recommended hypothesis test: one-sample *t*-test.

One-Group Pretest-Posttest Design

The next pre-experimental design is the *one-group pretest-posttest design.*

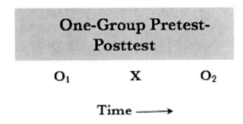

O_1 X O_2

Time ⟶

Major sources of internal invalidity: history, maturation, testing, and instrumentation.

Recommended hypothesis test: dependent *t*-test, DV = scores and IV = observation.

Static Group Comparison Design

The final pre-experimental design is the static group comparison design.

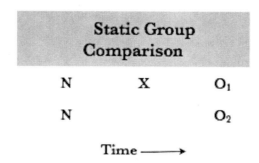

Major sources of internal invalidity: instrumentation, selection, interactions with selection, and experimental mortality.

Recommended hypothesis test: independent t-test, DV = posttest scores and IV = group.

Single-Case Designs

Single-case (single-subject) studies represent research that focuses on the study of a single organism, rather than a group or groups of participants. Researchers observe a participant under one condition, then they change conditions and make further observations. (The number of conditions introduced depends on the levels of the IV and the specific design.) When a participant reacts differently to the different conditions, this is evidence that the IV may influence the DV.

A single-case design is a type of time-series design. A participant is observed repeatedly to establish a baseline (A). Then different treatments or the same treatment are introduced (B) or withdrawn, depending on the specific design. Common single-case designs include the A-B design, the A-B-A design, the A-B-A-B design, the B-A-B design, and the A-B-C-B design (Heppner, Kivlighan, & Wampold, 1999).

A-B Design

The *A-B design* is a single-case design that begins with baseline observations (A) before the introduction of an intervention (B).

A-B Design							
Baseline (A)				Treatment (B)			
O	O	O	O	XO	XO	XO	XO

Time ─────────────→

The A-B design lacks control of extraneous variables. What is not known is whether it was the treatment (IV) that led to any change or other possibilities (i.e., concurrent history).

Other Single-Case Designs

The *A-B-A design* is a single-case design that begins with baseline observations (A) before the introduction of an intervention (B). After repeated observations are made on the participant during the intervention period, the intervention is withdrawn and more observations are made (A). If the treatment (IV) is effective, there will be a positive change in the condition being measured (DV) after treatment is introduced. There will be a return to the baseline level when the treatment is withdrawn.

The *A-B-A-B design* is a single-case design that begins with baseline observations (A) before the introduction of an intervention (B). After repeated observations are made on the participant during the intervention period, the intervention is withdrawn and more observations are made (A). Finally, the intervention is re-introduced (B) and more observations are made.

The *A-B-C-B design* is a single-case design that includes a baseline period (A) and two intervention periods (B and C). The study begins with baseline observations (A) before the introduction of an intervention (B). After repeated observations are made of the participant during the intervention period, the intervention is altered (C) and more observations are made.

Finally, the original intervention is restored (B) and additional observations are made.

A multiple-baseline design is a single-case design that includes several baseline periods. Multiple-baseline designs are used when it is not possible or ethical to withdraw a treatment and return to baseline. For one variation of the design, observations are made during a baseline period for several behaviors of interest. The treatment is implemented first for one behavior, but the baseline period is continued for the other behaviors. Later, the treatment is implemented for another behavior, and so on until it has been implemented for all behaviors. By staggering the introduction of the treatment for different behaviors, the researcher can ascertain that it is truly the treatment that is making the difference (Heppner, Kivlighan, & Wampold, 1999).

Additional design variations are possible, such as randomized AB designs. This design involves two phases, A and B, that are repeated in a randomized fashion over an extended period of time so that the presence of an A or B phase at any point of time is random (Heppner, Kivlighan, & Wampold, 1999).

The most important characteristics of single-case designs are summarized below (McMillan & Schumacher, 1997):

- Reliable measurement. Observations of behavior using standardized, reliable techniques are conducted throughout the study.

- Repeated measurement. Numerous measurements are made with a fixed interval.

- Description of conditions. A rich description of the setting and all conditions are recorded to assist in the analysis.

- Duration and stability of baseline and treatment condition. Typically, each condition (A and B) last the same amount of time and contain the same number of observations.

- Single variable rule. Only one variable is manipulated during the study.

Mixed Methods Designs

Mixed methods research is a methodology for conducting research that involves collecting, analyzing, and integrating quantitative and qualitative research in a single study. The basis for this form of research is that both qualitative and quantitative research, in combination, provide a better understanding of a research problem or issue than either research approach alone.

There are two primary approaches:

1. Sequential design consists of quantitative and qualitative methods are used sequentially.

2. Parallel design consists of quantitative and qualitative methods are used at the same time.

Typically, the mixed methods research study will have separate quantitative and qualitative research questions.

Quantitative Research Report

A quantitative research report (including theses, dissertations, and research grant reports) often consists of front matter and the following five chapters or sections:

1. Introduction
2. Literature review
3. Methodology
4. Results
5. Discussion

A research proposal often consists of the first three chapters. Once approved, the researcher then conducts the study and adds the final two chapters for the complete report.

Institutions normally have their own specific policies regarding the format of research proposals and reports as well as the style manual to be followed. What is provided here is a sampling of the contents and organization of typical research reports and proposals.

The first three chapters represent a written plan for the research. It enables interested parties (including funding agencies and university dissertation committees) to obtain information about the proposed study and offer suggestions for improvement. These chapters address three major questions:

- What problem is to be studied?
- Why is it worth studying?
- How will it be studied?

Each major part of the report is summarized below.

Front Matter

Content will vary depending on the purpose of the document.

- *Title page*. The title page should show the title of the study, identification of the researcher, and date of submission. The title should include:
  - Precise identification of the problem area, including specification of IVs, DVs, and target population.
  - Sufficient clarity and conciseness for indexing purposes.

- *Copyright page*.

- *Abstract*. The abstract is a condensed summary of the report that is normally limited to 350 words. This is the length preferred by Dissertation Abstracts, University Microfilms International Publications. It should be accurate, self-contained, and readable.

- *Dissertation committee approval page*.

- *Acknowledgements*.

- *Table of contents*.

- *List of tables*.

- *List of figures*.

Introduction

The introduction provides readers with background information for the study. Its purpose is to establish a framework for the research. The researcher should:

- Create reader interest in the topic.

- Lay the broad foundation for the problem that leads to the study.

- Place the study within the context of the scholarly professional literature.

An introduction often includes the following sections:

- *Background.* A concise description of the background and need organized from the general to the specific. Includes an explanation of the theoretical framework for the research by identifying the broad theoretical concepts and principles underpinning the research. The background logically leads to the problem statement.

- *Problem statement.* This is a description of the current issue that needs a solution. The target population and constructs are identified.

- *Significance of the problem.* This section is a statement that addresses why the problem merits investigation and the importance of the study.

- *Purpose.* A one or two sentence description of the goal to be gained from the research.

- *Research question(s).* Research questions flow from the problem statement and specify precise relations or differences between identified constructs that the study will address. Below are examples of quantitative research questions and identification of the research designs and hypotheses tests they imply.

Is there a difference in sense of classroom community among university students enrolled in fully online programs and the national norm for university students, $\mu \neq$ [test value]?

> [Implies a *descriptive design* and *one-sample t-test*]

Is there a difference in mean sense of classroom community between online and traditional on campus university students, $\mu_1 \neq \mu_2$?

> [Implies a *static group comparison design* (pre-experimental) and *independent t-test*]

Is there a difference between sense of classroom community pretest and sense of classroom community posttest among university students, $D \neq 0$? (Note: D represents the mean difference between paired observations.)

> [Implies a *one-group pretest-posttest design* (pre-experimental) and *dependent t-test*]

Is there a difference in sense of classroom community between graduate students based on type program (fully online, blended, traditional), $\mu_1 \neq \mu_2 \neq \mu_3$?

> [Implies a *static group comparison design* with three groups (pre-experimental or causal-comparative) and one-way between subjects *analysis of variance (ANOVA)*]

Is there a difference in sense of classroom community between graduate students based on type program (fully online, blended, traditional) after controlling for student age, $\mu_1 \neq \mu_2 \neq \mu_3$?

> [Implies a *nonequivalent pretest-posttest control group design* with three groups (quasi-experimental) and one-way between-subjects *analysis of covariance (ANCOVA)*]

Is there a difference in sense of classroom community over time (observation 1, observation 2, observation 3, observation 4) among undergraduate students, $\mu_1 \neq \mu_2 \neq \mu_3 \neq \mu_4$?

> [Implies a *time series design* (quasi-experimental) and one-way within-subjects *analysis of variance (ANOVA)*]

Is there a relationship between sense of classroom community and grade point average among freshmen students?

> [Implies a *correlational design* and *Pearson product-moment correlation test*]

Is there a relationship between sense of classroom community and grade point average in online students after controlling for student age?

> [Implies a *correlational design* and *partial correlation*]

Can sense of classroom community predict grade point average among university students?

> [Implies a *correlational design* (regression analysis) and *bivariate regression*]

Can one reliability predict whether a university student is an online or on campus student based on classroom community spirit and classroom community trust?

> [Implies a *correlational design* (regression analysis) and *discriminant analysis*]

- *Limitations and delimitations.* A limitation identifies potential weaknesses of the study. A delimitation addresses how a study is bounded.

- *Assumptions.* Assumptions typically are related to study limitations and delimitations and they are likely to influence study results. Limitations and delimitations should not be repeated in this section.

- *Definition of terms.* Constitutive definitions are provided for important terms or concepts used in the study. References should be cited, as appropriate.

- *Organization of the study.* This section summarizes the main chapters of the report (or the introduction, literature review, and methodology if a proposal) so that readers will know where to find specific information.

Literature Review

This chapter includes summarizes literature that is relevant to the research and expands on the information provided in the introduction. It emphasizes recent developments and avoids the researcher's personal opinions. Consequently, citations to the professional literature are required throughout this chapter.

The literature review need not be lengthy; however, it should be comprehensive. It is organized (often under headings) to facilitate understanding, starts with a short paragraph outlining the organization of the chapter, forms a connected argument, and has a conclusion at the end in which the researcher:

- Provides a summary of the main issues and findings of the review.

- Discusses the existing scientific knowledge base related to the research problem.

- Supports the problem statement.

Poor reviews lose the reader in details and give the impression the researcher is meandering. This chapter describes important threads rather than simply providing summaries of prior research. Good reviews also relate the professional literature to the research problem. An acceptable structure provides a funnel effect, which goes from general to more specific, ending with the research problem.

Methodology

The methodology chapter usually contains the following sections:

- *Introduction.* A concise description of the contents and organization of the chapter.

- *Population and sample.* Identification of the target population, sample, sample size, and sampling methodology.

- *Setting.* A description of the research setting.

- *Instrumentation.* A description of all instruments and apparatus used in the research. Includes reliability and validity characteristics.

- *Procedures.* Identification of the process used by the researcher to conduct the study. Details should be sufficient for study replication. If lengthy, the details can be provided in an appendix.

- *Research question(s).* The researcher repeats the research question(s) from the first chapter. Following each research question there should be a null hypothesis.

- *Variables.* The researcher identifies the constructs and their operational definitions. For example, an operational definition of intelligence could be "intelligence quotient as measured by the Wechsler Intelligence Scale for Children (WISC-III)."

- *Design.* Identification of the type of study and design. For example, the study might use a true experimental pretest-posttest with a control group design. The design must be appropriate for the problem and allow for adequate controls.

- *Data Analysis.* It is often useful to organize this section according to hypotheses, explaining how one will analyze the data to respond to each hypothesis.

- *Threats to validity.* Major threats to the internal and external validity of the study and how they will be controlled are listed here. Threats not adequately controlled are study limitations.

- *Summary.*

Results

This chapter is limited to statistical results. All relevant results should be included, including nonsignificant findings and findings that are counter to the study's hypotheses. It is not a place for interpretations, opinions, conclusions, or recommendations. Typically, it will include multiple tables and figures. It is often divided into the following sections:

- *Introduction.* A brief description of the purpose and organization of the chapter.

- *Background information.* Includes demographic information and data collection response rates.

- *Descriptive statistics.* As a minimum, this section includes the best measures of central tendency and dispersion for each variable. It also includes appropriate graphs and charts.

- *Hypothesis tests.* This section should be organized by each hypothesis that is tested. Results of evaluating test assumptions should be included.

- *Summary.* The results are summarized in this section, to include identification of null hypotheses that were rejected as well as those that were not rejected.

Discussion

This chapter is the place to evaluate and interpret the results and provide conclusions and recommendations. It often consists of the following sections.

- *Introduction.* Addresses the organization of this chapter.

- *Study summary.* Summarizes the entire study. Includes a clear statement of support or nonsupport for the research hypotheses.

- *Conclusions.* Findings from the previous chapter are not restated. Instead, the researcher draws from the results chapter to formulate conclusions. References should be made to the problem statement in the first chapter.

- *Discussion.* The researcher organizes this section by research question. Links are provided to the literature review. The researcher compares and contrasts findings from previous studies and describes how the study's findings advance knowledge in the field. The researcher's personal ideas and interpretations are expected in this section.

- *Limitations.* Limitations (i.e., threats to validity that have not been fully controlled) are listed here.

- *Recommendations.* Recommendations should be prescriptive in nature. If appropriate, recommendations for further study are included.

End Matter

End matter typically includes the following:

- *References.* Most references should be no older than five years. Only references cited in the report or proposal are to be included.

- *Appendices.* Appendices should contain copies of documents that have been used in the research, such as copies of instruments used, transcripts of interviews, informed consent form used in the research, cover letters, permission letters, Institutional Review Board approval letter, etc.

3.3: Threats to Validity

Overview

The challenge to the social science researcher is to select a design and implement procedures that are as valid as possible, recognizing that no research project is perfect. Where weaknesses become evident, controls need to be put in place to reduce/eliminate threats to validity. When threats remain or cannot be fully controlled, they need to be listed as study limitations in one's research report, dissertation, or journal article.

There are two major types of threats to the validity of research studies.

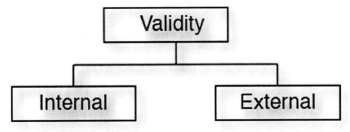

Internal Validity

Internal validity is the extent to which one can accurately state that an intervention (i.e., the IV) produced the observed effect (Campbell & Stanley, 1963). It reflects the extent of control over confounding variables (possible rival hypotheses) in a research study. The results of research with high internal validity will have high credibility for the tested sample. Whether or not the results can be generalized to the target population is an issue of external validity. Internal validity is more important than external validity because without internal validity, generalizations are meaningless. As internal validity increases (approaching laboratory conditions), external validity tends to decrease. However, since a research finding may be valid in one setting but not in another, the researcher needs to balance the requirements of internal validity with those of external validity.

All threats to internal validity listed below are not necessarily mutually exclusive. There are varying degrees of overlap. These threats can be used to evaluate any type of quantitative research design. Also, this list of threats is not comprehensive. Some studies have threats that simply don't fit into one of the listed categories. When one encounters such a threat one should simply describe it. Frequently, it helps to discuss a proposed study in a small group environment and brainstorm potential threats to validity.

The blind study, also known as the single blind study) is a common standard used by researchers to protect against bias in experimental research. In blind studies, the participants or the investigators are unaware of the nature of the treatment the participants are receiving; e.g., whether participants are in a treatment or control group. The double blind study takes this precaution one step further, by ensuring that both investigators and participants are unaware of the nature of the treatment the participants are receiving.

Additionally, internal validity is enhanced by:

- random assignment of participants to groups
- maximizing the effects of the IV by making the levels of the IV as different as possible
- minimizing the effects of random error
- controlling extraneous variables; e.g., controlling the threats to internal validity described below

The most common threats to the internal validity of quantitative studies are summarized below (Campbell & Stanley, 1963; Gall, Gall, & Borg, 2007).

History

The history threat to internal validity consists of specific events external to the treatment occurring between observations (measurements) that affect the DV (Campbell & Stanley, 1963). The threat consists of changes in the environment outside of the treatment that could produce changes in the variable under study. For example, the Head Start program started and Sesame Street began airing on television during the 1970s. Any evaluation of the educational effectiveness of the Head Start program could have been confounded by Sesame Street if some research participants watched Sesame Street and others did not.

Educational achievement attributed to Head Start might, in fact, been the result of Sesame Street.

The longer the time lapse between the pretest and posttest, the more like history will be a threat. Attitude surveys are particularly subject to this influence since opinions may largely be influenced by recent events and media presentation of topical issues.

Possible actions:

- Reduce the length of time between observations.

- Use a control or comparison group. Make sure the groups are likely to be exposed to the same outside events.

- Form groups that experience the same concurrent history.

- Standardize the conditions under which the research study is carried out.

Maturation

The maturation threat to internal validity is a threat produced by internal (physical or psychological) changes in research participants not related to the experimental intervention (Campbell & Stanley, 1963). It consists of the processes within participants that act as a function of time – e.g. if the project lasts a for a long time – such that participants may improve their performance regardless of intervention based on biological, psychological, or social processes that naturally take place with the passage of time. If these changes are related to the variable under study, then a false picture is obtained. It is particularly serious when adolescents are research participants. Longitudinal designs are especially vulnerable to the maturation threat.

Possible actions:

- Minimize the length of the study.

- Use a control group. Maturation is controlled because the two groups undergo the same changes, assuming they are equivalent.

- Use a true experimental design.

Testing

The testing threat to internal validity consists of the effects of taking a pretest upon scores of a posttest (Campbell & Stanley, 1963). The impact may be from remembering or sensitizing to a subject area. Consequently, participants' performance on a measure at the end of the study may differ from an initial testing, not because of the experimental intervention, but because they are more familiar with the instrument or have increased experience gained while taking the pretest. Therefore, the rival hypothesis is that taking the pretest, instead of the experimental intervention, accounted for an improvement recorded at the posttest.

Possible actions:

- Eliminate pretest (use a true experimental design).

- Use unobtrusive measures for the pretest.

- Use parallel test forms of the instrument by randomly assigning a parallel form to each participant for the pretest and using the parallel form for the posttest.

- Use a Solomon 4-group design.

- Use a control group. The reactive effect of measurement, if present, will be present in both groups.

Instrumentation

The instrumentation threat to internal validity consists of changes in calibration of the measuring instrument or use of an unreliable instrument (Campbell & Stanley, 1963). For example, changes over time in how observers/scorers measure the DV is an instrumentation threat. Raters become more skillful, or less attentive, or bored during subsequent testing. Raters may experience fatigue, knowledge about experiment, maturation, or acquire more relaxed or stringent standards at subsequent measurements.

Possible actions:

- Make observational instruments objective (rating scales, true/false, etc.).

- Minimize experimenter interaction with the subjects.

- Use a standard set of written instructions.

- Standardize data collection procedures.

- Use multiple raters who rate the same phenomenon and conduct periodic inter-observer agreement checks.

- Train observers.

- Use grading rubrics.

- Use a test instrument that is reliable (e.g., evidence of reliability should be included in test manuals).

Statistical Regression

The statistical regression threat to internal validity can occur when selecting participants on the basis of extremely low (or extremely high) scores on some test, giving them some intervention, and then retesting them (Campbell & Stanley, 1963). If scores have gone up (or down) significantly, a false conclusion can be drawn that this is due to the intervention. It may actually be a statistical artifact known as regression to the mean. Extreme scores tend to move toward the center of the distribution the next time people are measured. The more extreme the initial selection, the greater will be the regression toward the mean at the time of the next measurement. This phenomenon occurs because measurable characteristics do not have constant values but vary above and below the average value.

For example, a math program for the bottom 25% of third graders on a standardized math achievement test is likely to result in increased scores on the standardized math achievement posttest because of the statistical regression effect alone, regardless of any experimental intervention.

Statistical regression can occur when a sample is selected for their extreme scores on one variable and then tested on an unrelated variable.

Possible actions:

- Randomly assign participants to both experimental and control groups from the same extreme pool.

- Avoid the use of extreme scores.

Experimental Mortality

The experimental mortality threat to internal validity occurs when there is a differential loss of participants by group from the study through attrition. The result is that group equivalence formed at the start of the study may be destroyed (Campbell & Stanley, 1963). Consequently, differences between groups at the end of the study may be due to differences in those who remained in each group rather than to the effects of the experimental intervention. Moreover, dropout problems prevent the researcher from obtaining complete information on all participants exposed to an intervention.

Possible actions:

- Use random assignment of participants to groups.

- Provide incentives for study completion.

- Use matching and omission procedures.

- Increase the sample size.

- Pretesting can assist in determining if dropouts and non-dropouts differ at the start of the study.

Selection

The selection threat to internal validity results from nonrandom assignment of research participants to groups (i.e., use of non-equivalent or intact groups; Campbell & Stanley, 1963). Biases are introduced as the result of the differential selection. Self-selection of participants to groups is an example of this threat. Another example is assigning the first 20 names on a list to the treatment group and the next 20 names to a control group. Group differences become alternative explanations for any differences observed between groups at the end of the study.

Possible actions:

- Use random assignment to groups (true experimental design).

- Don't allow self-selection of research participants to specific groups.

- Use statistical covariance to statistically equate groups on a pretest.

- Use a matched pairs design where participants are matched on a known extraneous variable(s) and then one member of each matched pair is randomly assigned to each group. The researcher is thus assured that the groups are initially equivalent on the variables used in the matching procedure.

Interactions with Selection

This is a family of threats that occur when the selection threat combines with other threats.

The selection-maturation interaction threat to internal validity comes about if one group matures at a faster rate than the other group, even though groups might be identical at the pretest (Campbell & Stanley, 1963). For example, adolescent females tend to mature more quickly than adolescent males on certain constructs. If one group consisted of adolescent females and the other consisted of adolescent males and the DV was related to sexual maturity, one can assume that the selection-maturation interaction threat is a threat to validity.

The selection-history interaction threat results when the experimental group and the control group are selected from different settings with different histories that might affect their response to the treatment.

Possible actions:

- Use random assignment (true experimental design).

Experimental Treatment Diffusion

The experimental treatment diffusion threat to internal validity (also known as contamination) occurs when experimental and control groups become aware of both treatments and treatments are diffused throughout participants and groups (Gall, Gall, & Borg, 2007). This threat occurs when there is communication about the treatment between groups of participants. It is most likely when members of treatment and control groups are in close proximity to each other and regularly interact on a social level.

Possible actions:

- Minimize (eliminate) contact between groups.

Compensatory Rivalry

The compensatory rivalry to internal validity occurs when it is common knowledge among participants that one of the treatment groups is expected to perform better than the control group and a competitive environment results in which the control group uses extraordinary means not to be beaten (Gall, Gall, & Borg, 2007). This threat is also known as the John Henry effect, which comes from the story of John Henry trying to lay railroad track faster than a machine.

Possible actions:

- Minimize (eliminate) contact between groups.

- Keep experimenters unaware of the specifics of the research.

Other Threats to Internal Validity

Other threats unique to a particular quantitative study may also be present that cannot be easily categorized by one of the threats described above, such as faulty research design, sampling, or statistical testing.

A very common threat is the use of an inadequate number of study participants. Gay (1987) recommends the following minimum sample sizes for the respective types of research:

- Descriptive – 10% of population.

- Correlational – 30 participants (for prediction studies, higher sample sizes may be required based on the number of predictor variables).

- Causal-comparative – 30 participants per group.

- Experimental – 15 subjects per group (note: some researchers believe 20-25 subjects are required for quasi-experimental studies).

Statistical considerations will also affect optimum sample size. Inadequate sample sizes can lead to low statistical power resulting in insufficient power to reject a false null hypothesis

(Type II error). For example, if the effect being measured in the population is very small, increased sample size is required. Also, for survey research, a low response rate introduces the possibility of bias since those who did not respond to the survey might be significantly different than those who did respond on variables that are important to the study.

The following additional threats may be encountered.

Compensatory Equalization of Treatments

The compensatory equalization of treatments threat to internal validity occurs when one treatment condition seems more desirable to those who are responsible for administering the experiment. As a result, there may be a tendency on the part of researchers to compensate in the other treatment condition.

Possible actions:

- Use a double blind study.

Resentful Demoralization

The resentful demoralization threat to internal validity occurs when there is demoralization and/or resentment that influences the outcome of the research when participants in one group feel that they are receiving less benefit than are those in another group (Gall, Gall, & Borg, 2007).

Possible actions:

- Minimize (eliminate) contact between groups.
- Provide benefits unrelated to the study to the group receiving the less desirable treatment.
- Keep experimenters unaware of the specifics of the research.

Implementation

The implementation threat to internal validity occurs when the treatment and/or control conditions are not implemented objectively and consistently across all groups (Wallen & Fraenkel, 2001). In particular, the treatment group might be treated in unintended ways that are not part of the intervention but gives one group an advantage (or disadvantage) over other groups.

Possible actions:

- Document the intervention.
- Use observers to confirm the accuracy of treatment implementation.
- Train observers.
- Ensure treatment fidelity.

Halo Effect

The halo effect threat to internal validity occurs as a result of the tendency for an irrelevant feature of a research participant to influence a relevant feature (Rosenzweig, 2007). When one considers a person good (or bad) in one category – e.g., attractiveness – he or she is likely to make a similar evaluation in other categories; e.g., teaching ability. Typically, a strong initial positive or negative impression of a person, group, or event tends to influence ratings on subsequent observations. For example, a student that received high grades on earlier papers may receive a higher than deserved grade on a substandard paper because the earlier work created a halo effect that biased the rater.

Possible actions:

- Use specific and clearly defined data collection procedures.
- Use grading rubrics.
- Train raters.
- Avoid any situation that diminishes objectivity of data collection.

External Validity

External validity is the generalizability of study findings to the target population (i.e., can the experiment be replicated with the same results?; Campbell & Stanley, 1963). It is the ability to generalize across categories or classes of individuals and across settings within the same target population. External validity is enhanced by random selection of participants from the target population and maintaining experimental realism in so far as possible.

> **Key Point**
> Random selection enhances external validity while random assignment enhances internal validity.

For most social science research, the selection of research designs strong in both internal and external validity is the goal, but cannot always be realized. A major issue is that as internal validity is enhanced by introducing more controls, procedures are implemented that tend to make research conditions more and more artificial, thereby adversely affecting generalizability.

The major components of the external validity of quantitative studies are summarized below (Bracht & Glass, 1968; Campbell & Stanley, 1963; Cook & Campbell, 1979; Gall, Gall, & Borg, 2007).

Population Validity

Population validity is a type of external validity that describes how well the sample used is representative of the target population. The focus is on the extent to which the results of a study can be generalized from the specific sample to a larger population (Bracht & Glass, 1968).

Possible actions:

- Specify targets of generalizability in advance, then plan the selection of persons, settings, and times so that there is a clear relationship between the planned targets and the sample.

- Be more representative of the target population. Employ random selection of the research sample from the target population.

- Achieve maximum similarity of experiments to the conditions of application.

Ecological Validity

Ecological validity is closely related to external validity. It looks at the testing environment and determines how much it influences behavior (Brewer, 2000). The extent to which a research context resembles or takes place in a naturally occurring (i.e., unmanipulated) and frequently experienced contexts is referred to as ecological validity (Brooks & Baumeister, 1977). Methods, materials, and the setting of the study must approximate the real-life situation that is under investigation. The focus is on the extent to which the results of a research study can be generalized from the set of environmental conditions created by the researcher to the environmental conditions characteristic of the target population. In other words, ecological validity is concerned with the degree to which research results generalize to different settings. Ecological validity includes the following components (Bracht & Glass, 1968; Gall, Gall, & Borg, 2007).

Explicit Description of the Experimental Treatment

If the researcher fails to adequately describe how he or she conducted a study, it is difficult to determine how well the results are applicable to the target population. Moreover, the intervention may not be able to be implemented as evaluated.

Possible actions:

- The description of the intervention must be precise enough for study replication.

Multiple Treatment Interference

Multiple treatment interference involves the effects of previous treatments, which are not usually erasable, on research outcomes. Consequently, the research findings may be generalized only to persons who experience the same sequence of treatments.

Possible actions:

- Attempt to select a research design in which only one treatment is assigned to each participant.
- Use different groups for different treatments.

Hawthorne Effect

The Hawthorne effect refers to the tendency of some people to work harder and perform better when they are being observed. Therefore, it represents the increase in efficiency/achievement/productivity due to awareness that one is a participant in a research study.

Possible actions:

- Use a control group.

- Provide the control group with some type of special treatment (placebo) that is comparable to the experimental group but does not influence the DV.

- Use nonreactive measures. A measurement is reactive whenever the participant is directly involved in a study and he or she is reacting to the measurement process itself. A measurement is nonreactive when it does not change that which is being measured. It is a passive or unobtrusive measure of behavior and does not introduce stimulus factors to which the subject might otherwise react. For classroom research, consider the following nonreactive strategies:

  - Build the research measures into the regular classroom routine.

  - Involve alternative teaching procedures presented without announcing changes.

  - Use the regular school staff to collect data.

Placebo Effect

The placebo effect is a measurable improvement caused by the expectations of participants rather than by any provided intervention.

Possible actions:

- Use a blind study.

- Provide the experimental and control groups the same information regarding the study.

Reactive Effects of Experimental Arrangements

The responses or performance of study participants may be different from what they would have been otherwise as a result of the awareness by participants that they are involved in a study. The effectiveness of a new treatment may also increases because the treatment is new or different. This novelty effect tends to diminish with time.

Additionally, the effects of the intervention may be influenced by an experimental setting if it is not representative of that of the target population. Consequently, individuals exposed to the same intervention in a different setting may not get the same results.

Possible actions:

- Ensure the experimental setting approximates the target population setting.

- Use unobtrusive measures in a natural setting.

- Extend the duration of the treatment to allow any novelty effects to wear off.

Reactive Effects of Testing

The pretest can contribute to this threat by increasing or decreasing the sensitivity of the research participants to the treatment. In other words, the pretest becomes a learning experience. Consequently, these participants may no longer be representative of the un-pretested population. The pretest, in essence, becomes a part of the treatment and the treatment, without this sensitization, is less effective.

Posttest sensitization is similar to pretest sensitization. In this case the effectiveness of the treatment is due, in part, to the administration of a posttest.

Possible actions:

- Use a pretest that does not increase the sensitivity or awareness of participants to the behaviors that the treatment is designed to change. Alternatively, eliminate the pretest.

- Use a posttest that does not increase the sensitivity of participants to the behaviors that the treatment is designed to change.

Experimenter Effect (Rosenthal Effect)

The Rosenthal effect occurs when the researcher unintentionally modifies the behavior of research participants through verbal or nonverbal cues.

Possible actions:

- Use unobtrusive measures.

- Implement a double blind study.

- Build into the experiment simultaneous replication by another researcher.

Measurement of the DV

All measurement instruments must be described in sufficient detail to allow another researcher to replicate the study. Deficiencies adversely impact the ability to generalize study results.

Possible actions:

- Carefully document how the DV is measured, to include retaining copies of instruments, observation forms, etc., as well as all instructions.

Interaction of History and Treatment Effects

History can influence the generalizability of research study results if the historical environment during the conduct differs significantly from the target population. Issues that are in the news may render the treatment more effective. When the issue becomes less visible, the treatment may be less effective. For example, if sexual harassment is a major issue on TV and the newspapers, any treatment to sensitize one to sexual harassment may be more effective.

Possible actions:

- Avoid reactive arrangements and history-treatment interactions.

- Build into the experiment simultaneous replication in another setting.

Interaction of Time of Measurement and Treatment Effects

Treatment effectiveness can vary based on when the treatment is conducted. For example, if the treatment takes place early in the morning, when participants are alert, it is likely to be more effective than a treatment conducted at the end of the day when participants are tired and less alert. Also, the full effect of the treatment may be delayed and may not be immediately apparent at the end of the treatment.

Possible actions:

- Implement the study using the same conditions that will be used to implement the intervention in the target population.

3.4: Chapter 3 Review

The answer key is at the end of this section.

1. What is a construct?

    A. A construct is any characteristic or quality that varies

    B. A construct is a categorization or concept for a set of behaviors or characteristics of an individual

    C. A construct is a method for making decisions about the target population

    D. A construct refers to how a characteristic is defined in a study

2. What is the most inaccurate and unreliable type of measurement?

    A. Self-report measurements

    B. Physiological measurements

    C. Behavioral measurements

    D. Parallel measurements

3. What is the best method for controlling extraneous variables in a research study?

    A. Matching

    B. Random selection

    C. Random assignment

    D. Counterbalancing

4. What type of bias reflects a conscious or subconscious attempt by the respondent to create a certain impression?

    A. Acquiescence response style bias

    B. Social desirability bias

    C. Extreme and central tendency responding bias

    D. Negative affectivity bias

5. Organizational research is especially vulnerable to what type of self-report bias?

    A.   Extreme and central tendency responding bias

    B.   Negative affectivity bias

    C.   Acquiescence response style bias

    D.   Social desirability bias

6. What type of variable cannot take on all values within the limits of the variable?

    A.   Discrete variable

    B.   Interval scale variable

    C.   Ratio scale variable

    D.   Quantitative variable

7. Which of the following is NOT a measure of internal consistency reliability?

    A.   Cronbach's alpha

    B.   Split-half

    C.   Parallel

    D.   Stability

8. What is NOT a characteristic of causal-comparative studies?

    A.   Involve at least two groups

    B.   Determine cause and effect

    C.   Involve making comparisons

    D.   Researcher does not manipulate the IV

9. What is a characteristic of correlational studies?

A.   Involve two or more groups

B.   Attempts to determine the cause for pre-existing differences

C.   Typically involve two or more variables

D.   Random assignment

5. Random assignment of participants to groups is a characteristic of what type of study?

    A.   Descriptive studies

    B.   Causal-comparative studies

    C.   Correlational studies

    D.   Experimental studies

6. *Z*-scores of 0 to 1 define approximately what % of a population?

    A.   68%

    B.   34%

    C.   95%

    D.   14%

7. *Z*-scores of 0 to 2 define approximately what % of a population?

    A.   68%

    B.   34%

    C.   14%

    D.   48%

8. What scale of measurement is U.S.D.A. quality of beef ratings (good, choice, prime)?

    A.   Nominal

    B.   Ordinal

    C.   Interval

    D.   Ratio

9. What scale of measurement is used for number of events per minute?

    A.   Nominal

    B.   Ordinal

    C.   Interval

    D.   Ratio

10. What scale of measurement is undergraduate student status (freshman, sophomore, junior, senior)?

    A.   Nominal

B. Ordinal

C. Interval

D. Ratio

11. What scale of measurement are the numbers on the jerseys of players on a football team?

A. Nominal

B. Ordinal

C. Interval

D. Ratio

12. What scale of measurement is degrees centigrade?

A. Nominal

B. Ordinal

C. Interval

D. Ratio

13. In what scale of measurement is division and multiplication permissible?

A. Nominal

B. Ordinal

C. Interval

D. Ratio

19. What is the biggest threat to the internal validity of the following research design?

O X O

A. History

B. Selection

C. Implementation

D. Maturation

20. What is the biggest threat to the internal validity of the following research design?

```
N   X   O
N       O
```

A. Testing

B. Instrumentation

C. Selection

D. History

21. What is the biggest threat to the internal validity of the following research design?

```
O  O  O  X  O  O  O
```

A. Selection

B. Mortality

C. History

D. Instrumentation

22. Select the threat to internal validity from the following list of threats.

A. The pretest decreases the sensitivity of the research participants to the treatment

B. The pretest increases the sensitivity of the research participants to the treatment

C. Taking the pretest influences posttest scores

D. None of the above

23. Identify the following threat to internal validity: changes occur within participants over time during a study.

A. History

B. Selection

C. Maturation

D. Multiple treatment interference

24. Identify the following threat to internal validity: assigning of participants to groups results in systematic differences between the groups at the beginning of the study.

A. History

B. Selection

C. Maturation

D. Experimental mortality

25. What type of instrument validity is frequently assessed using a panel of experts that evaluate the degree to which the items on the instrument address the intended domain, nothing less and nothing more?

   A. Face validity

   B. Content validity

   C. Construct validity

   D. Criterion validity

26. Which of the following is NOT a characteristic of a normal curve?

   A. Bell-shaped

   B. Multi-modal

   C. Symmetric about the mean

   D. Involves a large number of cases

27. Which of the following is NOT a characteristic of all density curves?

   A. Symmetric

   B. Smooth

   C. On or above the x-axis

   D. Area under the curve equals 1

28. What type of sampling occurs when participants are selected on the basis of the researcher's knowledge of the target population?

   A. Probability sampling

   B. Convenience sampling

   C. Purposive sampling

   D. Quota sampling

29. What is the *z*-score that equals one standard deviation above the mean?

    A.   1

    B.   0

    C.   2

    D.   Cannot be determined without more information

Chapter 3 Answers

1B, 2A, 3C, 4B, 5D, 6A, 7D, 8B, 9C, 10D, 11B, 12D, 13B, 14D, 15B, 16A, 17C, 18D, 19A, 20C, 21C, 22C, 23C, 24B, 25B, 26B, 27A, 28C, 29A

Chapter 4: Evaluation Research

Evaluation research is closely related to traditional social research and utilizes may of its tools and methodologies. However, unlike traditional research, evaluation research takes place within an organizational context that requires consideration of the needs of multiple program stakeholders.

4.1: Basic Concepts

Overview

Social science research seeks conclusions based on empirical research. It does not seek evaluative conclusions. It establishes standards or values and then integrates them with empirical results to reach evaluative conclusions and recommendations regarding social programs.

> **Key Point**
> Evaluation research determines the merit, worth, or value of programs.

A program is a collection of organizational resources that is geared to accomplish a certain major goal or set of goals (Fitzpatrick, Sanders, & Worthen, 2004). A program is both an organization and a system.

According to Posavac and Carey (2002), evaluation is a collection of methods, skills, and sensitivities necessary to determine whether a human service is needed and likely to be used, whether it is conducted as planned, and whether the service helps people.

Evaluations of programs are conducted to answer questions and address issues that are raised by stakeholders. Stakeholders are individuals who have:

- a real, active interest in the program

- an investment in the program; e.g., employees, donors, clients, and board members

- a commitment to the program's success (Fitzpatrick, Sanders, & Worthen, 2004)

Involving stakeholders in the evaluation process helps to "create ownership" and "buy-in." Since there may be tension between the evaluator and key stakeholders on various issues, both should agree to an evaluation plan at the start of a program evaluation.

Program evaluation is the process of making a judgment (i.e., regarding merit, worth, and value) concerning the quality of a social program. Rossi, Lipsey, and Freeman (2004) refine this definition by suggesting program evaluation as the use of social research procedures to systematically investigate the effectiveness of social intervention programs. Program evaluation results typically support management and funding agency decisions regarding program improvement, continuation, and/or funding. Evaluators begin planning program evaluations by identifying the program goals, objectives, and performance indicators (types of evidence) by which the program will be evaluated and by identifying the data sources to be used for the measurements, comparisons, and analyses that will be required. At this point, four problems may emerge according to Fitzpatrick, Sanders, and Worthen (2004):

- Evaluators and intended users of the evaluation report fail to agree on the goals, objectives, and performance criteria to be used in evaluating the program.

- Program goals and objectives are found to be unrealistic given the resources that have been committed to them and the program activities that have been implemented.

- Information on program performance required for a credible evaluation is not available to the evaluators.

• Administrators at the policy or operating levels are unable or unwilling to change the program on the basis of evaluation information.

To the extent that these problems exist, evaluation research is unlikely to result in program improvement. Consequently, preliminary negotiation and investigation conducted jointly by the evaluator, the evaluation sponsor, and possibly other stakeholders is required to determine if a program meets preconditions for evaluation. This negotiation is frequently conducted concurrently with an evaluability assessment, described later in this section.

Program evaluation focuses on collecting information about a specific program. Usually there is little interest in generalizing results. Consequently, the focus is on internal validity with little or no attention given to external validity, unless there is a need to generalize findings to multiple program locations and clients.

Informal program evaluations conducted by practitioners are referred to as collaborative action research (or simply action research). Action research, therefore, is the process by which practitioners attempt to study their problems scientifically in order to improve their programs.

The Joint Committee on Standards for Educational Evaluation (JCSEE), a coalition of major professional associations concerned with the quality of evaluation, has developed a set of standards to guide program evaluations. These standards are available at the JCSEE Web site at http://www.jcsee.org/program-evaluation-standards/program-evaluation-standards-statements.

EVALUATION TYPES

Types of evaluation vary depending on the program being evaluated and the purpose of the evaluation. Different authors tend to advocate different models. For example, Scriven (1967) introduced the concept of a "goal-free" evaluation in which the evaluator explores all possible aspects of a program without knowledge of program goals and objectives. Stufflebeam (2000) advocates the context, input, product, and process (CIPP) model. The model provided below is a synthesis from the professional literature and is based largely on a systems approach.

Formative Evaluations

Formative evaluations strengthen or improve the program being evaluated by examining the delivery of the program, the quality of its implementation, and the assessment of the organizational context, personnel, procedures, inputs, etc. (Fitzpatrick, Sanders, & Worthen, 2004). Formative evaluation includes three evaluation types:

- An input evaluation determines the resources needed to deliver the program and determines whether staff and available resources are adequate to implement the program. It also identifies and evaluates system capabilities to include equipment and technical expertise, alternative program strategies, and the resources used to satisfy client needs. Its purpose is to provide information on the quality and adequacy of resources used by the program and to determine how to best use these resources to achieve program objectives. Input evaluations assist in making program structuring decisions.

- A needs assessment refers to the identification of workforce or client needs for products and services. The need can be based on the requirement to improve performance, to correct a deficiency, or to improve alignment of program services with client needs. Its goal is to eliminate a gap between a present and ideal end state. A needs assessment can also address the issue or whether there is a need for the program to be evaluated.

  - What is the scope of the need?

  - Do program goals and objectives adequately address the need?

  - Could a different program better fulfill the need?

- A process evaluation investigates the process of delivering a program in order to determine how it produces the results that it does. The evaluator must examine not only what is happening within the program as it is being implemented but also what should be happening and is not. It provides information about the state of all components of the program. Included in a process evaluation are judgments regarding program efficiency (e.g., cost-benefit analysis, cost effectiveness analysis, return on investment, etc.) as well as program conceptualization and design. It helps identify and diagnose the barriers that inhibit achieving program goals and objectives. Process evaluations help in making decisions regarding how best to implement a program.

Summative Evaluations

Summative evaluations, in contrast, examine the effects or outcomes of a program by describing what happens subsequent to delivery of the program, assessing whether the program can be said to have influenced the outcome, and, estimating the relative costs associated with the program. Summative evaluation can be subdivided as follows:

- An outcomes evaluation investigates the program's demonstrable effects on clients. It consists of collecting, analyzing, and judging program results in order to determine the extent to which program activities are properly aligned with program goals and objectives.

- An impact evaluation is broader and assesses the overall or net effects, intended or unintended, of the program as a whole. It addresses the longer-term results of the program and the extent to which the program reduced or eliminated client needs and the effects of the program on society at large.

EVALUATION STRATEGIES

Within the context of the type of evaluation described above, specific evaluation strategies are used to collect data. In selecting the strategy or combination of strategies, the evaluator must consider the interests of all stakeholders and how these interests can best be served. Worthen et al. (1997) identifies six evaluation strategies that are frequently used to collect data for program evaluations. These six strategies are described below (Rovai, 2003):

1. *Objectives-oriented* – arguably, the most popular strategy is the objectives-oriented evaluation strategy. The distinguishing feature of this strategy is that the evaluation focuses on determining the extent to which program objectives have been met. Major weaknesses often cited regarding this strategy include the difficulty of evaluators to operate in a program environment with ill-defined objectives, to identify unintended program outcomes, and to measure learning in educational and training programs. For example, grades, often used to operationalize learning, can have little relationship to what students have learned as students may already know the material when they enroll, or their grades may be more related to class participation, or work turned in late, than to learning.

2. *Management-oriented* – the management-oriented strategy is meant to serve decision-makers and is particularly useful for making decisions about the reallocation of funds. The rationale for using this strategy is that

    > evaluative information is an essential part of good decision making and that the evaluator can be most effective by serving administrators, policy makers, boards, practitioners, and others who need good evaluative information" (Worthen et al., 1997, p. 97).

    A weakness of this strategy is that it tends to reinforce the status quo of management rather than balancing the interests of management with those of other internal and external stakeholders.

3. *Consumer-oriented* – the market-driven, consumer-oriented strategy, typically summative, adheres to the type of evaluation used by the Consumers Union. Consequently, the central theme of this strategy is the development of information on products and services for use by consumers.

4. *Expertise-oriented* – the expertise-oriented approach to evaluation, widely used by accrediting agencies, depends primarily upon professional expertise to judge a program. For example, the worth of a curriculum is evaluated by curriculum experts who observe the curriculum in action, examine its content and underlying learning theory, and

render a judgment about its value. However, this strategy has a potential weakness in the limited reliability of expert testimony. Different experts may not make the same judgments and recommendations regarding the program.

5. *Adversary-oriented* – the adversary-oriented strategy attempts to reduce bias by attempting to assure fairness by incorporating both positive and negative views into the evaluation itself. Several models have been used for adversary evaluations, to include structured public debates, such as town hall meetings, and the use of opposing evaluators that debate the issues. The idea of using this model is not so much to win a verdict as it is for all stakeholders and evaluators to acquire a better appreciation of the issues involved and to gain insights into other points of view (Worthen et al., 1997).

6. *Participant-oriented* – the participant-oriented or naturalistic strategy involves all stakeholders. Huxley (1959) wrote an excellent description that accurately captures the spirit of this strategy.

> The best way to find things out... is not to ask questions at all. If you fire off a question, it is like firing off a gun—bang it goes, and everything takes flight and runs for shelter. But if you sit quite still and pretend not to be looking, all the little facts will come and peck round your feet, situations will venture forth from the thickets, and intentions will creep out and sun themselves on a stone and if you are patient, you will see and understand a great deal more than a man with a gun does (p. 272).

A weakness of the participant-oriented approach is that each stakeholder is likely to have different criteria regarding program value and effectiveness. If the evaluator attempts to find common ground and to satisfy all stakeholders, the evaluation is likely to become ineffective, and those designing and conducting evaluations may focus on answering questions that are not relevant, but to which everyone agrees.

EVALUATION FRAMEWORK

The figure below outlines the program evaluation framework (Rovai, 2003).

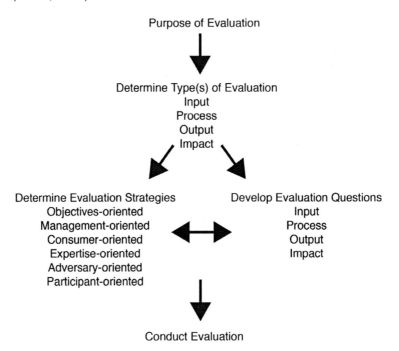

The process starts with identification of the purpose of the program evaluation. Why is the evaluation necessary and what decisions will be made about the program? Should emphasis be placed on input, process, outcome, or impact issues? Once the purpose of the evaluation is understood, the type of evaluation can be determined. Then, evaluation strategies and questions can be developed in parallel.

Evaluation Questions

The specific evaluation questions to be used for any program evaluation should be based on the information needs of the evaluation's sponsor, and the strategies used to respond to these questions should be selected based on an understanding of the broader context in which the program operates. For example, there may be a variety of complex issues involving a program that requires inclusion of an adversary-oriented strategy to ensure that all views are presented and considered during the evaluation process.

Posavac and Carey (2002) suggest that responses to the following questions often help inform the development of evaluation questions:

- What program will be evaluated?

- Who will use the results of the evaluation?

- What is the purpose of the evaluation? What issues have been raised? How will the results be used? What decisions need to be made regarding the program (e.g., continuance, expansion, reducing costs)?

- Who is going to conduct the program evaluation?

- How will the program evaluation be conducted? What method(s) should be used? What are the available resources? What are the constraints (e.g., time and money)?

Evaluation questions tend to be broader and less specific than research questions. Since program evaluations support the decision-making process, specific questions must be aligned with the decisions that need to be made regarding the program. It is often useful to identify both main questions and supporting questions. It is also useful to negotiate a list of questions with program stakeholders. As a minimum, evaluation questions must be approved by the agency sponsoring (i.e., paying for) the program evaluation.

Types of evaluation that respond to specific evaluation questions are not mutually exclusive and may be combined. Below are examples of a variety of evaluation questions regarding a distance education program and identification of the types of evaluation and evaluation strategies they imply (Rovai, 2003).

Is the program's admission policy sufficiently rigorous? What types of students and instructors are attracted to the program? How many students are served by the program? Is the program reaching its intended audience? Why or why not? How effective was student pre-enrollment counseling? Does the school provide students with advertising, recruiting, and admissions information that adequately and accurately represent the program and services available?

[*Implies an input evaluation; possible strategies include consumer- and management-oriented*]

Are course materials current? How efficient is the course development process? How does the school ensure that students admitted possess the knowledge and equipment necessary to use the technology employed by the program? What evaluation and assessment methods does the school use to measure student learning? How does the program ensure the integrity of student work and the credibility of the degrees and credits awarded?

[*Implies an input evaluation; possible strategies include objectives-, management-, consumer-, expertise-, and participant-oriented.*]

What are the educational needs of students targeted by the program? Are program and course objectives sufficiently responsive to these needs? What are the needs of instructors? What is the extent to which these needs are satisfied? What relevant professional development activities and support services are provided instructors? Are these activities and services adequate? Do the instructors feel adequately prepared to use the e-learning system? Are instructors sufficiently competent in designing courses for delivery using the e-learning system? Have instructors adopted the specialized teaching techniques considered appropriate for the e-learning system? What is the nature and extent of support services needed for instructor success?

[*Implies a needs assessment; possible strategies include consumer-, expertise-, and participant-oriented.*]

How were faculty selected to teach at a distance? Are instructors qualified to teach the content of their courses? Are instructors qualified to teach online? What is the extent to which instructors control the content of their courses? What are the administrative and teaching burdens of instructors?

[*Implies a process evaluation; possible strategies include management-, consumer-, expertise-, and participant-oriented.*]

Is the program implemented as intended? How efficiently is the program being implemented? Is there a gap in student satisfaction between distance education and on campus students? What is the level of interaction between students and instructors and among students? Does the instructor provide timely feedback to students? What program components or activities are the most and least effective? To what extent is the learner involved in setting goals and in choosing the tasks, assessments, and standards to reach those goals? How is the integrity of student work assured?

[*Implies a process evaluation; possible strategies include objectives-, management-, consumer-, and participant-oriented.*]

What is the nature and extent of support services needed for student and instructor success? Are these support services responsive to student and instructor needs? To what extent are these resources used? Does the school monitor the use and quality of support services?

[*Implies a process evaluation and needs assessment; possible strategies include expertise-, consumer-, and participant-oriented.*]

What are the program results? Are courses transferable? Are certificates or degrees awarded by the program recognized by the appropriate profession? What structures or policies in the school or e-learning environment are supporting or hindering outcomes and overall program effectiveness? Were program objectives achieved? What program and course design components appear to contribute the most and least to the attainment of these objectives? Do students feel that they gained the desired knowledge and skills? Is there a gap in learning outcomes between distance education and on campus students?

[*Implies an outcomes evaluation; possible strategies include objectives-, management-, expertise-, and participant-oriented.*]

What are the effects of the program on graduates? As a result of completing the program did they receive increased pay, acquired professional certifications, received promotions, etc.? Did the program have any unintended impacts?

[*Implies an impact evaluation; possible strategies include participant-oriented.*]

EVALUABILITY ASSESSMENT

In order for program evaluation to be carried out successfully, it is important that a program be ready for evaluation. One way to determine its readiness is to conduct an evaluability assessment. Developed by Joseph Wholey in 1979, the evaluability assessment is a tool that can help an evaluator determine whether a program meets the criteria for a meaningful evaluation. According to Wholey (1979),

> Evaluability assessment explores the objectives, expectations, and information needs of program managers and policy makers; explores program reality; assesses the likelihood that program activities will achieve measurable progress toward program objectives; and assesses the extent to which evaluation information is likely to be used by program management. The products of evaluability assessment are: (1) a set of agreed-on program objectives, side effects, and performance indicators on which the program can realistically be held accountable; and (2) a set of evaluation/management options which represent ways in which management can change program activities, objectives, or uses of information in ways likely to improve program performance. (p. xiii)

The primary purpose of an evaluability assessment is to determine if the program can be managed for results (Wholey, 1994). Evaluability assessments also help determine:

- The extent to which a program is ready for evaluation.
- The changes that are needed to increase its readiness.
- The type(s) of evaluation and evaluation strategies most suitable to judge a program.

Steps

Smith (1989) offers the following steps in conducting an evaluability assessment. The steps are not meant to suggest that an evaluability assessment is a rigid linear process. Depending on the context and purpose, some steps can be omitted or re-ordered. These steps, with short explanations, are as follows.

1. Determine evaluation purpose, secure commitment, and identify work group members. A clearly articulated purpose will help secure buy-in and foster commitment.

2. Define boundaries of the program to be studied. This step sets limits on evaluability assessment work and further clarifies the purpose of the evaluability assessment. Boundaries may vary based on such factors as geographic location or program objectives. Boundaries might also be constructed to focus the evaluability assessment on a program component rather than the entire program.

3. Identify and analyze program documents. Documents could include documentation or legislation authorizing a program, grant applications, evaluations, audits, brochures, program Web sites with program descriptions and claims, and internal memoranda. Documents provide a sense of the intent of the program as well as what is actually occurring.

4. Develop/clarify program theory and logic. Identifying assumptions and values, available resources, program activities, objectives, and how these components relate to one another to produce outcomes, are the major features of developing a program theory.

5. Identify and interview stakeholders. Interviews should focus on what stakeholders know and perceive to be true about the program.

6. Describe stakeholder perceptions of the program. Descriptions and comparisons of stakeholder perceptions is important for further understanding of the program.

7. Identify stakeholder needs, concerns, and differences in perceptions. Differences can indicate misperceptions of the program and intent, or a program that is not sufficiently meeting the needs of one or more stakeholder groups.

8. Determine plausibility of program model. Data from program staff, documentation, and stakeholder interviews are used to determine plausibility of the program. That is, data are analyzed to determine the extent to which the program is properly implemented, sufficiently developed, and activities are appropriate to predict that desired outcomes can be achieved.

9. Draw conclusions and make recommendations. Conclusions and recommendations are drawn from qualitative and quantitative data analysis.

10. Plan specific steps for utilization of evaluability assessment data. The next step might be to continue with an evaluation of the program, revise the program, or recommend that no action be taken.

Format

Title Page (one page only). Include the title of the program, evaluator's name, affiliation, and date. One may include additional information such as the identification of the sponsor of the evaluation (person or organization).

Executive Summary (one page only). Executive summaries are not overviews. They provide a brief synopsis that highlights key facts, issues, and conclusions.

Program Background (one page only). Provides a concise identification and description of the program. As a minimum, it includes the program's purpose, short history, target audience, and size. It also describes the reason for the proposed program evaluation; e.g. an external evaluation is needed in order to support a continuation of funding request to a government agency.

Program Goals and Objectives (one or two pages only). Identifies program goals and objectives as documented by the program. Goals are broad, general statements of what the program intends to accomplish. They are disaggregated by priority, if possible. Objectives are tied to specific goals and identify the activities or action steps needed to attain the goals. SMART objectives are specific, measurable, achievable, realistic, and time-oriented. The evaluator must work with the goals and objectives that direct the program. The quality of program goals and objectives impact the abilities of the program director to manage the program for results and the program evaluator to evaluate the program.

Document Model (one or two pages only). Key to this stage of the evaluation is the construction of the program's theory (Wholey, 1979). The document model depicts the program as defined by the program's documentation. It is a logic model that displays program components and effects and identifies major program components, immediate goal effects, and ultimate goal effects using a flowchart. The model should show that there are plausible logical links between client needs, program activities, and program goals.

Below is an example of a document model for a family-centered, values-based human sexuality program consisting of two components: curricula and outreach services. The goal of this program is to provide adolescent girls with the knowledge, skills, and support they need to commit to sexual abstinence until marriage. The program respects the right of parents as primary sexuality educators of their children and seeks to affirm their adequacy in that role. Consequently both girls and their mothers participate in this program.

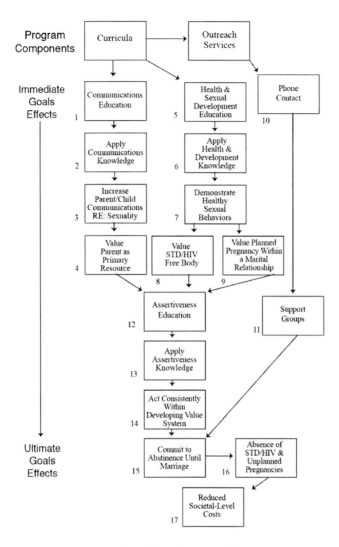

It is important to identify effects, and not topics, processes, or activities in the document model. The effects are numbered so one may refer to them in the evaluability assessment.

A brief discussion of the program logic follows the model.

Program Manager's Model (one or two pages only). Often a program manager will make modifications to the program as originally established. This model depicts the program as it is implemented by the program manager. Elements may be added and others may be deleted from the document model. The evaluator depicts the program manager's model followed by discussion in which he or she identifies and describes deviations from the document model, if any, and the reasons for these deviations. The document model and the program manager model will be identical if the program is being executed as described by the program documentation. If this is the case the discussion will identify this situation and one need not duplicate the document model to portray the program manager's model.

Evaluable Program Model (two to three pages only). This model identifies the program model that will be evaluated in the program evaluation, if one is conducted. One graphically depicts the evaluable program model followed by a discussion. Portions of the model that will not be evaluated are shown with dotted lines rather than solid lines. The discussion describes the reasons for these deviations; e.g., the effect is a longer term effect that cannot be measured during the program evaluation. If there are no deviations from the program manager's model and all effects will be evaluated, the program manager's model and the evaluable program model are identical.

The evaluation questions that will guide the program evaluation (analogous to research questions in a research study) are included at the end of this section.

Key Performance Indicators (one or two pages only). A table is used to identify each effect of the evaluable program model that will be evaluated with performance indicators (variables that can be measured) and data sources. An example for the first effect from the above document model is provided below:

- Effect (i.e., immediate and ultimate goal effects):
  - #1. Learn communication skills
- Key Performance Indicators (i.e., what one can measure to generate evidence):
  - Attendance (persistence rate)
  - Relevance (i.e., the extent to which the skills correspond to client perception of needs)

- Gratification (i.e., the extent to which the skills enhance the client's self esteem and sense of integrity)

- Learning outcomes (i.e., cognitive and affective gains).

• Data Methods/Sources (i.e., from whom or where the evidence will be generated):

  - Program records
  - Program stakeholder surveys
  - Perceived Learning Scale
  - Student grades
  - Interviews
  - Focus groups

One should use the same effects (with numbers) from the evaluable program model. Naturally any key performance indicators table needs to address all the program effects that will be evaluated, to include ultimate goal effects.

Even if the program is well planned and has a logical theory, a program evaluation is not possible without the data needed to conduct the evaluation. Consequently, the program evaluator must take steps to ensure that if a program evaluation is conducted, data and sources identified in the key performance indicators table will be available.

Analysis Procedures (one or two pages only). Includes a description of all the major analytical procedures (both quantitative and qualitative, as appropriate) that will be used to analyze the data. Addresses all of the performance indicators from the key performance indicators table. The focus of this section is on data analysis, not sampling, design, or data collection efforts. It shows how the evaluator intends to analyze indicators to permit an evaluation of effects to answer the evaluation questions.

Summary and Conclusions (one or two pages only). This section addresses the following questions:

• Can the program be managed and evaluated for results?

• Is the causal assumption for the program as implemented plausible?

- Is the target population and program participants well defined?

- Are effects measurable?

- Is there sufficient information available upon which to base a credible evaluation and will this information be made available to the program evaluator?

One of two conclusions can be drawn:

1. The program is deemed evaluable, and is ready for an evaluation.

2. The program is not ready for an evaluation due to fundamental planning and implementation issues.

If the program is not ready for evaluation, the evaluator should direct the program manager to areas of the program that need further development. The evaluator should point out why this is so and what can be done to bring the program to the appropriate level. From here, program managers can begin rethinking their programs and making plans to implement the necessary changes.

4.2: Chapter 4 Review

The answer key is at the end of this section.

1. 1. What evaluation strategy is meant to serve decision-makers and is particularly useful for making decisions about the reallocation of funds?

    A.   Objectives-oriented

    B.   Management-oriented

    C.   Consumer-oriented

    D.   Expertise-oriented

    E.   Adversary-oriented

    F.   Participant-oriented

2. What evaluation strategy employs structured public debates, such as town hall meetings?

    A.   Objectives-oriented

    B.   Management-oriented

    C.   Consumer-oriented

    D.   Expertise-oriented

    E.   Adversary-oriented

    F.   Participant-oriented

3. What evaluation strategy typically involves all stakeholders?

    A.   Objectives-oriented

    B.   Management-oriented

    C.   Consumer-oriented

    D.   Expertise-oriented

    E.   Adversary-oriented

    F.   Participant-oriented

4. What evaluation strategy tends to reinforce the status quo?

    A.   Objectives-oriented

B. Management-oriented

C. Consumer-oriented

D. Expertise-oriented

E. Adversary-oriented

F. Participant-oriented

5. What type evaluation determines the extent to which program activities are properly aligned with program goals?

A. Input evaluation

B. Process evaluation

C. Outcomes evaluation

D. Impact evaluation

6. What type of evaluation helps in making decisions regarding how best to implement a program?

A. Input evaluation

B. Process evaluation

C. Outcomes evaluation

D. Impact evaluation

7. What type of evaluation assists in making program structuring decisions?

A. Input evaluation

B. Process evaluation

C. Outcomes evaluation

D. Impact evaluation

8. What evaluation type provides information about the state of all components of the program?

A. Input evaluation

B. Process evaluation

C. Outcomes evaluation

D. Impact evaluation

9. What type evaluation does the following evaluation question for a distance education program imply: Are instructors qualified to teach online?

   A. Input evaluation

   B. Process evaluation

   C. Outcomes evaluation

   D. Impact evaluation

10. What type evaluation does the following evaluation question for a distance education program imply: Is there a gap in student evaluation of teaching between online and on campus courses?

    A. Input evaluation

    B. Process evaluation

    C. Outcomes evaluation

    D. Impact evaluation

11. Which of the following is a type of formative evaluation?

    A. Objectives-oriented evaluation

    B. Adversary-oriented evaluation

    C. Process evaluation

    D. Outcomes evaluation

12. Which of the following is a type of summative evaluation?

    A. Input evaluation

    B. Process evaluation

    C. Outcomes evaluation

    D. None of the above

13. What evaluability assessment model depicts the program as it is presently implemented?

    A. Document model

    B. Program manager's model

    C. Evaluable program model

D. Output model

14. What evaluability assessment model depicts the program as it will be evaluated?

    A. Document model

    B. Program manager's model

    C. Evaluable program model

    D. Output model

15. What is the primary purpose of an evaluability assessment?

    A. To determine if the program can be managed for results

    B. To determine the extent to which a program is ready for evaluation

    C. To determine the changes that are needed to increase a program's readiness for evaluation

    D. To determine the type(s) of evaluation and evaluation strategies most suitable to judge a program

16. What is the purpose of a program evaluation?

    A. To determine whether a human service is needed

    B. To determine whether a human service is likely to be used

    C. To determine whether a human service is conducted as planned

    D. To determine whether a human service helps people

    E. All of the above

17. How do evaluation questions differ from research questions?

    A. They are broader

    B. They are more narrow

    C. They are more specific

    D. They are less specific

    E. Choices A and D above

    F. Choices B and C above

18. What are the characteristics of a good program goal?

    A. Specific

    B. Measurable

    C. Achievable

    D. Realistic

    E. Broad

    F. Choices A through E above

19. The key performance indicator table of an evaluability assessment lists all the effects from which program model?

    A. Document model

    B. Program manager's model

    C. Evaluable program model

    D. All of the above

20. When should a goals-free evaluation be conducted?

    A. When the program has no goals

    B. When the program has no objectives

    C. When the program manager refuses to inform the program evaluator of program goals

    D. When the program evaluator is interested in unintended program outcomes

Chapter 4 Answers

1B, 2E, 3F, 4B, 5C, 6B, 7A, 8B, 9B, 10B, 11C, 12C, 13B, 14C, 15A, 16E, 17E, 18E, 19C, 20D

Chapter 5: Descriptive Statistics

There are two types of statistics: descriptive statistics and inferential statistics. This chapter describes measures of central tendency, measures of dispersion, measures of relative position and supporting graphs and charts.

5.1: Introduction

Overview

Descriptive statistics are used to describe what is or what the data shows. It is divided into the four subcategories shown below.

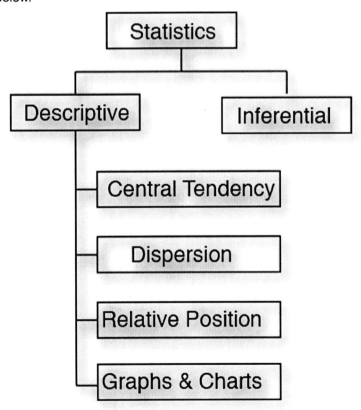

The first step in data analysis is to describe data using descriptive statistics. Descriptive statistics are a way to summarize large datasets and to detect patterns in the data in order to convey their essence to others and/or to allow for further analysis using inferential statistics.

> **Key Point**
> Descriptive statistics summarize data collected from a sample while inferential statistics reach conclusions that extend beyond the sample.

It is customary to describe any dataset descriptively in any research report or journal article. Results sections of quantitative research reports describe the distributions obtained from measuring a sample on one or more variables, to include demographic variables, by reporting, as a minimum, the sample size (N), group sizes (n), and the best measures of central tendency and dispersion for each variable. Additionally, graphs and charts are used to display the shape of distributions. A comprehensive description can also include the following distribution characteristics:

- *Symmetry* (symmetrical, skewed positively, or skewed negatively)
- *Kurtosis* (leptokurtic, mesokurtic, or platykurtic)
- *Modality* (unimodal, bimodal, multimodal)
- *Presence of outliers* (mild or extreme)

These terms are described in this chapter.

SPSS Procedure

SPSS can calculate descriptive statistics for each variable that one specifies.

SPSS > Analyze > Descriptive Statistics > Frequencies, Descriptives, Explore

The *Frequencies* procedure provides statistics and graphical displays that are useful for describing many types of variables. The frequencies procedure is a good place to start looking at data.

The *Descriptives* procedure displays univariate summary statistics for several variables in a single table. Reported statistics include sample size, mean, minimum, maximum, standard deviation, variance, range, sum, standard error of the mean, and kurtosis and skewness statistics with their standard errors.

The *Explore* procedure produces summary statistics and graphical displays, either for all or separately for groups of cases. There are many reasons for using this procedure; e.g., data screening, outlier identification, description, assumption checking, and characterizing differences among subpopulations (groups of cases). Data screening may show that there are unusual values, extreme values, gaps in the data, or other peculiarities. Exploring the data can also help to determine whether or not the statistical techniques that one is considering for more sophisticated data analysis are appropriate.

Data with Missing Values

SPSS treats blank values as missing. The researcher can control how SPSS treats missing values in the following ways:

- *Exclude cases listwise* (this is the default). Cases with missing values are excluded from all analyses.

- *Exclude cases pairwise*. Cases with no missing values for variables in a group (cell) are included in the analysis of that group. The case may have missing values for variables used in other groups.

Data Preparation

Data preparation is the manipulation of data collected from a research study into a form suitable for further analysis and processing as well as engaging in steps necessary to ensure quality control. It includes actions regarding:

- Data accuracy and verification.

  - Cleaning the data by finding and correcting coding errors.

- Dataset structure and preparation.

  - Preparing a codebook (a map to help one figure out the structure of the data).

  - Using the SPSS *Define Variable Properties* tool to set up data dictionary information (such as value labels, variable labels, and variable types).

- Using the SPSS *Recode* tool to create a new variable that rearranges the values of an existing variable by assigning them new values; e.g., merge categories of categorical variables or create a collapsed ordinal scale.

  - Reversing the ratings for some of the scale items when reverse scoring is employed by the test instrument.

  - Creating new variables, such as scale and subscale totals.

- Missing value handling.

  - Determining patterns of missing data.

  - Using the the SPSS *Missing Values property* to code missing values.

  - Replacing missing values of nominal variables with the mode, ordinal variables with the median, and continuous variables with the mean.

  - Excluding cases with missing values from the analysis.

- Outlier handling.

  - Trimming extreme outliers that lie beyond the cutoff value (3 standard deviations from the mean) to the cutoff value.

  - Excluding extreme outliers.

- Data transformations, if appropriate.

5.2: Measures of Central Tendency

Measures of central tendency indicate where the middle of a distribution lies. Researchers typically report the best measures of central tendency and dispersion for each variable in research reports.

Mean

The *mean* or arithmetic average is a statistic such that the sum of deviations from it is zero. It is based on the sum of the deviation scores raised to the first power, or what is known as the first moment of the distribution.

The sample mean may be thought of as an estimate of the population mean from which the sample was drawn. By convention, the population mean is denoted by the Greek letter μ (mu) and the sample mean is denoted by M or $\bar{x}$.

The formula for the sample mean is given below. It shows that the sum of all scores is divided by the total number of scores (N) in the sample.

$$\bar{X} = \frac{\sum X}{N}$$

The mean is always located more toward the skewed (tail) end of skewed distributions in relation to the median and mode. For symmetric distributions, mean = mode = median.

The mean can be thought of as the balance point of the distribution. If one places the observations on an imaginary see-saw with the mean at the center point, then the two sides of the see-saw should be balanced (that is, both sides are off the ground and the see-saw is level).

> **Key Point**
> For interval/ratio variables, the mean is normally the best measure of central tendency. For strongly skewed variables, both mean and median should be reported.

SPSS Procedure

SPSS > Analyze > Descriptive Statistics > Descriptives

SPSS > Analyze > Descriptive Statistics > Frequencies > Statistics > Mean

5% Trimmed Mean

The *5% trimmed mean* is the mean that would be obtained if the lower and upper 2.5% of values of the variable were deleted. If the value of the 5% trimmed mean is substantially different from the mean, it is reasonable to conclude the presence of outliers in the original dataset. However, one cannot assume that all outliers have been removed from the trimmed mean.

SPSS Procedure

SPSS > Analyze > Descriptive Statistics > Explore

Median

The *median* (*Md*) is the score that divides the distribution into two equal halves. It is the midpoint of the distribution when the distribution has an odd number of scores. It is the number halfway between the two middle scores when the distribution has an even number of scores. The median is useful to describe a skewed distribution.

> **Key Point**
> For ordinal variables, the median is
> the best measure of central tendency.

SPSS Procedure

SPSS > Analyze > Descriptive Statistics > Descriptives

SPSS > Analyze > Descriptive Statistics > Explore

Mode

The *mode (Mo)* is the most frequently occurring score in a distribution. A distribution is called unimodal if there is only one major peak in the distribution of scores when displayed as a histogram. If the distribution is symmetrical and unimodal (i.e., a normally-shaped bell curve), the mode equals the mean.

The mode is useful when describing nominal variables and in describing a bimodal or multimodal distribution (use of the mean or median only can be misleading).

- *Major mode* = most common value, largest peak.
- *Minor mode(s)* = smaller peak(s).
- *Unimodal* (i.e., having one peak or mode)
- *Bimodal* (i.e., having two peaks or modes)
- *Multimodal* (i.e., having two or more peaks or modes)
- *Rectangular* (i.e., having no peaks or modes)

> **Key Point**
> For nominal variables, the mode is
> the best measure of central tendency.

SPSS Procedure

SPSS > Analyze > Descriptive Statistics > Frequencies >
Statistics > Mode

Summary

The table below identifies the measures of central tendency
that are most appropriate for various scales of measurement.

Measure	Ratio	Interval	Ordinal	Nominal
Mean	X	X		
5% trimmed mean	X	X		
Median	X	X	X	
Mode	X	X	X	X

5.3: Measures of Dispersion

Measures of dispersion describe the variability of a distribution. Researchers typically report the best measures of central tendency and dispersion for each variable in research reports.

Standard Deviation

Standard deviation is a measure of variability or dispersion of a set of data. It is calculated from the deviations between each data value and the sample mean. It is also the square root of the variance.

$$\sigma = \sqrt{\frac{\sum(X-\mu)^2}{N}}$$

$$S = \sqrt{\frac{\sum(X-\overline{X})^2}{N}}$$

$$\hat{s} = \sqrt{\frac{\sum(X-\overline{X})^2}{N-1}}$$

Note that the top formula is for the population standard deviation, σ, where μ is the population mean. The middle formula is for the sample standard deviation, *s*, and the bottom formula is for the sample estimate of the population standard deviation, s-hat. The sample mean minimizes the sum of squared (*SS*) deviations. Therefore, $N-1$ is used in the bottom formula since the SS from the sample will underestimate the population SS.

For normally distributed data values, approximately 68.2% of the distribution falls within ± 1 standard deviation of the mean, 95.4% of the distribution falls within ± 2 standard deviations of the mean, and 99.6% of the distribution falls within ± 3 standard deviations of the mean.

> **Key Point**
> Standard deviation is the best measure of dispersion for interval/ratio scale variables.

SPSS Procedure

SPSS > Analyze > Descriptive Statistics > Descriptives > Options > Standard Deviation

SPSS > Analyze > Descriptive Statistics > Explore

Variance

Variance is a measure of variability derived from the sum of the deviation scores from the mean raised to the second power (i.e., the second moment of the distribution).

The formula for the population and sample variances are given below

$$\sigma^2 = \frac{\sum (X - \mu)^2}{N}$$

$$S^2 = \frac{\sum \left(X - \overline{X}\right)^2}{N}$$

where σ^2 is the symbol for population variance, s^2 is the symbol for sample variance, and μ is the symbol for population mean.

Adding or subtracting a constant to/from each score just shifts the distribution without changing the variance.

SPSS Procedure

SPSS > Analyze > Descriptive Statistics > Descriptives > Options > Variance

SPSS > Analyze > Descriptive Statistics > Explore

Standard Error of the Mean

Standard error of the mean is the standard deviation of the sampling distribution of the mean. It is used in the computation of confidence intervals and significance tests for the mean.

The precision of the mean of a sample of data, as an estimate of some unknown or true value of the population mean, is described using the standard error of the mean. Note that as the sample size increases, the sample mean becomes a better estimate of the population mean.

$$\sigma_M = \frac{\sigma}{\sqrt{N}}$$

There is a 68.26% probability that the true population mean is ± one standard error of the mean from the sample mean.

SPSS Procedure

SPSS > Analyze > Descriptive Statistics > Descriptives > Options > SE Mean

Skewness

Skewness is based on the third moment of the distribution, or the sum of cubic deviations from the mean. It measures deviations from perfect symmetry.

- *Positive skewness* indicates a distribution with a heavier positive (right-hand) tail than a symmetrical distribution (mode < median < mean). A frequency distribution with a negative skew can result from a set of scores from a difficult examination.

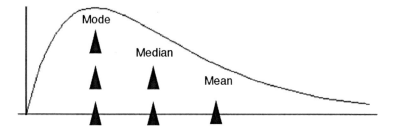

- *Negative skewness* indicates a distribution with a heavier negative tail (mean < median < mode). A frequency distribution with a negative skew can result from a set of scores from an easy examination.

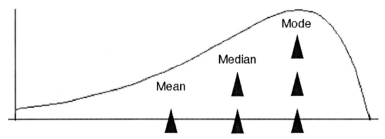

- *Symmetrical distributions* (i.e., zero skewness) have approximately equal numbers of observations above and below the middle with approximately equal tails. Skewness statistic = 0 for a perfectly normal distribution (mean = median = mode). A symmetrical distribution has the appearance of a bell-shaped curve.

Kurtosis

Kurtosis is derived from the fourth moment (i.e., the sum of quartic deviations). It captures the heaviness or weight of the tails relative to the center of the distribution. Kurtosis measures heavy-tailedness or light-tailedness relative to the normal distribution. A heavy-tailed distribution has more values in the tails (away from the center of the distribution) than the normal distribution, and will have a negative kurtosis. A light-tailed distribution has more values in the center (away from the tails of the distribution) than the normal distribution, and will have a positive kurtosis.

Kurtotic shapes of distributions are generally recognized with various labels and associated kurtosis statistics.

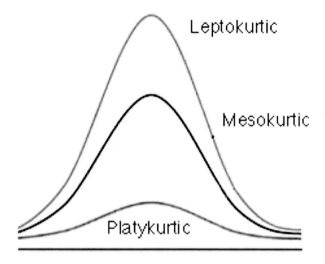

- *Leptokurtic* – peaked shape, kurtosis statistic above 0, small standard deviation.

- *Mesokurtic* – between extremes, normal shape. Kurtosis statistic = around 0 for an approximately normal distribution.

- *Platykurtic* – flat shape, kurtosis statistic below 0, large standard deviation.

SPSS Procedure

SPSS > Analyze > Descriptive Statistics > Descriptives > Options > Kurtosis, Skewness

SPSS > Analyze > Descriptive Statistics > Explore

Range

The *range* of a distribution is calculated by subtracting the minimum score from the maximum score:

$$Range = X_{Max} - X_{Min}$$

The range is not very stable (reliable) because it is based on only two scores. Consequently, outliers have a significant effect on the range of variable.

> **Key Point**
> For ordinal and nominal variables,
> the range is the best measure of
> dispersion.

SPSS Procedure

SPSS > Analyze > Descriptive Statistics > Descriptives > Options > Range

SPSS > Analyze > Descriptive Statistics > Explore

Interquartile Range

The *interquartile range* (*IQR*) is the distance between the 75th percentile (P_{75}) and the 25th percentile (P_{25}). In other words, the *IQR* is the range of the middle 50% of the data and is used to summarize the extent of data spread.

- $IQR = Q_3 - Q_1$ = middle 50% of the distribution
- Not affected by a few outliers
- Used with ratio and interval scales

The *semi-interquartile range* (or quartile deviation) is half the *IQR*. It is sometimes preferred over the range as a measure of dispersion because it is not affected by extreme scores.

The boxplot, depicted below for the variable social isolation, identifies the *IQR*. The central rectangle spans the first quartile (Q_1) to the third quartile (Q_3), thus providing a graphical representation of the *IQR* for this variable.

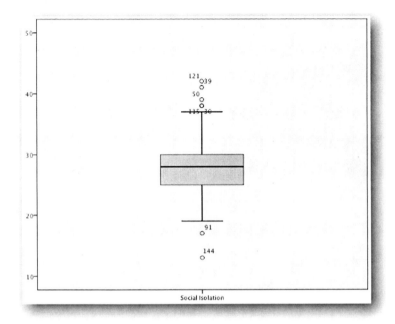

SPSS Procedure

SPSS > Analyze > Descriptive Statistics > Explore

SPSS > Graphs-> [Legacy Dialogs] > Boxplot

SPSS > Analyze > Descriptive Statistics > Explore > Plots > Boxplot

Outliers

Outliers are extreme values. There are regular or mild outliers and extreme outliers. Scatter plots and boxplots are graphical techniques for identifying outliers.

- *Extreme outliers* are any data values that lie more than 3.0 times the *IQR* below Q_1 or above Q_3. Extreme outliers normally pose a serious threat to the validity of parametric tests.

- *Mild outliers* are any data values that lie between 1.5 times and 3.0 times the *IQR* below Q_1 or above Q_3.

SPSS Procedure

SPSS > Analyze > Descriptive Statistics > Explore > Statistics > Outliers

SPSS > Graphs-> Boxplot

SPSS > Graphs-> Scatter/Dot

Summary

The table below identifies the measures of dispersion appropriate for various scales.

Measure	Ratio	Interval	Ordinal	Nominal
Standard deviation	X	X		
Variance	X	X		
Standard error of the mean	X	X		
Skewness	X	X		
Kurtosis	X	X		
Outliers	X	X	X	
Range	X	X	X	X
Interquartile range	X	X		

5.4: Measures of Relative Position

Measures of relative position indicate how high or low a score is in relation to other scores in a distribution. These measures not only include percentiles and quartiles described in this section, but also standard scores; e.g., z-scores, T-scores, NCE-scores, stanines, etc.

Percentiles

A *percentile* (*P*) is a measure that tells one the percent of the total frequency that scored below that measure. Percentiles divide the data into 100 equal parts based on their statistical rank and position from the bottom. It is the value of a variable below which a given percent of the cases lie. For example, the 50th percentile, P_{50}, which represents the median value, indicates that 50% of scores are below P_{50}. Therefore, a percentile is a cutoff score and not a range of values.

A percentile rank is a number between 0 and 100 that shows the percent of cases falling at or below that score. Percentile scores are ordinal scale data; they are not interval scale data. The difference between any two scores is not the same between any other two percentile scores.

SPSS Procedure

SPSS > Analyze > Descriptive Statistics > Frequencies > Statistics > Percentile(s)

SPSS > Analyze > Descriptive Statistics > Explore > Statistics > Percentiles

Deciles

A *decile* (*D*) divides the data into ten equal parts based on their statistical ranks and position from the bottom, where $D_1 = P_{10}$ and $D_5 = P_{50} = Q_2$.

Quartiles

A *quartile* (*Q*) divides the data into four equal parts based on their statistical ranks and position from the bottom. In other words, quartiles are the values that divide a list of numbers into quarters, $Q_1 = P_{25}$, $Q_2 = P_{50} = Md$, $Q_3 = P_{75}$. Like the percentile, the quartile is a cutoff score and not a range of values. One may be above or below Q_2, but not in Q_2.

SPSS Procedure

SPSS > Analyze > Descriptive Statistics > Frequencies > Statistics > Quartiles

Summary

The table below identifies the measures of relative position that are appropriate for various scales of measurement.

Measure	Ratio	Interval	Ordinal	Nominal
Quartiles	X	X		
Percentiles	X	X		
Deciles	X	X		

5.5: Graphs and Charts

Line Chart

A *line chart* allows one to visually examine the mean (or other statistic) of a continuous variable across the various levels of a categorical variable. Line charts are ideally suited to show trends for data over time in longitudinal studies. For example, the *x*-axis can be observation; e.g., observation 1, observation 2, observation 3, etc. Data points are connected by lines.

Below is an example of a line chart produced by SPSS representing mean self-esteem among university students (*y*-axis) across various student age categories (*x*-axis). A single line chart can include multiple lines (variables).

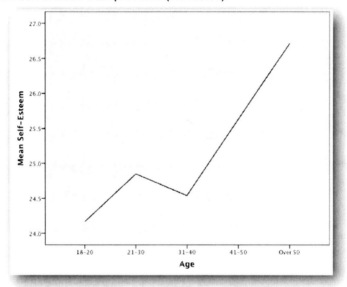

SPSS Procedure

SPSS > Graphs-> [Legacy Dialogs] > Line

Line charts are included as an option in various SPSS outputs; e.g., *ANOVA* output.

Bar Chart

A *bar chart* is made up of columns positioned over a label that represents a categorical variable. The height of the column represents the size of the group defined by the column label.

Below is an example of a bar chart produced by SPSS representing the number of participants in a research study disaggregated by ethnicity.

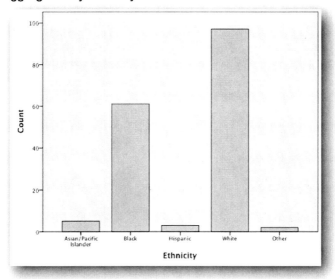

SPSS Procedure

SPSS > Graphs-> [Legacy Dialogs] > Bar

Histogram

A *histogram* is an example of a frequency curve that displays a univariate dataset. It is constructed by dividing the range of continuous data into equal-sized adjacent bins (classes or groups). It is helpful to view these bins as containers that accumulate data that causes the bins to increase in height. For each bin, a rectangle is constructed with an area proportional to the number of observations falling into that bin. Bins are plotted on the *x*-axis and frequencies (the number of cases accumulated in each bin) are plotted on the *y*-axis. The *y*-axis ranges from 0 to the greatest number of cases deposited in any bin. The *x*-axis includes the entire data range.

Histograms are similar to bar charts. However, with bar charts, each column represents a group defined by a categorical variable. In contrast, with histograms, each column represents a group defined by a continuous variable. Typically, there are no spaces between columns in a histogram while bar charts include spaces.

Below is an example of a histogram produced by SPSS representing the self-esteem of university students enrolled in a distance education program. Note that SPSS also provides *M*, *SD*, and *N*.

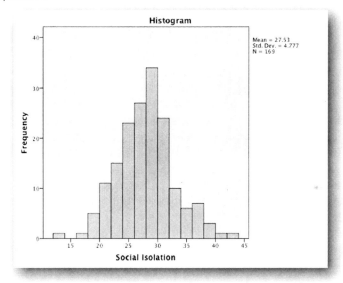

Histograms are useful for evaluating:

- The shape of a distribution
- Symmetry, skewness, and kurtosis
- Modality
- Presence of outliers

SPSS Procedure

SPSS > Graphs-> [Legacy dialogs] > Histogram

SPSS > Analyze > Descriptive Statistics > Frequencies > Charts > Histograms

SPSS > Analyze > Descriptive Statistics > Explore > Plots > Histogram

Boxplot

A *boxplot* is another graphical way depicting a univariate dataset of a continuous variable. It identifies the following values:

- high outliers
- largest case not an outlier
- upper quartile (Q_3)
- median (Q_2)
- lower quartile (Q_1)
- smallest case not an outlier
- low outliers

Boxplots are vertically oriented with a box that extends from the first to the third quartiles and with the median (Q_2) indicated by a black center line. This box represents the inter-quartile range (*IQR*). Vertical lines (whiskers) extend from the top and bottom of the box. These whiskers represent the highest and lowest values that are not outliers. The location of the box between the whiskers shows how the data are distributed. If the box is midway between the whiskers, the data are more evenly distributed. If the box is closer to the lower whisker, the data are positively skewed. If the box is closer to the upper whisker, the data are negatively skewed.

Mild outliers (values that are between 1.5 and 3 times the *IQR*) and extreme outliers (values that are more than 3 times the *IQR*) are represented by small circles (i.e., mild outliers) and asterisks (i.e., extreme outliers) respectively beyond the whiskers in SPSS generated boxplots. SPSS output also identifies case numbers adjacent to the circles and asterisks.

Below is an example of a boxplot produced by SPSS representing social isolation of university distance education students.

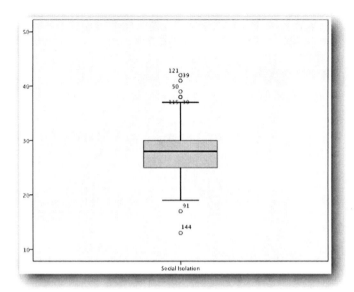

The above example shows the presence of five high mild outliers and two low mild outliers together with their dataset case numbers. There are no extreme outliers.

SPSS Procedure

SPSS > Graphs-> [Legacy Dialogs] > Boxplot

SPSS > Analyze > Descriptive Statistics > Explore > Plots > Boxplot

Stem-and-Leaf Plot

A *stem-and-leaf plot* is a type of graph that is similar to a histogram. The purpose is to allow one to identify exact scores in the plot and also get a sense of the shape of the distribution. It depicts the shape of a dataset in a sideway orientation and provides detail regarding individual values.

Below is a stem-and-leaf plot generated by SPSS depicting the same variable displayed in the histogram and boxplot shown above. The numbers on the left side of the decimal place represent the stems. The numbers on the right side of the decimal are the leaves. SPSS displays how many leaves are on each stem. It also identifies outliers as extremes.

In the plot below, the stems are the scores on the test and the leaves are tenths. For example, there are five scores of 19.0, the stem is 19 and the leaf is the tenths decimal place. Each leaf represents one case.

Social Isolation Stem-and-Leaf Plot

Frequency	Stem & Leaf	
2.00	Extremes	(= < 17.0)
5.00	19 .	00000
6.00	20 .	000000
5.00	21 .	00000
3.00	22 .	000
12.00	23 .	000000000000
7.00	24 .	0000000
16.00	25 .	0000000000000000
16.00	26 .	0000000000000000
11.00	27 .	00000000000
16.00	28 .	0000000000000000
18.00	29 .	000000000000000000
16.00	30 .	0000000000000000
8.00	31 .	00000000
5.00	32 .	00000
5.00	33 .	00000
4.00	34 .	0000
2.00	35 .	00
6.00	36 .	000000
1.00	37 .	0
5.00	Extremes	(> = 38.0)

Stem width: 1
Each leaf: 1 case(s)

SPSS Procedure

SPSS > Analyze > Descriptive Statistics > Explore > Plots > Stem-and-leaf

Scatterplot

Scatterplots (also called scattergrams) show the relationship between two continuous variables. For each case, scatterplots depict the value of the IV on the *x*-axis and the value of the DV on the *y*-axis. Each dot on a scatterplot is a case. The dot is placed at the intersection of each case's scores on *x* and *y*.

There are several types of scatter plots. The simple scatterplot allows one to plot one variable as a function of another as described above. It the most frequently used type of scatterplot for producing graphical representations of bivariate correlation and linear regression. The matrix scatterplot allows one to plot several simple scatter plots organized in a matrix. This is useful for depicting all possible scatter plots for a set of variables. The overlay scatterplot allows one to plot several variables as a function of another single variable. Finally, the 3D scatterplot allows one to produce three dimensional (i.e., three variable) scatterplots.

Below is an example of a simple boxplot produced by SPSS representing social isolation (*x*-axis) and alienation (*y*-axis).

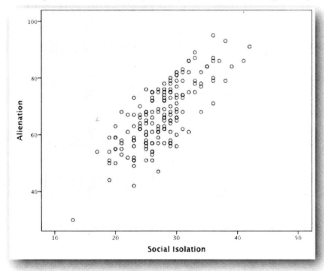

The above scatterplot suggests a linear relationship between social isolation and alienation.

SPSS Procedure

SPSS > Graphs-> Scatter/Dot

Q-Q Plot

The *Q-Q plot* (Quantile-Quantile plot) plots the quantiles of a variable's distribution against the quantiles of a normal distribution (or other specified distribution). If the two sets come from a population with the same distribution, the points should fall approximately along the reference line depicted on the plot. The greater the departure from this reference line, the greater the evidence for the conclusion that the two data sets come from populations with different distributions. When generating a Q-Q plot for a variable, SPSS:

- Arranges observed data values from smallest to largest, and calculates the percentile occupied by each value.

- Plots each data point (observed value) against its corresponding standardized score (expected value if a normal distribution).

Interpreting normality is based on a visual inspection of the Q-Q plot. One should focus on the middle two-thirds of the line and determine how closely the data points depict a straight line.

If the data distribution approximates a normal distribution, the plotted points will reflect a straight line, usually a 45 degree line. Normal plots compare the obtained scores (on the x-axis) with expected z-scores (on the y-axis). That is, a normal plot compares the actual scores with z-scores that would have been obtained if the scores were normally distributed. Systematic deviations from this line indicate a non-normal distribution (Moore & McCabe, 1999). Outliers appear as points lying far away from the overall pattern of the plot. When examining a Q-Q plot, it is important to appreciate that real-world data will almost always show some variation from the theoretical normal model. Consequently, one should not be overly concerned about minor wiggles in the line (Moore & McCabe, 1999).

Q-Q plots are used with interval or ratio level data. Below is an example of a Q-Q plot produced by SPSS showing a non-normal distribution.

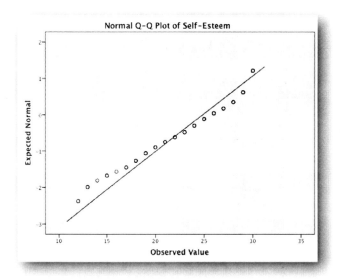

The boxplot for the same variable is provided below, which provides additional visual evidence of non-normality. Clearly, the distribution is negatively skewed.

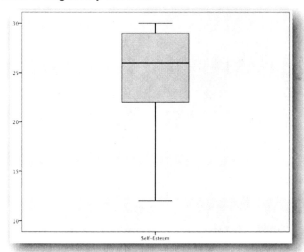

SPSS Procedure

SPSS > Analyze-> Descriptive Statistics > Explore (select normality plots with tests)

SPSS > Analyze > Descriptive Statistics > Q-Q Plots

Detrended Q-Q Plot

Detrended Q-Q plots provide information that is similar to that provided by the Q-Q plot. The *y*-axis represents standard deviations from the 45-degree line seen in the non-detrended Q-Q plot and the *x*-axis represents values. The plot shows the difference between an observation's expected *z*-score under normality and its actual z-score. If the distribution were perfectly normal, the points should cluster in a horizontal band around y = 0 with no specific pattern. If the data were spread evenly around y = 0 without a pattern (e.g. the absence of curvature), it would be an indication that the sample data likely came from a population that is approximately normal. This plot is very sensitive and very easy to misinterpret.

Below is an example of a detrended Q-Q plot produced by SPSS showing a non-normal distribution (note the distinct curvature).

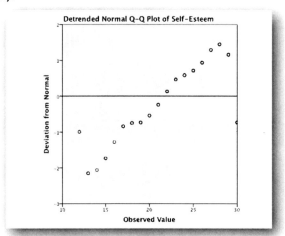

SPSS Procedure

SPSS > Analyze-> Descriptive Statistics > Explore (select normality plots with tests)

SPSS > Analyze > Descriptive Statistics > Q-Q Plots

P-P Plot

P-P plots (Probability-Probability plots) are very similar to Q-Q plots. The P-P plot plots two cumulative distribution functions against each other. They are used with interval or ratio level data. If the data points do not all fall on the diagonal line, then one can use this plot to visually determine where the data do and do not follow the distribution. P-P plots tend to magnify deviations from the normal distribution in the middle while Q-Q plots tend to magnify deviations from the normal distribution in the tails.

Below is an example of a P-P plot using normal as the test distribution produced by SPSS. It shows a non-normal distribution.

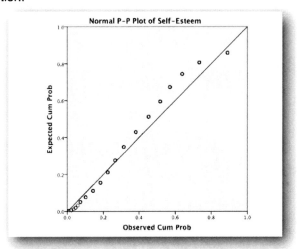

SPSS Procedure

SPSS > Analyze-> Descriptive Statistics > Explore

SPSS > Analyze > Descriptive Statistics > P-P Plots

5.6: Chapter 5 Review

The answer key is at the end of this section.

1. What measure of central tendency is most appropriate for ordinal data?

   A. Mean

   B. 5% trimmed mean

   C. Median

   D. Mode

2. What measure of dispersion is most appropriate for interval data?

   A. Standard deviation

   B. Range

   C. Mode

   D. Standard error

3. How would adding 5 to every observation affect the mean of a variable?

   A. No effect

   B. Increase mean by 5

   C. Increase mean by 25

   D. Decrease mean by 5

4. How would adding 5 to every observation affect the variance of a variable?

   A. No effect

   B. Increase variance by 5

   C. Increase variance by 25

   D. Decrease variance by 5

5. How would multiplying 5 to every observation affect the variance of a variable?

   A. No effect

B. Increase variance by 5

C. Increase variance by 25

D. Decrease variance by 5

6. Which of the following symbols is used to represent the population variance?

   A. σ

   B. σ^2

   C. s

   D. s^2

7. Which of the following graphs produced by SPSS is most useful in identifying extreme outliers?

   A. Line chart

   B. Histogram

   C. Scatterplot

   D. Boxplot

8. Which of the following graphs produced by SPSS is most useful in examining the relationship between two variables?

   A. Line chart

   B. Histogram

   C. Boxplot

   D. Scatterplot

9. The median is the value that...

   A. occurs most often

   B. divides an ordered dataset into two equal halves

   C. is the arithmetic average

   D. none of the above

10. What is the most accurate description of the distribution displayed in the following histogram?

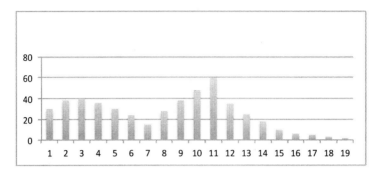

A.   Unimodal, positive skew

B.   Unimodal, negative skew

C.   Bimodal, positive skew

D.   Bimodal, negative skew

11. What is the interquartile range for a distribution with the following percentiles: $P_{25} = 25$, $P_{50} = 50$, $P_{75} = 75$?

A.   50

B.   25

C.   75

D.   100

12. The interquartile range allows one to make a statement about...

A.   the top 50% of observations

B.   the middle 75% of observations

C.   the middle 50% of observations

D.   the middle 25% of observations

13. Which of the following qualitative sampling strategies may occur after data collection has begun?

A.   the balancing point of a distribution

B.   the same as arithmetic average

C.   often, the best measure of central tendency for interval scale data

D.   none of the above

14. The mode is...

A.   the typical way of measuring central tendency for ordinal data

B.   the typical way of measuring central tendency for nominal data

C.   the middle value in a group of scores

D.   affected by outliers

15. What statement is correct regarding variance?

A.   The average amount that scores differ from the mean

B.   Point at which half the scores are above and half are below

C.   Unaffected by the extremity of individual scores

D.   The average of the squared deviations from the mean

16. Which of the following is not a measure of dispersion?

A.   Median

B.   Range

C.   Standard deviation

D.   Standard error of the mean

17. A distribution with a kurtosis statistic = 0 is best described using what term?

A.   Leptokurtic

B.   Platykurtic

C.   Mesokurtic

D.   None of the above

18. Which statement about skewness is correct?

A.   Skewness is a measure of modality

B.   Skewness measures deviations from perfect symmetry

C.   Skewness is a measure of whether the data are peaked or flat relative to a perfectly normal distribution

D. Negative skewness reflects a heavy positive tail

19. If a distribution were perfectly normal, the detrended Q-Q plot would show...

   A. the points should cluster in a horizontal band around $y = 0$ with no pattern

   B. the points should cluster in a 45 degree band with no pattern

   C. the points should cluster in a vertical band with no pattern

   D. the points should reflect a curvilinear pattern around $x = 0$

20. Which statement is NOT correct?

   A. Q-Q plots are used with interval or ratio level data

   B. Q-Q plots tend to magnify deviations from the normal distribution in the tails

   C. P-P plots tend to magnify deviations from the normal distribution in the middle

   D. P-P plots are used with nominal or ordinal level data

Chapter 5 Answers

1C, 2A, 3B, 4A, 5A, 6B, 7D, 8D, 9B, 10C, 11A, 12C, 13D, 14B, 15D, 16A, 17A, 18B, 19A, 20D

Chapter 6: Inferential Statistics

Inferential statistics goes beyond the sample and draws conclusions about the population from which the sample was drawn. This chapter describes point and interval estimation, hypothesis testing, and the evaluation of test assumptions.

6.1: Basic Concepts

Introduction

The purpose of inferential statistics is to reach conclusions that extend beyond the sample measured to a target population. It is divided into estimation and hypothesis testing.

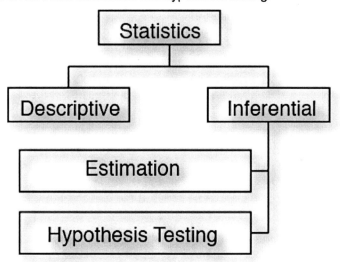

Inferential statistics are used to address the following issues:

- How confident can one be that statistical results are not due to chance? One looks at the statistical test's significance level. If $p \leq$ the à priori significance level (usually .05 for social science research), the results are statistically significant.

- Is a statistically significant effect of any practical significance? One calculates and reports the effect size statistic as a proxy measure to assess practical significance. Effect size is a measure of the magnitude of a research result.

- What is the direction of the effect? For a difference research question, one compares each group's best measure of central tendency (usually mean for interval or ratio data). For a relationship question, one examines the sign of the correlation coefficient. A plus sign indicates a positive (direct) relationship in which both variables covary in the same direction. A negative sign indicates an inverse relationship in which both variables covary in opposite directions.

There are two types of inferential tests: parametric tests and nonparametric tests. A parametric test is a statistical procedure that assumes data come from a probability distribution and makes inferences about the parameters of the distribution. It also assumes data are normally distributed and the DV(s) are interval or ratio scale. Robustness studies have established that mild to moderate violations of parametric assumptions have little effect on substantive conclusions in many instances (e.g., Cohen, 1988).

Since all common parametric statistics are relational, the range of procedures used to analyze one continuous DV and one or more IVs (continuous or categorical) are mathematically similar. The underlying model is called the general linear model (GLM).

A nonparametric test does not make assumptions regarding the distribution. Consequently, a nonparametric test is considered a distribution-free method because it does not rely on any underlying mathematical distribution. Nonparametric tests do, however, have various assumptions that must be met.

A nonparametric test is limited in its ability to provide the researcher with grounds for drawing conclusions – parametric tests provide more detailed information. Consequently, researchers prefer parametric to nonparametric tests because generally they are more powerful. However, nonparametric tests are useful when parametric test assumptions, most often the assumption of normality, cannot be met.

```
Key Point
Findings are statistically significant
only when they are unlikely to be
explained by chance.
```

Types of Variables

There are several important types of variables used in inferential statistics. Independent variables (IVs) make up one type. These are the predictor variables that one expects to influence other variables. In an experiment, the researcher manipulates the IV(s), which typically involve an intervention of some type. For example, if a researcher sets up two classes using two different teaching methods for the purpose of comparing the effectiveness of these methods, the IV is teaching method (method A, method B).

Dependent variables (DVs) make up a second type of variable. These are outcome variables, or those that one expects to be affected by IVs. For example, if different teaching methods (the IV) result in different student achievement as measured by test scores, then student achievement (or, operationally, test score) is the DV.

IVs are variables that are manipulated whereas DVs are variables that are measured. The terms IV and DV apply especially to experimental research where some variables are manipulated or to regression studies where one addresses prediction. In this case the IV is the predictor variable and the DV is the criterion variable. IV's and DV's can be summarized by the following example:

IV > DV

Cause > Effect (Outcome)

Level of Education > Income Level

Moderating variables are introduced to account for situations where the relationship between the IV and the DV is presumed to depend on some third variable.

In general terms, a moderator is a qualitative (e.g., sex, race, class) or quantitative (e.g., level of reward) variable that affects the direction and/or strength of the relation between an independent or predictor variable and a dependent or criterion variable. Specifically within a correlational analysis framework, a moderator is a third variable that affects the zero-order correlation between two other variables. ... In the more familiar analysis of variance (*ANOVA*) terms, a basic moderator effect can be represented as an interaction between a focal independent variable and a factor that specifies the appropriate conditions for its operation. (Baron & Kenny, 1986, p. 1174)

For example, gender can act as a moderator variable in the following relationship as it influences both level of education and income level.

Level of Education > Income Level

Mediating variables (also called intervening variables) may be introduced to explain why an antecedent variable affects a consequent variable.

In general, a given variable may be said to function as a mediator to the extent that it accounts for the relation between the predictor and the criterion. Mediators explain how external physical events take on internal psychological significance. Whereas moderator variables specify when certain effects will hold, mediators speak to how or why such effects occur" (Baron & Kenny, p. 1176).

Cause > Mediating Variable(s) > Effect

Level of Education > Occupation > Income Level

Extraneous variables are additional variables relevant to a research study that the researcher needs to control. Extraneous variables are related, in a statistical sense, with both the DV and the IV. An extraneous variable becomes a confounding variable when the researcher cannot or does control for it, thereby adversely affecting the internal validity of a study by increasing error. Confounding variables are sometimes called lurking variables. For example, confounding can occur when a researcher does not randomly assign participants to groups and a type of difference between groups, which is not controlled, affects research results (e.g., motivation, ability, etc.).

Gain and Loss Scores

Gain and loss scores are sometimes used as DVs by researchers in pretest-posttest designs. It makes intuitive sense to subtract the pretest from the posttest measures (or vice versa) and then determine whether the gain (or loss) is statistically significant between groups. However, this is a controversial procedure; e.g., Cronbach and Furby (1970) and Nunnally (1975).

Cronbach and Furby (1970) wrote that when the pretest and post scores are well correlated, the gain scores have a dramatic loss in reliability. Cronbach and Furby argued that: "gain scores are rarely useful, no matter how they may be adjusted or refined" (p. 68) and "investigators who ask questions regarding gain scores should ordinarily be better advised to frame their questions in other ways" (p. 80).

Estimation

Estimation is a way to estimate a population parameter based on measuring a sample. It can be expressed in two ways:

- A point estimate of a population parameter is a single value of a statistic.

- An interval estimate is defined by two numbers, between which a population parameter is said to lie.

An estimate is called a point estimate when it is a single number. For example, the sample mean is a point estimate of the population mean μ. The estimate is called an interval estimate when it is a range of numbers. For example, confidence intervals are a type of interval estimates.

An unbiased estimator is one that produces the right answer, on average, over a set of replications. Bias occurs when there is a systematic error in the measure that shifts the estimate more in one direction than another, on average. One should randomly sample from the target population to avoid bias.

In addition to being on target, one also wants the distribution of an estimator to have a small variance; i.e., to be efficient, precise. More efficient statistics have smaller sampling variances, smaller standard error, and are preferred because if both are unbiased, one is closer to the parameter, on average. Larger sample sizes tend to be more efficient.

Additionally, one wants the estimator to be consistent (i.e., reliable) so that as the number of observations gets large, the variability around the estimate approaches zero and the estimate approaches more closely the parameter that one is trying to estimate. The estimator is consistent if its bias and variance both approach zero. In other words, we expect the mean square error (MSE) to approach zero.

Drawing from probability theory, a probability distribution is a function that describes the probability of a random variable taking certain values. Probability distributions are a fundamental concept in statistics as they serve several useful purposes including:

- The calculation of point estimates and confidence intervals for parameters and to calculate critical regions for hypothesis tests.

- Determining a model for the distribution; e.g., normal distribution or binomial distribution. Inferential tests assume certain distribution models that require evaluation before using the specific test.

If one draws all possible samples of size N from a given population and computes a statistic – e.g., mean, for each sample – the resultant probability distribution of this statistic is called a sampling distribution.

Central Limit Theorem

A sampling distribution is a distribution of a sample statistic, such as a sample of means created by various samples drawn from the same population. According to the central limit theorem, the sampling distribution of sample means is approximated by a normal distribution when the sample is a simple random sample and the sample size is large. In this case, the mean of the sampling distribution is the population mean, μ, and the standard deviation of the sampling distribution is the population standard deviation, σ.

> **Key Point**
> The sampling distribution of any statistic will be normal or nearly normal if the sample size is large enough.

The central limit theorem is the basis for inferential statistics. Assuming a large sample, it allows one to use hypothesis tests that assume normality, even if the data appear non-normal. This is because the tests use the sample mean, which the central limit theorem posits is approximately normally distributed.

A sample size of 100 or more units is generally considered sufficient to permit applying the central limit theorem. If the population from which the sample is drawn is symmetrically distributed, $N > 30$ may be sufficient.

Confidence Intervals

A confidence interval gives an estimated range of values that is likely to include an unknown population parameter. For example, the 95% confidence interval for the mean provides the estimated range of values that is 95% likely to include the population mean.

The following steps are necessary to construct an interval estimate for a population mean, μ:

- Obtain the point estimate of μ. This is usually the sample mean.

- Evaluate the distribution of the sample mean. If N is large, then the central limit theorem can be used and the sampling distribution of means is normally distributed with mean µ and standard deviation σ.

- Select a confidence level; e.g., 95%.

- Use the following formula (point estimate of parameter ± margin of error) to calculate confidence intervals for an unknown population mean

$$\overline{X} \pm C \frac{\sigma}{\sqrt{N}}$$

where x-bar is the point estimate of the population mean, C is the critical value for the required confidence interval in standard deviation units (z-values), σ is the population standard deviation, and N is the sample size. The critical value times the standard error of the statistic is referred to as the margin of error.

The critical value for a 95% confidence interval is 1.96 (the value of 1.96 is based on the fact that 95% of the area of a normal distribution is within 1.96 standard deviations of the mean).

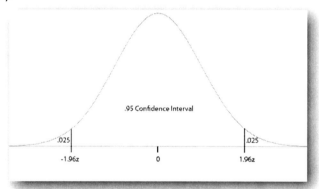

In the above figure, the 95% confidence interval in the standard normal distribution is displayed for a two-tailed test at the .05 significance level. Thus, the significance level is the sum of probabilities that a sample statistic goes beyond the critical value (larger than 1.96 and less than -1.96).

- The critical value for a 90% confidence interval is 1.645 (the value of 1.645 is based on the fact that 90% of the area of a normal distribution is within 1.645 standard deviations of the mean).

- The critical value for a 99% confidence interval is 2.58 (the value of 2.58 is based on the fact that 99% of the area of a normal distribution is within 2.58 standard deviations of the mean).

When the population standard deviation is not known but must be estimated from sample data one should use the *t*-distribution rather than the normal distribution to obtain critical values. When the sample size is large – e.g. > 100 – the *t*-distribution is similar to the standard normal distribution and the critical values provided above are adequate. The critical values of *t* to be used in a confidence interval can be looked up in a table of the *t*-distribution based on degrees of freedom and confidence level.

SPSS Procedure

SPSS > Analyze > Descriptive Statistics > Explore

This procedure will display the 95% confidence interval of the mean.

Hypothesis Testing

Hypothesis testing is a method for making decisions about the target population based on the characteristics of a random sample drawn from that population. The overall goal of a hypothesis test is to rule out chance (sampling error) as a plausible explanation for the research results. All hypothesis tests are based on probability theory and have risks of reaching a wrong conclusion.

> **Key Point**
> No amount of statistical skill will overcome research design flaws.

Probability

Probability is the chance that something random will occur in order to predict the behavior of defined systems. The basic rules of probability are (Gall, Gall, & Borg, 2007):

- Any probability of any event, $p(E)$, is a number between 0 and 1.

- The probability that all possible outcomes can occur is 1.

- If there are k possible outcomes for a phenomenon and each is equally likely, then each individual outcome has probability of $1/k$.

- The chance of any (one or more) of two or more events occurring is the union of the events. The probability of the union of events is the sum of their individual probabilities.

- The probability that any event E does not occur is $1 - p(E)$.

- If two events E_1 and E_2 are independent, then the probability of both events is the product of the probabilities for each event, $p(E1 \text{ and } E2) = p(E_1)p(E_2)$.

For example, in a population with 50 males and 40 females, the probability of randomly selecting a male is $p(M) = 50/90 = .56$ and the probability of not selecting a male (i.e., selecting a female) is $p(F) = 1 - p(M) = .44$. The probability of selecting two males $= p(M)p(M) = .31$.

Odds are defined as the ratio of the probability that an event will occur divided by the probability that an event will not occur. In other words, odds are described by the ratio of the probability that something is true divided by the probability that it is not true. If there is a 30% chance of rain, then there is a 70% chance of no rain. The odds for rain are $.30/.70 = .43$.

The odds ratio is calculated by the following formula

$$odds\_ratio = \frac{a/b}{c/d}$$

where a and c are "yes" frequency counts (probability that the event will occur) and b and d are "no" frequency counts derived from a treated condition (a/b) and an untreated condition (c/d).

For example, take the following two groups measured dichotomously.

	Improved	Not Improved
Treated	$a = 13$	$b = 4$
Not treated	$c = 8$	$d = 7$

Odds for the treated group = $a/b = 13/4 = 3.25$

Odds for the control (not treated) group = $c/d = 8/7 = 1.14$

Odds ratio = $3.25/1.14 = 2.85$

Therefore, the odds of improving were 2.85 times when treated versus not treated. Also see the discussion on relative risk in Section 2 (Nonparametric Tests) of Chapter 9 (Correlation and Prediction Tests).

Logits are the natural logs of odds ratios. They contain exactly the same information as odds ratios, but because they are symmetrical, they can be compared more easily. For example, in logistic regression, a positive logit means the IV (predictor) has the effect of increasing the odds that the DV (criterion) equals a given value. A negative logit means the IV has the effect of decreasing the odds that the DV equals the given value.

Hypotheses

There are two types of statistical hypotheses.

1. The research or alternate hypothesis, denoted by H_1 or H_a or H_A, is the hypothesis that sample observations are influenced by a nonrandom cause; i.e., the intervention.

2. The null hypothesis, denoted by H_0, is the hypothesis of no difference or no relationship.

Bartos (1992) identifies the following characteristics of a usable hypothesis:

- Possesses explanatory power
- States the expected relationship between variables
- Must be testable
- Is linked to the professional literature
- Is stated simply and concisely

Hypothesis tests have four possible outcomes. Probabilities for each statistical outcome are depicted in the following table:

	H_0 is True	H_0 is False
Reject H_0	Type I Error (α)	No Error ($1 - \beta$)
Fail to Reject H_0	No Error ($1 - \alpha$)	Type II Error (β)

Statistical tests involve Type I (α) and Type II (β) risks or errors. Type I error is the probability of deciding that a significant effect is present when it is not. Type II error is the probability of not detecting a significant effect when one exists. In other words, Type I error is committed when one rejects the null hypothesis (H_0) when it is true. The probability of the Type I error is denoted by the Greek letter alpha (α). Type II error is committed when one fails to reject the null hypothesis when the alternative hypothesis (i.e., the research hypothesis) is true. The probability of the Type II error is shown by the Greek letter beta (β).

Researchers usually begin by formulating H_0 and assuming it is true. This is analogous to the presumption of innocence if one is a defendant at a trial. If the H_0 is true, what is the biggest difference between the sample means that can occur by chance at a reasonable level of probability? In other words, how different can we expect the means to become simply as a result of chance?

The next step is to determine if the data support rejecting or not rejecting H_0 as true. If the statistical analysis suggests that the differences or relationships one sees are unlikely to be due to chance, then one rejects H_0 and accepts H_1. Since hypothesis testing deals with probabilities, there is a chance that the statistical conclusion will be wrong.

Suppose that a researcher believes that teachers are more likely to adopt technology in their teaching if they possess greater knowledge of computers. The researcher could conduct a study that compares the level of teacher technology adoption in one group (e.g., teachers who have a high level of computer knowledge) to those in another group (e.g., teachers with a lower level of computer knowledge). Accordingly, the IV is group (high computer knowledge, low computer knowledge) and the DV is a measure of classroom technology use. H_0 would be there is no difference in the mean technology adoption scores of teachers in the two groups. The research hypothesis could be that teachers in the high computer knowledge group will have a higher mean technology adoption score than teachers in the low computer knowledge group (implying a one-tailed test), or more simply, that there will be a difference between the mean scores of the two groups (implying a two-tailed test).

If one has a correlation study (i.e., a study that seeks to determine if there is a relationship between variables), the process of developing hypotheses is similar For example, if the research question is:

Is there a relationship between intelligence and GPA?

then the null hypothesis is:

H_0: There is no relationship between intelligence and GPA.

Significance Level

The significance level is the probability of making a Type I error (α). A researcher needs to assign a value to the significance level before he or she can conduct any statistical analysis (*à priori* assignment). For social science research this value is typically set at .05 (.10 is sometimes used for exploratory research, .01 for more precise research). A significance level of .05 means that if one rejects H_0, one is willing to accept no more than a 5% chance that one is wrong (if the significance level were set at .01, one is willing to accept no more than a 1% chance that one is wrong). In other words, with a .05 significance level, one wants to be at least 95% confident that if one rejects H_0 the correct decision was made. The confidence level in this situation is .95.

For some tests, SPSS reports an asymptotic significance, which means that the asymptotic method was used to calculate this statistic. This method is considered to be accurate with large samples, but less so with smaller samples. In both large and small samples the exact test is the most accurate method of calculating significance.

One- and Two-Tailed Hypotheses

Hypotheses can be one- or two-tailed, based on how the research question is worded:

- *Two tailed* – this hypothesis is non-directional (i.e., the direction of difference or association is not predicted), e.g., H_0: $\mu_1 = \mu_2$, Ha: $\mu_1 \neq \mu_2$. The test determines whether or not the mean of the sample group is either less than or greater than the mean of the control group.

- *One-tailed* – this hypothesis is directional (i.e., the direction of difference or association is predicted); e.g., H_0: $\mu_1 \gtrless \mu_2$, Ha: $\mu_1 > \mu_2$. For example, sense of classroom community in graduate students is higher in face-to-face courses than online courses. Here the DV is sense of classroom community and the IV is type course (face-to-face, online).

The figure below depicts a one-tailed test with a .95 confidence interval and a .05 significance level using the standard normal distribution. The significance level is the probability that a sample statistic goes beyond the critical value (larger than 1.645 in this situation). A one-tailed test tests either if the sample mean is significantly greater than x or if the mean is significantly less than x, but not both as in a two-tailed test. Then, depending on the chosen tail, the mean is significantly greater than or less than x if the test statistic is in the top 5% of its probability distribution or bottom 5% of its probability distribution, depending on the direction specified in the hypothesis.

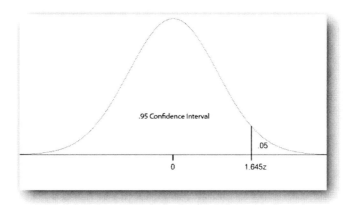

.95 Confidence Interval

.05

0   1.645z

SPSS offers the researcher the opportunity to select the type of test, either one-tailed or two-tailed, in the dialog box associated with many hypothesis tests. The issue of two- versus one-tailed hypotheses becomes important when performing the statistical test and determining the p-value. For example, in a two-tailed test when α is set at .05, the .05 is actually divided equally between the left and right tails of the sample distribution curve. The condition being tested is that the group A mean is different from the group B mean. In the case of a one-tailed test with $\alpha = .05$, the entire .05 appears in the right or high tail of the curve if the directional hypothesis were $H_a: \mu_1 > \mu_2$ or in the left tail if the directional hypothesis were $H_a: \mu_1 < \mu_2$. The result is that the calculated p-value will be lower and it will be easier to reject t H_0 if a one-tailed test is used instead of a two-tailed test, all else being equal.

Degrees of Freedom

Statistical analysis can be based upon different amounts of information. The number of independent pieces of information that go into the estimate of a parameter is called the degrees of freedom (df). In general, the degrees of freedom of an estimate is equal to the number of independent scores that go into the estimate minus the number of parameters estimated as intermediate steps in the estimation of the parameter itself. The higher the degrees of freedom, the more representative the sample will be of the population.

Statistical Conclusions

The purpose of the hypothesis test is to decide between the following two conclusions:

- Failure to reject H_0

  - When the calculated significance level (p-value) is larger than the *à priori* significance level, one concludes any observed results (e.g., differences in means) are not statistically significant and are therefore probably due to sampling error or chance.

  - Failure to reject H_0 does not necessarily mean that H_0 is true. It simply means that there is not sufficient evidence to reject H_0. A H_0 is not accepted just because it is not rejected. Data not sufficient to show convincingly that a difference between means is not zero do not prove that the difference is zero. Such data may even suggest that H_0 is false but not be strong enough to make a convincing case that it is false. In this situation one had insufficient statistical power to reject a false H_0. Consider ways of increasing statistical power.

- Rejection of H_0

  - One concludes that the observed results are statistically significant and are probably due to some determining factor or condition other than chance.

  - Rejection of H_0 does not necessarily mean that the alternative hypothesis is true. There is always the probability of a Type I error.

The ability to reject H_0 depends upon:

- Significance level (α) – usually set to be .05, although this is somewhat arbitrary. This is the probability of rejecting H_0 given that H_0 is true.

- Sample size (N) – a larger sample size leads to more accurate parameter estimates and more statistical power.

- Effect size – the bigger the size of the effect in the population, the easier it will be to find and reject a false H_0.

When H_0 is rejected, the outcome is said to be "statistically significant;" when H_0 is not rejected then the outcome is said be "not statistically significant." However, keep in mind that an event that has a 5% chance of occurring should occur, on average, 1 in 20 times. Therefore, one may have falsely rejected H_0 because an event with a 5% probability has occurred. One's response to this problem may be to set α to some lower value such as .01 to lower the risk of rejecting a true H_0. This may be needed if an important decision, such as expenditure of resources, is to be made based on the results of the study. For example, in medical research where life may be placed in jeopardy based on a wrong decision, significance levels are normally set at a very low level; e.g., .0001.

> **Key Point**
> The *p*-value cannot be zero. A p-value of zero represents certainty that no Type I error took place.

Inferential statistics is based on probabilities, not certainties. However, SPSS truncates values beyond three decimal places. Consequently, SPSS output may include a significance level of .000. This is to be interpreted and reported as $p < .001$.

When one enters edit mode in SPSS output and clicks the cell with .000, a value such as 2.661e-5 appears instead of .000. This will only happen for cells with .000. The value is shown in scientific notation. Scientific notation is based on powers of the base number 10. The value after e indicates how many places to move the decimal place to the left in order to view the actual *p*-value. In mathematical terms, the value is $2.661 \times 10\text{-}5$. In this example one would move the decimal place five places to the left. The significance level in general notation would then be .00002661.

Statistical Power

The statistical power (or observed power) of a statistical test is the probability rejecting a false H_0. It is equal to 1 minus the probability of accepting a false H_0 $(1 - \beta)$. Low power results in relationships that may be true but are not significant. Desired power is .80 or higher. Many SPSS procedures will report observed power, if requested as optional output.

Three factors are considered in any determination of statistical power.

- *Level of significance*, normally .05 – smaller alpha levels (e.g., .01) produce lower power levels (that is, the greater the likelihood of Type II error) for a given sample size.

- *Sample size* – the smaller the sample, the greater the likelihood of Type II errors and the lower the power.

- *Effect size* – the smaller the effect size, the more likely the Type II error and thus the lower the power for a given sample size.

One can increase statistical power by:

- Increasing the sample size.

- Increasing the significance level.

- Using all the information provided by the data (e.g., do not transform interval scale variables to ordinal scale variables prior to the analysis).

- Using a one-tailed (versus a two-tailed) test.

- Using a parametric (versus nonparametric) test.

Effect Size

In very large samples, small differences are likely to be statistically significant. This sensitivity to sample size is a weakness of hypothesis testing and has led to the use of an effect size statistic to complement interpretation of a significant hypothesis test.

Key Point
Statistical significance does not
imply meaningful or important

Effect size is a measure of the magnitude of a treatment effect. Researchers frequently refer to effect size as practical significance in contrast to statistical significance. While statistical significance is concerned with whether a statistical result is due to chance, practical significance is concerned with whether the result is useful in the real world.

Key Point
There is no practical significance
without statistical significance.

The effect size helps policymakers and educators decide whether a statistically significant difference between programs translates into enough of a difference to justify adoption of a program. It is the degree to which H_0 is false. In general, effect size can be measured in one of the following four ways (Kline, 2004):

1. the standardized difference between two means; e.g., Cohen's *d*.

2. the correlation between the independent variable and the individual scores on the dependent variable; e.g., Pearson *r*, Spearman's rank order correlation coefficient, Kendall's tau, phi coefficient, Cramér's *V*, and eta square (η^2).

3. estimates corrected for error; e.g., adjusted R^2.

4. risk estimates; e.g., relative risk (risk ratio) and odds ratio.

The *Publication Manual of the American Psychological Association* (APA, 2010) notes that

> For the reader to appreciate the magnitude or importance of a study's findings, it is almost always necessary to include some measure of effect size in the results section. Whenever possible, provide a confidence interval for each effect size reported to indicate the precision of estimation of the effect size. Effect sizes may be expressed in the original units (e.g., the mean number of questions answered correctly; kg/month for a regression slope) and are most easily understood when reported in original units. It can often be valuable to report an effect size not only in original units but also in some standardized or units-free unit (e.g., as a Cohen's *d* value) or a standardized regression weight. (p. 34)

The guidelines for interpreting various effect size statistics are meant to be flexible. Cohen's caution regarding the assignment of standardized interpretations to effect size values is relevant:

> The terms 'small,' 'medium,' and 'large' are relative, not only to each other, but to the area of behavioral science or even more particularly to the specific content and research method being employed in any given investigation....In the face of this relativity, there is a certain risk inherent in offering conventional operational definitions for these terms for use in power analysis in as diverse a field of inquiry as behavioral science. This risk is nevertheless accepted in the belief that more is to be gained than lost by supplying a common conventional frame of reference which is recommended for use only when no better basis for estimating the *ES* index is available. (p. 25)

A generic formula for calculating effect size using standard deviation units follows

$$ES = \frac{(M_E - M_C)}{SD_C}$$

where ES = effect size, M_E = mean of the experimental group, M_C = mean of the control group, and SD_C = standard deviation of the control group (or pooled standard deviation).

This measure of effect size is equivalent to a z-score. For example, an effect size of .50 indicates that the score of the average person in the experimental group is .50 standard deviations above the average person in the control group. A small effect size is between .2 and .5 standard deviation units, a medium effect size is one that is between .5 and .8 standard deviation units, and a large effect size is one that is .8 or more standard deviation units (Rosenthal & Rosnow, 1991).

Cohen's d is frequently used in conjunction with t-tests and also represents standard deviation units. Cohen (1988) defined the magnitude of d as small, d = .20; medium, d = .50; and large, d = .80. The formula for Cohen's d for one-sample and dependent t-tests follows

$$d = \frac{t}{\sqrt{N}}$$

where t = t-statistic reported by SPSS and N = sample size.

The formula for Cohen's d for the independent t-test is

$$d = t\sqrt{\frac{N_1 + N_2}{N_1 N_2}}$$

where N represents the size of each group.

The coefficient of multiple correlation (R) and the coefficient of multiple determination (R²) are commonly used as effect size statistics for regression analyses.

The correlation coefficient (r) and the coefficient of determination (r²) are also suitable for estimating effect size when analyzing continuous, normally distributed variables. Cohen's d and Pearson r can be converted one from another using the following formulas

$$r = \sqrt{\frac{d^2}{(d^2 + 4)}}$$

$$d = \frac{2r}{\sqrt{(1 - r^2)}}$$

Effect size can also be measured by eta square (η^2) and partial eta square (η_p^2) statistics, where .01 = small effect size, .06 = medium effect size, and .14 = large effect size (Tabachnick & Fidell, 2007). These statistics are very frequently used in conjunction with *ANOVA*, *MANOVA*, *ANCOVA*, and *MANCOVA*. Eta square represents the effect size of the model and partial eta square is the effect size of a specific effect; e.g., a main effect or interaction effect. However, it should be noted that η_p^2 statistics are non-additive and can add to over 100% of total variance explained.

The formula for eta square follows

$$\eta^2 = \frac{SS_{effect}}{SS_{total}}$$

where SS_{effect} is sum of squares for a specific effect and SS_{total} is the total sum of squares for all effects (main, interaction, and error).

The formula for partial eta square is

$$\eta_p^2 = \frac{SS_{effect}}{SS_{effect} + SS_{error}}$$

Leech and Onwuegbuzie (2002) write:

Reporting effect sizes is no less important for statistically significant nonparametric findings than it is for statistically significant parametric results… However, it should be noted that just as parametric tests are adversely affected by departures from [general linear model] assumptions, so too are parametric effect sizes… Therefore, researchers should consider following up statistically significant nonparametric *p*-values with nonparametric effect sizes. Nonparametric effect sizes include Cramer's *V*, the phi coefficient, and the odds ratio. (pp. 14-15)

Phi can be used as an effect size statistic for 2 x 2 contingency tables. Cramér's V can be used for larger tables and corrects for table size. For 2 x 2 tables, Cramér's *V* equals phi.

The Spearman rank order correlation coefficient, gamma, Kendall's tau, and Somer's d can be used to estimate effect size with ordinal data.

The odds ratio and relative risk are suitable for an effect size measure when comparing two dichotomous groups and the outcomes are binary (e.g., 0 = no, 1 = yes).

Steps in Inferential Statistics

1. Identify a problem or issue and form a research question and a research hypothesis based on a theoretical rationale.

2. Identify the target population.

3. Operationalize the variables by determining how each will be measured. Measuring instruments should be valid and reliable.

4. Develop a null hypothesis; e.g., H_0: $\mu_1 = \mu_2$. The null hypothesis is the one tested. This is the hypothesis that one hopes to reject by the statistical test, assuming the research hypothesis is correct.

5. Decide on the appropriate statistical test to use in order to evaluate the null hypothesis. When selecting an appropriate test keep the following issues in mind:

   - What type of hypothesis is being tested: (a) hypothesis of difference or (b) hypothesis of association?

   - How many variables are there?

   - What are the scales of measurement for each variable? For categorical variables, how many categories (i.e., levels or groups) are there?

   - Are the data related (e.g., pretest-posttest or a matching procedure was used) or independent (e.g., independent groups)?

   - Evaluate test assumptions for the selected test. If assumptions are not tenable for the test, select another test if one is available.

6. Determine the number of participants required and collect an appropriate sample from the target population.

7. Decide on the *à priori* significance level. If potentially serious consequences could occur if a wrong decision is made, a researcher may choose to decrease the significance level; e.g., from .05 to .01 or to .001.

8. Decide whether to use a one-tailed test or two-tailed test. This decision is based on the wording of the research and null hypotheses to be tested. Normally, one selects a two-tailed test.

9. Conduct the statistical test and make a decision. If the calculated *p*-value is less than or equal to the significance level, one has sufficient evidence to reject the null hypothesis.

> **Key Point**
> Failure to reject the null hypothesis does not constitute proof that the research hypothesis is false. It only indicates that the data were not sufficient to reject the null hypothesis.

10. Report the statistical results to include effect size if the results are significant.

6.2: Evaluating Test Assumptions

Introduction

Various hypothesis tests make different assumptions about the distribution of the variable(s) being analyzed. These assumptions must be addressed when choosing a test and when interpreting the results. Parametric tests have more assumptions than non parametric tests and are more powerful than nonparametric tests.

Below is a list of the more common test assumptions that require evaluation as well as a description of how they can be evaluated.

Independence of Observations

Observations are independent if the sampling of one observation does not affect the choice of the second observation. Independence of observations (i.e., absence of autocorrelation) means that multiple observations are not acted on by an outside influence. A small violation of this assumption produces a substantial effect on both the level of significance and statistical power of a test (Stevens, 2002).

Independence can be evaluated by the Durbin-Watson d coefficient or by the Wald-Wolfowitz runs test.

- The Durbin-Watson test uses studentized residuals (i.e., raw residuals that are divided by their estimated standard deviation). The value of d can range from 0 to 4. Values close to 0 indicate extreme positive residuals; close to 4 indicates extreme negative autocorrelation; and close to 2 suggests no serial autocorrelation. Generally, d should be between 1.5 and 2.5 to support independence of observations.

- The Wald-Wolfowitz runs test estimates the number of runs (i.e., a series of similar responses for a given variable) that one would expect by chance and compares that figure to the number of runs in a sample. A nonsignificant test provides evidence of random order and supports the assumption of independence of observations.

SPSS Procedure

SPSS > Analyze > Nonparametric Tests > [Legacy Dialogs] > Runs

SPSS > Analyze > Nonparametric Tests > One Sample > Runs Test

Measurement Without Error

The assumption of measurement without error refers to the need for error-free measurement when using the general linear model. Measurement without error in social science research is difficult to achieve because of the reliability characteristics of most instruments that are used to measure social phenomena. Pedhazur (1997) writes "the presence of measurement errors in behavioral research is the rule rather than the exception" and "reliabilities of many measures used in the behavioral sciences are, at best, moderate" p. 172). Unreliable measurements can create problems, especially in correlation and regression analyses and in adjusting the effects of the covariate in *ANCOVA*. When IVs are measured with error in regression analysis, both the least squares estimators and the variance estimators are biased.

It is therefore important that researchers pay attention to the reliability characteristics of all instruments used in their research and select instruments with high reliability – e.g., .70 or higher – and confirm instrument reliability as part of their research. Whenever this is not possible, errors in measurement should be identified as a study limitation.

SPSS Procedure

SPSS > Analyze > Scale > Reliability Analysis > Alpha

SPSS > Analyze > Scale > Reliability Analysis > Split-half

SPSS > Analyze > Scale > Reliability Analysis > Guttman

SPSS > Analyze > Scale > Reliability Analysis > Parallel

SPSS > Analyze > Scale > Reliability Analysis > Strict Parallel

Normality

The assumption of normality refers to the shape of the distributions of variables. The shape is symmetrical and appears like a bell. Parametric tests assume a normal distribution. This means that a variable or variables are normally distributed. For example, the DV is distributed normally as in the one-sample *t*-test, or residuals (random errors) are distributed normally as in *ANOVA* and regression analysis, or differences are distributed normally as in the dependent *t*-test.

Research suggests that many parametric procedures – e.g., one-way *ANOVA* – are robust in the face of light to moderate departures from normality (e.g, Tiku, 1971).

Normality is evaluated by statistical and/or graphical methods. Normality can be assessed visually using various charts and graphs, especially the Q-Q plot, P-P plots, detrended plots, the boxplot, and the histogram.

Two common inferential tests for normality are:

- One sample Kolmogorov-Smirnov test (Chakravarti, Laha, & Roy, 1967)

- One sample Shapiro-Wilk W test (Shapiro & Wilk, 1965)

The one-sample Kolmogorov-Smirnov test is calculated for samples with 50 or larger observations. This test is an inferential test used to decide if a sample of data comes from a specific distribution. (The Kolmogorov-Smirnov test can test goodness-of-fit against many theoretical distributions, not just the normal distribution.) This test has several important limitations:

- It only applies to continuous distributions.

- It tends to be more sensitive near the center of the distribution than it is at the tails.

- It is a conservative test (i.e., there is an increased likelihood of a finding of non-normality).

Because the Kolmogorov-Smirnov Z test is conservative, the Kolmogorov-Smirnov D test with the Lilliefors correction is preferred over the non-corrected test. The test is defined by:

H_0: The data follow a specified distribution (typically, this is specified as the normal distribution).

H_a: The data do not follow the specified distribution.

The Shapiro-Wilk W test, another test for normality, is more reliable than the Kolmogorov-Smirnov test when $N < 50$.

SPSS Procedure

SPSS > Analyze > Nonparametric Tests > [Legacy Dialogs] > 1-Sample KS

SPSS > Analyze > Nonparametric Tests > One Sample > Kolmogorov-Smirnov Test

SPSS > Analyze > Descriptive Statistics > Explore > Plots > Normality plots with tests

SPSS > Analyze-> Descriptive Statistics > Explore (select normality plots with tests)

SPSS > Analyze > Descriptive Statistics > Q-Q Plots

Multivariate Normality

With multivariate statistics, the assumption of normality is that the combination of variables follows a multivariate normal distribution. Multivariate normality is the assumption that all variables and all combinations of the variables are normally distributed. When the assumption is met, residuals are normally distributed and independent, the differences between predicted and obtained scores (the errors or residuals) are symmetrically distributed around a mean of zero, and there is no pattern to the errors. In addition to establishing univariate normality, all possible subsets of variables should be normally distributed and the linear relationship of any combination of variables should be distributed normally (Stevens, 2002).

> **Key Point**
> If variables are not univariate normal,
> they are not multivariate normal.

Multivariate normality can be evaluated by examining residuals to assess the normality of errors. A Q-Q plot of the residuals with the comparison to a normal distribution is also useful.

SPSS Procedure

SPSS > Analyze > Descriptive Statistics > Explore (select normality plots with tests)

SPSS > Analyze > Descriptive Statistics > Q-Q Plots

Kurtosis and Skewness

Kurtosis measures heavy-tailedness or light-tailedness relative to the normal distribution. A heavy-tailed distribution has more values in the tails (away from the center of the distribution) than the normal distribution. A light-tailed distribution has more values in the center (away from the tails of the distribution) than the normal distribution. The ratio of kurtosis to its standard error is used as a test of normality. If this ratio is < -2 or $> +2$, normality is not tenable.

If the data are not distributed symmetrically, the distribution is said to be skewed. One way of determining skewness is by looking at the frequency distribution of the data. Another way of determining skewness is by comparing the values of the mean, median and mode. If the three are equal, then the data are symmetrical. The ratio of skewness to its standard error is used as a test of normality. If this ratio is < -2 or $> +2$, normality is not tenable.

SPSS Procedure

SPSS > Analyze > Descriptive Statistics

Outliers

Univariate outliers are anomalous observations that have extreme values with respect to a single variable. Chatterjee and Hadi (1988) defined an outlier as an observation with a large residual. It is common to define extreme univariate outliers as cases that are more than three standard deviations above the mean of the variable or less than three standard deviations from the mean.

> **Key Point**
> Outliers represent a very serious threat to normality. Extreme scores can have dramatic effects on the accuracy of correlations and regressions.

Boxplots are used to identify outliers. The ends of the box (hinges) of a boxplot are at Q_1 and Q_3. The two vertical lines (called whiskers) outside the box extend to the smallest and largest observations that don't exceed 1.5 x *IQR* below Q_1 or 1.5 x *IQR* above Q_3. Scores that fall below the bottom whisker or above the top whisker are outliers.

- *Mild outliers* fall between 1.5 x *IQR* and 3 x *IQR* either above the top hinge or below the bottom hinge and are identified by a circle and a SPSS case number (i.e., dataset row number).

- *Extreme outliers* are greater than 3 x *IQR* either above the top hinge or below the bottom hinge and are identified by an asterisk and a case number in SPSS.

Converting raw scores to *z*-scores and evaluating the degree of deviation of the *z*-scores is another method of identifying outliers.

Multivariate outliers are cases that have an unusually high or low combination of values for multiple variables. The value for an individual variable may not be a univariate outlier, but in combination with other variables, the case may be a multivariate outlier. For example, an annual salary of $25,000 may not be an extreme outlier for a salary variable; likewise, $600,000 for the purchase of a home may not be an extreme outlier for a home cost variable. However, someone purchasing a $600,000 home and having an annual salary of $25,000 may be an extreme multivariate outlier.

Cook's distance (D_i) is a measure for identifying multivariate outliers, which are operationally defined as cases that have a Cook's distance greater than some cutoff (some use a cutoff of 1; some use $4/[n - p]$, where p is the number of parameters in the model; some use $4/[n - k - 1]$, where n is the number of cases and k is the number of independents). It identifies the influence of suspected outliers on regression coefficients by examining regression coefficients that would exist if the outlier were deleted.

Mahalanobis distance (D^2) is another measure for identifying multivariate outliers. It measures the distance of a case from the centroid (multidimensional mean) of a distribution, given the covariance (multidimensional variance) of the distribution. A case is a multivariate outlier if the probability associated with its D^2 is 0.001 or less. D^2 follows a chi-square distribution with degrees of freedom equal to the number of variables included in the calculation.

Leverage is another related way of identifying multivariate outliers, with outliers defined as having a leverage value greater than some cutoff (some use .5; others use $2p/n$, where p is the number of parameters including the intercept).

The absence of multivariate outliers is a common assumption in multivariate tests such as multiple regression and correlation.

SPSS Procedure

Univariate outliers:

SPSS > Graphs-> [Legacy Dialogs] > Boxplot

SPSS > Analyze > Descriptive Statistics > Explore > Plots > Boxplot

Multivariate outliers:

SPSS > Analyze > Regression > Linear (one can save Cook's distances, Mahalanobis distances, and leverage as separate variables using the SPSS Linear Regression Save option).

Linearity

The assumption of linearity is that there is an approximate straight line relationship between two continuous variables. That is, the amount of change, or rate of change, between scores on two variables are constant for the entire range of scores for the variables. It is a common assumption in many bivariate and multivariate tests, such as correlation and regression analysis, because solutions are based on the general linear model (GLM). If a relationship is nonlinear, the statistics that assume it is linear will either underestimate the strength of the relationship or fail to detect the existence of a relationship.

There are relationships that are best characterized as curvilinear rather than linear. For example, the relationship between learning and time is not linear. Learning a new subject shows rapid gains at first but then the pace slows down over time. This is often referred to as the learning curve.

Pedhazur (1997) recommends three primary ways of detecting nonlinearity. The first is the use of theory or prior research. However, this method has drawbacks in so far as other researchers may not have adequately evaluated the assumption of linearity.

A second method is the use of graphical methods that include the examination of residual plots and scatterplots, often overlaid with a trend line. However, this strategy is sometimes difficult to interpret. Outliers may fool the observer into believing a linear model may not fit. Alternatively, true changes in slope are often difficult to discern from only a scatter of data. The key is to determine central patterns without being strongly influenced by outliers.

The third method of detecting nonlinearity is the use of statistical methods. A relationship is linear if the difference between the linear correlation coefficient (Pearson r) and the nonlinear correlation coefficient eta (η) is small. If the two coefficients are the same, the relationship is perfectly linear.

A less stringent assumption is one of monotonicity. A monotonic relationship is one where the value of one variable increases as the value of the other variable increases or the value of one variable increases as the value of the other variable decreases, but not necessarily in a linear fashion. Consequently, a monotonic relationship can be either linear or curvilinear.

SPSS Procedure

SPSS > Graphs > Scatter/Dot

Homogeneity of Variance

Homogeneity of variance (or error variance) is the assumption that two or more groups have equal or similar variances. The assumption is that the variability in the DV is expected to be about the same at all levels of the IV.

$$s_1^2 = s_2^2 = s_3^2 ... = s_n^2$$

This is a common assumption for many parametric tests such as the independent t-test (but not the dependent *t*-test). One can get a feel for whether this assumption is tenable by comparing the standard deviations or variances of each group. However, this is not a reliable procedure. The problem one will encounter is the determination of how much the variances can differ before the assumption is no longer tenable.

Levene's test, which tests the null hypothesis that the variance of the DV is equal across groups determined by the IV, is robust in the face of departures from normality. If the data satisfy the assumption of homogeneity of variance, the significance level of Levene's test should not be significant. If the significance level equals .05 or lower, the results are significant and one has evidence to reject the null hypothesis. Under these circumstances one can conclude that the assumption of homogeneity of variance is not tenable.

Homogeneity of variance-covariance matrices is the multivariate equivalent of homogeneity of variance and is an assumption of multivariate analysis of variance (*MANOVA*). It assumes that the variance/covariance matrix in each cell of the design is sampled from the same population so they can be reasonably pooled together to make an error term. Box's *M* test of equality of covariance matrices tests this assumption. If Box's *M* test is significant at $p < .001$, one concludes a violation has occurred.

SPSS Procedure

SPSS will automatically run Levene's Test for many statistical procedures, such as the independent *t*-test. For the GLM Multivariate procedure, checking homogeneity tests produces Levene's test for each DV across all level combinations of the between subjects factors.

SPSS will run Box's *M* test as part of the GLM multivariate, GLM repeated measures, and discriminant analysis procedures, if homogeneity tests are requested as an option.

Homoscedasticity

The assumption of homoscedasticity is that the variability in scores for one variable is roughly the same at all values of a second variable. Variables are homoscedastic when the variability in scores for one continuous variable is roughly the same at all values of another continuous variable.

Homoscedasticity is evaluated with scatterplots or boxplots for pairs of variables. One can also produce a scatterplot of the standardized residuals against the fitted values and a scatterplot of the standardized residuals against each of the independent variables. If homoscedasticity is satisfied, residuals should vary randomly around zero and the spread of the residuals should be about the same throughout the plot, with no systematic patterns.

SPSS Procedure

SPSS > Graphs-> Scatter/Dot

SPSS > Graphs > [Legacy Dialogs] > Boxplot

SPSS > Analyze > Descriptive Statistics > Explore > Plots > Boxplot

Sphericity

Sphericity is an assumption in repeated measures *ANOVA/ MANOVA* designs. In a repeated measures design, the univariate *ANOVA* tables will not be interpreted properly unless the variance/covariance matrix of the DVs is circular in form. In other words, the variance of the difference between all pairs of means is constant across all combinations of related groups. The sphericity assumption is always met for designs with only two levels of a repeated measures factor but must be evaluated for designs with three or more levels. Sphericity is also an assumption of principal components and factor analysis. Sphericity can be evaluated by the following tests (Tabachnick & Fidell, 2007):

- *Bartlett's test of sphericity* – the null hypothesis is that the correlation matrix is an identity matrix. A significant p-value provides evidence that the assumption of sphericity is supported.

- *Mauchly's test of sphericity* – the null hypothesis is that the variances of the differences between pairs of means are equal. The null hypothesis supports the assumption of sphericity. A significant p-value provides evidence that the assumption of sphericity is not supported.

SPSS Procedure

SPSS will automatically run Bartlett's test of sphericity and Mauchly's test of sphericity for specific procedures, such as principal components and factor analysis and GLM repeated measures procedures.

Homogeneity of Regressions

In *ANCOVA* and *MANCOVA*, the slopes of the regression lines (slopes) should be the same for each group formed by the categorical variables and measured on the dependents. The more this assumption is violated, the more likely for the covariate procedure to make Type I errors (i.e., not rejecting a false null hypothesis).

Homogeneity of regressions assumes the absence of an interaction between the covariate and IV. The homogeneity of regression assumption can be tested by including an interaction term between the covariate and the IV. If the regression coefficients differ across groups, this interaction will be significant. A significant interaction between the covariate and the IV suggests that the differences on the DV among groups vary as a function of the covariate. If the interaction is significant, the results from an *ANCOVA* or *MANCOVA* are not meaningful, and *ANCOVA* or *MANCOVA* should not be conducted.

SPSS Procedure

SPSS > Analyze > General Linear Model > Univariate (Multivariate for *MANCOVA*)

Use the *Model* option to create a *Custom* model that includes an IV by covariate interaction to evaluate the assumption of homogeneity of regressions.

Multicollinearity

Multicollinearity occurs when variables are very highly correlated ($r = 0.90$ and above), and singularity occurs when the variables are perfectly correlated ($r = 1.00$). Likewise, high multicollinearity is indicated when high R^2 and significant F-tests of the model occur in combination with non-significant t-tests of coefficients. Multicollinearity and singularity indicate redundancy of variables and the need to remove variables from the analysis.

Absence of multicollinearity is an important assumption in multiple correlation and regression procedures and related tests such as discriminant analysis and logistic regression. High multicollinearity leads to large variances and covariances, large confidence intervals, large standard errors, and small t-statistics. Regression coefficients and their standard errors will be sensitive to changes in just a few observations and the regression model will unlikely be stable across multiple samples from the same population.

The following collinearity statistics, produced by SPSS when collinearity diagnostics are requested as part of the statistical output, are useful in assessing multicollinearity (Pedhazur, 1997; Tabachnick & Fidell, 2007):

- *High bivariate correlation coefficients* – One should avoid variables with a bivariate correlation of greater than 0.70 in tests where absence of multicollinearity is an assumption.

- *Tolerance* – Tolerance identifies "the proportion of the variability in one independent variable not explained by the other independent variables" (Vogt, 2005, p. 325). It is mathematically defined as $1 - R^2$, where R^2 is the multiple R of a given independent regressed on all other independent variables. If the tolerance value is less than some cutoff value, usually .20, the independent should be dropped from the analysis due to multicollinearity. This is better than just using simple $r > .90$ since tolerance looks at the IV in relation to all other independents and thus takes interaction effects into account in addition to simple correlations.

- *Variance Inflation Factor (VIF)* – The variance inflation factor (reciprocal of tolerance) quantifies how much the variance is inflated and reflects the presence or absence of multicollinearity. The VIF has a range 1 to infinity. When VIF is high there is high multicollinearity and instability of the *b* and beta coefficients. A common cutoff threshold is a VIF value of 10, which corresponds to a tolerance value of .10. VIF and tolerance are found in the SPSS output on collinearity statistics.

- An *eigenvalue* is used "to indicate how much of the variation in the original group of variables is accounted for by a particular factor" (Vogt, 2005, pp. 103–104). Eigenvalues close to 0 indicate dimensions that explain little variance. Multiple eigenvalues close to 0 indicate an ill-conditioned crossproduct matrix, meaning there may be a problem with multicollinearity and the condition indices should be examined as described below.

- *Condition indices* are used to flag excessive collinearity in the data. Condition indices over 15 indicate possible multicollinearity problems and over 30 indicate serious multicollinearity problems. If a dimension has a high condition index, one looks in the variance proportions columns to see if that factor accounts for a sizable proportion of variance in two or more variables (that is, if two or more variables are most heavily loaded on that dimension). If this is the case, these variables have high linear dependence and multicollinearity is a problem, with the effect that small data changes may translate into very large changes or errors in the regression analysis.

- *Variance proportions* represent the proportion of variance for each regression coefficient (and its associated variable) attributable to each condition index. Coefficients that have high proportions for the same condition index are largely responsible for the amount of multicollinearity identified by the condition index. A value of .50 is commonly used as a cut-off threshold.

Dealing with Deviations

Independence of Observations

This is a sampling issue and is controlled during measurement. Generally, implementation of a survey questionnaire minimizes possibilities of dependence among the observations provided the researcher implements controls to prevent respondents from discussing their responses prior to completing the survey.

Normality

One should ensure that a non-normal distribution has not occurred due to a data coding or entry error. If such errors are not detected, a decision must be made in terms of how to deal with a non-normal distribution. Several options are available (Tabachnick & Fidell, 2007). Whatever option is selected, the research must report the procedure used.

- Option 1 – use nonparametric statistical tests that do not assume variables have a normal distribution. These tests are less powerful than parametric tests.

- Option 2 – delete the extreme outliers that create the problem. The major limitation associated with this option is that it involves removing participants from the research.

- Option 3 – replace the extreme score(s) with more normal score(s); e.g., replace extreme outliers with mild outliers. Once again, the major limitation associated with this option is that it involves altering scores generated by research participants.

- Option 4 – analyze data with and without extreme score(s) and compare results. Many of the parametric statistical tests are considered to be robust to violations in the assumption of normality. If results from the two analyses are similar, the extreme scores are retained. However if discrepancies are evident in the two outputs, another option should be considered.

- Option 5 – increase sample size. Distributions tend to more closely reflect the characteristics of a normal distribution as the sample size increases.

- Option 6 – transform data. Data transformation is a process designed to change the shape of a distribution so that it more closely approximates a normal curve. A new variable is created by altering the original scores in a consistent manner. After data transformation is conducted on a variable, the distribution is reexamined to determine how well it approximates a normal distribution. Although transformed variables may satisfy the assumption of normality of distribution, they tend to complicate the interpretation of findings as scores no longer convey the same meaning as the original values. Tabachnick and Fidell (2007) suggest the following guidelines for transforming variables:

Data Transformations		
Problem	**Severity**	**Transformation**
Positive skew	Moderate	Square root
	Substantial	Logarithm
	Severe	Inverse
Negative skew	Moderate	Square root*
	Substantial	Logarithm*
	Severe	Inverse*

Note: *reflect first. To reflect a variable: (a) find the largest score in the distribution, (b) add one to it to form a constant that is larger than any score in distribution, (c) create a new variable by subtracting each score from this constant.

Outliers

Outliers should be removed if there is reason to believe that other variables not in the model explain why the outlier cases are unusual. Alternatively, outliers may suggest that additional explanatory variables need to be brought into the model (that is, the model needs to be re-specified). Extreme outliers should be dealt with as follows:

- Temporarily remove the outliers from the dataset.

- Repeat the analysis and determine whether the same general results are obtained. If similar results are obtained, one can conclude that the outliers are not distorting the results. Report the results of the original analysis, adding a note that removal of outliers did not greatly affect the statistical model.

- If different general results are obtained, accurate interpretation requires collection of additional data. Report the results of both analyses and note that the interpretation of the data is uncertain. The outliers may represent a subpopulation for which the effects of interest are different from those in the main population. This group will need to be identified and, if possible, a sample collected from it so that it can be compared with the main population.

> **Key Point**
> Always report and justify removal or modification of cases.

Linearity

When a relationship is not linear, one can transform one or both variables to achieve a linear relationship. Four common transformations to induce linearity are the square root transformation, the logarithmic transformation, the inverse transformation, and the square transformation. These transformations produce a new variable that is mathematically equivalent to the original variable, but expressed in different measurement units; i.e. logarithmic units instead of decimal units.

Homoscedasticity

When the assumption of homoscedasticity is not supported, one can transform the variables and test again for homoscedasticity. The three most common transformations used are the logarithmic transformation, the square root transformation, and the inverse transformation.

Sphericity

Violations of sphericity can be adjusted based on corrections developed by Greenhouse and Geisser and Huynh and Feldt. They adjust the degrees of freedom in order to produce a more accurate p-value based on the amount of departure from the sphericity assumption. This is accomplished by way of the epsilon (ε) statistic. When $\varepsilon = 1$ there is no violation of sphericity and no correction is required. However, the departure from sphericity becomes more pronounced the more epsilon drops in value from 1. For less severe departures from sphericity ($\varepsilon > .75$), the Huynh-Feldt ε is used, while Greenhouse-Geisser ε is used for more severe violations of the sphericity assumption.

Multicollinearity

Multicollinearity is a serious problem. The researcher needs to understand the cause of multicollinearity and remove or reduce it. If one of the offending variables is not essential to the model, removing it should eliminate the problem. Alternatively, the researcher may be able to replace two offending variables with a different variable that combines the essences of the original variables. Additionally, one can also reduce multicollinearity by centering the variables. Centering is a data transformation that subtracts the mean from each case.

6.3: Test Decision Tree

The following decision tree will assist one in identifying an appropriate inferential test.

1. **What type of hypothesis is being tested?**

   - If testing a hypothesis of difference, go to Step 2

   - If testing a hypothesis of goodness of fit to a theoretical distribution or norm, go to Step 17.

   - If testing a hypothesis of association or relationship, go to Step 19.

   - If testing a hypothesis of prediction, go to Step 23.

2. **How many categories are there in the independent variable (IV)?**

   - If two categories, go to Step 3.

   - If three or more categories, go to Step 8

3. **How many dependent variables (DVs) are there?**

   - If one DV, go to Step 4.

   - If two or more DVs, go to Step 14.

4. **Are there any covariates?**

   - If no, go to Step 5.

   - If yes, go to Step 12.

5. **Are the data dependent (repeated observations of the same group or use of a matched pairs design) or independent?**

   - If data are dependent, go to Step 6.

   - If data are independent, go to Step 7.

6. **Is the DV a continuous variable and normally distributed?**

   - If yes, conduct the dependent t-test.

   - If no, conduct the Wilcoxon signed ranks test or the related samples sign test.

7. Is the DV a continuous variable and normally distributed?

- If yes, conduct the independent *t*-test.
- If no, conduct the Mann-Whitney *U* test or the median test.

8. Are there any covariates?

- If no, go to Step 9.
- If yes, go to Step 12.

9. Is the DV a continuous variable and normally distributed?

- If yes, go to Step 10.
- If no, go to Step 11.

10. Are the data dependent (repeated observations of the same group or use of a matched pairs design) or independent?

- If data are dependent, conduct the one-way within subjects analysis of variance (*ANOVA*).
- If data are independent, conduct the one-way between subjects analysis of variance (*ANOVA*).

11. Are the data dependent (repeated observations of the same group or use of a matched pairs design)?

- If data are dependent, conduct the Friedman test or Cochran's *Q* test.
- If data are independent, conduct the Kruskal-Wallis *H* test.

12. Are the DVs continuous variables and normally distributed?

- If yes, go to Step 13.
- If no, there is no omnibus nonparametric test.

13. Are the data dependent (repeated observations of the same group or use of a matched pairs design) or independent?

- If data are dependent, conduct the one-way within subjects analysis of covariance (*ANCOVA*).

- If data are independent, conduct the one-way between subjects analysis of covariance (*ANCOVA*).

14. Are there any covariates?

- If no, go to Step 15.

- If yes, go to Step 16.

15. Are the DVs continuous variables and normally distributed?

- If yes, conduct the multivariate analysis of variance (*MANOVA*).

- If no, there is no omnibus nonparametric test.

16. Are the DVs continuous variables and normally distributed?

- If yes, conduct the multivariate analysis of covariance (*MANCOVA*).

- If no, there is no omnibus nonparametric test.

17. Is the DV a continuous variable and normally distributed?

- If yes, conduct the one-sample *t*-test.

- If no, go to Step 18.

18. What is the purpose of the test?

- If the intent is to determine if a sample of data comes from a specific distribution, conduct the one-sample Kolmogorov-Smirnov test ($N \geq 50$) or the one-sample Shapiro-Wilk test ($N < 50$).

- If the intent is to evaluate randomness of a distribution, conduct the Wald-Wolfowitz runs test for randomness.

- If the intent is to determine if a sample of data for one categorical variable comes from a population with a specific distribution, conduct the chi-square (χ^2) goodness of fit test.

- If the intent is to determine if the proportion of individuals in one of two categories is different from a hypothesized test proportion, conduct the binomial test.

19. Are the variables continuous and normally distributed?

- If yes, go to Step 20.
- If there is one continuous variable and one dichotomous variable, conduct the point-biserial correlation test.
- If no, go to Step 21.

20. How variables are there?

- If there are two variables, conduct the Pearson product-moment correlation test.
- If there are two variables and a third control variable, conduct the partial correlation test.
- If there are one dependent variable and multiple independent variables, conduct the multiple regression and correlation test.
- If there are multiple dependent variables and multiple independent variables, conduct canonical correlation analysis or principal components and factor analysis.

21. Are the variables nominal?

- If no go to Step 22.
- If both variables are nominal, conduct Pearson chi-square (χ^2) contingency table analysis, or the phi (Φ), Cramér's *V*, lambda, or the contingency coefficient procedure.
- If both variables are dichotomous, conduct the gamma procedure.

22. Are the variables ordinal scale or a mix of nominal and ordinal or non-normal interval/ratio scales?

- If one variable is nominal and the other ordinal, conduct the lambda procedure.

- If one variable is nominal and the other continuous, conduct the eta procedure.

- If both variables are ordinal scale, conduct the Spearman rank order correlation test or Kendall's tau-b or tau-c procedure.

- If both variables are categorical ordinal variables, conduct the gamma or Somers' *d* procedure.

- If both variables are within the same class, conduct the intraclass correlation coefficient procedure.

23. How many variables are there?

- If there are two normally distributed variables, conduct the bivariate regression procedure.

- If there is one normally distributed criterion variable and multiple normally distributed predictor variables, conduct the multiple regression procedure.

- If there is one categorical criterion variable and multiple normally distributed predictor variables, conduct the discriminant analysis procedure.

- If there is one dichotomous criterion variable and multiple predictor variables, conduct the binomial logistic regression procedure.

6.4: Chapter 6 Review

The answer key is at the end of this section.

1. If one rejects the null hypothesis, one is proving that...

    A.   the research hypothesis is true

    B.   the null hypothesis is false

    C.   the IV has an impact on the DV

    D.   none of the above

2. What is a variable called that is presumed to cause a change in another variable?

    A.   Dependent variable

    B.   Independent variable

    C.   Criterion variable

    D.   Categorical variable

3. In hypothesis testing, one...

    A.   attempts to prove the research hypothesis

    B.   attempts to prove the null hypothesis

    C.   attempts to obtain evidence to reject the null hypothesis

    D.   attempts to obtain evidence to accept the research hypothesis

4. What does a significance level of .01 mean?

    A.   If the null hypothesis is true, one will reject it 1% of the time

    B.   If the null hypothesis is true, one will not reject it 1% of the time

    C.   If the null hypothesis is false, one will reject it 1% of the time

    D.   If the null hypothesis is false, one will not reject it 1% of the time

5. For a given hypothesis test, the *p*-value of the test statistic equals 0.04. This implies a 0.04 probability of making a...

    A.   Type I error

    B.   Type II error

    C.   correct decision in rejecting the null hypothesis

    D.   choices B and C are correct

6. What confidence interval do social science researchers tend to use in their hypothesis testing?

    A.   5%

    B.   90%

    C.   95%

    D.   10%

7. In a population with 50 males and 40 females, what is the probability of randomly selecting a female?

    A. $p(F) = 0.56$

    B. $p(F) = 0.44$

    C. $p(F) = 0.40$

    D. $p(F) = 0.35$

8. If there is a 40% chance of rain, what are the odds for rain?

    A.   .40

    B.   .54

    C.   .67

    D.   .73

9. What is a Type I error?

    A.   The probability of deciding that a significant effect is not present when it is present

    B.   The probability of deciding that a significant effect is present when it is not present

    C.   The probability that a true null hypothesis (H_0) is not rejected

    D.   The probability that a false H_0 is rejected

10. What is a Type II error?

A. The probability that a true null hypothesis (H_0) is not rejected

B. The probability of deciding that a significant effect is present when it is not present

C. The probability of deciding that a significant effect is not present when it is present

D. The probability that a false H_0 is rejected

11. What is a confidence level?

A. The probability of deciding that a significant effect is not present when it is present

B. The probability of deciding that a significant effect is present when it is not present

C. The probability that a true null hypothesis (H_0) is not rejected

D. The probability that a false H_0 is rejected

12. What is statistical power?

A. The probability of deciding that a significant effect is not present when it is present

B. The probability of deciding that a significant effect is present when it is not present

C. The probability that a true null hypothesis (H_0) is not rejected

D. The probability that a false H_0 is rejected

13. What is the cutoff called that a researcher uses to decide whether or not to reject the null hypothesis?

A. Alpha

B. Significance level

C. Confidence level

D. choices A and B are correct

14. You are researching the following research question: Is sense of classroom community higher in on campus rather than online courses? What kind of test would you use?

A. Two-tailed test

B. One-tailed test

C. Either choice A or B

D. None of the above

15. What is the best graphical technique to use in order to evaluate linearity?

A. Line chart

B. Histogram

C. Boxplot

D. Scatterplot

16. What is the best graphical technique to use in order to evaluate homoscedasticity?

A. Line chart

B. Histogram

C. Boxplots for pairs of variables

D. Q-Q plot

17. What is the best graphical technique to use in order to identify extreme outliers?

A. Line chart

B. Histogram

C. Boxplot

D. Scatterplot

18. What is NOT a measure used to identify multivariate outliers?

A. Leverage

B. Cook's distance

C. Condition index

D. Mahalanobis distance

19. Which symbol represents a population parameter?

A. Σ

B. M

C. s^2

D. μ

20. What measure does NOT increase statistical power?

    A. Increase sample size

    B. Increase significance level

    C. Use a two-tailed rather than one-tailed test

    D. Use a parametric rather than non-parametric test

21. What occurs when variables are highly correlated?

    A. Sphericity

    B. Heteroscedasticity

    C. Multicollinearity

    D. Homogeneity of regressions

22. What value is at the center of a confidence interval?

    A. Point estimate

    B. Population parameter

    C. Margin of error

    D. Standard error

23. The 95% confidence interval for μ, calculated from sample data, produces an interval estimate that ranges from 115 to 131. What does this NOT suggest?

    A. The margin of error is 8

    B. The sample mean is 123

    C. There is a 95% chance that the population mean ranges between 115 and 131

    D. One should reject the null hypothesis for any value between 115 and 131

24. When will a confidence interval widen?

   A. The confidence level is increased from 95% to 99%

   B. Sample standard deviation is higher

   C. Sample size is decreased

   D. All of the above

25. What measures can assist in evaluating multicollinearity?

   A. Pearson correlation coefficients

   B. Eigenvalues

   C. Variance proportions

   D. All of the above

26. You have a sample distribution, $N = 200$. What is the best test for evaluating normality?

   A. Levene's test

   B. Shapiro-Wilk W test

   C. Kolmogorov-Smirnov Z test

   D. Kolmogorov-Smirnov D test with Lilliefors correction

27. Effect size is used to determine...

   A. Statistical significance

   B. Practical significance

   C. Reliability

   D. Validity

Chapter 6 Answers

1D, 2B, 3C, 4A, 5A, 6C, 7B, 8C, 9B, 10C, 11C, 12D, 13D, 14B, 15D, 16C, 17C, 18C, 19D, 20C, 21C, 22A, 23D, 24D, 25D, 26D, 27B

Chapter 7: Goodness of Fit Tests

Goodness of fit tests are one-sample tests that have the goal of determining how well sample data fits theoretical distributions or population norms. This chapter describes common one-sample procedures.

7.1: Introduction

The goodness-of-fit test measures the extent to which an empirical distribution fits the distribution expected under the null hypothesis, such as a normal distribution. The null hypothesis typically is that they do and the alternate hypothesis is that they do not. Parametric tests assume a normal distribution and prior to conducting such a test the researcher can evaluate a sample dataset for normality. Additionally, a goodness of fit test can be used to determine whether two or more subgroups share the same distribution.

One sample (one group) tests are examples of goodness of fit tests where one is comparing a dataset to hypothesized values. For example, the Trait Form of the State-Trait Anxiety Inventory (STAI) measures trait anxiety. The STAI Manual includes several trait anxiety norms based on working adults, college students, high school students, etc. Given these norms on this test a researcher can administer the STAI to a local sample – e.g., college students – and compare local results to the published national norms.

Goodness of Fit Tests

Chi-Square (χ2) Goodness of Fit

(one categorical variable)

Binomial Test

(one dichotomous variable)

Wald-Wolfowitz Runs Test for Randomness

(numeric data recorded in the order sampled)

One-Sample t-Test

(one continuous variable)

One-Sample Kolmogorov-Smirnov Test

(determines whether a sample of data comes from a specific distribution; $N \geq 50$)

One-Sample Shapiro-Wilk W Test

(determines whether a sample of data comes from a specific distribution; $N < 50$)

7.2: Nonparametric Tests

Chi-Square (χ^2) Goodness of Fit Test

Purpose

The χ^2 goodness of fit test is a nonparametric procedure that determines if a sample of data for one categorical variable comes from a population with a specific distribution (Snedecor & Cochran, 1989). The researcher compares observed values with theoretical or expected values.

Below is the formula for the test statistic

$$\chi^2 = \sum \left(\frac{(O-E)^2}{E} \right)$$

where O = observed frequency and E = expected frequency.

The χ^2 goodness of fit test is an alternative to the Kolmogorov-Smirnov goodness-of-fit test when discrete distributions, such as the binomial and the Poisson, are used.

Degrees of freedom. This test has ($k - c$) degrees of freedom where k = number of non-empty cells and c = number of estimated parameters.

Effect size.

$$Effect\_size = \frac{\chi^2}{N(Categories - 1)}$$

where χ^2 is the chi-square statistic reported by SPSS and N = total sample size across all categories.

Key Assumptions & Requirements

Random selection of samples (probability samples) to allow for generalization of results to a target population.

Variables. One categorical variable where categories are reported in raw frequencies. Values/categories of the variable must be mutually exclusive and exhaustive.

Sample size. Observed frequencies must be sufficiently large ($N > 30$). Each cell should have an expected frequency of five or more. Applying chi-square to smaller samples results in a higher Type II error rates.

Example Research Question

Is there a difference in how online college students report perceived learning on a scale of 1 to 10?

Example Null Hypothesis

H_0: There is no difference in how online college students report perceived learning on a scale of 1 to 10.

SPSS Procedure

SPSS > Analyze > Nonparametric Tests > [Legacy Dialogs] > Chi-square

SPSS > Analyze > Nonparametric Tests > One Sample > Chi-Square Test

SPSS Output & Analysis

Descriptive Statistics.

Descriptive Statistics

	N	Mean	Std. Deviation	Minimum	Maximum	Percentiles		
						25th	50th (Median)	75th
Perceived Learning	168	6.51	1.761	1	9	6.00	7.00	8.00

Frequencies (observed *N*, expected *N*, and residual for each category).

Test Statistics.

Test Statistics

	Perceived Learning
Chi-Square	181.167[a]
df	9
Asymp. Sig.	.000

a. 0 cells (0.0%) have expected frequencies less than 5. The minimum expected cell frequency is 16.8.

The above SPSS output shows significant test results, $\chi^2(9, N = 168) = 181.17$, $p < .05$. There is sufficient evidence to reject the null hypothesis. One can conclude that the data vary from the expected values and there is a significant difference in how online college students report perceived learning based on 10 categories. Effect size is $181.167/(168*9) = .12$.

Binomial Test

Purpose

The binomial test is a nonparametric procedure that determines if the proportion of individuals in one of two categories is different from a hypothesized test proportion; e.g., different from .5. The specified test proportion entered in SPSS is for the first category. If no test proportion is entered, SPSS assumes $P = .5$ for both categories.

Continuous variables can be set up dichotomously with only two values by specifying a cut point where everything less than or equal to the cut point is in the first category and everything above the cut point is in the second category.

Degrees of freedom. This test has $(k - c)$ degrees of freedom where $k =$ number of non-empty cells and $c =$ number of estimated parameters.

Effect size. Green and Salkind (2008) recommend reporting an effect size as the difference between the observed and hypothesized proportions

$$Effect\_size = P_{Observed} - P_{Hypothesized}$$

Key Assumptions & Requirements

Random selection of samples (probability samples) to allow for generalization of results to a target population.

Variables. One dichotomous DV.

Sample size. A relatively large sample size ($N > 30$).

Example Research Question

Is the proportion of college students who prefer distance online courses over traditional on campus courses different, $P \neq .5$?

Example Null Hypothesis

H_0: There is no difference in the proportion of college students who prefer distance online courses over traditional on campus courses, $P = .5$.

SPSS Procedure

SPSS > Analyze > Nonparametric Tests > [Legacy Dialogs] > Binomial

SPSS > Analyze > Nonparametric Tests > One Sample > Binomial Test

SPSS Output & Analysis

Descriptive Statistics (N, mean, standard deviation, minimum, maximum, and P_{25}, P_{50}, P_{75}).

Binomial Test.

Binomial Test

		Category	N	Observed Prop.	Test Prop.	Exact Sig. (2-tailed)
Type course	Group 1	Distance	103	.84	.50	.000
	Group 2	Traditional	20	.16		
	Total		123	1.00		

The above SPSS output shows the observed proportions differed significantly from the hypothesized proportion of .50, *p*

< .001. A greater proportion of students prefer distance online courses. Effect size is .84 − .50 = .34.

One-Sample Kolmogorov-Smirnov Test

Purpose

The Kolmogorov-Smirnov test is a nonparametric procedure that determines whether a sample of data comes from a specific distribution; i.e., normal, uniform, Poisson, or exponential (Chakravarti, Laha, & Roy, 1967). One can also examine a normal Q-Q plot in order to evaluate normality graphically.

This test is mostly used for evaluating test assumptions.

Key Assumptions & Requirements

Random selection of samples (probability samples) to allow for generalization of results to a target population.

Variables. One DV.

Sample size. Large sample sizes ($N \geq 50$).

Example Research Question

Is sense of classroom community data normally distributed?

Note: $N \geq 50$. Use the one-sample Shapiro-Wilk W test if $N <$ 50.

Example Null Hypothesis

H_0: There is no difference between the distribution of sense of classroom community data and a normal distribution.

Alternatively, H_0: Sense of classroom community data are normally distributed.

SPSS Procedure

SPSS > Analyze > Nonparametric Tests > [Legacy Dialogs] > 1-Sample KS

SPSS > Analyze > Nonparametric Tests > One Sample > Kolmogorov-Smirnov Test

SPSS > Analyze > Descriptive Statistics > Explore > Plots > Normality plots with tests

Note: This test available under nonparametric tests computes Kolmogorov-Smirnov Z without the Lilliefors correction while the D test available under the explore menu computes the test with Lilliefors correction. The Kolmogorov-Smirnov Lilliefors D test, is more appropriate for very large datasets.

SPSS Output & Analysis

Descriptive Statistics (*N*, mean, standard deviation, minimum, maximum, and P_{25}, P_{50}, P_{75}).

One-sample Kolmogorov-Smirnov Test.

- The "Most Extreme Differences" values are the largest positive and negative differences between the sample distribution.

- The Kolmogorov-Smirnov Z statistic is calculated by multiplying the square root of sample size by the largest absolute difference.

One-Sample Kolmogorov-Smirnov Test

			Classroom Community
N			169
Normal Parameters[a,b]	Mean		28.84
	Std. Deviation		6.242
Most Extreme Differences	Absolute		.089
	Positive		.089
	Negative		-.073
Kolmogorov-Smirnov Z			1.153
Asymp. Sig. (2-tailed)			.140

a. Test distribution is Normal.

b. Calculated from data.

The above SPSS output shows that the test is not significant, $p = .14$. Consequently, it can be assumed that the tested dataset is normally distributed.

One-Sample Shapiro-Wilk *W* Test

Purpose

The Shapiro-Wilk *W* test is a nonparametric procedure that determines if a sample of data comes from a normal distribution. It is more appropriate for small sample sizes (< 50), but can also handle larger sample sizes, although the one-sample Kolmogorov-Smirnov test is preferred in this situation (Shapiro & Wilk, 1965).

The *W* statistic is the ratio of the best estimator of the variance (based on the square of a linear combination of the order statistics) to the usual corrected sum of squares estimator of the variance (Shapiro & Wilk; 1965). Small values of *W* are evidence of departure from normality. One can also examine a normal Q-Q plot in order to evaluate normality graphically.

This test is mostly used for evaluating test assumptions.

Key Assumptions & Requirements

Random selection of samples (probability samples) to allow for generalization of results to a target population.

Variables. One continuous variable.

Sample size. Small sample sizes ($N < 50$).

Example Research Question

Is sense of classroom community data normally distributed?

Note: $N < 50$. Use the one-sample Kolmogorov-Smirnov test test if $N \geq 50$.

Example Null Hypothesis

H_0: There is no difference between the distribution of sense of classroom community data and a normal distribution.

Alternatively, H_0: Sense of classroom community data are normally distributed.

SPSS Procedure

SPSS > Analyze > Descriptive Statistics > Explore > Plots > Normality plots with tests

SPSS Output & Analysis

Descriptives (mean, 95% confidence interval for mean, 5% trimmed mean, median, variance, standard deviation, minimum, maximum, range, interquartile range, skewness, kurtosis).

Tests of Normality.

Tests of Normality

	Kolmogorov-Smirnov[a]			Shapiro-Wilk		
	Statistic	df	Sig.	Statistic	df	Sig.
Classroom Community	.131	49	.035	.950	49	.038

a. Lilliefors Significance Correction

The above SPSS output shows Shapiro-Wilk (as well as Kolmogorov-Smirnov Lilliefors) test results are significant, $W(49) = .95$, $p = .04$. Consequently, it can be assumed that the tested dataset is not normally distributed.

Plots (histogram, stem-and-leaf plot, normal Q-Q plot, detrended normal Q-Q plot, boxplot).

Wald-Wolfowitz Runs Test for Randomness

Purpose

The Wald-Wolfowitz runs test is a nonparametric procedure that tests if a sequence of values is in random order (Bradley, 1968). A run is any sequence of cases having the same value. The total number of runs in a sample is a measure of randomness in the order of the cases in the sample. Too many or too few runs can suggest a nonrandom ordering.

Below is the formula for the test statistic

$$Z = \frac{R_o - R_e}{s_R}$$

where R_O is the observed number of runs, R_e is the expected number of runs, and s_R is the standard deviation of the number of runs.

The original runs test required that data be a dichotomy. However, the SPSS runs test does not require true dichotomies.

The researcher or SPSS dichotomizes continuous variables by identifying cut points; e.g., mean, median, or mode.

This test is mostly used for evaluating independence of observations.

Key Assumptions & Requirements

Random selection of samples (probability samples) to allow for generalization of results to a target population.

Variables. Numeric data. Data are recorded in the order sampled and are not aggregated (grouped).

Example Research Question

Is the sequence of values in the perceived learning dataset random?

Example Null Hypothesis

H_0: The sequence of values in the perceived learning dataset is random.

SPSS Procedure

SPSS > Analyze > Nonparametric Tests > [Legacy Dialogs] > Runs

SPSS > Analyze > Nonparametric Tests > One Sample > Runs Test

SPSS Output & Analysis

Descriptive Statistics (N, mean, standard deviation, minimum, maximum, and P_{25}, P_{50}, P_{75}).

Runs Test.

Runs Test

	Perceived Learning
Test Value[a]	7
Cases < Test Value	59
Cases >= Test Value	109
Total Cases	168
Number of Runs	68
Z	-1.624
Asymp. Sig. (2-tailed)	.104

a. Median

The above SPSS output shows that the test is not significant using the z-approximation, $Z = -1.62$, $p = .10$. The test provides evidence that the sequence of values in the perceived learning dataset is random.

7.3: Parametric Tests

One-Sample *t*-Test

Purpose

The one-sample *t*-test is a parametric procedure that compares a calculated sample mean to a known population mean or a previously reported value in order to determine if the difference is statistically significant. In the SPSS *One Sample T Test* dialog box, the researcher must enter both the test variable(s) in the Test Variable(s): box and the test value in the *Test Value* box. SPSS places a default value of zero in this box, so the test will run with this default test value if the researcher does not enter a test value.

The *t*-statistic is calculated as follows

$$t = \frac{(\overline{X} - X_0)}{\dfrac{s_X}{\sqrt{N}}}$$

where x̄ is the mean of the DV, X_0 is the comparison value, s_X is the standard deviation of the DV, and *N* is the sample size.

Degrees of freedom. The degrees of freedom for this test are $N - 1$.

Effect size. Cohen's *d* is used to report effect size, where *d* values of .2, .5, and .8 are regarded as small, medium, and large effect sizes respectively.

$$d = \frac{t}{\sqrt{N}}$$

where *t* = *t*-statistic reported by SPSS and *N* = sample size.

Key Assumptions & Requirements

Random selection of samples (probability samples) to allow for generalization of results to a target population.

Variables. One continuous DV measured on the interval or ratio scale.

Normality. One DV, normally distributed. The one sample *t*-test is robust to minor violations of the assumption of normally distributed data with sample sizes > 50 (Diekhoff, 1992).

Example Research Question

Is there a difference in the mean sense of classroom community score among university students enrolled in fully online programs and the norm for university students, $\mu \neq 30$?

Example Null Hypothesis

H_0: There is no difference in the mean sense of classroom community score of university students enrolled in fully online programs and the norm of 30, $\mu = 30$.

SPSS Procedure

SPSS > Analyze > Compare Means > One-Sample *T* Test

SPSS Output & Analysis

One-Sample Statistics.

- The standard error of the mean provides an estimate of the spread of all possible random sample means.

One-Sample Statistics

	N	Mean	Std. Deviation	Std. Error Mean
Classroom Community	169	28.84	6.242	.480

The above SPSS output shows there is a 68.26% probability that the true population mean is ± .48 from the sample mean of 28.84.

One-Sample Test.

One-Sample Test

	Test Value = 30					
					95% Confidence Interval of the Difference	
	t	df	Sig. (2-tailed)	Mean Difference	Lower	Upper
Classroom Community	-2.42	168	.017	-1.160	-2.11	-.21

The above SPSS output shows that the test is significant, $t(168) = -2.42$, $p = .02$. Therefore, there is a statistically significant difference between the sample mean, 28.84, and the test value of 30. The effect size is small, $d = 2.42/13 = .19$.

7.4: Chapter 7 Review

The answer key is at the end of this section.

1. Which of the following tests is a parametric test?

   A. One-sample t-test

   B. Binomial test

   C. One-sample Kolmogorov-Smirnov test

   D. Wald-Wolfowitz runs test for randomness

2. What is the best statistical test for normality for a small sample size?

   A. Chi-square (x^2) goodness of fit test

   B. One-sample Kolmogorov-Smirnov test

   C. One-sample Shapiro-Wilk W test

   D. Cohen's Kappa (κ) measure of agreement

3. What is the best test to address the following null hypothesis: H_0: Online college students are equally likely to report low, medium, or high sense of classroom community.

   A. Chi-Square (x^2) goodness of fit test

   B. Binomial test

   C. One sample t-test

   D. One-sample Kolmogorov-Smirnov test

4. What is the best test to answer the following research question: Is the proportion of college students who prefer online courses different from the proportion of college students who prefer traditional on campus courses?

   A. Runs test for randomness

   B. Chi-square (x^2) goodness of fit test

   C. One-sample Shapiro-Wilk test

   D. Binomial test

5. What is a conservative test for normality?

A. Chi-square (χ^2) goodness of fit test

B. Binomial test

C. One-sample Kolmogorov-Smirnov test

D. One-sample Shapiro-Wilk W test

6. What test determines if the proportion of individuals in one of two categories is different from a specified test proportion?

A. Chi-square goodness of fit test

B. Binomial test

C. One-sample t-test

D. Runs test for randomness

7. What test assumes normality?

A. Binomial test

B. One-sample Shapiro-Wilk test

C. One-sample t-test

D. Wald-Wolfowitz runs test

8. Below is an extract from SPSS one-sample t-test output. What is the correct finding?

	Test Value = 100		
	t	df	Sig. (2-tailed)
Alienation	-38.005	168	.000

A. $t(-38) = 168, p = .000$

B. $t(168) = -38, p = .000$

C. $t(168) = -38, p < .05$

D. $t(-38) = 168, p < .05$

9. Below is an extract from SPSS chi-square goodness of fit test output. What is the correct finding?

Test Statistics

	Ethnicity
Chi-Square	223.905[a]
df	4
Asymp. Sig.	.000

A. $\chi^2(223.91) = 4, p = .000$

B. $\chi^2(223.91) = 4, p < .001$

C. $\chi^2(4) = 223.91, p = .000$

D. $\chi^2(4) = 223.91, p < .001$

10. What is the best test for evaluating the normality assumption for samples with $N \geq 50$?

A. χ^2 goodness of fit test

B.   One-sample Shapiro-Wilk test

C.   One-sample Kolmogorov-Smirnov test

D.   Wald-Wolfowitz runs test

Chapter 7 Answers

1A, 2C, 3A, 4D, 5C, 6B, 7C, 8C, 9B, 10C

Chapter 8: Difference Tests

Difference tests are used to compare two or more groups with the goal of determining how the groups differ from each other. This chapter summarizes common difference procedures.

8.1: Introduction

Overview

Difference tests, in general, are used to determine if two or more groups differ from each other on one or more variables or whether there are differences in one or more groups measured repeatedly over time. These tests use statistics that reflect a signal-to-noise ratio, or how much variance in the DV is accounted for by the IV, compared to what is left.

Data can be independent (i.e., scores in one group cannot be matched or paired to scores in another group) or data can be dependent. Observations are linked in this second approach. The primary way to achieve this linkage is to use a repeated measures design, e.g., pretest-posttest design, in which the same research participants are observed more than once. A second, less common, approach is to pair research participants in a matched pairs design.

Matched pairs designs use randomization to control for confounding by extraneous variables. The design is achieved when participants are paired based on some blocking variable(s), such as socioeconomic status, gender, etc. This type of randomized block design is in contrast to a completely randomized design. Participants in each block or subgroup are randomly assigned to treatment conditions, e.g., treatment group and control group. For example, the researcher could assign research participants to two blocks based on gender, (i.e., a male block and a female block). Then, within each block, participants are randomly assigned to treatment conditions. This procedure ensures that each treatment condition has an equal representation of males and females and that gender is not a confounding variable.

Difference Tests

McNemar Chi-Square Test

(two dependent samples, nominal DV)

Related Samples Sign Test

(two dependent samples, nominal or ordinal DV)

Cochran's Q Test

(multiple dependent samples, nominal DV)

Mann-Whitney U Test

(two independent samples, ordinal DV)

Wilcoxon Signed Ranks Test

(two dependent samples, ordinal DV)

Median Test

(multiple independent samples, ordinal DV)

Kruskal-Wallis H Test

(multiple independent samples, ordinal DV)

Friedman Test

(multiple dependent samples, ordinal DV)

Levene's Test

(multiple independent samples, interval or ratio DV)

Independent t-Test

(two independent samples, interval or ratio DV)

Dependent t-Test

(two dependent samples, interval or ratio DV)

Between Subjects ANOVA

(multiple independent samples, one interval or ratio DV)

Within Subjects ANOVA

(multiple dependent samples, one interval or ratio DV)

Multivariate ANOVA

(MANOVA; multiple independent and/or dependent samples, multiple interval or ratio DVs)

Analysis of Covariance

(ANCOVA; one interval or ratio DV; multiple DVs for MANCOVA; interval or ratio covariate(s); multiple independent samples)

Multivariate Tests

SPSS provides the following measures (test criteria) of group differences with multivariate procedures (Norusis, 2011). The null hypothesis is that the centroids do not differ between groups.

- *Wilks' lambda* is the most frequently used measure and performs the same role of the *F*-test in one-way *ANOVA*. Use if assumptions appear to be met. It shows the amount of variance accounted for in the DV(s) by the IV. The value ranges from 0 to 1. The smaller the value, the larger the difference between groups. It is interpreted as the proportion of the variance in the outcomes that is not explained by an effect. One minus Wilks' lambda reflects the amount of variance in the DV(s) explained by the IV(s).

- *Pillai's trace* is useful if sample sizes are small, cell sizes are unequal, or covariances are not homogeneous. Olson (1976) found Pillai's trace to be the most robust of the four measures and is sometimes preferred for this reason.

- *Hoteling's trace* provides a relationship between the effect and the model. The larger the statistic, the greater the effect contributes to the model.

- *Roy's largest root* only uses the variance from the dimension that separates the groups most (the largest "root" or difference). Appropriate and very powerful when the DVs are strongly interrelated on a single dimension. Most likely to be affected by violations of assumptions. Use only if *MANOVA* assumptions are tenable. Because it is based only on the largest root, it can behave differently than the other three measures. In cases where the other three are not significant and Roy's largest root is significant, the effect should not be considered significant.

Factorial Designs

Much of social science research examines the effect of one explanatory variable (IV) at a time. Studying factors separately does not allow for a full examination of how factors interact with each other. Consequently, social science researchers often use factorial designs to assess the effects of interventions that also take into account the influence of other categorical factors, such as socioeconomic status and gender.

A factor is simply a categorical variable with two or more values, referred to as levels, e.g., gender with two levels, male and female. A study that consists of two factors with two levels each uses a 2 x 2 factorial design. The two-way *ANOVA* procedure would be used to analyze the data (as opposed to a one-way *ANOVA* with only one IV). Factorial designs include several advantages.

- Such designs represent the complexity of the real world more accurately.

- A parsimonious approach is achieved by addressing multiple related issues in a single study.

- Interaction effects between different factors can be studied.

- Additional factors can extend the validity of research findings.

When there is one IV (factor) there is only one H_0. For example, the following is the H_0 for a difference question in which the IV is counseling service (referred, not referred) and the DV is graduation rate:

> H_0: There is no difference in college graduation rates between students who were referred to the counseling service and students who utilized the counseling service on their own initiative.

However, when there are two IVs, as in a two-way factorial design, there are three null hypotheses. For example, the following three null hypotheses apply to a difference question in which the IVs are type course (traditional, distance) and gender (male, female), and the DV is community spirit posttest:

H_{01}: There is no difference in community spirit posttest between students based on type course (traditional, distance). (This hypothesis addresses the first IV or main effect or factor.)

H_{02}: There is no difference in sense of classroom community between students based on gender (male, female). (This hypothesis addresses the second IV or main effect or factor.)

H_{03}: The difference in community spirit posttest between students based on type course (traditional, distance) remains constant regardless of gender (male, female). (This hypothesis addresses the interaction effect; i.e., how the IVs affect each other).

Below is a profile plot of a significant gender x type course interaction. It shows that male students score higher than female students on posttest community spirit in a traditional course. However, in an online distance education course, female students score higher than male students. Inspection of the plot clearly shows that the two lines are not parallel, which is the defining feature of an interaction. Parallel lines or approximately parallel lines suggest no interaction.

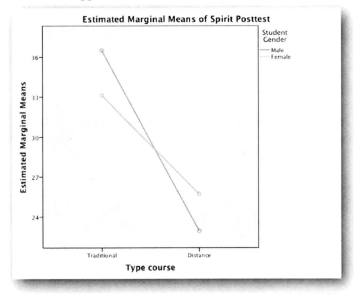

So, the rule is simple. If one is conducting research in differences between groups and has one IV and one DV, one tests one H_0, a main effect hypothesis. If one has two IVs and one DV, one tests three null hypotheses: two main effect null hypotheses and one interaction hypothesis, which addresses the first order interaction. These three outcomes (one for each null hypothesis) produce eight possible results:

1. No significant effects (there is no evidence to reject any null hypothesis).

2. Only the null hypothesis associated with the first main effect can be rejected.

3. Only the null hypothesis associated with the second main effect can be rejected.

4. Only the null hypothesis associated with the interaction effect can be rejected.

5. Only the null hypothesis associated with the two main effects can be rejected.

6. Only the null hypothesis associated with the first main effect and the interaction effect can be rejected.

7. Only the null hypothesis associated with the second main effect and the interaction effect can be rejected.

8. All null hypotheses can be rejected.

If one has three IVs and one DV, one tests seven null hypotheses: three main effect null hypotheses (one for each IV), three first order interaction hypotheses, and one second order interaction hypothesis. The first order interactions address interactions between all possible pairs of IVs. The second order interaction involves all three IVs. For example:

> H_{01}: There is no difference in sense of community between graduate students based on type of distance education course (synchronous, asynchronous). (This hypothesis addresses the first main effect or IV.)

> H_{02}: There is no difference in sense of community between graduate students based on gender (male, female) . (This hypothesis addresses the second main effect or IV.)

H_{03}: There is no difference in sense of community between graduate students based on type of school (public, private). (This hypothesis addresses the third main effect or IV.)

H_{04}: The difference in sense of community between students based on type of distance education course (synchronous, asynchronous) remains constant regardless of gender (male, female). (This hypothesis addresses the first two-way or first order interaction effect.)

H_{05}: The difference in sense of community among graduate students based on type of distance education course (synchronous, asynchronous) remains constant regardless of type of school (public, private). (This hypothesis addresses the second two-way or first order interaction effect.)

H_{06}: The difference in sense of community between graduate students based on gender (male, female) remains constant regardless of type of school (public, private). (This hypothesis addresses the third two-way or first order interaction effect.)

H_{07}: The difference in sense of community between students based on type of distance education course (synchronous, asynchronous) remains constant regardless of gender (male, female) and type of school (public, private). (This hypothesis addresses the three-way or second order interaction effect.)

Post Hoc Multiple Comparison Tests

> **Key Point**
> A significant difference test – e.g., ANOVA with three groups – provides evidence that there is a significant difference between groups, but it does not identify pairwise differences (i.e., differences between pairs of groups).

Post hoc (or follow-up) multiple comparison tests are used following a significant omnibus test – e.g., one-way *ANOVA* – in order to determine which groups differ from each other when there are three or more groups. A post hoc test following a significant independent t-test is not required because this test only involves two groups and if the t-test is significant it is clear what two groups are different. However, in a test involving three or more groups, a significant omnibus test only provides evidence to the researcher that the groups differ, not where the groups differ. In a three group test the researcher does not know if group A differs significantly from group B and group C or if group B differs significantly from group C. Hence there is a need to conduct post hoc tests to identify pairwise differences.

At this point it is important for researchers to understand the difference between planned (*à priori*) and unplanned (*à posteriori*) multiple comparison tests. If the comparisons are planned in advance, the groups can be tested using à priori procedures. Planned comparisons use the Bonferroni correction or Holm's sequential Bonferroni correction. The revised *p*-value is the one used when evaluating test results.

If the comparison is unplanned – i.e., it takes place only if the omnibus test, *ANOVA*, is significant – the researcher uses standard post hoc procedures. As long as post hoc tests are only conducted following a significant *ANOVA* – i.e., they are unplanned – a correction to control for Type I error is not required.

Here is a partial list of the post hoc multiple comparison tests one can use when the assumption of homogeneity of variances is met for a parametric test (Norusis, 2011):

- The *Bonferroni test* sets the α error rate to the experimentwise error rate (usually .05) divided by the total number of comparisons to control for Type I error when multiple comparisons are being made. If the Bonferroni test is requested, SPSS will print out a table of "Multiple Comparisons" giving the mean difference in the dependent variable between any two groups. The significance of this difference is also printed, and an asterisk is printed next to differences significant at the .05 level or better.

- The *Sidak test* is a variant on the Bonferroni approach, using a *t*-test for pairwise multiple comparisons. The α significance level for multiple comparisons is adjusted to tighter bounds than for the Bonferroni test.

- If the *Tukey Honestly Significant Difference* (*HSD*) test is requested (identified only by Tukey by SPSS), SPSS will produce a table similar to that for the Bonferroni test of all pairwise comparisons between groups, interpreted in the same way. The Tukey method is preferred when the number of groups is large as it is a very conservative pairwise comparison test, and researchers prefer to be conservative when the large number of groups threatens to inflate Type I errors.

- *Tukey's Wholly Significant Difference* (*WSD*) test, also called Tukey-*b* in SPSS, is a less conservative version of Tukey's *HSD* test.

- The *Scheffé test* is a widely-used method for controlling Type I errors in post hoc testing of differences in group means. It works by first requiring the overall *F*-test of the null hypothesis be rejected. If the null hypothesis is not rejected overall, then it is not rejected for any comparison null hypothesis. While the Scheffé test maintains an experimentwise .05 significance level in the face of multiple comparisons, it does so at the cost of a loss in statistical power (more Type II errors may be made). The

Scheffé test is very conservative (even more conservative than Tukey).

- The *Least Significant Difference* (*LSD*) test, also called Fisher's *LSD* test, is based on the t-statistic and thus can be considered a form of t-test. It compares all possible pairs of means after the F-test rejects the null hypothesis that groups do not differ. *LSD* is the most liberal of the post-hoc tests (it is most likely to reject the null hypothesis). It controls the experimentwise Type I error rate at a selected α level, but only for the omnibus (overall) test of the null hypothesis. Most researchers recommend against any use of *LSD* on the grounds that it has poor control of experimentwise α significance, and better alternatives exist.

When the assumption of homogeneity of variances is not met, SPSS provides these alternate post hoc methods for the researcher (Norusis, 2011):

- The *Games-Howell test* can be liberal when sample size is small. Because this test is more powerful than Dunnett's *C* or *T3* tests, it is recommended over these tests.

- *Dunnett's T3 and Dunnett's C* tests might be used in lieu of the Games-Howell test only if it were essential to maintain strict control over the alpha significance level (e.g., exactly .05 or better).

- *Tamhane's T2* is a conservative test based on the student t-distribution.

Contrasts

A contrast is a linear combination of means. In addition to or in place of post hoc multiple comparison tests, SPSS can also produce one or more of the following contrasts (Norusis, 2011):

- The *deviation contrast* compares the mean of each level (except a reference category) to the mean of all of the levels (grand mean). The levels of the factor can be in any order.

- The *simple contrast* compares the mean of each level to the mean of a specified level. This type of contrast is useful when there is a control group.

- The *Helmert contrast* compares the mean of each level of the factor (except the last) to the mean of subsequent levels.

- The *difference contrast* compares the mean of each level (except the first) to the mean of previous levels. (Sometimes called reverse Helmert contrast.)

- The *polynomial contrast* (also called orthogonal polynomial contrast) is used to estimate polynomial trends following a significant within-subjects main effect. It is used to test for linear, quadratic, cubic, and higher-order trends in means across repeated measures groups (categories). The first degree of freedom contains the linear effect across all groups; the second degree of freedom contains the quadratic effect; and so on. In other words, the magnitude and significance of the linear component tells one about the general upward or downward trend in the DV across the repeated observations, while the quadratic component tells one how measurements are leveling off or changing direction over time.

Controlling Type I Error

Type I error is the probability of deciding that a significant effect is present when it isn't. That is, it is the probability of rejecting a true null hypothesis. Type I error is controlled by the researcher by specifying an *à priori* significance level for a single hypothesis test. This is known as the experimentwise Type I error rate.

When several tests are conducted simultaneously using the same dataset, they constitute a family of tests. Familywise Type I error rate is the probability for a family of tests that at least one null hypothesis will be rejected assuming that all of the null hypotheses are true. However, unless the researcher takes steps to control for familywise error, the Type I error rate becomes inflated. This happens because the more statistical tests one performs the more likely one is to reject the null hypothesis when it is true (i.e., commit a Type I error).

Bonferroni Correction

The Bonferroni correction is a simple procedure for controlling familywise Type I error for multiple pairwise comparisons. It requires the following steps (Green & Salkind, 2008):

- Identify familywise Type I error rate; e.g., $p = .05$.
- Determine the number of pairwise comparisons (n).
- Compute p-values for each individual test, $p_1, p_2,...p_n$.
- Reject the null hypothesis for each test if

$$p < \frac{p^*}{n}$$

where p^* = familywise Type I error rate and n = number of pairwise comparisons.

However, the Bonferroni method is often considered too conservative.

Holm's Sequential Bonferroni Correction

A variant of the Bonferroni correction that is less conservative is the Holm's sequential Bonferroni correction. Holm (1979) observes:

> Except in trivial non-interesting cases the sequentially rejective Bonferroni test has strictly larger probability of rejecting false hypotheses and thus it ought to replace the classical Bonferroni test at all instants where the latter usually is applied (p. 65).

This procedure involves the following steps (Green & Salkind, 2008; Holm, 1979):

- Identify familywise Type I error rate; e.g., $p = .05$.
- Determine the number of pairwise comparisons (n).
- Conduct the pairwise comparisons.
- Rank-order the comparisons on the basis of their p-values from smallest to highest.

- Evaluate the comparison with the smallest p-value. Compare the p-value to the *à priori* modified familywise Type I error rate as calculated using the Bonferroni method. Reject the null hypothesis for the test if

$$p < \frac{p^*}{n}$$

where p^* = familywise Type I error rate and n = number of pairwise comparisons.

- Evaluate the comparison with the next smallest p-value. Reject the null hypothesis for the test if

$$p < \frac{p^*}{n-1}$$

where p^* = familywise Type I error rate and n = number of pairwise comparisons.

- Continue as above by rejecting the next smallest p-value if

$$p < \frac{p^*}{n-2}$$

where p^* = familywise Type I error rate and n = number of pairwise comparisons.

- Continue this procedure until all comparisons have been evaluated, making sure to evaluate each p-value based on the number of completed comparisons.

8.2: Nonparametric Tests

McNemar Test

Purpose

The McNemar test is a nonparametric chi-square procedure that compares proportions obtained from a 2 x 2 contingency table where the row variable (A) is the DV and the column variable (B) is the IV. The McNemar test can be used to test if there is a statistically significant difference between the probability of a (0,1) pair and the probability of a (1,0) pair. The two tested proportions are:

- $P_A = (a + b)/N$
- $P_B = (a + c)/N$

The data are dependent. Either a single sample of participants measured twice; e.g., using a pretest-posttest design or matched-pair samples.

Dichotomous variables are employed where data are coded as "1" for those participants that display the property defined by the variable in question and "0" for those who do not display that property. The test addresses two possible outcomes (presence/absence of a characteristic) on each measurement.

Degrees of freedom. The McNemar test has one degree of freedom.

Effect size. The phi coefficient can be used for effect size following a significant McNemar test.

Key Assumptions & Requirements

Random selection of samples (probability samples) to allow for generalization of results to a target population.

Variables. Two dependent dichotomous variables coded in the same manner.

Example Research Question

Is there a difference in the proportion of university students by gender who completed extra credit work, $P_1 \neq P_2$?

Example Null Hypothesis

H_0: There is no difference in the proportions of university students by gender who completed extra credit work $P_1 = P_2$.

SPSS Procedure

SPSS > Analyze > Nonparametric Tests > [Legacy Dialogs] > Two-Related-Samples Tests > McNemar

SPSS > Analyze > Descriptive Statistics > Crosstabs > Statistics > McNemar

SPSS Output & Analysis

Descriptive Statistics (*N*, mean, standard deviation, minimum, maximum, P_{25}, P_{50}, P_{75}).

Crosstabs.

Completed Extra Credit & Gender

	Gender	
Completed Extra Credit	FEMALE	MALE
NO	53	30
YES	11	11

The above SPSS output displays a 2 x 2 crosstabulation showing frequency counts for each cell. A greater proportion of males than females completed extra credit work.

Test Statistics.

Test Statistics[a]

	Completed Extra Credit & Gender
N	105
Chi-Square[b]	7.902
Asymp. Sig.	.005

a. McNemar Test

b. Continuity Corrected

The above SPSS output shows a significant McNemar test, $\chi^2(1, N = 105) = 7.90, p = .005$. These results provide evidence that the null hypothesis of no difference in the proportions of university students by gender who completed extra credit work can be rejected. Effect size is weak, $\Phi = .12$.

Related Samples Sign Test

Purpose

The related samples sign test is a nonparametric procedure that compares the signs (plus, minus, or tied) of the differences between data pairs of dependent data (e.g., pretest-posttest observations) or median differences of independent paired observations. It does not measure magnitude of differences. It tests for a median difference of zero. The related samples sign test is used with nominal or ordinal data and may be used with interval data, but the Wilcoxon signed ranks test is preferred in this situation. Wilcoxon's signed rank test is more powerful than the related samples sign test and is generally preferred.

As an example, a related samples sign test can be used to determine if there is a difference between the ratings that raters each give on two products when the ratings represent ordinal or nominal data.

Parametric Equivalent

Dependent *t*-test

Key Assumptions & Requirements

Random selection of samples (probability samples) to allow for generalization of results to a target population.

Variables. DV: one ordinal or nominal scale variable. IV: one categorical variable consisting of one group or two matched-pairs groups. Use of dependent variables.

Sample size. Large sample size (because paired differences equalling 0 are omitted from the analysis, having a relatively large number of paired differences equal to 0 can significantly reduce the effective sample size).

Example Research Question

Are the number of positive difference scores and negative difference scores in computer anxiety different?

Note: the researcher used a pretest/posttest design.

Example Null Hypothesis

H_0: The number of positive difference scores and negative difference scores in computer anxiety are equal.

SPSS Procedure

SPSS > Analyze > Nonparametric Tests > [Legacy Dialogs] > Two-Related-Samples Tests > Sign

SPSS Output & Analysis

Descriptive Statistics (N, mean, standard deviation, minimum, maximum, P_{25}, P_{50}, P_{75}).

Frequencies.

Frequencies

		N
Computer Anxiety Posttest – Computer Anxiety Pretest	Negative Differences[a]	60
	Positive Differences[b]	23
	Ties[c]	3
	Total	86

a. Computer Anxiety Posttest < Computer Anxiety Pretest

b. Computer Anxiety Posttest > Computer Anxiety Pretest

c. Computer Anxiety Posttest = Computer Anxiety Pretest

The above SPSS output shows that there are more negative differences than positive differences when comparing pretest and posttest computer anxiety scores. Negative differences are interpreted as less computer anxiety. The issue is whether these differences are statistically significant.

Test Statistics.

Test Statistics[a]

	Computer Anxiety Posttest – Computer Anxiety Pretest
Z	-3.952
Asymp. Sig. (2-tailed)	.000

a. Sign Test

Drawing on the normal approximation, the above SPSS output provides evidence to reject the null hypothesis that the number of positive difference scores and negative difference scores in computer literacy are equal, $Z = -3.95$, $p < .001$. Therefore, there is a significant decline in computer anxiety between pretest and posttest observations.

Wilcoxon Signed Ranks Test

Purpose

The Wilcoxon signed ranks test is a nonparametric procedure that compares differences between data pairs of dependent data from two dependent samples. It is similar to the related samples sign test except that this test factors in the size as well as the sign of the paired differences. This procedure involves ranking all nonzero difference scores disregarding sign, reattaching the sign to the rank, and then evaluating the mean of the positive and the mean of the negative ranks. Consequently, the Wilcoxon signed ranks test is more powerful than the related sample sign test and is the preferred test.

Effect size. An approximation of the r coefficient can be obtained using the value of z, as reported by SPSS, and the following formula

$$r = \frac{z}{\sqrt{N}}$$

where N = number of paired observations.

Alternatively, the difference in mean ranks between groups can be used for effect size.

Parametric Equivalent

Dependent *t*-test

Key Assumptions & Requirements

Random selection of samples (probability samples) to allow for generalization of results to a target population.

Variables. DV: one continuous variable that is ordinal, interval, or ratio scale. IV: one categorical variable with two observations. The distribution of difference scores should be continuous and symmetrical. Use of dependent variables.

Example Research Question

Is there a difference in ranks between computer anxiety pretest and computer anxiety posttest among university students?

Example Null Hypothesis

H_0: There is no difference in ranks between computer anxiety pretest and computer anxiety posttest among university students.

SPSS Procedure

SPSS > Analyze > Nonparametric Tests > [Legacy Dialogs] > 2 Related Samples > Wilcoxon

SPSS > Analyze > Nonparametric Tests > One Sample > Wilcoxon Signed Ranks Test

SPSS Output & Analysis

Descriptive Statistics (*N*, mean, standard deviation, minimum, maximum, P_{25}, P_{50}, P_{75}).

Ranks.

Ranks

		N	Mean Rank	Sum of Ranks
Computer Anxiety Posttest - Computer Anxiety Pretest	Negative Ranks	60[a]	49.20	2952.00
	Positive Ranks	23[b]	23.22	534.00
	Ties	3[c]		
	Total	86		

a. Computer Anxiety Posttest < Computer Anxiety Pretest

b. Computer Anxiety Posttest > Computer Anxiety Pretest

c. Computer Anxiety Posttest = Computer Anxiety Pretest

The above SPSS output shows the mean of the ranks of the difference scores in which posttest computer anxiety decreased is 49.20 and the mean of the ranks of the difference scores in which posttest computer anxiety increased is 23.22.

Test Statistics.

Test Statistics[a]

	Computer Anxiety Posttest - Computer Anxiety Pretest
Z	-5.492[b]
Asymp. Sig. (2-tailed)	.000

a. Wilcoxon Signed Ranks Test

b. Based on positive ranks.

The above SPSS output shows that the test is significant using the z-approximation, $Z = -5.49$, $p < .001$. Consequently, there is evidence to conclude that there a statistically significant difference in ranks between computer anxiety pretest and computer anxiety posttest among university students. Posttest computer anxiety is significantly lower than pretest computer anxiety. Effect size using the r-approximation is .59, suggesting a moderate effect size.

Cochran's *Q* Test

Purpose

Cochran's *Q* test is a nonparametric procedure for dependent data that tests for differences between three or more matched sets of frequencies or proportions. The DV can be any dichotomy, such as pass-fail, presence-absence, hit-miss, etc. It is an extension of the McNemar test. The data must be coded with 0 to represent failure (or absence), and 1 to represent success (or presence). Rows containing only 1's or only 0's do not influence the value of Q.

The dependent data should be the result of either repeated observations of the same group or matching multiple groups as part of an experimental design.

Degrees of freedom. Cochran's Q has $k - 1$ degrees of freedom where k = number of frequencies or proportions.

Post hoc multiple comparison tests. For pairwise post hoc comparisons, the McNemar test is appropriate following a significant Q test.

Effect size. Kendall's W (Kendall's coefficient of concordance) can be used as an effect size statistic. The coefficient ranges from 0 to 1, with stronger relationships indicated by higher values. (See SPSS procedure below.)

Parametric Equivalent

One-way within-subjects *ANOVA*

Key Assumptions & Requirements

Random selection of samples (probability samples) to allow for generalization of results to a target population.

Variables. DV: one categorical variable with two categories. IV: one categorical variable with multiple dependent groups. Use of dependent variables.

Example Research Question

Did the probability of passing differ among the four examinations taken by statistics students?

Note: Examinations (A, B, C and D) are assessed on a pass/fail basis.

Example Null Hypothesis

H_0: There is no difference in the passing proportions of statistics students among four examinations, $P_1 = P_2 = P_3 = P_4$.

Alternatively, H_0: The mean differences between examinations equals 0, $P_1 = P_2 = P_3 = P_4$.

SPSS Procedure

SPSS > Analyze > Nonparametric Tests > [Legacy Dialogs] > K Related Samples > Cochran's Q

SPSS > Analyze > Nonparametric Tests > [Legacy Dialogs] > K Related Samples > Kendall's W

SPSS Output & Analysis

Descriptive Statistics (N, mean, standard deviation, minimum, maximum, P_{25}, P_{50}, P_{75}).

Frequencies.

Test Statistics.

Test Statistics

N	44
Cochran's Q	33.764[a]
df	3
Asymp. Sig.	.000

a. 1 is treated as a success.

The above SPSS output shows that Cochran's Q results are significant, $Q(3) = 33.76$, $p < .001$, and the null hypothesis that the mean differences between examinations equals 0 can be rejected. Data were coded as fail = 0 and pass = 1.

Test Statistics

N	44
Kendall's W[a]	.256
Chi-Square	33.764
df	3
Asymp. Sig.	.000

a. Kendall's Coefficient of Concordance

The above SPSS output is the result of requesting Kendall's *W*. Effect size, based on Kendall's *W*, is .26.

Test Statistics.

Test Statistics^a

	A & B	A & C	A & D	B & C	B & D	C & D
N	44	44	44	44	44	44
Exact Sig. (2-tailed)	.250^b	.002^b	.000^b	.016^b	.000^b	.031^b

a. McNemar Test

b. Binomial distribution used.

The above SPSS output displays the results of the McNemar test requested separately and used as a post hoc multiple comparison test. By applying the Bonferroni correction (see controlling Type I error in Section 1 (Introduction) of this chapter), the adjusted significance level becomes .05/4 = .0125. Pairwise comparisons A & B and C & D are not significant based on this significance level.

Mann-Whitney *U* Test

Purpose

The Mann-Whitney *U* test is a nonparametric procedure that determines if ranked scores in two independent groups differ.

This test is equivalent to the Kruskal-Wallis *H* test when two independent groups are compared. It is a useful nonparametric test when the assumptions of the independent *t*-test are not tenable.

Degrees of freedom. Degrees of freedom = $k - 1$, where $k =$ number of groups.

Effect size. An approximation of the *r* coefficient can be obtained using the value of *z*, as reported by SPSS, using the following formula

$$r = \frac{z}{\sqrt{N}}$$

where N = total number of cases.

Alternatively, the difference in mean ranks between groups can be used for effect size.

Parametric Equivalent

Independent t-test

Key Assumptions & Requirements

Random selection of samples (probability samples) to allow for generalization of results to a target population.

Variables. DV: one continuous variable measured on the ordinal, interval, or ratio scale. IV: one categorical variable with two categories; e.g., Group (Treatment, Control). The distributions of the DV for the two groups are the same (except for the medians).

Independence. Independent observations and independent samples.

Example Research Question

Are the ranks of computer knowledge pretest dispersed differently between male and female university students?

Example Null Hypothesis

H_0: There is no difference in how the ranks of computer knowledge pretest are dispersed between online and on campus university students.

SPSS Procedure

SPSS > Analyze > Nonparametric Tests > [Legacy Dialogs] > 2 Independent Samples > Mann-Whitney U Test

SPSS Output & Analysis

Descriptive Statistics (N, mean, standard deviation, minimum, maximum, P_{25}, P_{50}, P_{75}).

Ranks.

Ranks

	Student gender	N	Mean Rank	Sum of Ranks
Computer Knowledge Pretest	Male	24	52.50	1260.00
	Female	68	44.38	3018.00
	Total	92		

The above SPSS output displays the mean rank for each group. Male participants reported an average rank of 52.50 while females averaged 44.38.

Test Statistics.

- The Wilcoxon *W* test determines whether the median of one group is significantly different from the median of the second group.

- *Z* represents the normal approximation of the Mann-Whitney *U* statistic. It requires a large sample size and includes a correction for ties.

Test Statistics[a]

	Computer Knowledge Pretest
Mann–Whitney U	672.000
Wilcoxon W	3018.000
Z	–1.283
Asymp. Sig. (2–tailed)	.199

a. Grouping Variable: Student gender

The above SPSS output shows that, using the normal approximation, the results of the Mann-Whitney *U* test are not significant, $Z = -1.28$, $p = .20$. Therefore, there is insufficient evidence to reject the null hypothesis of no difference in how the ranks of computer knowledge pretest are dispersed between online and on campus university students. Alternatively, the results could be reported as $U = 672.00$, $p = .20$ (or $p > .05$).

Median Test

Purpose

The median test is a nonparametric procedure that compares the number of instances greater than or less than the grand median value between two or more independent groups when the DV is either ordinal or interval/ratio. It then performs a chi-square test. Some researchers apply the Yates-corrected chi-square statistic to the results of this test in order to adjust results to provide better control over Type I error.

Degrees of freedom. Degrees of freedom = $k - 1$, where $k =$ number of groups.

Post hoc multiple comparison tests. For pairwise post hoc comparisons, the Mann-Whitney U test or median test is appropriate following a significant omnibus median test.

Effect size. Grissom and Kim (2012) recommend the following effect size statistic

$$effect\_size = \frac{U}{n_a n_b}$$

where $U =$ the Mann-Whitney U statistic and where n_a and n_b are the two sample sizes.

Parametric Equivalent

Independent t-test

One-way between subjects *ANOVA*

Key Assumptions & Requirements

Random selection of samples (probability samples) to allow for generalization of results to a target population.

Variables. DV: one continuous variable measured on the ordinal, interval, or ratio scale. IV: one categorical variable with two or more categories. The distributions of the two groups have the same shape.

Independence. Independent observations. Independent samples.

Example Research Question

Is there a difference in median computer knowledge pretest between online and on campus university students, $md_1 \neq md_2$?

Example Null Hypothesis

H_0: There is no difference in median computer knowledge pretest between online and on campus university students, $md_1 = md_2$.

Alternatively, H_0: The distribution of computer knowledge is the same for online and on campus students.

SPSS Procedure

SPSS > Analyze > Nonparametric Tests > [Legacy Dialogs] > K-Independent Samples > Median Test

SPSS Output & Analysis

Descriptive Statistics (N, mean, standard deviation, minimum, maximum, P_{25}, P_{50}, P_{75}).

Frequencies.

- SPSS output displays frequencies for the DV > median and frequencies for the DV <= median for each group.

Frequencies

		Student gender	
		Male	Female
Computer Knowledge Pretest	> Median	13	30
	<= Median	11	38

Test Statistics.

Test Statistics[a]

		Computer Knowledge Pretest
N		92
Median		9.00
Chi-Square		.720
df		1
Asymp. Sig.		.396
Yates' Continuity Correction	Chi-Square	.373
	df	1
	Asymp. Sig.	.542

a. Grouping Variable: Student gender

The above SPSS output shows that the median test results, with continuity corrected chi-square, are not significant, $\chi^2(1, N = 92) = .37$, $p = .54$. Consequently, there is insufficient evidence to reject the null hypothesis of no difference in median computer knowledge between online and on campus university students. If the results were significant, the researcher should also calculate and report effect size.

Kruskal-Wallis *H* Test

Purpose

The Kruskal-Wallis *H* test is a nonparametric procedure that compares total ranks between multiple independent groups when the DV is either ordinal or interval/ratio scale. It is an extension of the Mann-Whitney *U* test for multiple groups.

Degrees of freedom. Degrees of freedom = $k - 1$, where $k =$ number of groups.

Post hoc multiple comparison tests. For pairwise post hoc comparisons, the Mann-Whitney *U* test is appropriate following a significant Kruskal-Wallis *H* test.

Effect size. Eta square calculated on ranked data is a suitable effect size statistic. The following formula, using the chi-square statistic reported in the Kruskal-Wallis *H* test output, can be used

$$\eta^2 = \frac{\chi^2}{N - 1}$$

Parametric Equivalent

One-way between-subjects *ANOVA*

Key Assumptions & Requirements

Random selection of samples (probability samples) to allow for generalization of results to a target population.

Variables. DV: one continuous variable measured on the ordinal, interval, or ratio scale. IV: one categorical variable with multiple categories. The group distributions have the same shape.

Independence. Independent observations. Independent samples.

Sample size. Adequate cell size.

Example Research Question

Is there a difference in the sum of ranks of computer knowledge pretest among four undergraduate computer literacy classes?

Example Null Hypothesis

H_0: There is no difference between the sum of ranks of computer knowledge pretest pretest among four undergraduate computer literacy classes.

SPSS Procedure

SPSS > Analyze > Nonparametric Tests > [Legacy Dialogs] > *K*-Independent Samples > Kruskal-Wallis *H*

SPSS Output & Analysis

Descriptive Statistics (*N*, mean, standard deviation, minimum, maximum, P_{25}, P_{50}, P_{75}).

Ranks.

Ranks

	Class	N	Mean Rank
Computer Knowledge Pretest	Class A	39	44.13
	Class B	19	42.68
	Class C	20	44.73
	Class D	14	60.82
	Total	92	

The above SPSS output displays sample size and mean ranks for each of four groups.

Test Statistics.

Test Statistics[a,b]

	Computer Knowledge Pretest
Chi-Square	4.833
df	3
Asymp. Sig.	.184

a. Kruskal Wallis Test

b. Grouping Variable: Class

The above SPSS output shows that the Kruskal-Wallis H test is not significant, $\chi^2(3, N = 92) = 4.83$, $p = .18$. Therefore, there is insufficient evidence to reject the null hypothesis of no difference in the sum of ranks of computer knowledge pretest among four undergraduate computer literacy classes. If the test were significant, post hoc multiple comparison tests using the Mann-Whitney U test are required to identify pairwise differences using the Bonferroni correction or the Holm's sequential Bonferroni correction (see controlling Type I errors in Section 1 (Introduction) of this chapter).

Friedman Test

Purpose

The Friedman test, also known as the Friedman one-way *ANOVA*, is a nonparametric procedure that compares average rank of groups between multiple sets of dependent data when the DV is either ordinal or interval/ratio. It is an extension of the Wilcoxon signed ranks test. The test uses the ranks of the data rather than their raw values to calculate the statistic.

The dependent data should be the result of either repeated observations of the same group or matching multiple groups as part of an experimental design.

Post hoc multiple comparison tests. For pairwise post hoc comparisons, the Wilcoxon signed-ranks test is appropriate following a significant Friedman test.

Effect size. Kendall's W (Kendall's coefficient of concordance) can be used as an effect size statistic. The coefficient ranges from 0 to 1, with stronger relationships indicated by higher values. (See SPSS procedure below.)

Parametric Equivalent

One-way within subjects *ANOVA*

Key Assumptions & Requirements

Random selection of samples (probability samples) to allow for generalization of results to a target population.

Variables. DV: one continuous variable that is ordinal, interval, or ratio scale. IV: one categorical variable with multiple dependent categories. The group distributions have the same shape. Use of dependent variables.

Example Research Question

Is there a difference in average computer anxiety rank among undergraduate students based on observation (end of year 1, end of year 2, end of year 3)?

Null Hypothesis

H_0: There is no difference in average computer anxiety rank among undergraduate students based on observation (end of year 1, end of year 2, end of year 3).

SPSS Procedure

SPSS > Analyze > Nonparametric Tests > [Legacy Dialogs] > *K* Related Samples > Friedman

SPSS > Analyze > Nonparametric Tests > [Legacy Dialogs] > *K* Related Samples > Kendall's *W*

SPSS Output & Analysis

Descriptive Statistics (*N*, mean, standard deviation, minimum, maximum, P_{25}, P_{50}, P_{75}).

Ranks.

Ranks

	Mean Rank
Computer Anxiety Pretest	2.50
Computer Anxiety Posttest	1.97
Computer Anxiety Delayed Test	1.53

SPSS output displays mean ranks for each observation.

Test Statistics.

Test Statistics[a]

N	75
Chi-Square	36.962
df	2
Asymp. Sig.	.000

a. Friedman Test

The above SPSS output shows that Friedman's test is significant, $\chi^2(2, N = 75) = 36.96$, $p < .001$. These results provide evidence that the null hypothesis of no difference in average computer anxiety rank among undergraduate students based on three observations can be rejected. Post hoc multiple comparison tests using the Wilcoxon signed ranks test are required to identify pairwise differences using the Bonferroni correction or the Holm's sequential Bonferroni correction (see controlling Type I errors in Section 1 (Introduction) of this chapter).

8.3: Parametric Tests

Levene's Test of Equality of Variances

Purpose

Levene's test of equality of variances is a parametric procedure that tests the null hypothesis that k groups have the same variance ($\sigma 2$) on an interval/ratio scale DV (Brown & Forsythe, 1974). If Levene's statistic is significant at the .05 level, the researcher rejects H_0 and concludes the groups have unequal variances.

Levene's test is typically used to evaluate the assumption of homogeneity of variances, which is a precondition for parametric tests, such as *t*-tests and *ANOVAs*.

Degrees of freedom. Degrees of freedom are $df_1 = t - 1$ and $df_2 = N - t$, where $t =$ number of groups.

Key Assumptions & Requirements

Random selection of samples (probability samples) to allow for generalization of results to a target population.

Variables. DV: one continuous variable on an interval or ratio scale. IV: categorical variable with multiple categories.

Independence. Independence of observations. Independent samples.

Normality. The test is fairly robust to violations of normality.

Example Research Question

Is there a difference in the classroom community variances of a sample consisting of two groups, $\sigma_1^2 \neq \sigma_2^2$?

Example Null Hypothesis

H_0: The classroom community variances of the two groups are homogeneous, $\sigma_1^2 = \sigma_2^2$.

SPSS Procedure

The Levene test is available in the "Explore" procedure by requesting spread-level plots; in the "Compare Means" procedure by requesting *t*-test for independent samples; in the "Compare Means" procedure by requesting one-way *ANOVA* and choosing homogeneity of variance test from the statistics options; and in the "General Linear Model" procedure by choosing homogeneity tests from the options.

SPSS Output & Analysis

Levene's Test.

	Levene's Test for Equality of Variances	
	F	Sig.
Classroom Community	.627	.430

The above SPSS output shows that Levene's test is not significant, $p > .05$, and, consequently, there is insufficient evidence to reject the null hypothesis that the classroom community variances of the two groups are homogeneous. In other words, the assumption of homogeneity of variances is tenable.

Independent *t*-Test

Purpose

The independent *t*-test, also known as student's *t*-test, is a parametric procedure that assesses whether the means of two independent groups are statistically different from each other. Independent means that each sample consists of a different set of cases and the composition of one sample is not influenced by the composition of the other sample (Diekhoff, 1992).

The *t*-statistic is computed as follows

$$t = \frac{\overline{X}_1 - \overline{X}_2}{S_{\overline{X}_1 - \overline{X}_2}}$$

where where x-bar$_1$ is the mean of the first group, x-bar$_2$ is the mean of the second group, and the denominator is the sampling error (the standard deviation of the difference score).

Degrees of freedom. The degrees of freedom for this test are $N_1 + N_2 - 2$.

Effect size. Cohen's *d* is a test that measures effect size and is used following a significant test. The formula for Cohen's *d* for the independent *t*-test is

$$d = t \sqrt{\frac{N_1 + N_2}{N_1 N_2}}$$

where *N* represents the size of each group. This formula expresses the distance between the means of the two groups in terms of the size of the standard deviation. For example, $d = .6$ would means that the two group means are 6/10th of a standard deviation apart. By convention, Cohen's *d* values of .2, .5, and .8 are considered small, medium, and large effect sizes, respectively.

Nonparametric Equivalent

Mann-Whitney *U* test

Median test

Key Assumptions & Requirements

Random selection of samples (probability samples) to allow for generalization of results to a target population.

Variables. DV: one continuous variable, interval/ratio scale. IV: one categorical IV with two categories; e.g., Group (Treatment, Control).

Independence. Independent observations. Independent data.

Normality. DV is normally distributed.

Outliers. Outliers can distort the mean difference and the *t*-statistic. They tend to inflate the variance and depress the value and corresponding statistical significance of the *t*-statistic.

Homogeneity of variance.

Sample size. When sample sizes are large (i.e., when both groups have > 25 participants each) and are approximately equal in size, this test is robust to violations of the assumptions of normality and homogeneity of variance (Diekhoff, 1992). Formal analysis and simulations offer the following guidelines describing the extent to which the assumptions of normality and equal population variances can be violated without affecting the validity of this test (Miller, 1986):

- If sample sizes are equal, non-normality is not a problem and the *t*-test can tolerate population standard deviation ratios of 2 without showing any major ill effect.

- Serious distortion of the *p*-value can occur when the skewness of the two populations differs.

Example Research Question

Is there a difference in mean computer knowledge pretest between online and on campus university students, $\mu_1 \neq \mu_2$?

Example Null Hypothesis

H_0: There is no difference in mean computer knowledge pretest between online and on campus university students, $\mu_1 = \mu_2$.

Alternatively, H_0: The distribution of computer knowledge pretest is the same for online and on campus students.

SPSS Procedure

SPSS > Analyze > Compare Means > Independent-Samples *T* Test

SPSS Output & Analysis

Group Statistics (category, *N*, mean, standard deviation, and standard error of the mean).

Independent Samples Test.

- If Levene's Test is not statistically significant (i.e., *p* > .05), the results of the *t*-test conducted with equal variances assumed (first row of SPSS output) is used.

- If Levene's test is significant, the results of the *t*-test conducted with equal variances not assumed (second row of SPSS output) is used.

Independent Samples Test

		Levene's Test for Equality of Variances		t-test for Equality of Means						
									95% Confidence Interval of the Difference	
		F	Sig.	t	df	Sig. (2-tailed)	Mean Difference	Std. Error Difference	Lower	Upper
Computer Knowledge Pretest	Equal variances assumed	1.131	.290	1.152	90	.253	1.613	1.400	−1.169	4.395
	Equal variances not assumed			1.220	45.166	.229	1.613	1.322	−1.049	4.274

The above SPSS output shows that equal variances can be assumed because Levene's test is not significant, $p = .29$. However, the independent *t*-test shows that the difference between groups is not significant, $t(90) = 1.15$, $p = .25$. If the results were significant, the researcher would also calculate and report effect size using Cohen's *d*.

Dependent *t*-Test

Purpose

The dependent *t*-test, also called a paired-samples *t*-test, is a parametric procedure that compares mean scores obtained from two dependent (related) samples. Dependent or related data are obtained by:

- Measuring participants from the same sample on two different occasions (i.e., using a repeated-measures or within-subjects design).

- Using a matching procedure by pairing research participants and dividing them so one member of the pair is assigned to each group.

For example, the DV is test scores and the IV is observation (pretest, posttest).

The *t*-statistic is computed as follows

$$t = \frac{\overline{X}_1 - \overline{X}_2}{\dfrac{s_{\overline{X}_1 - \overline{X}_2}}{\sqrt{N}}}$$

where where $\bar{x}_1$ is the mean of the first measurement, $\bar{x}_2$ is the mean of the second measurement, and the denominator is the standard deviation of the difference score, divided by the square root (N) of the sample size.

Degrees of freedom. The degrees of freedom for this test are $N-1$.

Effect size. Effect size can be determined by calculating Cohen's d. The formula for Cohen's d for a dependent t-test is

$$d = \frac{t}{\sqrt{N}}$$

where N represents the number of pairs in the analysis. By convention, d values of .2, .5, and ,8 are considered small, medium, and large effect sizes, respectively.

Nonparametric Equivalent

Wilcoxon signed ranks test

Related samples sign test

Key Assumptions & Requirements

Random selection of samples (probability samples) to allow for generalization of results to a target population.

Variables. Interval or ratio scale measurements.

Normality. The sampling distribution of the differences between scores is normally distributed. Use of dependent variables.

Example Research Question

Is there a difference between computer confidence pretest and computer confidence posttest among university students, $\mu_1 - \mu_2 \neq 0$?

Example Null Hypothesis

H_0: There is no difference between computer confidence pretest and computer confidence posttest among university students, $\mu_1 - \mu_2 = 0$.

SPSS Procedure

SPSS > Analyze > Compare Means > Paired Samples *T* Test

SPSS Output & Analysis

Paired Samples Statistics (mean, *N*, standard deviation, standard error of the mean).

Paired Samples Correlations.

Paired Samples Correlations

		N	Correlation	Sig.
Pair 1	Computer Confidence Pretest & Computer Confidence Posttest	86	.694	.000

The above SPSS output shows a significant relationship between the pretest and posttest, $r(86) = .69$, $p < .001$.

Paired Samples Test.

- SPSS subtracts posttest results from pretest results in order to determine difference. If the value of *t* is negative it is because the posttest scores are lower than the pretest scores. Otherwise, the sign of the *t*-statistic is not relevant.

- The standard error of the mean is the standard deviation of the sampling distribution of the mean. It is a measure of the stability of the sample means.

Paired Samples Test

		Paired Differences						
					95% Confidence Interval of the Difference				
		Mean	Std. Deviation	Std. Error Mean	Lower	Upper	t	df	Sig. (2–tailed)
Pair 1	Computer Confidence Pretest – Computer Confidence Posttest	-1.430	4.383	.473	-2.370	-.490	-3.026	85	.003

The above SPSS output shows a statistically significant difference between the pretest and posttest, $t(85) = -3.03$, $p = .003$. Effect size is small, Cohen's $d = .33$.

Between Subjects Analysis of Variance

Purpose

Between subjects analysis of variance (*ANOVA*) is a parametric procedure that assesses whether the means of multiple independent groups are statistically different from each other (Keppel, 2004). This analysis is appropriate whenever one wants to compare the means of three or more groups (the independent *t*-test is used to compare the means of two independent groups). Since both *t*-test and *ANOVA* are based on similar mathematical models, both tests produce identical *p*-values when two means are compared.

An *ANOVA* with one IV is a one-way *ANOVA*. A factorial *ANOVA* is used when there is more than one (more than one IV); e.g., a two-way *ANOVA* is a factorial *ANOVA* with two IVs. (See factorial designs in Section 1 (Introduction) of this chapter.) A two-way *ANOVA* analyzes one quantitative DV in terms of the levels (groups) formed by two IVs, one of which may be thought of as a control variable. A factorial *ANOVA* can show whether there is a significant main effect for each of the IVs and whether there are significant interactions between IVs. According to Keppel (2004), an interaction is present when the effects of one IV on behavior change at the different levels of the second IV.

An IV is either a fixed factor or random factor IV based on whether the levels of the IV are randomly selected from all the possible levels of the IV (random factor) or represent all the levels (fixed factor). Most *ANOVA* designs are fixed effect models with data collected on all levels of the IVs.

When a DV is measured for independent groups where each group is exposed to a different intervention, the set of interventions or conditions is called a between-subjects factor (IV). The groups correspond to interventions that are categories or levels of this IV.

The total variation consists of the sum of squares (*SS*) of the differences of each mean with the grand mean. SPSS uses four methods to calculate *SS*. These methods are labeled Type I, Type II, Type III, and Type IV. One can request any of the four types of *SS* to be used in the analysis by selecting the appropriate method in the *SS* drop down menu. Type III is the default and is the most commonly used option for balanced or unbalanced models with no missing cells. When missing cells are present, the Type IV *SS* method should be used.

The key test in all *ANOVA*s is the *F*-test of the difference of group means, testing if the means of the groups formed by values of the IV are different enough not to have occurred by chance.

$$F = \frac{MS_b}{MS_w}$$

where MS_b is the between groups mean square and MS_w is the within groups mean square (mean square equals the *SS* divided by degrees of freedom).

If the computed *F*-statistic is approximately 1.0, differences in group means are only random variations. If the computed *F*-statistic is greater than 1, then there is more variation between groups than within groups, from which one infers that the grouping variable (IV) does make a difference. If the *F*-statistic is enough above 1, it will be found to be significant and the null hypothesis that the population means between groups are equal can be rejected.

Degrees of freedom. Two degrees of freedom parameters are associated with *ANOVA*: *dfn* (between group variation) = $a - 1$ and *dfd* (within group variation) = $N - a$, where a is the number of groups and N is the total number of participants in all groups.

Effect size. SPSS provides effect sizes for all main effects and interaction effects, if requested as an option. Eta square (η^2)

and partial eta square (η_p^2) are used to measure *ANOVA* effect size. Partial eta-square is the percent of total variance in the DV accounted for by the variance between categories formed by the IV(s). The coefficient is "partial" because it reflects effect size after controlling for other variables in the model. A common rule of thumb is that eta square and partial eta square values of .01, .06, and .14 represent small, medium, and large effect sizes.

Nonparametric Equivalent

Kruskal-Wallis *H* test (one-way)

Median test (one-way)

Key Assumptions & Requirements

Random selection of samples (probability samples) to allow for generalization of results to a target population.

Variables. DV: one continuous variable, interval/ratio scale. IV: one or more categorical variables with multiple categories; e.g., Group (Treatment A, Treatment B, Control).

Independence. Independent observations. Independent data.

Multivariate normality. The DV is normally distributed in each subpopulation or cell.

Homogeneity of variance. Two-way *ANOVA* is less sensitive than one-way *ANOVA* to moderate violations of the assumption of homogeneity of variances across the groups.

Sample size. When sample sizes are relatively large and approximately equal in size, this test is fairly robust to violations of the assumptions of normality and homogeneity of variance provided distributions are symmetric (Diekhoff, 1992). This means that although power is decreased, the probability of a Type I error is as low or lower than it would be if its assumptions were met. There are exceptions to this rule. For example, a combination of unequal sample sizes and a violation of the assumption of homogeneity of variance can lead to an inflated Type I error rate.

Example Research Question

Is there a difference in sense of classroom community between graduate students based on gender (male, female) and age (18-20, 21-30, 31-40, 41-50, over 50)?

Note: this research question implies a two-way 2 x 5 factorial *ANOVA* because it involves two IVs (one with 2 levels and the other with 5 levels).

Example Null Hypothesis

H_{01}: There no difference in sense of classroom community between graduate students based on gender (male, female).

H_{02}: There no difference in sense of classroom community between graduate students based on age (18-20, 21-30, 31-40, 41-50, over 50).

H_{03}: The difference in sense of classroom community between students based on gender remains constant regardless of age.

SPSS Procedure

SPSS > Analyze > General Linear Model > Univariate

SPSS > Analyze > Compare Means > One-Way *ANOVA*

SPSS Output & Analysis

SPSS output varies based on options selected by the user.

Between-Subjects Factors (value label, *N*).

Descriptive Statistics (categories, *N*, mean, standard deviation, standard error, 95% confidence interval, minimum, maximum).

Levene's Test of Equality of Error Variances.

- Levene's test is run by choosing homogeneity tests from the options menu in the "Univariate" SPSS dialog box or homogeneity of variance test in the "One-Way *ANOVA*" SPSS dialog box. It tests the null hypothesis that the error variance of the DV is equal across groups. A significant Levene's test is evidence that the assumption of homogeneity of variance has been violated.

Levene's Test of Equality of Error Variances[a]

Dependent Variable: Classroom Community

F	df1	df2	Sig.
.824	9	158	.595

Tests the null hypothesis that the error variance of the dependent variable is equal across groups.

a. Design: Intercept + gender + age + gender * age

The above SPSS output shows Levene's test is not significant, $F(9,158) = .82$, $p = .60$. Therefore, the *ANOVA* assumption of homogeneity of variance is tenable.

Tests of Between-Subjects Effects.

- The "Corrected Model" is the overall model. It includes the variance due to all main and interaction effects.

- The "Intercept" term provides a test of whether the grand mean is different from zero.

- Each main effect is listed. Each main effects row represents between-group variance. If the effect is significant, post hoc analysis is required to determine pairwise differences if there are three or more groups.

- Each interaction effect is listed (interaction effects only apply if there are two or more IVs). If any interaction is significant, one can conclude that any observed differences among groups on one factor depend on differences in the levels of the other factor(s).

- The "Error" term represents the within-group variance.

- The "Type III Sums of Squares" for the total effect includes the sums of squares for the intercept, the main effects, the interaction, and the error term.

- "Partial Eta Squared" is an effect size measure that shows the proportion of the variance in the DV that is attributable to the identified source.

Tests of Between-Subjects Effects

Dependent Variable: Classroom Community

Source	Type III Sum of Squares	df	Mean Square	F	Sig.	Partial Eta Squared
Corrected Model	1431.691[a]	9	159.1	4.976	.000	.221
Intercept	54691.919	1	54692	1711	.000	.915
gender	8.247	1	8.247	.258	.612	.002
age	827.787	4	206.9	6.473	.000	.141
gender * age	65.846	4	16.46	.515	.725	.013
Error	5051.161	158	31.97			
Total	146671.000	168				
Corrected Total	6482.851	167				

a. R Squared = .221 (Adjusted R Squared = .176)

The above SPSS output shows the overall *ANOVA* test was significant, $F(9,158) = 4.98$, $p < .001$, $\eta_p^2 = .22$. The age main effect was significant, $F(4,158) = 6.47$, $p < .001$, $\eta_p^2 = .14$. Consequently, there is sufficient evidence to reject the null hypothesis of no difference in sense of classroom community between graduate students based on age. However, the gender main effect, $F(1,158) = .26$, $p = .61$, $\eta_p^2 = .002$, and the interaction effect, $F(4,158) = .52$, $p = .73$, $\eta_p^2 = .01$, were not significant.

The corrected model, with 9 degrees of freedom, is the overall model. It includes the variance due to the two main effects (1 + 4) and the interaction effect (4), hence the 9 degrees of freedom. The effect size, as measured by partial eta-squared, shows that 14% of the total variability can be attributed to the age main effect.

Parameter Estimates (parameter, *B*, standard error, *t*, significance level, 95% confidence interval, partial eta square, noncentrality parameter, observed power).

- If the null hypothesis is not true, then the *F*-statistic has a noncentral sampling distribution and an associated noncentrality parameter. Noncentrality parameters are used in power and sample size calculations and reflect the extent to which the null hypothesis is false.

- Observed power is the probability of correctly rejecting the null hypothesis.

Lack of Fit Tests (source, sum of squares, degrees of freedom, mean square, *F*, significance level, partial eta square, noncentrality parameter, observed power).

- Lack of fit tests are used to select the best model.

Multiple Comparisons.

- The multiple comparisons table provides the post hoc pairwise multiple comparison tests requested by the researcher.

- SPSS flags (*) mean differences that are significant.

- The 95% confidence interval provides confidence intervals centered on mean differences.

Multiple Comparisons

Dependent Variable: Classroom Community

Tukey HSD

(I) Age	(J) Age	Mean Difference (I-J)	Std. Error	Sig.	95% Confidence Interval Lower Bound	Upper Bound
18-20	21-30	-2.56	1.348	.322	-6.28	1.16
	31-40	-5.91*	1.395	.000	-9.76	-2.06
	41-50	-8.33*	1.736	.000	-13	-3.54
	Over 50	-10.62*	2.429	.000	-17	-3.92
21-30	18-20	2.56	1.348	.322	-1.16	6.28
	31-40	-3.35*	1.048	.014	-6.24	-.46
	41-50	-5.77*	1.472	.001	-9.83	-1.71
	Over 50	-8.06*	2.248	.004	-14	-1.86
31-40	18-20	5.91*	1.395	.000	2.06	9.76
	21-30	3.35*	1.048	.014	.46	6.24
	41-50	-2.42	1.516	.500	-6.61	1.76
	Over 50	-4.71	2.276	.239	-11	1.57
41-50	18-20	8.33*	1.736	.000	3.54	13.12
	21-30	5.77*	1.472	.001	1.71	9.83
	31-40	2.42	1.516	.500	-1.76	6.61
	Over 50	-2.29	2.500	.891	-9.18	4.61
Over 50	18-20	10.62*	2.429	.000	3.92	17.32
	21-30	8.06*	2.248	.004	1.86	14.26
	31-40	4.71	2.276	.239	-1.57	10.99
	41-50	2.29	2.500	.891	-4.61	9.18

Based on observed means.
The error term is Mean Square(Error) = 31.969.

*. The mean difference is significant at the .05 level.

The above SPSS output of post hoc tests shows significant pairwise differences exist between the groups highlighted with an asterisk (*) in the "Mean Difference (I–J)" column.

Homogeneous Subsets.

- Provides groupings for the means that are not significantly different from each other.

Classroom Community

Tukey HSD[a,b,c]

Age	N	Subset 1	Subset 2	Subset 3
18–20	24	24.67		
21–30	66	27.23	27.23	
31–40	52		30.58	30.58
41–50	19			33.00
Over 50	7			35.29
Sig.		.645	.379	.090

Means for groups in homogeneous subsets are displayed.
Based on observed means.
The error term is Mean Square(Error) = 31.969.

a. Uses Harmonic Mean Sample Size = 18.414.

b. The group sizes are unequal. The harmonic mean of the group sizes is used. Type I error levels are not guaranteed.

c. Alpha =

The above SPSS output summarizes the major differences among the means. It organizes the means of the five groups into homogeneous subsets. Subsets of means that do not differ from each other at $p < .05$ are grouped, and subsets that do differ go into separate columns. Groups that do not show up in the same column are significantly different from each other at $p < .05$.

Spread-Versus-Level Plots.

- For each DV, the spread-versus-level plots show observed cell means (level) versus standard deviations (spread), observed cell means (level) versus variance (spread), and a observed versus predicted versus standard residual plot.

Within Subjects Analysis of Variance

Purpose

Within subjects analysis of variance (*ANOVA*) also known as a repeated measures *ANOVA*, is a parametric procedure that assesses whether the means of multiple dependent groups are statistically different from each other. It differs from a between subjects *ANOVA* in that one or more of the IVs are within-subject variables.

Sphericity is an assumption of this test. Sphericity is tenable when the variance of the difference between the estimated means for any pair of groups is the same as for any other pair. SPSS automatically does a sphericity test for designs with within subjects factors with three or more categories. If the significance of the sphericity test is less than .05 the researcher rejects the null hypothesis that the data are spherical, thereby violating the sphericity assumption, and the researcher must correct for sphericity. The Mauchly test for sphericity is automatically included in all output for repeated measures designs. To correct the univariate *F*-test results to compensate for departures from sphericity, the researcher uses the Huynh-Feldt or Greenhouse-Geisser epsilon (ε) adjustment. To correct *F* given a finding of lack of sphericity, SPSS multiplies the between-groups degrees of freedom by the value of ε.

Like between subjects *ANOVAs*, within subjects *ANOVAs* can also have factorial designs if there are multiple IVs. (See factorial designs in Section 1 (Introduction) of this chapter.) Mixed design is a term that refers to *ANOVAs* that include both within subjects and between subjects factors. In mixed designs, sphericity is frequently violated and therefore epsilon adjustments to degrees of freedom are routine prior to computing *F*-test significance levels.

Polynomial contrasts are appropriate following a significant within-subjects *ANOVA* (post hoc multiple comparison tests are appropriate for any significant between subjects factor in a mixed design). (See contrasts in Section 1 (Introduction) of this chapter.)

Degrees of freedom. Two degrees of freedom parameters are associated with within-subjects *ANOVA*. The degrees of freedom for between-groups is $k - 1$, where $k =$ the number of groups. The degrees of freedom for within-groups is $k(n - 1)$, where n is the number of cases in each group.

Effect size. Two effect size statistics are typically used with *ANOVA*: eta square (η^2) and partial eta square (η_p^2). A common rule of thumb is that eta square and partial eta square values of . 01, .06, and .14 represent small, medium, and large effect sizes.

Nonparametric Equivalent

Friedman test (one-way)

Wilcoxon signed ranks test (one-way)

Related samples sign test (one-way)

Cochran's *Q* test (one-way)

Key Assumptions & Requirements

Random selection of samples (probability samples) to allow for generalization of results to a target population.

Variables. DV: one continuous variable, interval/ratio scale. IV: one or more categorical variables with multiple categories; e.g., Group (Treatment A, Treatment B, Control). At least one IV must be a within-subjects variable. Use of dependent variables.

Multivariate normality. The DV is normally distributed in each subpopulation or cell.

Independence. Independent observations.

Homogeneity of variance. Groups have equal or similar variances.

Sphericity. The variance of the difference between all pairs of means is constant across all combinations of related groups.

Example Research Question

Is there a difference in mean computer confidence over time (observation 1, observation 2, and observation 3, $\mu_1 \neq \mu_2 \neq \mu_3$?

Note: This is an example of a one-way within subjects *ANOVA*. The research hypothesis is that at least two of the means are different from each other.

Example Null Hypothesis

H_0: There no difference in mean computer confidence over time (observation 1, observation 2, and observation 3), $\mu_1 = \mu_2 = \mu_3$.

Note: *ANOVAs* may have more than one factor; e.g., two-way *ANOVA*, three-way *ANOVA*, etc. There would be three null hypotheses for a two-way *ANOVA*, seven null hypotheses for a three-way *ANOVA*, etc.

SPSS Procedure

SPSS > Analyze > General Linear Model > Repeated Measures

SPSS Output & Analysis

SPSS output varies based on options selected by the user.

Within-Subjects Factors.

Descriptive Statistics (mean, standard deviation, *N*).

Bartlett's Test of Sphericity (likelihood ratio, approximate chi-square, degrees of freedom, significance level).

- This output addresses the null hypothesis that the residual covariance matrix is proportional to an identity matrix.

Multivariate Tests.

- See multivariate tests in Section 1 (Introduction) of this chapter for a description of each test.

Multivariate Tests[a]

Effect		Value	F	Hypothesis df	Error df	Sig.
obs	Pillai's Trace	.224	10.524[b]	2.000	73.000	.000
	Wilks' Lambda	.776	10.524[b]	2.000	73.000	.000
	Hotelling's Trace	.288	10.524[b]	2.000	73.000	.000
	Roy's Largest Root	.288	10.524[b]	2.000	73.000	.000

a. Design: Intercept
   Within Subjects Design: obs

b. Exact statistic

The above SPSS output shows that the value for Wilks' lambda is .776, with $p < .001$. Assuming an *à priori* significance level of .05, one can conclude that there is a statistically significant effect for main effect observation (obs).

Mauchly's Test of Sphericity.

- Mauchly's test of sphericity tests the null hypothesis that the error covariance matrix of the orthonormalized transformed DVs is proportional to an identity matrix. The null hypothesis is that there is no assumption violation. When this test is not significant, the researcher concludes that sphericity has not been violated and no correction is necessary.

- The sphericity assumption cannot be violated if the within-subjects factor has only two levels because there is only a single covariance between the two measures, so testing for sphericity in this situation is inappropriate.

Mauchly's Test of Sphericity[a]

Measure: MEASURE_1

Within Subjects Effect	Mauchly's W	Approx. Chi-Square	df	Sig.	Epsilon[b]		
					Greenhouse-Geisser	Huynh-Feldt	Lower-bound
Obs	.697	26.399	2	.000	.767	.780	.500

Tests the null hypothesis that the error covariance matrix of the orthonormalized transformed dependent variables is proportional to an identity matrix.

a. Design: Intercept
   Within Subjects Design: Obs

b. May be used to adjust the degrees of freedom for the averaged tests of significance. Corrected tests are displayed in the Tests of Within-Subjects Effects table.

The above SPSS output shows that Mauchly's test is significant and the assumption of sphericity has been violated, $\chi^2(2) = 26.40$, $p < .001$. Therefore, degrees of freedom should be corrected based on the value of epsilon (ε). If $\varepsilon > 0.75$, use the Huynh-Feldt correction; if $\varepsilon < 0.75$, use the Greenhouse-Geisser correction.

Tests of Within Subjects Effects.

Tests of Within-Subjects Effects

Measure: MEASURE_1

Source		Type III Sum of Squares	df	Mean Square	F	Sig.	Partial Eta Squared
Obs	Sphericity Assumed	186.107	2	93.053	11.113	.000	.131
	Greenhouse-Geisser	186.107	1.534	121.291	11.113	.000	.131
	Huynh-Feldt	186.107	1.560	119.265	11.113	.000	.131
	Lower-bound	186.107	1.000	186.107	11.113	.001	.131
Error (Obs)	Sphericity Assumed	1239.227	148	8.373			
	Greenhouse-Geisser	1239.227	113.544	10.914			
	Huynh-Feldt	1239.227	115.473	10.732			
	Lower-bound	1239.227	74.000	16.746			

The above SPSS output shows a significant within-subjects effect for observation. Consequently, the test provides evidence that the null hypothesis of no difference in mean computer confidence over time can be rejected, $F(1.56,115.47) = 11.11$, $p < .001$, $\eta_p^2 = .13$. In the above case, the Hunyh-Feldt correction was used because $\varepsilon > 0.75$ (see sphericity in Section 2 (Evaluating Test Assumptions) of Chapter 6 (Inferential Statistics)).

Tests of Within Subjects Contrasts.

Tests of Within-Subjects Contrasts

Measure: MEASURE_1

Source	obs	Type III Sum of Squares	df	Mean Square	F	Sig.
obs	Linear	185.927	1	185.927	17.037	.000
	Quadratic	.180	1	.180	.031	.861
Error(obs)	Linear	807.573	74	10.913		
	Quadratic	431.653	74	5.833		

The above SPSS output provides the results of polynomial contrasts for the within-subjects conditions. The linear trend is significant, but the quadratic trend is not. The linear *SS* is 185.927, which accounts for $185.927/(185.927 + .180) = 99.90\%$ of variability between the two trends. Consequently, the relationship among the three observations is considered mostly linear.

Tests of Between Subjects Effects (source, type III sum of squares, degrees of freedom, mean square, *F*, significance level, partial eta square, noncentrality parameter, observed power).

- If the null hypothesis is not true, then the *F*-statistic has a noncentral sampling distribution and an associated noncentrality parameter.

- Noncentrality parameters are used in power and sample size calculations and reflect the extent to which the null hypothesis is false.

Tests of Between-Subjects Effects

Measure: MEASURE_1
Transformed Variable: Average

Source	Type III Sum of Squares	df	Mean Square	F	Sig.	Partial Eta Squared	Noncent. Parameter	Observed Power[a]
Intercept	236196.000	1	236196.000	3888.721	.000	.981	3888.721	1.000
Error	4494.667	74	60.739					

a. Computed using alpha =

The above SPSS output displays the tests of between subjects factors. Since there are no such factors in the present model, this table can be ignored.

Parameter Estimates (DV, parameter, *B*, standard error, *t*, significance level, 95% confidence interval, partial eta square, noncentrality parameter, observed power).

Estimated Marginal Means (category, mean, standard error, 95% confidence interval).

- Provides confidence intervals centered on each category's mean separately.

Observed*Predicted*Standardized Residual Plots.

Profile Plot.

- The profile plot displays the main effects in a line chart. SPSS calls the within subjects variable "MEASURE_1" in the plot.

- No noticeable bends in the plot suggest a linear effect. One noticeable bend suggests a quadratic effect and two noticeable bends suggest a cubic effect.

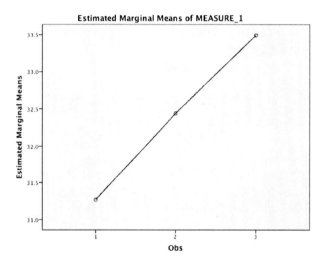

The above profile plot clearly displays the linear relationship of the within-subjects conditions as indicated by the polynomial contrasts.

Multivariate Analysis of Variance

Purpose

Multivariate analysis of variance (*MANOVA*) is a parametric procedure used to determine if multiple DVs are changed by manipulation of the IV(s). *MANOVA* is an extension of *ANOVA* in which main effects and interactions are assessed on a combination of DVs. *MANOVA* uses one or more categorical IVs as factors, like *ANOVA*, but unlike *ANOVA*, there are multiple DVs. (See factorial designs in Section 1 (Introduction) of this chapter.)

MANOVA is preferred over multiple *ANOVAs* (one for each DV) in order to:

- Control experiment-wise Type I error.

- Test the pattern of DVs (individual *ANOVAs* may not be significant, but the combination might be significant).

- Take into account intercorrelations among the DVs.

According to Tabachnick and Fidell (2007), *MANOVA* is best used when DVs are moderately correlated ($r = .4$ to $.7$; positive or negative correlation). *MANOVA* is not the best test if DVs are very highly correlated or not correlated.

Where *ANOVA* tests the differences in means of the quantitative DV for various levels of the IV(s), *MANOVA* tests the differences in the centroid (i.e., mean vector) of the multiple quantitative dependents, for various levels of the independent(s).

Reasons for conducting multivarate analyses (Fish, 1988):

- Multivariate statistics can be useful in controlling experimentwise Type I error rates.

- Multivariate methods often best honor the reality about which the researcher is trying to generalize.

MANOVA is the mathematical reversal of discriminant analysis:

- *MANOVA* asks, "Does being a member of this group influence scores on the DVs?"

- Discriminant analysis asks, "Can I predict group membership on the basis of a series of continuous predictors?"

The omnibus or overall *F*-test is the first of the two-step *MANOVA* process of analysis. It tests the null hypothesis that there is no difference in the pattern of DVs for the different groups formed by levels of the IVs.

Tests of group differences are the second step in *MANOVA*. If the overall F-test shows the centroid (vector) of means of the DVs is not the same for all the groups formed by the levels of the IVs, post hoc univariate *ANOVA*s and multiple comparison tests of group differences are used to explore the nature of the differences.

The power of a *MANOVA* decreases with an increase in the number of DVs.

Effect size. SPSS provides effect sizes for all main effects and interaction effects, if requested as an option. Eta square (η^2) and partial eta square (η_p^2) are used to measure *MANOVA* effect size.

Key Assumptions & Requirements

Random selection of samples (probability samples) to allow for generalization of results to a target population.

Variables. DV: continuous variables, interval/ratio scale. IV: one or more categorical variables with multiple categories; e.g., Group (Treatment A, Treatment B, Control).

Measurement without error.

Multivariate normality. The DV is normally distributed in each subpopulation or cell.

Outliers. MANOVA is sensitive to the presence of outliers. Outliers can produce either Type I or Type II errors.

Independence. Independent observations.

Linearity. There should be linear relationships between all pairs of DVs.

Multicollinearity. Multicollinearity between DVs indicates the presence of redundant DVs, which decreases statistical efficiency.

Homogeneity of variance-covariance matrices. If sample sizes are equal, the robustness of *MANOVA* is expected and the results of Box's *M* test can be disregarded (Tabachnick & Fidell, 2007). However, if sample sizes are unequal and Box's *M* test is significant at $p < .001$, then robustness is not guaranteed.

Sphericity (an assumption only if a within subjects factor is included in the model). The variance of the difference between all pairs of means is constant across all combinations of related groups.

Homogeneity of regressions (an assumption only if a covariate is included in the model). Assumes the interaction of the IV(s) by covariates(s) is not significant. Slopes relating each covariate to the DV are equal across all levels if a IV. In other words, for each level of the IV, the slope of the prediction of the DV from the covariate must be equal.

Sample size. Each cell size should include more participants than the number of DVs.

Example Research Question

Is there a difference in classroom social community and classroom learning community between graduate students based on ethnicity (white, other), $\mu_1 \neq \mu_2$?

Note: This is an example of a one-way *MANOVA*.

Example Null Hypothesis

H_0: There no difference in classroom social community and classroom learning community between graduate students based on ethnicity (white, other), $\mu_1 = \mu_2$.

SPSS Procedure

SPSS > Analyze > General Linear Model > Multivariate

SPSS Output & Analysis

SPSS output varies based on options selected by the user.

Between Subjects Factors.

Descriptive Statistics.

Descriptive Statistics

	Ethnicity	Mean	Std. Deviation	N
Classroom Social Community	Other	12.54	3.910	63
	White	15.18	3.567	106
	Total	14.20	3.902	169
Classroom Learning Community	Other	14.25	3.676	63
	White	14.88	3.829	106
	Total	14.64	3.774	169

Ideally, cell sizes should be approximately equal, although not a requirement. Cell sizes with ratios greater 1:1.5 can be problematic, as indicated in the above SPSS output for the "Other" category, which has a ratio of 1:1.68.

Box's Test of Equality of Covariance Matrices.

- Box's *M* test tests the multivariate homogeneity of variances and covariances assumption. When the test is not significant, the researcher assumes equality of covariance matrices and uses the Wilks' lambda measure.

- This is a very conservative (i.e., sensitive) test. A threshold of .01 or .001 is frequently used for identifying violations of this assumption.

Box's Test of Equality of Covariance Matrices[a]

Box's M	8.513
F	2.797
df1	3
df2	603316.070
Sig.	.039

Tests the null hypothesis that the observed covariance matrices of the dependent variables are equal across groups.

a. Design: Intercept + ethnicity

The above SPSS output shows that Box's M test is not significant at the .01 level, $F(3,603316.07) = 2.80$, $p = .04$. Although cell sizes are not equal (i.e., the design is not balanced), there is insufficient evidence to conclude that the assumption of homogeneity of variance-covariance matrices is not tenable.

Multivariate Tests.

- The "Multivariate Tests" table reports the results of the tests for each effect. See multivariate tests in Section 1 (Introduction) of this chapter for a description of each test. If tests are significant, post hoc tests are required.

- The intercept term is a test of whether the grand mean is different from zero.

Multivariate Tests[a]

Effect		Value	F	Hypothesis df	Error df	Sig.
Intercept	Pillai's Trace	.954	1731.186[b]	2.000	166.000	.000
	Wilks' Lambda	.046	1731.186[b]	2.000	166.000	.000
	Hotelling's Trace	20.858	1731.186[b]	2.000	166.000	.000
	Roy's Largest Root	20.858	1731.186[b]	2.000	166.000	.000
ethnicity	Pillai's Trace	.108	10.084[b]	2.000	166.000	.000
	Wilks' Lambda	.892	10.084[b]	2.000	166.000	.000
	Hotelling's Trace	.121	10.084[b]	2.000	166.000	.000
	Roy's Largest Root	.121	10.084[b]	2.000	166.000	.000

a. Design: Intercept + ethnicity

b. Exact statistic

The above SPSS output shows the effect of ethnicity (white, other) on classroom social community and classroom learning community is significant, $F(2,166) = 10.08$, $p < .001$. These results mean that there is a significant ethnicity effect on the pattern of classroom social community and classroom learning community grouped together. There are no interaction effects because there is only one IV.

Levene's Test of Equality of Error Variances.

- Levene's test is applicable to the tests of between subjects effects, since homogeneity of variances is a univariate *ANOVA* assumption.

- Levene's test is run by choosing homogeneity tests from the options menu in the "Multivariate" SPSS dialog box. It tests the null hypothesis that the error variance of the DV is equal across groups. A significant Levene's test is evidence that the assumption of homogeneity of variance has been violated.

Tests of Between-Subjects Effects.

- This table provides the results of the univariate *ANOVA* tests for each DV.

- "Type III Sum of Squares" (*SS*) is the sum of the squared deviations from the mean. "Mean Square" (*MS*) is *SS* divided by degrees of freedom.

Tests of Between–Subjects Effects

Source	Dependent Variable	Type III Sum of Squares	df	Mean Square	F	Sig.
Corrected Model	Classroom Social Community	275.311[a]	1	275.311	20.137	.000
	Classroom Learning Community	15.356[b]	1	15.356	1.079	.300
Intercept	Classroom Social Community	30360.755	1	30360.755	2220.631	.000
	Classroom Learning Community	33533.605	1	33533.605	2355.619	.000
ethnicity	Classroom Social Community	275.311	1	275.311	20.137	.000
	Classroom Learning Community	15.356	1	15.356	1.079	.300
Error	Classroom Social Community	2283.245	167	13.672		
	Classroom Learning Community	2377.342	167	14.236		
Total	Classroom Social Community	36613.000	169			
	Classroom Learning Community	38639.000	169			
Corrected Total	Classroom Social Community	2558.556	168			
	Classroom Learning Community	2392.698	168			

a. R Squared = .108 (Adjusted R Squared = .102)

b. R Squared = .006 (Adjusted R Squared = .000)

The above SPSS output shows that differences in classroom social community by ethnicity are significant, $F(1,167) = 20.14$, $p < .001$, while differences in classroom learning community by race are not, $F(1,167) = 1.08$, $p = .30$. The results presented in this table are the results of separate *ANOVAs*, one for each DV. Since the IV consists of only two levels (white, other), post hoc multiple comparison tests are not required.

Parameter Estimates (parameter, *B*, standard error, t, significance level, 95% confidence interval).

Post Hoc Tests and Contrasts.

- Post hoc tests and contrasts are used to identify significant pairwise differences following a significant *MANOVA*. The researcher should also conduct univariate *ANOVAs* for each main effect.

- SPSS flags (*) differences that are significant.

- See post hoc multiple comparison tests and contrasts in Section 1 (Introduction) of this chapter.

Homogeneous Subsets.

- Provides groupings for the means that are not significantly different from each other.

Plots.

- Spread-versus-level plots depict standard deviations vs. means, or variances vs. means, for each DV. This is useful in testing the homogeneity of variances assumption, and in identifying cells that deviate substantially from the assumption.

- Observed*Predicted*Standardized residual plots display for each DV, a plot that shows the comparisons among observed, predicted, and standardized residuals. For observed by predicted plots, one would like to see a clear pattern, but for the plots involving standardized residuals, one would like to not to see a pattern.

- A plot of standardized residual values against values expected by the *MANOVA* model tests the assumption of *MANOVA* that residuals are randomly distributed. If there are any observable systematic patterns, the model is questionable even if significant.

- Profile plots are line plots of the predicted means of each DV across levels of each factor. When two or three factors are involved, these are called interaction plots.

Analysis of Covariance

Purpose

Analysis of covariance (*ANCOVA*) is a parametric procedure that assesses whether the means of multiple groups are statistically different from each other after controlling for the effects of one or more control variables (potentially confounding variables). This procedure is similar to *ANOVA* with the exception of the inclusion of additional IVs (known as covariates) into the model.

A covariate is a continuous variable that is included in the analysis to adjust for relevant differences in study participants that exist at the start of the study. Covariates must not be selected arbitrarily, but rather selected based on theoretical considerations. Moreover, covariates should correlate significantly with the DV.

ANCOVA is especially useful in analyzing the results of pretest-posttest control group designs where the pretest measure(s) are the covariates and the posttest measure(s) are the DV(s). In this situation, the covariate(s) are used to control pre-existing differences between groups by statistically equating the groups on the pretest. This procedure may also be useful when random assignment to groups is not possible and the researcher needs to equate groups on attributes important to the research. However, selection of covariates in this situation can become a contentious issue (Stevens, 2002).

ANCOVA may employ a between subjects design, a within subjects design, or a mixed methods design based on the presence or absence of between subjects and within subjects factors. (See factorial designs in Section 1 (Introduction) of this chapter.) It incorporates regression analysis using the covariate(s) to predict the DV, then completes an *ANOVA* on the residuals (the predicted minus the actual DV) to see if the factors are still significantly related to the DV after the variation due to the covariates has been removed.

Multiple analysis of covariance (*MANCOVA*) is a *MANOVA* with one or more covariates present.

Degrees of freedom. Two degrees of freedom parameters are associated with *ANCOVA*: *dfn* and *dfd* (between group variation): $dfn = a - 1$, dfd (within group variation) $= N - a$, where *a* is the number of groups and *N* is the total number of participants in all groups.

Effect size. Two effect size statistics are typically used with *ANCOVA*: eta square (η^2) and partial eta square (η_p^2).

Key Assumptions & Requirements

Random selection of samples (probability samples) to allow for generalization of results to a target population.

Variables. DV: one continuous variable, interval/ratio scale. IV: one or more categorical variables. Limited number of continuous, interval/ratio scale covariates; significant correlation with the DV and low correlation with other covariates, if any.

Linear relationship of covariate(s) with the DV. Covariates measured before the intervention is conducted.

Measurement without error. The covariate(s) should be measured with high reliability.

Multivariate normality. The DV is normally distributed in each subpopulation or cell.

Independence. Independence of observations. Independent data.

Linearity. There should be linear relationships between each covariate and DV as well as between all covariates. Additionally, there should be linear relationships between all pairs of DVs if *MANCOVA* is conducted.

Homogeneity of regressions. Assumes the interaction of the IV(s) by covariates(s) is not significant. Slopes relating each covariate to the DV are equal across all levels of an IV. In other words, for each level of the IV, the slope of the prediction of the DV from the covariate is equal.

Multicollinearity (an assumption only if multiple DVs are included in the model and *MANCOVA* is conducted). Multicollinearity between DVs indicates the presence of redundant DVs, which decreases statistical efficiency.

Homogeneity of variance (an assumption only if a between subjects factor is included in the model). Groups have equal or similar variances.

Homogeneity of variance-covariance matrices (an assumption only if multiple DVs are included in the model and *MANCOVA* is conducted). If sample sizes are equal, the robustness of *MANCOVA* is expected and the results of Box's *M* test can be disregarded (Tabachnick & Fidell, 2007). However, if sample sizes are unequal and Box's *M* test is significant at $p < .001$, then robustness is not guaranteed.

Sphericity (an assumption only if a within subjects factor is included in the model).

Example Research Question

Is there a difference in mean sense of classroom community between graduate students based on gender (male, female) after controlling for student grade point average, $\mu_1 \neq \mu_2 \neq \mu_3$?

Alternatively,

Holding student grade point average constant, are mean differences in sense of classroom between males and females larger than expected by chance?

Note: This is an example of a between subjects *ANCOVA*.

Null Hypothesis

H_0: There no difference in mean sense of classroom community between graduate students based on gender (male, female) after controlling for student grade point average, $\mu_1 = \mu_2 = \mu_3$.

Note: *ANCOVAs* may have more than two factors; e.g., three-way *ANCOVA*, four-way *ANCOVA*, etc. There would be three null hypotheses for a two-way *ANCOVA*:

H_{01}: there is no difference in group means across the first IV after controlling the covariate(s).

H_{02}: there is no difference in group means across the second IV after controlling the covariate(s).

H_{03}: there is no interaction effect after controlling the covariate(s).

MANCOVA includes multiple DVs in addition to multiple IVs (factors and covariates).

SPSS Procedure

SPSS > Analyze > General Linear Model > Univariate (Multivariate for *MANCOVA*)

SPSS Output & Analysis

SPSS output varies based on options selected by the user.

Between-Subjects Factors (value label, *N*).

Descriptive Statistics.

Descriptive Statistics

Dependent Variable: Classroom Community

Gender	Mean	Std. Deviation	N
Female	28.84	6.181	144
Male	29.17	6.651	24
Total	28.89	6.231	168

Levene's Test Results.

- Levene's test is run by choosing homogeneity tests from the options menu in the "Univariate" SPSS dialog box. It tests the null hypothesis that the error variance of the DV is equal across groups. A significant Levene's test is evidence that the assumption of homogeneity of variance has been violated.

Levene's Test of Equality of Error Variances[a]

Dependent Variable: Classroom Community

F	df1	df2	Sig.
.457	1	166	.500

Tests the null hypothesis that the error variance of the dependent variable is equal across groups.

a. Design: Intercept + gender * gpa + gender

The above SPSS output provides evidence that the assumption of homogeneity of variance is tenable.

Tests of Between-Subjects Effects.

- The covariate effect evaluates the relationship between the covariate and the IV (factor) on the DV. If this effect is significant, one concludes that there is a relationship between the covariate and the DV. If the effect is not significant, the appropriateness of the covariate is questioned.

- The grouping variable effect evaluates the adjusted means for the total number of groups.

- The interaction effect (if requested) between the covariate and the IV is used to evaluate the homogeneity of regressions assumption. If this effect is significant, the assumption is not tenable and *ANCOVA* results are not meaningful.

- If a test involving three or more groups is significant, post hoc multiple comparison tests are required.

Tests of Between-Subjects Effects

Dependent Variable: Classroom Community

Source	Type III Sum of Squares	df	Mean Square	F	Sig.	Partial Eta Squared	Noncent. Parameter	Observed Power[b]
Corrected Model	936.257[a]	3	312.086	9.228	.000	.144	27.683	.996
Intercept	1329.951	1	1329.95	39.32	.000	.193	39.324	1.000
gender * gpa	934.066	2	467.033	13.81	.000	.144	27.618	.998
gender	61.437	1	61.437	1.817	.180	.011	1.817	.268
Error	5546.594	164	33.821					
Total	146671.000	168						
Corrected Total	6482.851	167						

a. R Squared = .144 (Adjusted R Squared = .129)

b. Computed using alpha =

The above SPSS output shows a significant gender * gpa interaction effect. Therefore, the assumption of homogeneity of regressions is not tenable and *ANCOVA* results are not meaningful. If the assumption of homogeneity of regressions were tenable, results would be reported as follows: The predicted main effect of gender was not significant, $F(1,164) = 1.82$, $p = .18$, $\eta_p^2 = .14$.

Estimated Marginal Means.

- The "Estimated Marginal Means" table displays the adjusted means of the DV for each group after the effect of the covariate has been statistically removed.

Gender

Dependent Variable: Classroom Community

Gender	Mean	Std. Error	95% Confidence Interval	
			Lower Bound	Upper Bound
Female	28.623[a]	.487	27.662	29.584
Male	29.926[a]	1.263	27.433	32.419

a. Covariates appearing in the model are evaluated at the following values: GPA = 3.3956.

Parameter Estimates (*B*, standard error, *t*, significance level, 95% confidence interval, partial eta square, noncentrality parameter, observed power).

- For each level of the factor, SPSS calculates the parameter estimate (*b* coefficient).

- The noncentrality parameter is used in calculating the observed power.

Contrast Coefficients.

Lack of Fit Tests (source, sum of squares, degrees of freedom, mean square, *F*, significance level, partial eta square, noncentrality parameter, observed power).

Post Hoc Tests.

- Post hoc tests are used to identify significant pairwise differences following a significant *ANCOVA* or *MANCOVA* involving three or more groups.

- SPSS flags (*) differences that are significant.

Spread-Versus-Level Plots.

8.4: Chapter 8 Review

The answer key is at the end of this section.

1. What test is implied by the following research question: Is there a difference in the proportion of university students by gender who completed extra credit work?

    A.   Dependent *t*-test

    B.   McNemar test

    C.   Friedman test

    D.   Median test

2. The larger the value of the *F*-ratio,...

    A.   the more the sample distributions overlap

    B.   the less the sample distributions overlap

    C.   the larger the total variance

    D.   the smaller the total variance

3. The ANOVA null hypothesis states...

    A.   the means of specific groups are equal

    B.   the means of at least two groups are equal

    C.   the means of all groups are different

    D.   the means of all groups are equal

4. Which of the following hypothesis tests is a parametric test?

    A.   Friedman test

    B.   Median test

    C.   Dependent *t*-test

    D.   Mann-Whitney *U* test

5. What is the best test to analyze data from the following research design?

    N   X O
    N   O

    A.   *ANCOVA*

B. *ANOVA*

C. Independent *t*-test

D. Dependent *t*-test

6. What is the best test to analyze data from the following research design?

O X O

A. *ANOVA*

B. Independent *t*-test

C. Dependent *t*-test

D. *ANCOVA*

7. What is the best test to analyze data from the following research design?

O O O X O O O

A. Between-subjects *ANOVA*

B. Within-subjects *ANOVA*

C. Mixed between-within-subjects *ANOVA*

D. Dependent *t*-test

8. What is the best test to analyze data from the following research design?

O X O
O   O

A. Dependent *t*-test

B. Independent *t*-test

C. *ANOVA*

D. *ANCOVA*

9. What is the best test to analyze data from the following research design?

O O O X O O O
O O O   O O O

A. Within-subjects *ANOVA*

B. Between-subjects *ANOVA*

C. Mixed between-within-subjects *ANOVA*

D. Dependent *t*-test

10. What is the best contrast to use following a significant within-subjects *ANOVA*?

A. Simple contrast

B. Difference contrast

C. Repeated contrast

D. Polynomial contrast

11. What is the best contrast to use when comparing the mean of each level to the mean of a specified level?

A. Simple contrast

B. Difference contrast

C. Repeated contrast

D. Polynomial contrast

12. What is the most conservative post hoc multiple comparison test?

A. Bonferroni

B. Sidak

C. Scheffé

D. Tukey honestly significant difference

13. What is the least conservative post hoc multiple comparison test?

A. Bonferroni

B. Sidak

C. Tukey honestly significant difference

D. Fisher's least significant difference

14. What post hoc multiple comparison test should be used when the assumption of homogeneity of variances is met?

A. Games-Howell

    B.   Dunnett's *T*3

    C.   Tukey's wholly significant difference

    D.   Tamehane's *T*2

15. *ANOVA* is a test of the equality of what statistics?

    A.   Variances

    B.   Means

    C.   Medians

    D.   Standard deviations

16. What statistic could one examine to evaluate the assumption of homogeneity of variance?

    A.   Mean

    B.   Mode

    C.   Standard deviation

    D.   Range

17. What is the best statement regarding *t*-tests?

    A.   Restricted to one IV

    B.   Restricted to one DV

    C.   Restricted to two groups

    D.   All the above statements are correct

18. Which of the following tests is used to analyze dependent data?

    A.   Kruskal-Wallis *H* test

    B.   Mann-Whitney *U* test

    C.   Wilcoxon signed-ranks test

    D.   Median test

19. The Kruskal-Wallis *H* test is the nonparametric counterpart of what test?

    A.   One-way *ANOVA*

    B.   Dependent *t*-test

C. Friedman test

D. One-sample *t*-test

20. Below is an extract from SPSS independent t-test output. What is the correct finding?

		Levene's Test for Equality of Variances				
		F	Sig.	t	df	Sig. (2-tailed)
Alienation	Equal variances assumed	.508	.477	1.384	166	.168
	Equal variances not assumed			1.471	32.79	.151

A. $t(.48) = 1.38$, $p = .17$

B. $t(32.79) = 1.47$, $p = .15$

C. $t(166) = 1.38$, $p = .17$

D. $t(166) = 1.47$, $p = .17$

21. Below is an extract from SPSS Mann-Whitney U-test output. What is the correct finding?

	GPA
Mann–Whitney U	1330.500
Wilcoxon W	1630.500
Z	-1.814
Asymp. Sig. (2-tailed)	.070

a. Grouping Variable: Gender

A. $U(2) = 1330.50$, $p = .07$

B. $U(2) = -1.81$, $p = .07$

C. $U(1) = -1.81$, $p = .07$

D. $U(1) = 1330.50$, $p = .07$

Chapter 8 Answers

1B, 2B, 3D, 4C, 5C, 6C, 7B, 8D, 9C, 10D, 11A, 12C, 13D, 14C, 15B, 16C, 17D, 18C, 19A, 20C, 21D

Chapter 9: Correlation and Prediction Tests

Correlation is a technique used to measure the relationship (association) between two or more variables. Correlation techniques are also used for prediction. This chapter summarizes common correlation and regression procedures.

9.1: Introduction

Overview

Tests of association and regression are used to estimate strength and direction of relationships between variables or to predict outcomes.

Regression and Association Tests

Pearson Chi-Square (χ^2) Two-Way Contingency Table Analysis

(symmetric relationship between two nominal variables)

Relative Risk

(relative risk between two dichotomous variables)

Phi (Φ)

(symmetric relationship between two dichotomous variables)

Cramér's *V*

(monotonic symmetric relationship between two nominal variables)

Lambda (λ)

(asymmetric measure between two nominal variables; proportional reduction of error measure)

Contingency Coefficient (C)

(test of independence between two categorical variables)

Point-Biserial Correlation (r_{pb})

(symmetric linear relationship between one dichotomous variable and one continuous variable)

Eta (η) Correlation Coefficient

(total linear and nonlinear asymmetric relationship between one nominal and one interval/ratio variable)

Cohen's Kappa (κ) Measure of Agreement

(measures consistency of two raters; one categorical variable with equal number of categories for each rater)

Spearman Rank Order Correlation

(monotonic symmetric relationship between two ranked variables)

Gamma

(monotonic symmetric relationship between two categorical ordinal variables or two dichotomous variables; ignores ties)

Somers' d

(monotonic asymmetric relationship between two categorical ordinal variables;adjusts for ties in the DV only)

Kendall's tau-b

(monotonic symmetric relationship between two ordinal variables; used when the number of rows and number of columns are equal)

Kendall's tau-c

(monotonic symmetric relationship between two ordinal variables; used when the number of rows and number of columns are not equal)

Pearson Product-Moment Correlation

(symmetric linear relationship between two interval/ratio variables)

Intraclass Correlation Coefficient

(two or more ratio, interval, or ordinal variables of the same class; measures consistency of raters)

Partial Correlation

(relationship between two interval/ratio variables after controlling for one or more interval/ratio variables)

Bivariate Regression

(predicting one interval/ratio DV with one interval/ratio IV)

Multiple Regression and Correlation

(predicting one interval/ratio DV with multiple interval/ratio IVs)

Discriminant Analysis

(predicting one categorical DV with multiple interval/ratio IVs)

Binomial Logistic Regression

(predicting one dichotomous DV with multiple continuous and/or categorical IVs)

Principal Components and Factor Analysis

(identifying latent variables among multiple interval/ratio variables)

Canonical Correlation Analysis

(CCA; relationship between a set of multiple interval/ratio IVs and a set of multiple interval/ratio DVs)

Two-Step Cluster Analysis

(natural groupings among multiple continuous and categorical variables)

Correlation

Correlation is a statistical technique that measures and describes the relationship (i.e., association, correlation) between variables. A relationship exists when changes in one variable tend to be accompanied by consistent and predictable changes in the other variable. In other words, if a significant relationship exists, the two variables covary in some nonrandom fashion.

A monotonic relationship is one in which the value of one variable increases as the value of the other variable increases or the value of one variable increases as the value of the other variable decreases, but not necessarily in a linear fashion.

A linear relationship means that any given change in one variable produces a corresponding change in the other variable. A plot of their values in a scatterplot approximates a straight line, or values that average out to be a straight line.

Bivariate correlation, multiple correlation, and canonical correlation are related statistical methods for modeling the relationship between two or more random variables. Bivariate correlation refers to a one on one relationship between two variables, multiple correlation refers to a one on many correlation, and canonical correlation refers to a many on many correlation.

There are three additional correlation terms that one is likely to encounter in viewing SPSS output:

- *Zero-order correlation* is the relationship between two variables, while ignoring the influence of other variables.

- *Partial correlation* is the relationship between two variables after removing the overlap of a third or more other variables from both variables.

- *Part (semi-partial) correlation* is the relationship between two variables after removing a third variable from just the IV (predictor).

Researchers generally choose the measure that is appropriate for the lower scale when selecting a correlation measure to assess the relationship between variables that are measured using different scales of measurement. For example, if one variable is nominal, and the other is interval, one would use a test appropriate for the nominal variable.

Strength of Relationship

A correlation measures the strength or degree of the relationship between X and Y. The strength of relationship (how closely they are related) is usually expressed as a number (correlation coefficient) between −1 and +1.

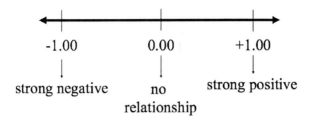

strong negative   no   strong positive
relationship

A zero correlation indicates no relationship. As the correlation coefficient moves toward either −1 or +1, the relationship gets stronger until there is a perfect correlation at either extreme. Perfect correlation is referred to as singularity.

A general interpretive guide that is often used to describe strength of statistically significant relationships (i.e., $p \le .05$) is provided below:

> Between 0 and ±0.20 – Very weak
> Between ±0.20 and ±0.40 – Weak
> Between ±0.40 and ±0.60 – Moderate
> Between ±0.60 and ±0.80 – Strong
> Between ±0.80 and ±1.00 – Very strong

However, other interpretive guides exist in the professional literature.

Various Correlation Coefficients (Hinkle, Wiersma, & Jurs, 1998)

> Little if any relationship < .30
> Low relationship = .30 to < .50
> Moderate relationship = .50 to < .70
> High relationship = .70 to < .90
> Very high relationship = .90 and above

Phi or Cramér's V (Rea & Parker, 2005)

> Negligible association < .10
> Weak association = .10 to < .20
> Moderate association = .20 to < .40
> Relatively strong association = .40 to < .60
> Strong association = .60 to < .80
> Very strong association = .80 and higher

Eta square (η2; Tabachnick & Fidell, 2007)

Small effect size = .01
Medium effect size = .06
Large effect size = .14

Cohen's d (Cohen, 1988)

Small effect = .2
Medium effect = .5
Large effect = .8

R² (Cohen, 1988)

Small effect = .0196
Medium effect -= .1300
Large effect = .2600

Key Point
If the results of a correlation test are not significant, there is no relationship, regardless of the correlation coefficient produced by the test.

Direction of Relationship

Positive linear correlation (a positive number) means that two variables tend to move in the same direction. That is, as one gets larger, so does the other. Negative or inverse linear correlation (a negative number) means that the two variables tend to move in opposite directions. That is, as one gets larger, the other gets smaller.

However, in a nonlinear or curvilinear relationship, as the scores of one variable change, the scores of the other variable do not tend to only increase or only decrease. At some point, the scores change their direction of change.

Tests for association can be symmetrical or asymmetrical. If the test is symmetrical, the coefficient of association – e.g.,

Pearson r – will be the same regardless of which variable is designated the IV (predictor variable). However, if the test is asymmetrical – e.g., Cramér's V – the designation of variables as IV and DV matters. Asymmetric tests measure strength of association in predicting the DV (criterion variable), while symmetric tests measure the strength of association when prediction is done in both directions.

Form of Relationship

The form of a relationship is either linear or nonlinear (i.e., curvilinear).

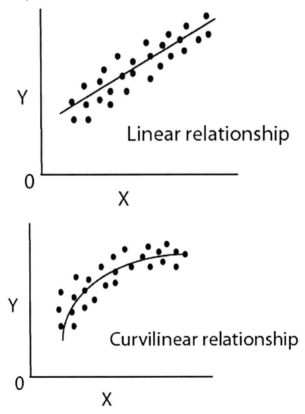

This book mostly addresses linear relationships, which means that linearity between variables is an assumption for many correlation tests. An example of a curvilinear relationship is age and health care usage. They are related, but the relationship does not follow a straight line. Young children and older people both tend to use much more health care than teenagers or young adults.

Reliability

Reliability is a necessary but not a sufficient condition for test validity (Fink, 1995; Pedhazur & Schmelkin, 1991). Reliability refers to the consistency or repeatability of an instrument or observation. It is the correlation between the observed variable and the true score when the variable is an imprecise indicator of the true score (Cohen & Cohen, 1983). Lack of precision (reliability) of measurement comes from error. The higher the error the more unreliable the measurement. These errors may come from random inattentiveness, guessing, differential perception, recording errors, etc. on the part of observers. These measurement errors are assumed to be random in classical test theory.

Accordingly, instrument reliability is the extent to which an item, scale, or instrument will yield the same score when administered in different times, locations, or populations, when the two administrations do not differ in relevant variables. In other words, it pertains to the consistency of measurement. Correlation procedures are used to assess reliability.

The measurement instrument should be both reliable and valid. The figure below displays the relationship between reliability and validity.

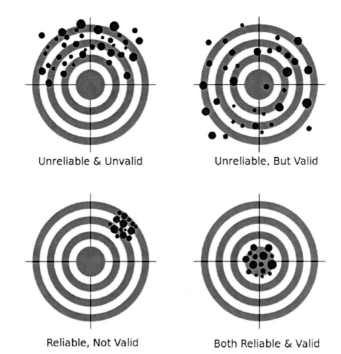

Unreliable & Unvalid

Unreliable, But Valid

Reliable, Not Valid

Both Reliable & Valid

Image: (c) Nevit Dilmen found at Wikimedia commons

Types of Reliability

There are five types of scale or instrument reliability:

1. *Internal consistency reliability* refers to the ability of each item on an instrument to measure a single construct or dimension. It assumes the equivalence of all items on the instrument. Internal consistency coefficients estimate how consistently individuals respond to the items within a scale. The reliability of the instrument is estimated by how well items that reflect the same construct produce similar results. There are three popular types of internal consistency reliability analyses: Cronbach's alpha, split-half, and Kuder-Richardson (K-R).

   • *Cronbach's alpha* is a model of internal consistency based on the average inter-item correlation. Alpha measures the extent to which item responses obtained at the same time correlate highly with each other. When the number of items in a scale is higher, alpha will be higher even when the estimated average correlations are equal. Also, the more consistent within-subject responses are, and the greater the variability between subjects in the sample, the higher Cronbach's alpha will be. Finally, alpha will be higher when there is homogeneity of variances among items than when there is not. It is generally the most appropriate form of internal consistency reliability for instruments in which there is a range of possible responses. It is not appropriate for dichotomously scored items; e.g., true-false responses. The widely-accepted social science cut-off is that Cronbach's alpha should be .70 or higher for a set of items to be considered an internally-consistent scale. When alpha is .70, the standard error of measurement is 0.55. The formula for Cronbach's alpha is

$$\alpha = \frac{n}{n-1}\left(1 - \frac{\Sigma s_i^2}{s_{Test}^2}\right)$$

where n = number of items, s_i^2 = variance of scores on each item, and s_{Test}^2 = total variance of all items on the scale.

- *Split-half* is a model of internal consistency that splits the scale into two parts and examines the correlation between the parts. Typically, responses on odd versus even items are employed and total scores on odd items are correlated with the scores obtained on even items. The correlation obtained, however, represents the reliability coefficient of only half the test, and since reliability is related to the length of the test, a correction must be applied in order to obtain the reliability for the entire test. The Spearman-Brown Prophecy formula is used to make this correction.

- *Kuder-Richardson* (K-R) reliability is used to assess reliability when all items on an instrument are scored dichotomously.

2. *Test-retest reliability*, also referred to as instrument stability) is a method of estimating the stability of scores generated by

a measurement instrument over time. It involves administering the same instrument to the same individuals at two different times. The test-retest method should only be used when the variables being measured are considered to be stable over the test-retest period. One issue with test-retest reliability is the memory effect, which is potentially more serious when the two test administrations are close together in time. Many respondents will remember their responses and when they take the retest will answer the way they did on the first test rather than evaluating each question carefully. This situation can create an artificially high reliability coefficient as participants respond from their memory rather than the test itself. The intraclass correlation coefficient (ICC) can be used to assess test-retest reliability.

3. *Inter-rater reliability* is used to assess the degree to which different raters/observers give consistent estimates of the same phenomenon. Cohen's kappa measure of agreement can be used used to assess inter-rater agreement when ratings are measured as categories. The ICC can be used when ratings are measured on the ratio, interval, or ordinal scales.

4. *Intra-rater reliability* is used to assess the degree to which the same raters/observers give consistent estimates of the same phenomenon over time. The ICC can be used when ratings are measured on the ratio, interval, or ordinal scales.

5. *Parallel forms reliability,* also referred to as equivalence, is used to measure consistency over two forms of an instrument. Parallel or alternate forms of an instrument are two forms that have similar kinds of items so that they can be interchanged. If these are reliable, then one can expect that administering the alternate forms to the same group of individuals will yield similar scores for each individual. The Pearson product-moment correlation coefficient can be used as a measure of parallel forms reliability. Although two forms of a test may be statistically similar, they are not identical. If parallel forms of a test are to be used in a pretest-posttest design, the researcher should avoid administering one form during the pretest and the other form during the posttest. To avoid a pattern effect, research participants should be administered the two forms on a random basis for the pretest

and administered the form not taken in the pretest for the posttest.

Measurement Error

Measurement error is the difference between the actual value of a quantity and the value obtained by a measurement. The scores generated by any measurement tool contain some degree of error. However the goal of measurement is to reduce this error as much as possible. A measure that has no random error (i.e., consists of all true scores) is perfectly reliable; a measure that includes no true score (i.e., is all random error) has zero reliability.

Measurement Error = True Score – Observed Score

Generally, measurement error is viewed as possessing two components.

1. *Random error* is caused by any factors that randomly affect measurement of the variable across the sample. For example, in a particular testing situation, some individuals may be tired while others are alert. If mood affects their performance on a measure, it may artificially inflate the observed scores for some individuals and artificially weaken them for others. Random error does not have consistent effects across the entire sample. Instead, it affects observed scores up or down randomly. Random error adds variability to the data but does not affect average performance of the group.

2. *Systematic error* is caused by any factors that systematically affect measurement of the variable across the entire sample in one direction. For example, if there is a loud noise where research participants are being measured, this noise is likely to affect all of the scores by systematically lowering them. Unlike random error, systematic errors tend to be consistently either positive or negative. Systematic error is a form of measurement bias.

Measurement error may occur due to a variety of factors (see the instrumentation threat to internal validity). These factors include:

- Undercoverage occurs when some members of the target population are not adequately represented in the sample

- Situational contaminants are present; e.g., time of day/ month differences in measurement.

- Personal factors change; e.g., fatigue or anxiety differences.

- Data collection varies; e.g., changes in how data are collected such as variations in the instructions given to different groups being tested.

- Volunteer bias occurs when sample members are self-selected. Volunteers tend to overrepresent individuals who have strong opinions. Additionally, Rosenthal and Rosnow (1975) report that volunteers, when compared to non-volunteers, tend to be:

  - better educated
  - of higher socioeconomic status
  - more intelligent, sociable, and unconventional
  - higher in need of social approval
  - less authoritarian and conforming

- Nonresponse bias occurs when some individuals selected for the sample are unwilling or unable to participate in the study. Nonresponse bias results when respondents differ in meaningful ways from nonrespondents.

- Response bias occurs when some individuals selected for the sample are unwilling or unable to respond in a truthful manner in reaction to questions or items on a survey. Kalton and Schuman (1982) and Lanyon and Goodstein (1997) identify the following major response biases:

  - Question ambiguity may lead to unreliability.

  - Questions that demand the impossible may also lead to unreliability; e.g., detailed recall of historical events.

  - Order effects occur when responses to a series of questions or items depend on the order in which the questions or items are presented.

  - Response set bias reflects a conscious or subconscious attempt by the respondent to create a certain impression; e.g., social desirability bias. Social desirability bias is the tendency to present oneself in a positive manner. Organizational research is especially vulnerable to social desirability bias.

- Response style bias implies bias in a certain direction. Acquiescence bias is the tendency to respond positively. Extreme and central tendency responding bias is the tendency to respond using only certain portions of the measurement scale. Negative affectivity bias is a manifestation of neuroticism and can affect self-reports regarding health matters, life events, etc.

Measurements must accurately assess the underlying attitudes or opinions of the respondent. It is important to avoid giving the respondent any cues or information that will prompt him or her to alter a true response (order effects) or to give a response perceived to be desired by the researcher or society (social desirability bias). For example, an instrument measuring racial discrimination is prone to social desirability bias as respondents who are racist may be reluctant to admit being a racist. This is referred to as response bias and is a concern in doing survey research because it potentially creates an inconsistent pattern of results in the data gathered and defeats the purpose of doing the survey in the first place (i.e., to identify people's true reactions to a certain topic/issue). Offering anonymity on surveys can reduce social desirability bias.

The standard error of measurement (SE_m) is used to determine the range of certainty around a reported score. If one SE_m is added to an observed score and one SE_m is subtracted from it, one can be 68% sure that the true score falls within the created range. The formula is

$$SE_m = \sigma\sqrt{1-r}$$

where σ = standard deviation and r = reliability coefficient.

Regression

Regression uses the relationship between variables in making predictions. If there is a relationship between two variables, it is possible to predict a person's score on one variable on the basis of their score on the other variable.

When one looks at a scatterplot of two variables that are associated, one can imagine a curve or line running through the data points that characterizes the general pattern of the data. A straight line reflects the pattern of linear relationships. The Pearson correlation summarizes how tightly clustered the points are around this imaginary line. The process of placing a best fit line onto a scatterplot is called bivariate linear regression.

Typically no single straight line will align with each data point (that is, one cannot draw a single line through all of the data points in a scatterplot). What one desires is the line that fits the best and minimizes error. In other words, one seeks the line that differs the least from all of the data points as the best fitting line. To do this one finds the least-squares solution, that is, the line that generates the least value if one adds the squares of all errors. Such a straight line is called the *line of best fit.*

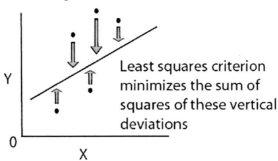

Least squares criterion minimizes the sum of squares of these vertical deviations

Characteristics of the best fit line:

- Line minimizes the sum of the squared distances between the data points and the line.

- Line goes through the mean scores for both the dependent (y) and the independent (x) variable.

- If one squares the vertical distance of each data point from the line, and then sums these values, the resulting value is smaller than the value obtained with any other line. This is known as the *ordinary least squares (OLS) criterion.*

Key Point
It doesn't matter which variable is assigned as the IV and which is assigned as the DV in correlation analysis. However, for regression analysis it does matter; one predicts the outcome of y (DV) based on x (IV).

Coefficient of Determination

The coefficient of determination tells us how much of the variance in Y is explained by X. It is the percentage of the variability among scores on one variable that can be attributed to differences in the scores on the other variable (or multiple variables in multiple regression). To compute the coefficient of determination one simply squares the correlation coefficient. For example, if the bivariate correlation is $r = .7$ (a high relationship), $r^2 = .7 * .7 = .49$. Therefore, 49% of the variation in the criterion variable is related to changes in the predictor variable. In other words, the IV is said to explain 49% of the variance in the DV.

The coefficient of nondetermination is the proportion of total variance in one variable that is not predictable from another variable. It is calculated by the formula $1 - r^2$.

Cross Validation

Cross-validation is used to ascertain how much shrinkage occurs in the multiple regression when the regression equation is applied to a new sample. Cross validation involves the following four steps (Pedhazur, 1997):

1. Determine the regression equation and R^2 (coefficient of multiple determination) using a screening sample (the original sample).

2. Apply the regression equation to the calibration sample (a new sample from the same population used to constitute the screening sample).

3. Calculate Pearson r (analogous to the multiple correlation coefficient R) between the observed criterion scores and the predicted criterion scores of the calibration sample. Square this figure to produce a coefficient of determination.

4. Calculate the difference between the coefficients of determination (an estimate of the amount of shrinkage). If the shrinkage is small and R^2 is meaningful, the screening and calibration samples can be combined to develop a new regression equation for use in future predictions.

9.2: Nonparametric Tests

Pearson Chi-Square (χ^2) Contingency Table Analysis

Purpose

Chi-square (χ^2) contingency table analysis, also known as the chi-square test of independence, is a nonparametric procedure to determine the association between two categorical variables. It is a test of independence that compares the frequencies of two nominal variables.

The dataset represents a R × C contingency table, where R is the number of rows (categories of one variable) and C is the number of columns (categories of the second variable). For example, two dichotomous variables will produce a 2 x 2 table. By convention, the row variable is considered the DV and the column variable is viewed as the IV.

SPSS will accommodate more than two variables in this procedure. Place additional variables in the SPSS dialog box labeled "Layer 1 of 1". These additional variables serve as control variables.

Degrees of freedom. The degrees of freedom = (number of rows − 1) x (number of columns − 1).

Effect size. Phi is used to report effect size for 2 x 2 contingency tables while Cramer's *V* is used for larger tables.

Key Assumptions & Requirements

Random selection of samples (probability samples) to allow for generalization of results to a target population.

Variables. Variables must be reported in raw frequencies (not percentages). Values/categories of the variable must be mutually exclusive and exhaustive.

Independence. Independence of observations.

Sample size. Observed frequencies must be sufficiently large. Each cell has an expected frequency of five or more (some statisticians prefer 10 or more). If the sample size is very small, the χ^2 value is overestimated; if it is very large, the χ^2

value is underestimated. To overcome this problem, Cramer's V and the contingency coefficient C are suggested when measuring very small or very large samples.

Example Research Question

Are the proportions associated with preference for online or on campus courses the same for male and female university students?

Example Null Hypothesis

H_0: The proportions associated with preference for online and on campus courses are the same for male and female university students.

SPSS Procedure

SPSS > Analyze > Descriptive Statistics > Crosstabs > Statistics > Chi-square

SPSS Output & Analysis

Crosstabulation.

Type course * Gender Crosstabulation

Count

		Gender		Total
		Male	Female	
Type course	Traditional	2	18	20
	Distance	18	82	100
Total		20	100	120

Chi-Square Tests.

- Pearson chi-square tests the hypothesis that the row and column variables in a crosstabulation are independent of one another. This is usually the primary test that the researcher should consider.

- Continuity correction (Yates' correction) is provided for 2 x 2 tables. The continuity correction is thought to give a better approximation to the theoretical sampling distribution for chi-square when the observed frequencies in any cell are small (less than 5).

- Likelihood ratio tests the hypothesis using a log-linear model. It is an alternative procedure for testing the hypothesis of no association of columns and rows.

- Fisher's exact test is used when one or more of the cells have an expected frequency of five or less. The chi-square test assumes that each cell has an expected frequency of five or more, but the Fisher's exact test does not have this assumption.

- Linear-by-linear association is only appropriate when data are ordinal (i.e., there is a logic to the order of the cases for a variable).

Chi-Square Tests

	Value	df	Asymp. Sig. (2-sided)	Exact Sig. (2-sided)	Exact Sig. (1-sided)
Pearson Chi-Square	.768[a]	1	.381		
Continuity Correction[b]	.300	1	.584		
Likelihood Ratio	.853	1	.356		
Fisher's Exact Test				.521	.306
Linear-by-Linear Association	.762	1	.383		
N of Valid Cases	120				

a. 1 cells (25.0%) have expected count less than 5. The minimum expected count is 3.33.

b. Computed only for a 2x2 table

The above SPSS output shows that the test is not significant, $\chi^2(1, N = 120) = .77, p = .38$. Note that one cell has an expected frequency of less than 5. The test does not provide evidence to reject the null hypothesis that the proportions associated with preference for online and on campus courses are the same for male and female university students.

Relative Risk

Purpose

Relative risk (also called the risk ratio) is nonparametric procedure used to determine the relative risk between two dichotomous variables (2 x 2 frequency table). It addresses the question of how much more likely is one condition if the person has a risk factor than if the person does not have the risk factor.

The row variable in the frequency table is the risk factor and the column variable is the condition. Conditions should be coded so that the first row variable is yes to the risk condition and the first column variable is yes to the risk factor (Rosnow & Rosenthal, 2003).

The formula for relative risk is

$$RR = \frac{[A/(A+B)]}{[C/(C+D)]}$$

where *a* and *c* are "yes" frequency counts (probability that the event will occur) and *b* and *d* are "no" frequency counts derived from a treated condition (*a/b*) and an untreated condition (*c/d*).

For example, take the following two groups measured dichotomously.

	Improved	Not Improved
Treated	*a* = 13	*b* = 4
Not Treated	*c* = 8	*d* = 7

Relative risk = .76/.53 = 1.43. Therefore, participants are 1.43 more likely to improve if they are treated.

Effect size. The odds ratio can be used as a measure of effect size.

Key Assumptions & Requirements

Random selection of sample (probability sample) to allow for generalization of results to a target population.

Variables. Variables are dichotomous.

Independence. Independence of observations.

Example Research Question

How much more likely is an online student to become a dropout by not attending the optional beginning of program on campus residency?

Example Null Hypothesis

H_0: Online students and on campus students are equally likely to become dropouts regardless of whether or not they attend the optional beginning of program on campus residency.

SPSS Procedure

SPSS > Analyze > Descriptive Statistics > Crosstabs > Statistics > Risk

SPSS Output & Analysis

Crosstabulation.

Attended residency? * Is a dropout? Crosstabulation

Count

		Is a dropout?		Total
		yes	no	
Attended residency?	yes	7	30	37
	no	10	11	21
Total		17	41	58

Chi-Square Tests.

- Pearson chi-square tests the hypothesis that the row and column variables in a crosstabulation are independent of one another. This is usually the primary test that the researcher should consider.

- Continuity correction (Yates' correction) is provided for 2 x 2 tables. The continuity correction is thought to give a better approximation to the theoretical sampling distribution for chi-square when the observed frequencies in any cell are small (less than 5).

- Likelihood ratio tests the hypothesis using a log-linear model. It is an alternative procedure for testing the hypothesis of no association of columns and rows.

- Fisher's exact test is used when one or more of the cells have an expected frequency of five or less. The chi-square test assumes that each cell has an expected frequency of five or more, but the Fisher's exact test does not have this assumption.

- Linear-by-linear association is only appropriate when data are ordinal (i.e., there is a logic to the order of the cases for a variable).

Chi-Square Tests

	Value	df	Asymp. Sig. (2-sided)	Exact Sig. (2-sided)	Exact Sig. (1-sided)
Pearson Chi-Square	5.33[a]	1	.021		
Continuity Correction[b]	4.031	1	.045		
Likelihood Ratio	5.211	1	.022		
Fisher's Exact Test				.035	.023
Linear-by-Linear Association	5.234	1	.022		
N of Valid Cases	58				

a. 0 cells (0.0%) have expected count less than 5. The minimum expected count is 6.16.

b. Computed only for a 2x2 table

The above SPSS output shows a significant relationship between the residency and dropout variables, $\chi^2(1, N = 58) = 5.33, p = .02$.

Risk Estimate.

Risk Estimate

	Value	95% Confidence Interval	
		Lower	Upper
Odds Ratio for Attended residency? (yes / no)	.257	.078	.842
For cohort Is a dropout? = yes	.397	.178	.888
For cohort Is a dropout? = no	1.548	1.000	2.395
N of Valid Cases	58		

The above SPSS output shows an odds ratio of .26. This means that the odds of being a dropout (yes) and attending the on campus residency (yes) are .26 the odds of being a dropout and not attending the on campus residency The output also shows a relative risk of 1.55. This means that online students who did not attend the on campus residency are 1.55 times more likely to become dropouts than online students who attended the residency.

Phi (Φ) and Cramér's *V*

Purpose

Phi (Φ) and Cramér's *V* tests are nonparametric symmetric procedures based on the chi-square statistic used to determine if there is an association between columns and rows in contingency tables. The values range between 0 and 1. Both coefficients are measures of nominal by nominal association based on the chi-square statistic. Phi is used for 2 x 2 contingency tables and is the equivalent of Pearson *r* for dichotomous variables. Cramér's *V* can be used for larger tables and corrects for table size. For 2 x 2 tables, Cramér's *V* equals phi. The tests are not sensitive to sample size.

Formulas for the two test statistics are given below

$$\phi = \sqrt{\frac{\chi^2}{N}}$$

$$V = \sqrt{\chi^2 \Big/ N(k-1)}$$

where *N* is the total number of cases and *k* is the lesser of number of rows and number or number of columns.

Both statistics are symmetric, so they will produce the same value regardless of how the variables are designated IV and DV. They are primarily used as post-hoc tests to determine strengths of association (effect size) after the chi-square test has determined significance in a contingency table analysis. Strength of relationship for Φ and Cramér's *V* are interpreted as follows (Rea & Parker, 2005):

Under .10, negligible association
.10 and under .20, weak association
.20 and under .40, moderate association
.40 and under .60, relatively strong association
.60 and under .80, strong association
above .80, very strong association

Key Assumptions & Requirements

Random selection of sample (probability sample) to allow for generalization of results to a target population.

Variables. Variables are categorical variables that generate a contingency table. Variables must be reported in raw frequencies (not percentages). Values/categories on the IV and DV must be mutually exclusive and exhaustive.

Independence. Independence of observations.

Example Research Question

Are student outcomes on the candidacy examination (pass, fail) the same for distance and traditional on campus students?

Example Null Hypothesis

H_0: Student outcomes on the candidacy examination (pass, fail) are independent of student program (distance, traditional on campus).

SPSS Procedure

SPSS > Analyze > Descriptive Statistics > Crosstabs > Statistics > Phi and Cramér's *V*

SPSS Output & Analysis

Crosstabulations.

Grade * Type course Crosstabulation

Count

		Type course		Total
		Traditional	Distance	
Grade	fail	2	18	20
	pass	18	82	100
Total		20	100	120

Symmetric Measures.

Symmetric Measures

		Value	Approx. Sig.
Nominal by Nominal	Phi	-.080	.381
	Cramer's V	.080	.381
N of Valid Cases		120	

a. Not assuming the null hypothesis.

b. Using the asymptotic standard error assuming the null hypothesis.

The above SPSS output shows that both phi and Cramér's *V* are not significant, *p* = .38. Therefore, there is insufficient evidence to reject the null hypothesis that student outcomes on the candidacy examination (pass, fail) are independent of student program (online, on campus).

Lambda (λ)

Purpose

Lambda (λ) is nonparametric asymmetric procedure used to determine if there is an association between two nominal (or a nominal and ordinal) variables. The values of lambda can range from 0 to 1. A value of 0 means no improvement in prediction. A value of 1 indicates that the prediction can be made without error.

Lambda is a proportional reduction in error (*PRE*) measure, defined as the improvement, expressed as a percentage, in predicting a DV based on knowledge of the IV. Multiplying the lambda coefficient by 100% results in a *PRE* percentage value. For example, if λ = .09, one can conclude that knowledge of the IV improves one's ability to predict the DV by a factor of 9%. (A non-*PRE* measure has no such interpretation.)

The formula for lambda is

$$\lambda = \frac{(P(1) - P(2))}{P(1)}$$

where *P*(1) is the overall probability of making an incorrect classification and *P*(2) is the probability of making an error after taking into account the classification variable.

Key Assumptions & Requirements

Random selection of sample (probability sample) to allow for generalization of results to a target population.

Variables. Variables are categorical.

Independence. Independence of observations.

Example Research Question

Is student computer experience the same for for students in different classes?

Example Null Hypothesis

H_0: Student computer experience is independent of different classes.

SPSS Procedure

SPSS > Analyze > Descriptive Statistics > Crosstabs > Statistics > Lambda

SPSS Output & Analysis

Crosstabulation.

Directional Measures.

- The Goodman and Kruskal tau coefficient is similar to lambda. It measures the proportional increase in accurately predicting the outcome of one categorical variable when one has information about a second categorical variable (Bishop, Feinberg, & Holland, 1975).

Directional Measures

			Value	Asymp. Std. Error[a]	Approx. T[b]	Approx. Sig.
Nominal by Nominal	Lambda	Symmetric	.107	.049	2.067	.039
		Class Dependent	.189	.068	2.590	.010
		Computer Experience Pretest Dependent	.051	.061	.819	.413
	Goodman and Kruskal tau	Class Dependent	.210	.025		.057[c]
		Computer Experience Pretest Dependent	.034	.010		.418[c]

a. Not assuming the null hypothesis.

b. Using the asymptotic standard error assuming the null hypothesis.

c. Based on chi-square approximation

The above SPSS output shows that the test is significant when class is the DV. A lambda of .19 means that there was a 19% reduction in error in predicting class when computer experience was taken into account. The test was not significant when computer experience is the DV.

Contingency Coefficient

Purpose

The contingency coefficient (C) is a chi-square-based measure of the relationship between two categorical variables. It determines whether the rows and columns of a two-way contingency table are independent (i.e., row and column variables are not associated). C is calculated as follows

$$C = \sqrt{\frac{\chi^2}{\chi^2 + N}}$$

where N is the total number of cases in the table.

The range of C is limited to 0 through 1 (where 0 means complete independence). However, an issue with this coefficient is that its maximum value depends upon the size of the table. It can reach the limit of 1 only if the number of categories is unlimited. Consequently, it does not give a meaningful description of the strength of relationship. Its primary use is for determining whether or not there is dependence.

The contingency coefficient cannot be compared across tables of different size.

Key Assumptions & Requirements

Random selection of sample (probability sample) to allow for generalization of results to a target population.

Variables. Variables are categorical variables that generate a contingency table. Variables must be reported in raw frequencies (not percentages). Values/categories of the IV and DV must be mutually exclusive and exhaustive.

Independence. Independence of observations.

Example Research Question

Is student computer experience the same for students in different classes?

Example Null Hypothesis

H_0: Student computer experience is independent of different classes.

SPSS Procedure

SPSS > Analyze > Descriptive Statistics > Crosstabs > Statistics > Contingency coefficient

SPSS Output & Analysis

Crosstabulations.

Symmetric Measures.

Symmetric Measures

		Value	Approx. Sig.
Nominal by Nominal	Contingency Coefficient	.596	.167
N of Valid Cases		92	

a. Not assuming the null hypothesis.

b. Using the asymptotic standard error assuming the null hypothesis.

The above SPSS output shows that test results are not significant, $C = .60$, $p = .17$. Consequently, there is insufficient evidence to reject the null hypothesis that student computer experience is independent of different classes.

Eta (η) Correlation Coefficient

Purpose

The eta (η) correlation coefficient is a nonparametric asymmetric measure that provides the strength of the total linear and nonlinear relationship between an interval DV and nominal IV. Eta varies from 0 to 1. For totally linear relationships, eta equals the Pearson r correlation coefficient. A relationship is linear if the difference between Pearson *r* and η is small. If the two coefficients are the same, the relationship is perfectly linear.

Eta square (η^2) is the coefficient of determination and is used as a measure of effect size in certain statistical tests; e.g., *ANOVA*. It is calculated as the ratio of the effect variance to the total variance and is interpreted as the percent of variance in the DV explained linearly and nonlinearly by the IV.

According to Tabachnick and Fidell (2007), eta square can be interpreted as follows:

Small effect size = .01
Medium effect size = .06
Large effect size = .14

Partial η^2 is the proportion of the effect plus error variance that is attributable to the effect. The formula differs from the η^2 formula in that the denominator includes the error effect (Tabachnick & Fidell, 2007).

Key Assumptions & Requirements

Random selection of samples (probability samples) to allow for generalization of results to a target population.

Variables. IV: one categorical variable (nominal, ordinal, or grouped interval). DV: one continuous variable. Absence of restricted range (data range is not truncated in any variable).

Independence. Independence of observations.

Sample size. Large cell sizes.

Example Research Question

Is there a relationship between grade point average and ethnicity, $\eta \neq 0$?

Example Null Hypothesis

H_0: There is no relationship between grade point average and ethnicity, $\eta = 0$

Alternatively, H_0: grade point average and ethnicity are independent of each other, $\eta = 0$.

SPSS Procedure

SPSS > Analyze > Descriptive Statistics > Crosstabs > Statistics > Eta

SPSS Output & Analysis

Crosstabulations.

Directional Measures.

Directional Measures

			Value
Nominal by Interval	Eta	GPA Dependent	.525
		Ethnicity Dependent	.741

The above SPSS output shows the values of the eta statistic. When grade point average (GPA) is the DV, the strength of relationship is moderate, η = .53; when ethnicity is the DV, the strength of relationship is strong, η = .74.

Spearman Rank Order Correlation Test

Purpose

The Spearman rank order correlation test is a nonparametric symmetric procedure that determines the monotonic strength and direction of the relationship between two ranked variables. This test is not based on the concordance pair concept. It can be used for any type of data, except categories that cannot be ordered. The Spearman rank order correlation coefficient varies from −1 to +1.0. It can be used instead of Pearson *r* if Pearson *r* parametric assumptions cannot be met. The symbol for the correlation coefficient is r_s (formerly Spearman rho). The formula for r_s is

$$r_s = 1 - \frac{6(\Sigma D^2)}{N(N^2 - 2)}$$

where *N* is the number of pairs of ranks and *D* is the difference between the two ranks in each pair.

Gamma is preferable to the Spearman rank order correlation test when the data contain many tied observations.

Degrees of freedom. The degrees of freedom for this test is *n* − 2, where *n* is the number of pairs in the analysis. The number of pairs equals sample size (*N*) provided there is no missing data.

Parametric Equivalent

Pearson product-moment correlation test

Key Assumptions & Requirements

Random selection of sample (probability sample) to allow for generalization of results to a target population.

Variables. Two ranked variables (ordinal, interval, or ratio data can be used). Absence of restricted range (data range is not truncated for any variable).

Independence. Independence of observations.

Monotonicity. Monotonic relationship between variables.

Example Research Question

Is there a relationship between sense of classroom community and grade point average, $r_s \neq 0$?

Example Null Hypothesis

H_0: There is no relationship between sense of classroom community and grade point average, $r_s = 0$

Alternatively,

H_0: sense of classroom community and grade point average are independent of each other, $r_s = 0$.

H_0: The ranks of one variable are not related to the ranks of the second variable, $r_s = 0$.

SPSS Procedure

SPSS > Analyze > Correlate > Bivariate > Spearman

SPSS Output & Analysis

Correlations.

Correlations

			Classroom Community	GPA
Spearman's rho	Classroom Community	Correlation Coefficient	1.000	.382**
		Sig. (2-tailed)	.	.000
		N	169	169
	GPA	Correlation Coefficient	.382**	1.000
		Sig. (2-tailed)	.000	.
		N	169	169

**. Correlation is significant at the 0.01 level (2-tailed).

The above SPSS output displays a significant but weak relationship between sense of classroom community and grade point average, $r_s(167) = .38$, $p < .001$.

Gamma (γ)

Purpose

Gamma (γ) is a nonparametric symmetric procedure that determines the monotonic strength and direction of association between two categorical ordinal variables (or with dichotomous nominal variables). The value of gamma varies from −1 to +1.

Gamma is based on the number of concordances and discordances in paired observations. Concordance occurs when paired observations vary together and discordance occurs when paired observations vary differently. Unlike Kendall's tau-*b*, gamma ignores ties. The formula for gamma is

$$\gamma = \frac{P - Q}{P + Q}$$

where P = number of concordant pairs and Q = number of discordant pairs.

Gamma is preferable to the Spearman rank order coefficient or to Kendall's tau when the data contain many tied observations.

Key Assumptions & Requirements

Random selection of sample (probability sample) to allow for generalization of results to a target population.

Variables. Two categorical ordinal variables. Absence of restricted range (data range is not truncated for any variable).

Independence. Independence of observations.

Monotonicity. Monotonic relationship between variables.

Example Research Question

Is there a relationship between sense of classroom community (strong, medium, weak) and assignment grade (A, B, C, F), $\gamma \neq 0$?

Example Null Hypothesis

H_0: There is no relationship between sense of classroom community (strong, medium, weak) and assignment grade (A, B, C, F), $\gamma = 0$.

Alternatively,

H_0: sense of classroom community and assignment grade are independent of each other, $\gamma = 0$.

H_0: The ranks of one variable are not related to the ranks of the second variable, $\gamma = 0$.

SPSS Procedure

SPSS > Analyze > Descriptive Statistics > Crosstabs > Statistics > Gamma

SPSS Output & Analysis

Symmetric Measures.

Symmetric Measures

		Value	Asymp. Std. Error[a]	Approx. T[b]	Approx. Sig.
Ordinal by Ordinal	Gamma	.143	.064	2.242	.025
N of Valid Cases		168			

a. Not assuming the null hypothesis.

b. Using the asymptotic standard error assuming the null hypothesis.

The above SPSS output shows that the test is significant, $\gamma = .14$, $p = .03$. Consequently, there is sufficient evidence to reject the null hypothesis that sense of classroom community and assignment grade are independent of each other. However, the strength of relationship is very weak.

Somers' d

Purpose

Somer's *d* is a nonparametric asymmetric procedure that determines the monotonic strength and direction of association between two categorical ordinal variables. The value of Somers' *d* varies from −1 to +1. The values +1 and - 1 indicate strict monotonic association.

Somers' *d* is based on the number of concordances and discordances in paired observations adjusted for ties in the dependent variable only. Concordance occurs when paired observations vary together and discordance occurs when paired observations vary differently. The formula for Somers' *d* is

$$Somers'd = \frac{P-Q}{P+Q+T_R}$$

where P = number of concordant pairs, Q = number of discordant pairs, and T_R = number of ties in the dependent variable (traditionally, the row variable).

Key Assumptions & Requirements

Random selection of sample (probability sample) to allow for generalization of results to a target population.

Variables. Two categorical ordinal variables. Absence of restricted range (data range is not truncated for any variable).

Independence. Independence of observations.

Monotonicity. Monotonic relationship between variables.

Example Research Question

Is there a relationship between perceived learning and assignment grade, $d \neq 0$?

Example Null Hypothesis

H_0: There is no relationship between perceived learning and assignment grade, $d = 0$.

Alternatively,

H_0: Perceived learning and assignment grade are independent of each other, $d = 0$.

H_0: The ranks of one variable are not related to the ranks of the second variable, $d = 0$.

SPSS Procedure

SPSS > Analyze > Descriptive Statistics > Crosstabs > Statistics > Somers' d

SPSS Output & Analysis

Directional Measures.

Directional Measures

			Value	Asymp. Std. Error[a]	Approx. T[b]	Approx. Sig.
Ordinal by Ordinal	Somers' d	Symmetric	.123	.055	2.242	.025
		grade Dependent	.133	.059	2.242	.025
		Perceived Learning Dependent	.114	.051	2.242	.025

a. Not assuming the null hypothesis.

b. Using the asymptotic standard error assuming the null hypothesis.

The above SPSS output shows significant test results; when grade is the DV, $d = .13$, $p = .03$, and when perceived learning is the DV, $d = .11$, $p = .03$. The strengths of relationship are very weak.

Kendall's Tau-*b* (τ_b) and Tau-*c* (τ_c)

Purpose

Kendall's tau-*b* test is a nonparametric symmetric procedure that determines the strength and direction of the monotonic association between two ordinal variables. It is often used with but not limited to 2 x 2 tables. This test is appropriate for collapsed ordinal data where the number of rows and number of columns are equal. Kendall's tau-*b* reaches 1.0 (or -1.0 for negative correlations) only for square tables. It equals 0 for statistical independence.

It is based on the number of concordances and discordances in paired observations adjusted for ties. Concordance occurs when paired observations vary together and discordance occurs when paired observations vary differently. The formula for Kendall's tau-b is

$$Tau_b = \frac{P-Q}{\sqrt{(P+Q+T_R)(P+Q+T_C)}}$$

where P = number of concordant pairs, Q = number of discordant pairs, T_R = number of ties in the row variable, and T_C = number of ties in the column variable.

Kendall's tau-c (τ_c), also called Stuart's tau-*c*, is a variant of tau-*b* for larger tables. It is used when the number of rows and number of columns are not equal.

It equals the excess of concordant over discordant pairs, multiplied by a term representing an adjustment for the size of the table. The formula for Kendall's tau-*c* is

$$Tau_c = \frac{2m(P-Q)}{N^2(m-1)}$$

where m = the smaller of the number of rows and columns and N = number of observations.

Gamma is preferable to Kendall's tau-*b* and Kendall's tau-*c* when the data contain many tied observations.

Key Assumptions & Requirements

Random selection of sample (probability sample) to allow for generalization of results to a target population.

Variables. Two categorical ordinal variables. Absence of restricted range (data range is not truncated in any variable).

Independence. Independence of observations.

Monotonicity. Monotonic relationship between variables.

Example Research Question

Is there a relationship between sense of classroom community (strong, medium, weak) and assignment grade (A, B, C, F), $\tau_b \neq 0$?

Example Null Hypothesis

H_0: There is no relationship between sense of classroom community (strong, medium, weak) and assignment grade (A, B, C, F), $\tau_b = 0$.

Alternatively,

H_0: Sense of classroom community and assignment grade are independent of each other, $\tau_b. = 0$.

H_0: The ranks of one variable are not related to the ranks of the second variable, $\tau_b = 0$.

SPSS Procedure

SPSS > Analyze > Correlate > Bivariate > Kendall's tau-*b*

SPSS > Analyze > Descriptive Statistics > Crosstabs > Statistics > Kendall's tau-*b*, Kendall's tau-*c*

SPSS Output & Analysis

Symmetric Measures.

Symmetric Measures

		Value	Asymp. Std. Error[a]	Approx. T[b]	Approx. Sig.
Ordinal by Ordinal	Kendall's tau–b	.123	.055	2.242	.025
	Kendall's tau–c	.117	.052	2.242	.025
N of Valid Cases		168			

a. Not assuming the null hypothesis.

b. Using the asymptotic standard error assuming the null hypothesis.

The above SPSS output shows significant test results with τ_b = .12, p = .03, and τ_c = .12, p = .03. Consequently, there is sufficient evidence to reject the null hypothesis that sense of classroom community and assignment grade are independent of each other. Strength of relationship, however, is very weak.

Intraclass Correlation Coefficient

Purpose

The intraclass correlation coefficient (*ICC*) is a nonparametric correlation procedure used to measure correlations within a class. A class is defined as variables that share a metric (scale) and variance. It represents agreements between two or more raters or evaluation methods on the same set of participants. The variables are different quantitative measurements of the same construct; e.g., repeated measures on the same participant, or measures on multiple individuals within the same group such as students in a classroom. Cases (rows) are the objects being measured, and the variables (columns) are the different measurements (raters) of each case. The *ICC* provides a scalar measure of agreement between all the methods. The value 1 represent perfect agreement and 0 represents no agreement. The procedure is often used to assess reliability, to include inter-rater and test-retest reliability.

If data are categorical, reliability should be assessed using Cohen's kappa measure of agreement. If interclass correlation is desired, the Pearson product moment correlation should be used.

The goal of *ICC* is to determine the proportion of variation in a measure that is due to being a member of a particular group. According to McGraw and Wong (1996), *ICC* estimates are based on mean squares obtained by applying *ANOVA* models to the data. According to Shrout and Fleiss (1979), the following models are used to calculate *ICC* (available as choices in SPSS):

- For the one-way random effects model raters are considered as sampled from a larger pool of potential raters and are treated as random effects. *ICC* is interpreted as the % of total variance accounted for by participants/items variance.

- For two-way random effects model, both factors (raters and items/participants) are viewed as random effects resulting in two variance components in addition to the residual variance. One further assumes that raters assess all items/participants. *ICC* gives in this case the % of variance attributable to raters + items/participants.

- For two-way mixed model (SPSS default model) raters are considered as fixed effects (no generalization beyond the sample) but items/participants are treated as random effects. The unit of analysis may be the individual or the average ratings.

The default type is consistency (as opposed to absolute agreement). Consistency addresses whether targets are ranked the same and absolute agreement addresses whether targets received the exact same scores.

The researcher enters a test value for testing the null hypothesis that there is no difference between the population *ICC* and the test value. The default value is 0.

Key Assumptions & Requirements

Random selection of samples (probability samples) to allow for generalization of results to a target population.

Variables. Two or more quantitative variables (ratio, interval, or ordinal) are used from the same class; i.e., they share a metric (scale).

Homogeneity of variance. Groups have equal or similar variances.

Example Research Question

What is the test-retest reliability of the classroom community scale, $ICC \neq 0$?

Example Null Hypothesis

H_0: The classroom community scale has no test-retest reliability, $ICC = 0$.

SPSS Procedure

SPSS > Analyze > Scale > Reliability Analysis > Statistics > Intraclass correlation coefficient

SPSS Output & Analysis

Intraclass Correlation Coefficient.

- Single measures reliability gives the reliability for a single judge's rating.

- Average measures reliability gives the average reliability of the mean of the ratings of all raters.

Intraclass Correlation Coefficient

	Intraclass Correlation[b]	95% Confidence Interval		F Test with True Value 0			
		Lower Bound	Upper Bound	Value	df1	df2	Sig
Single Measures	.782[a]	.715	.834	8.160	168	168	.000
Average Measures	.877[c]	.834	.910	8.160	168	168	.000

Two-way mixed effects model where people effects are random and measures effects are fixed.

a. The estimator is the same, whether the interaction effect is present or not.

b. Type C intraclass correlation coefficients using a consistency definition-the between-measure variance is excluded from the denominator variance.

c. This estimate is computed assuming the interaction effect is absent, because it is not estimable otherwise.

The above SPSS output shows *ICC* = .88 (high degree of test-retest reliability), using the following SPSS options: mixed model *ANOVA*, type consistency, and average measures.

Binomial Logistic Regression

Purpose

Binomial logistic regression is a nonparametric procedure that describes or predicts membership in two mutually exclusive groups from a set of predictors. It is very similar to multiple regression with the major difference being that in logistic regression the DV is categorical rather than continuous. It is also very similar to discriminant analysis with the major difference being that in logistic regression the IVs may be continuous variables, categorical variables, or both.

Logistic regression uses maximum likelihood estimation (MLE) rather than ordinary least squares (OLS) to derive parameters. MLE relies on large-sample asymptotic normality, which means that reliability of estimates decline when there are few cases for each observed combination of X variables (Hosmer & Lameshow, 2000).

Correct interpretation of coefficients using the odds ratio, represented by Exp(*B*), is important. Assuming an IV is coded as (0, 1), odds ratios greater than 1 show an increase in odds of an outcome of 1, with a one-unit increase in the predictor; odds ratios less than 1 show the decrease in odds of that outcome with a one-unit change. For example, an odds ratio of 1.5 shows that the outcome of 1 is 1.5 times as likely (or 50% more likely) with a one-unit increase in the IV. That is, the odds are increased by 50%. An odds ratio of 0.8 shows that an outcome of 1 is 0.8 times as likely (or 20% less likely; 1 - 0.8 = 0.2) with a one-unit increase in the predictor; the odds are decreased by 20%.

The default procedure SPSS uses for logistic regression is the "Enter" procedure in which all predictors are entered into the model simultaneously in a single block. Stepwise, forward, and backward procedures are also available.

Key Assumptions & Requirements

Random selection of samples (probability samples) to allow for generalization of results to a target population.

Independence. Independence of observations (errors).

Linearity. Logistic regression does not require linear relationships between the independents and the dependent, as does OLS regression, but it does assume a linear relationship between the logit of the independents and the dependent.

Outliers. Absence of extreme outliers.

Multicollinearity. No extreme multicollinearity or singularity between pairs of predictor variables.

Proper specification of the model. If relevant variables are omitted from the model, the common variance they share with included variables may be wrongly attributed to those variables, and the error term is inflated. If causally irrelevant variables are included in the model, the common variance they share with included variables may be wrongly attributed to the irrelevant variables. The more the correlation of the irrelevant variable(s) with other independents, the greater the standard errors of the regression coefficients for these independents. Omission and irrelevancy can both affect substantially the size of the b and beta coefficients.

Sample size. A large ratio of cases to variables is required.

Example Research Question

Do classroom community spirit, grade on final examination, and race predict the likelihood of a university student favoring online courses over on campus courses?

Example Null Hypothesis

H_0: One cannot predict whether a university student favors online courses over on campus courses based on classroom community spirit, grade on final examination, and race.

SPSS Procedure

SPSS > Analyze > Regression > Binary Logistic

SPSS Output & Analysis

SPSS output varies based on options selected by the user.

Block 0: Beginning Block, Iteration History.

- Block 0 shows the results of the logistic regression analysis without any of the predictor variables entered into the model, referred to as the null model.

Block 0: Beginning Block

Iteration History[a,b,c]

Iteration		-2 Log likelihood	Coefficients Constant
Step 0	1	105.235	1.350
	2	103.816	1.616
	3	103.806	1.640
	4	103.806	1.641

a. Constant is included in the model.

b. Initial -2 Log Likelihood: 103.806

c. Estimation terminated at iteration number 4 because parameter estimates changed by less than .001.

Block 0: Beginning Block, Classification Table.

- The classification table compares the predicted values for the DV, based on the regression model, with the actual observed values in the data. The overall percentage gives the percent of cases for which the DV was correctly predicted given the model.

Classification Table[a,b]

			Predicted		
			Favor Online		Percentage Correct
Observed			No	Yes	
Step 0	Favor Online	No	0	19	.0
		Yes	0	98	100.0
Overall Percentage					83.8

a. Constant is included in the model.

b. The cut value is .500

The above SPSS output indicates that the model with no predictors entered correctly classified 83.8% of the cases. Note that all predictions were placed in the category favoring online courses.

Block 0: Beginning Block, Variables in the equation.

Variables in the Equation

		B	S.E.	Wald	df	Sig.	Exp(B)
Step 0	Constant	1.641	.251	42.831	1	.000	5.158

Block 0: Beginning Block, Variables not in the equation.

Block 1: Method = Enter. Iteration History.

- Block 1 shows the results of the logistic regression analysis with the predictor variables entered into the model.

Block 1: Method = Enter

Iteration History[a,b,c,d]

Iteration		-2 Log likelihood	Coefficients			
			Constant	race	grade	spirit
Step 1	1	84.032	4.493	-.028	.019	-.118
	2	70.337	8.381	-.029	-.066	-.234
	3	66.016	12.041	-.019	-.244	-.337
	4	65.267	14.310	-.017	-.356	-.400
	5	65.235	14.895	-.018	-.380	-.416
	6	65.235	14.924	-.018	-.381	-.417
	7	65.235	14.924	-.018	-.381	-.417

a. Method: Enter

b. Constant is included in the model.

c. Initial -2 Log Likelihood: 103.806

d. Estimation terminated at iteration number 7 because parameter estimates changed by less than .001.

Block 1: Omnibus Tests of Model Coefficients.

Omnibus Tests of Model Coefficients

		Chi-square	df	Sig.
Step 1	Step	38.571	3	.000
	Block	38.571	3	.000
	Model	38.571	3	.000

The above SPSS output shows that the logistic regression model, with all predictors entered, significantly predicts the variation in course preference in the research sample.

Block 1: Model Summary.

- The Cox & Snell R^2 and the Nagelkerke R^2 indicate what percentage of the DV may be accounted for by all included predictor variables.

- Nagelkerke's R^2 is a further modification of the Cox and Snell coefficient to assure that it can vary from 0 to 1. That is, Nagelkerke's R^2 divides Cox and Snell's R^2 by its maximum in order to achieve a measure that ranges from 0 to 1.

- These measures are used to indicate how well the model fits the data. A likelihood is a probability, specifically the probability that the observed values of the DV may be predicted from the observed values of the IVs. Smaller −2 log likelihood values mean that the model fits the data better; a perfect model has a −2 log likelihood value of zero.

Model Summary

Step	−2 Log likelihood	Cox & Snell R Square	Nagelkerke R Square
1	65.235[a]	.281	.477

a. Estimation terminated at iteration number 7 because parameter estimates changed by less than .001.

The above SPSS output displays the model summary. It indicates that between 28.1% and 47.7% of the variability in predicting the criterion variable is explained by the set of predictor variables

Block 1: Hosmer and Lemeshow Test.

- The Hosmer-Lemeshow goodness-of-fit test produces a chi-square statistic that examines whether the observed counts in each risk group correspond with the count expected under linearity. If the observed and expected counts are close to one another, one should see a small Hosmer and Lemeshow statistic and a large p-value. The H_0 for this test is that the model fits the data.

Hosmer and Lemeshow Test

Step	Chi-square	df	Sig.
1	4.559	8	.803

The above SPSS output provides evidence that the model fits the data since $p > .05$.

Block 1: Contingency Table for Hosmer and Lameshow Test.

Block 1: Classification Table.

- The classification table compares the predicted values for the DV, based on the regression model, with the actual observed values in the data. The overall percentage gives the percent of cases for which the DV was correctly predicted given the model.

Classification Table[a]

			Predicted		
			Favor Online		Percentage Correct
	Observed		No	Yes	
Step 1	Favor Online	No	7	12	36.8
		Yes	5	93	94.9
	Overall Percentage				85.5

a. The cut value is .500

The above SPSS output indicates that the model with all predictors entered correctly classified 85.5% of the cases. However, the null model correctly classified 83.8% of the cases. The marginal increase in accuracy with all predictors entered suggests this model has little discriminatory power and no practical value. A contributing problem is that several cells have few cases, resulting in a model that is likely to be unstable.

Positive predictive value (% of cases that the model predicts has the characteristic that is observed to have the characteristic) = [93 / (12 +93)] x 100 = 88.57%.

Negative predictive value (% of cases that the model predicts not to have the characteristic that is observed not to have the characteristic) = [7 / (7 + 5)] x 100 = 58.33%.

Block 1: Variables in the Equation.

- This table provides information about the importance of each predictor variable based on the Wald chi-square test. The *B* values are equivalent to the *B* values produced by the multiple regression and correlation procedure. Wald is a measure of the significance of *B* for the identified variable. Higher values, in conjunction with degrees of freedom, suggest statistical significance.

- The Exp(B) is the exponentiation of the *B* coefficient and represents the odds ratio for each IV. Tabachnick and Fiddell (2007) report that the odds ratio represents

  the change in odds of being in one of the categories of outcome when the value of a predictor increases by one unit. (p. 461)

- The 95% confidence interval for Exp(*B*) provides the upper and lower bounds within which one has 95% confidence encompasses the true odds ratio.

Variables in the Equation

		B	S.E.	Wald	df	Sig.	Exp(B)	95% C.I.for EXP (B) Lower	Upper
Step 1[a]	spirit	-.417	.104	16.147	1	.000	.659	.538	.808
	grade	-.381	1.056	.130	1	.718	.683	.086	5.407
	race	-.018	.291	.004	1	.950	.982	.555	1.737
	Constant	14.924	3.893	14.696	1	.000	3030602.4		

a. Variable(s) entered on step 1: spirit, grade, race.

The above SPSS output shows that the only significant predictor of course preference is classroom community spirit.

The Exp(B) column shows the odds ratios of the row IV with the DV. Since the 0 value in the DV corresponds to favoring traditional courses and the 1 value favors distance courses, and since odds ratios less than 1 correspond to decreases, the odds ratio of .66 for community spirit indicates that with a unit increase (switching from traditional to distance courses), the odds of favoring distance courses are multiplied by .66, which is a 34% (1 − .66) decrease (34% less likely).

Block 1: Correlation Matrix.

- SPSS produces a correlation matrix for all variables in the regression equation, if requested. This matrix is useful for identifying highly correlated variables, which can result in multcollinearity and an unstable solution.

Correlation Matrix

		Constant	race	grade	spirit
Step 1	Constant	1.000	-.056	-.512	-.853
	race	-.056	1.000	-.101	.009
	grade	-.512	-.101	1.000	.008
	spirit	-.853	.009	.008	1.000

Block 1: Plot, Observed Groups and Predicted Probabilities.

Block 1: Casewise List.

Cohen's Kappa (κ)

Purpose

Cohen's kappa (κ) measure of agreement is a reliability coefficient generated by a nonparametric procedure that tests for inter-rater agreement between two raters using the same categorical rating scale. It produces a κ coefficient. This test compares the observed agreement to the expected agreement if the ratings are independent (Peat, 2001). Below is the formula for the test statistic

$$K = \frac{p - p_e}{1 - p_e}$$

where p is the proportion of units where there is agreement and p_e is the proportion of units that would be expected to agree by chance.

If agreement is less than agreement by chance, then κ is less than or equal to 0. The minimum possible value of κ is −1. Generally, a value of κ higher than 0.75 indicates excellent agreement while lower than 0.4 indicates poor agreement. According to Peat (2001), a significant κ may be interpreted as follows:

Moderate agreement – .5
Good agreement – above .7
Very good agreement – .8

There are two possible uses of κ: as a way to test rater independence and as a way to quantify the level of agreement.

- The first use involves testing the null hypothesis that there is no more agreement than might occur by chance given random guessing. Kappa is appropriate for this purpose.

- It is the second use of κ, quantifying actual levels of agreement, that is a source of concern. Kappa's calculation uses a term called the proportion of chance (or expected) agreement. This is interpreted as the proportion of times raters would agree by chance alone. However, the term is relevant only under the conditions of statistical independence of raters. Since raters are not independent (i.e., they are rating the same individuals), the appropriateness of this application is questionable.

As a test statistic, κ can verify that agreement exceeds chance levels; consequently κ is preferred over simple percentage agreement. However, as a measure of the level of agreement, κ is not chance-corrected.

As a measure of agreement, the value of к should be high (i.e., over .70), not merely statistically significant.

If data are continuous, reliability should be assessed using the intraclass correlation coefficient (*ICC*).

Key Assumptions & Requirements

Variables. Two raters who use the same categorical rating scale (i.e., both raters uses the same rating codes).

Independence. Independence of observations.

Example Research Question

How reliable are the raters in assigning grades of pass and fail for the spring semester candidacy examination?

Note: This question assumes a team of raters (rater 1, rater 2) graded each examination paper.

Example Null Hypothesis

H_0: there is no more agreement by raters in grading the spring semester candidacy examination than might occur by chance given random guessing.

SPSS Procedure

SPSS > Analyze > Descriptive Statistics > Crosstabs > Statistics > Kappa

SPSS Output & Analysis

Crosstabulations table.

Symmetric Measures.

Symmetric Measures

	Value	Asymp. Std. Error[a]	Approx. T[b]	Approx. Sig.
Measure of Agreement Kappa	.386	.042	9.448	.000
N of Valid Cases	350			

a. Not assuming the null hypothesis.

b. Using the asymptotic standard error assuming the null hypothesis.

The above SPSS output shows a significant к. However, the value of к suggests the level of agreement is only fair. Although not included in the output, one can determine the 95%

confidence interval by using the generic formula for 95% confidence intervals: value ± 1.96 standard errors, where value = kappa coefficient.

9.3: Parametric Tests

Pearson Product-Moment Correlation Test

Purpose

The Pearson product-moment correlation test (Pearson r) is a parametric procedure that determines the strength and direction of the linear relationship between two continuous variables. Pearson r is symmetric, with the same coefficient value obtained regardless of which variable is the IV and which is the DV.

Pearson r is calculated by taking cross-products of z-scores.

$$r = \frac{\sum Z_X Z_Y}{N}$$

The z-scores in the formula standardize the units of measure in both distributions.

According to Hinkle, Wiersma, and Jurs (1998), Pearson r can be interpreted as follows:

Little if any relationship < .30
Low relationship = .30 to < .50
Moderate relationship = .50 to < .70
High relationship = .70 to < .90
Very high relationship = .90 and above

Degrees of freedom. The degrees of freedom for this test is $n - 2$, where n is the number of pairs in the analysis. The number of pairs equals sample size (N) provided there is no missing data.

Nonparametric Equivalent

Spearman rank order correlation test

Key Assumptions & Requirements

Random selection of samples (probability samples) to allow for generalization of results to a target population.

Variables. Two interval/ratio scale variables. Absence of restricted range (i.e., data range is not truncated in any variable).

Many researchers support the use of this test with ordinal scale variables that have several levels of responses. For example, Nunnally and Bernstein (1994) assert that this test can be used with ordinal level variables that have more than 11 rank values.

Measurement without error.

Bivariate normality. Both variables should have an underlying distribution that is bivariate normal (bivariate normal distributions have a symmetric elliptical pattern). It indicates that scores on one variable are normally distributed for each value of the other variable, and vice versa.

Outliers. Absence of extreme outliers.

Independence. Independence of observations.

Homoscedasticity. The variability in scores for one variable is roughly the same at all values of a second variable.

Linearity.

Example Research Question

Is there a relationship between sense of classroom community and grade point average, $r = 0$?

Example Null Hypothesis

H_0: There is no relationship between sense of classroom community and grade point average, $r \neq 0$.

SPSS Procedure

SPSS > Analyze > Correlate > Bivariate > Pearson

SPSS Output & Analysis

Descriptive Statistics (mean, standard deviation, *N*).

Correlations.

Correlations

		Classroom Community	GPA
Classroom Community	Pearson Correlation	1	.360**
	Sig. (2-tailed)		.000
	N	169	169
GPA	Pearson Correlation	.360**	1
	Sig. (2-tailed)	.000	
	N	169	169

**. Correlation is significant at the 0.01 level (2-tailed).

The above SPSS output shows a low but significant direct relationship between sense of classroom community and grade point average, $r(167) = .36$, $p < .001$. As one variable goes up or down, so does the other variable.

Internal Consistency Reliability Analysis

Purpose

Internal consistency reliability analysis is a parametric procedure that measures the internal consistency reliability of a scale or subscale. See reliability in Section 1 (Introduction) of this chapter.

Reliability is the extent to which an item, scale, or instrument will yield the same score when administered at different times or locations, or to different populations, assuming the administrations do not differ on relevant variables being measured. Reliability coefficients are forms of correlation coefficients.

The following models of internal consistency reliability are available in SPSS:

- Cronbach's alpha model is based on the average inter-item correlation.

- Split-half model splits the scale into two parts and examines the correlation between the parts.

- Guttman model computes Guttman's lower bounds for true reliability.

- Parallel model assumes that all items have equal variances and equal error variances across replications.

- Strict parallel model makes the assumptions of the parallel model and also assumes equal means across items.

SPSS will produce statistics for any of these reliability models. Reliability coefficients can be interpreted as follows (Hinkle, Wiersma, & Jurs, 1998):

Little if any reliability < .30
Low reliability = .30 to < .50
Moderate reliability = .50 to < .70
High reliability = .70 to < .90
Very high reliability = .90 and above

> **Key Point**
> Many researchers consider scale reliability below .70 as inadequate and avoid using such scales.

Many researchers consider scale reliability below .70 as inadequate and avoid using such scales.

In addition to computing internal consistency reliability for a scale, one might also want to investigate the scale's dimensionality in order to determine if the scale is unidimensional or multidimensional (i.e., consists of homogeneous subsets that represent subscales of the instrument). Exploratory factor analysis is used for this purpose.

To obtain evidence of criterion validity, one should obtain the Pearson product-moment correlation coefficient between the tested scale and the criterion scale, assuming scores from both scales are normally distributed. The Spearman rank order correlation coefficient should be used for ordinal data.

Key Assumptions & Requirements

Variables. The instrument, representing an additive scale, should consist of multiple interval or ratio scale items. The items measure the same construct and are thus related to each other in a linear manner. Cronbach's alpha requires that items are not scored dichotomously.

Normality. Each item on the scale should be normally distributed. If this assumption is not tenable, Spearman rank order correlation should be considered for the reliability analysis.

Example Research Question

Is the Classroom Community Scale reliable, $r \geq .70$?

Example Null Hypothesis

H_0: The Classroom Community Scale is not reliable, $r < .70$.

SPSS Procedure

SPSS > Analyze > Scale > Reliability Analysis > Alpha

SPSS > Analyze > Scale > Reliability Analysis > Split-half

SPSS > Analyze > Scale > Reliability Analysis > Guttman

SPSS > Analyze > Scale > Reliability Analysis > Parallel

SPSS > Analyze > Scale > Reliability Analysis > Strict Parallel

SPSS Output & Analysis

Reliability Statistics.

Reliability Statistics

Cronbach's Alpha	Cronbach's Alpha Based on Standardized Items	N of Items
.926	.928	20

The above SPSS output shows internal consistency reliability results using Cronbach's alpha for the Classroom Community Scale (Rovai, 2002). The internal consistency reliability of .93 is very high.

Reliability Statistics

Cronbach's Alpha	Part 1	Value	.869
		N of Items	10[a]
	Part 2	Value	.862
		N of Items	10[b]
	Total N of Items		20
Correlation Between Forms			.842
Spearman–Brown Coefficient	Equal Length		.914
	Unequal Length		.914
Guttman Split–Half Coefficient			.910

This SPSS table reports the results of using the split-half model. The reliability of the total scale is reported as .91 (Spearman-Brown equal length coefficient), reflecting very high internal consistency

If Guttman is selected, SPSS reports lambda coefficients. If parallel or strict parallel is selected, SPSS reports common variance, true variance, error variance, common inter-item correlation, reliability of scale, and reliability of scale (unbiased).

Item Statistics (mean, deviation, *N*).

Item-Total Statistics.

- If Cronbach's alpha is higher when an item is removed, the researcher concludes that that item may not be part of the same construct as all of the other items and therefore may need to be removed from the scale if the scale's content validity is not adversely affected.

Item-Total Statistics

	Scale Mean if Item Deleted	Scale Variance if Item Deleted	Corrected Item-Total Correlation	Cronbach's Alpha if Item Deleted
q01	53.72	141.263	.583	.923
q02	53.57	139.780	.623	.922
q03	54.13	136.131	.716	.920
q04	53.80	137.386	.620	.922
q05	54.17	134.954	.710	.920
q06	54.06	139.799	.425	.927
q07	54.69	133.988	.701	.920
q08	54.16	140.808	.445	.926
q09	54.08	134.689	.723	.919
q10	53.91	139.907	.547	.923
q11	53.83	141.884	.609	.922
q12	53.82	137.922	.597	.922
q13	54.05	138.367	.645	.921
q14	53.54	142.342	.506	.924
q15	54.57	139.336	.533	.924
q16	53.60	140.712	.629	.922
q17	54.29	137.921	.625	.922
q18	53.77	138.705	.581	.923
q19	53.92	139.983	.608	.922
q20	53.62	140.029	.608	.922

The above SPSS output indicates all questions (items) on the survey appear reliable. There are no outlier questions that, if deleted, would significantly change the instrument's internal consistency reliability.

Inter-Item Correlation Matrix.

Inter-Item Covariance Matrix.

Summary Item Statistics.

Summary Item Statistics

	Mean	Minimum	Maximum	Range	Maximum / Minimum	Variance	N of Items
Item Means	2.84	2.11	3.265	1.153	1.546	.100	20
Item Variances	.922	.550	1.417	.867	2.577	.048	20
Inter-Item Covariances	.355	.113	.740	.627	6.569	.015	20
Inter-Item Correlations	.392	.093	.671	.578	7.220	.015	20

Scale Statistics.

- If split-half or Guttman is selected, SPSS reports statistics for part 1, part 2, and both parts. If parallel or strict parallel is selected, SPSS reports mean, variance, standard deviation, *N* of items)

Scale Statistics

Mean	Variance	Std. Deviation	N of Items
56.81	153.192	12.377	20

Hotellings T-Squared Test.

- Tests the null hypothesis that all items on the scale have the same mean.

Hotelling's T-Squared Test

Hotelling's T-Squared	F	df1	df2	Sig
1005.351	50.304	19	347	.000

The above SPSS output shows significant test results, $F(19, 347) = 50.30$, $p < .001$. There is sufficient evidence to reject Hotelling's *T*-squared null hypothesis that all items on the scale have the same mean.

Intraclass Correlation Coefficient.

- Single measures reliability gives the reliability for a single judge's rating.

- Average measures reliability gives the average reliability of the mean of the ratings of all raters.

Point-Biserial Correlation (r_{pb})

Purpose

The point-biserial correlation (r_{pb}) is the special case of the Pearson product moment correlation applied to a dichotomous and a continuous variable. The dichotomous variable is coded as 1 when the trait is present and 0 when the trait is not present; e.g., 1 = pass, 0 = fail. The correlation coefficients produced by the SPSS Pearson *r* correlation procedure is a point-biserial correlation when these types of variables are used.

Degrees of freedom. The degrees of freedom for this test is $n - 2$, where n is the number of pairs in the analysis. The number of pairs equals sample size (N) provided there is no missing data.

Nonparametric Equivalent

Spearman rank order correlation test

Key Assumptions & Requirements

Random selection of samples (probability samples) to allow for generalization of results to a target population.

Variables. One dichotomous and one continuous variable. Absence of restricted range (i.e., data range is not truncated in any variable).

Measurement without error.

Bivariate normality. The continuous variable should have an underlying distribution that is bivariate normal). It indicates that scores on the continuous variable are normally distributed for each value of the dichotomous variable.

Outliers. Absence of extreme outliers.

Independence. Independence of observations.

Homoscedasticity. The variability in scores for one variable is roughly the same at all values of a second variable.

Linearity.

Example Research Question

Is there a relationship between classroom spirit and type course (on campus, online), $r_{pb} \neq 0$?

Example Null Hypothesis

H_0: There is no relationship between classroom spirit and type course (on campus, online), $r_{pb} = 0$.

SPSS Procedure

SPSS > Analyze > Correlate > Bivariate > Pearson

SPSS Output & Analysis

Descriptive Statistics (mean, standard deviation, *N*).

Correlations.

Correlations

		Type course	Spirit Posttest
Type course	Pearson Correlation	1	-.495**
	Sig. (2-tailed)		.000
	Sum of Squares and Cross-products	16.748	-132.975
	Covariance	.137	-1.117
	N	123	120
Spirit Posttest	Pearson Correlation	-.495**	1
	Sig. (2-tailed)	.000	
	Sum of Squares and Cross-products	-132.975	4519.925
	Covariance	-1.117	37.983
	N	120	120

**. Correlation is significant at the 0.01 level (2-tailed).

The above SPSS output displays the Pearson product-moment correlation coefficient, $r(118) = -.50$, $p < .001$. These results are equal to r_{pb} since a continuous variable and a dichotomous variable (0 = on campus and 1 = online) were used in the analysis.

Partial Correlation

Purpose

Partial correlation is a parametric procedure that determines the correlation between two variables after removing the influences of a third or more variable from the relationship. If the partial correlation approaches 0, the inference is that the original correlation is spurious. That is, the original relationship (i.e., zero-order correlation) is computational only and there is no direct causal link between the original variables because confounding variable(s) were not considered.

One conducts partial correlation when the third variable is related to one or both of the primary variables and when there is a theoretical reason why the third variable would influence the results.

Degrees of freedom. The degrees of freedom for this test is $n - 3$, where n is the number of pairs in the analysis. The number of pairs equals sample size (N) provided there is no missing data.

Key Assumptions & Requirements

Random selection of samples (probability samples) to allow for generalization of results to a target population.

Variables. All variables are continuous. Absence of restricted range (i.e., data range is not truncated in any variable). Many researchers support the use of this test with ordinal level variables that have several levels of responses. For example, Nunnally and Bernstein (1994) assert that this test can be used with ordinal level variables that have more than 11 rank values.

Measurement without error.

Multivariate normality. The variables being compared should have an underlying distribution that is multivariate normal. It indicates that scores on one variable are normally distributed for each value of the other variables, and vice versa.

Outliers. Absence of extreme outliers.

Independence. Independence of observations.

Homoscedasticity. The variability in scores for one variable is roughly the same at all values of a second variable.

Linearity.

Example Research Question

Is there a relationship between sense of classroom community and grade point average in online students after controlling for student age, $r_{12.3} \neq 0$?

Null Hypothesis

H_0: There is no relationship between sense of classroom community and grade point average in online students after controlling for student age, $r_{12.3} = 0$.

SPSS Procedure

SPSS > Analyze > Correlate > Partial

SPSS Output & Analysis

Descriptive Statistics (mean, standard deviation, *N*).

Correlations.

Correlations

Control Variables			Classroom Community	GPA	Age
-none-[a]	Classroom Community	Correlation	1.000	.360	.457
		Significance (2-tailed)	.	.000	.000
		df	0	166	166
	GPA	Correlation	.360	1.000	.552
		Significance (2-tailed)	.000	.	.000
		df	166	0	166
	Age	Correlation	.457	.552	1.000
		Significance (2-tailed)	.000	.000	.
		df	166	166	0
Age	Classroom Community	Correlation	1.000	.146	
		Significance (2-tailed)	.	.060	
		df	0	165	
	GPA	Correlation	.146	1.000	
		Significance (2-tailed)	.060	.	
		df	165	0	

a. Cells contain zero-order (Pearson) correlations.

The above SPSS output displays a significant zero-order correlation between classroom community and grade point average, $r(166) = .36$, $p < .001$. However, when age is held constant, the relationship becomes insignificant, $r_{12.3}(165) = .15$, $p = .06$. Consequently, there is insufficient evidence to reject the null hypothesis of no relationship between sense of classroom community and grade point average in online students after controlling for student age.

Bivariate Regression

Purpose

Bivariate regression is a parametric procedure that predicts individual scores on a continuous DV based on scores of a continuous IV. Bivariate regression refers to the situation where there are only two distributions of scores, X and Y. By convention, X is the predictor variable (IV), and Y is the criterion (predicted) variable (DV). Bivariate regression analysis determines the fit of the best line to the bivariate scatterplot. That line represents the predicted relationship between two variables. Bivariate regression is a special case of the multiple regression procedure that uses only one IV instead of multiple IVs. See regression in Section 1 (Introduction) of this chapter for more information on the conceptual underpinnings of regression analysis.

Bivariate regression can incorporate a dichotomous variable as the IV that is coded using 1 and 0 and treated as a continuous variable. One codes this dummy variable with 1 if the characteristic is present and with 0 if the characteristic is absent. For example, maleness would be coded as 1 if present and 0 if absent. Conversely, femaleness could be coded as 1 if present and 0 if absent.

The unstandardized regression line derived from the regression of y on x (i.e., the bivariate regression prediction equation) takes the following form

$$Y' = a + bx$$

The equation for the standardized regression line takes the following form

$$Z_Y = \beta Z_X$$

where:

Y' = predicted value of the DV.

a = y-axis intercept, that is, the predicted value of y when x is zero. This is the point at which the regression line intersects with the vertical y-axis.

b = unstandardized regression coefficient, that is, the slope of the regression or best fit line. It signifies the amount of change in y associated with one unit change in x; i.e., the rise of the line over the run of the line.

x = a score on the IV.

β = the standardized regression coefficient

Z = standard z-score.

The more linear the relationship, the more accurate the prediction. Since a relationship between two variables can be approximately linear over a certain range, then change, one should be very cautious about predictions beyond the range of observed data that produces a regression equation. This practice of extrapolation may yield inaccurate answers.

Effect size. The coefficient of multiple correlation (R) and the adjusted coefficient of multiple determination (R^2) are appropriate effect size statistics for regression analysis.

Key Assumptions & Requirements

Random selection of samples (probability samples) to allow for generalization of results to a target population.

Gauss-Markov assumptions (Berry & Feldman, 1985):

- All variables are at least interval scale and are measured without error (one can use dummy variables for ordinal or nominal scale predictors). Measurement errors in the DV do not lead to estimation bias in the correlation coefficients, but they do lead to an increase in the standard error of the estimate, thereby weakening the test of statistical significance. Additionally, measurement errors in the IVs may lead to either an upward or a downward bias in the regression coefficients (Pedhazur, 1997).

- Mean value of the error term is zero.

- The variance of the error term is constant.

- Error terms are uncorrelated.

- Each predictor is uncorrelated with the error term.

- No extreme multicollinearity or singularity between pairs of predictor variables.

Note: When Gauss-Markov assumptions are met,

the least squares estimators of regression parameters are unbiased and efficient... The Gauss-Markov theorem holds only when the assumptions of the regression model are met. (Berry & Feldman, 1985, p. 15)

Normality. Both variables should have an underlying distribution that is bivariate normal (bivariate normal distributions have a symmetric elliptical pattern). It indicates that scores on one variable are normally distributed for each value of the other variable, and vice versa. Residuals (predicted minus observed values) are distributed normally.

Outliers. Absence of extreme outliers.

Linearity. If the relationship between the IV and the criterion variable is not linear, the results of the regression analysis will under-estimate the true relationship. This under-estimation carries an increased chance of a Type II error.

Homoscedasticity. Tthe variability in scores for one variable is roughly the same at all values of a second variable.

Proper specification of the model. If relevant variables are omitted from the model, the common variance they share with the included IV may be wrongly attributed to that variable and the error term will be inflated. In other words, one should have all the important variables in the model and no unimportant ones. This assumption is very often problematic in bivariate regression since many social phenomena involve multiple variables. The specification problem in regression is similar to the problem of spuriousness in correlation, where a given bivariate correlation may be inflated because one has not yet introduced control variables into the model by way of partial correlation.

Sample size. Various rules of thumb have been suggested regarding sample size, but much depends on the amount of noise in the data and the nature of the phenomena being investigated. Tabachnick and Fidell (2007) suggest researchers have 105 events for bivariate regression analysis. Stevens (2002) suggests regression analysis must include at least 15 events per predictor variable.

Example Research Question

Can perceived learning predict sense of classroom community among university students, $b \neq 0$?

Example Null Hypothesis

H_0: perceived learning cannot predict classroom community among university students, $b = 0$.

Alternatively,

H_0: The slope of the regression line fitting perceived learning and classroom community in the population is equal to zero, $b = 0$.

SPSS Procedure

SPSS > Analyze > Regression > Linear

SPSS Output & Analysis

Descriptive Statistics.

Descriptive Statistics

	Mean	Std. Deviation	N
Classroom Community	28.82	6.255	168
Perceived Learning	6.51	1.761	168

Correlations.

Correlations

		Classroom Community	Perceived Learning
Pearson Correlation	Classroom Community	1.000	.526
	Perceived Learning	.526	1.000
Sig. (1-tailed)	Classroom Community	.	.000
	Perceived Learning	.000	.
N	Classroom Community	168	168
	Perceived Learning	168	168

The above SPSS output shows a moderate positive relationship between classroom community and perceived learning, $r(166) = .53$, $p < .001$.

Model Summary.

- In bivariate regression analysis, R represents the Pearson r product-moment correlation coefficient between the DV and the IV. R square is the coefficient of determination. It identifies the portion of variance in the DV explained by variance in the IV.

- The Durbin–Watson statistic is used to detect the presence of autocorrelation of residuals. Generally, a Durbin-Watson statistic in the range of 1.5 to 2.5 means that one may assume independence of observations.

Model Summary[b]

	Change Statistics					
Model	R Square Change	F Change	df1	df2	Sig. F Change	Durbin–Watson
1	.277[a]	63.49	1	166	.000	1.599

a. Predictors: (Constant), Perceived Learning
b. Dependent Variable: Classroom Community

The above SPSS output shows that the regression model is statistically significant, $F(1,166) = 63.49$, $p < .001$. In particular, 27.7% of the variance in classroom community in the sample is accounted for by perceived learning. Additionally, the Durbin-Watson statistic provides evidence of independence of observations.

Coefficients.

- These coefficients provide the values needed to write the regression equation. The unstandardized coefficients are used to create an unstandardized prediction equation, where a = constant and slope (b) = unstandardized coefficient (B).

- Beta represents the standardized coefficient, which shows the impact of the IV in standard deviation units.

- A significant *t*-test is evidence that the coefficient is significantly different from zero.

- Collinearity diagnostics are useful in multiple regression when one evaluates the assumption of absence of multicollinearity among pairs of IVs. These diagnostics can be ignored in bivariate regression. See the multiple regression procedure for an explanation of collinearity statistics.

Coefficients[a]

Model		Unstandardized Coefficients		Standardized Coefficients	t	Sig.	Collinearity Statistics	
		B	Std. Error	Beta			Tolerance	VIF
1	(Constant)	16.647	1.58		10.520	.000		
	Perceived Learning	1.869	.235	.526	7.968	.000	1.000	1.000

a. Dependent Variable: Classroom Community

The above SPSS output provides evidence that perceived learning is a significant predictor of classroom community. The unstandardized prediction equation is

$$Y' = 1.87x + 16.65$$

where y = classroom community and x = perceived learning. Tolerance and variance inflation factor (*VIF*) statistics suggest multicollinearity is not an issue.

Residuals Statistics.

- This table displays descriptive statistics for predicted values, values, standardized predicted values, and standardized residuals.

Plots.

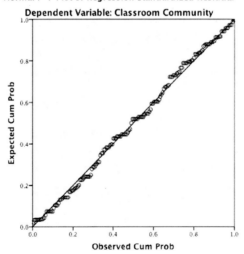

Normal P-P Plot of Regression Standardized Residual
Dependent Variable: Classroom Community

The above SPSS plot provides evidence that residuals are normally distributed. Violations of linearity and homogeneity of variance assumptions can cause residuals to depart from normality.

Multiple Regression and Correlation

Purpose

Multiple regression and correlation (*MRC*) is a parametric multiple correlation procedure that determines the relationship between a single continuous DV and multiple continuous IVs. It is also a multiple regression procedure that accounts for (i.e., predicts) the variance in a continuous DV (the criterion variable) based on linear combinations of continuous IVs (the predictor variables). It employs ordinary least squares (OLS) to minimize the sum of the squared residuals. See regression In Section 1 (Introduction) of this chapter for more information on the conceptual underpinnings of regression analysis.

MRC can incorporate a categorical variable as an IV as a dummy variable. A dummy variable is a nominal scale variable that is recoded using 1 and 0 and treated as a quantitative variable. One codes the dummy variable with 1 if the characteristic is present and with 0 if the characteristic is absent 0. A single nominal variable is recoded as $k-1$ dummy variables, where k = the number of levels in the nominal variable. For example, take the nominal variable gender (male, female). A dummy variable could be maleness, where each participant is coded 1 if the participant is male and 0 for female participants. Alternatively, the dummy variable could be femaleness where each participant is coded 1 if the participant is female and 0 for male participants. Only one of these dummy variables would be used as the IV. Incorporating both maleness and femaleness in the same model would create a multicollinearity problem.

The unstandardized regression line derived from the regression of y on x (i.e., the multiple regression prediction equation) takes the following form

$$Y' = a + b_1 X_1 + b_2 X_2 + ... b_i X_i$$

where y is the DV (the apostrophe indicates a predicted value via the equation); the b term is the unstandardized regression coefficient (reported as *B* by SPSS), representing the amount the DV (i.e., *y*) changes when the associated IV (i.e., *x*) changes one unit; the a term is the constant term and represents the point where the regression line intercepts the *y* axis (it represents the value of the DV when all the IVs are 0); and *i* = the number of IVs.

When the scores on X and Y have been converted to *z*-scores (standardized coefficients), then the constant term disappears and the equation for predicting Y from X becomes

$$Z_Y = \beta_1 Z_{X1} + \beta_2 Z_{X2} + ...\beta_i Z_{Xi}$$

where β is the standardized coefficient (beta) reported in the output and *i* = the number of IVs.

The standardized versions of the b coefficients are the beta coefficients or weights. The beta weights can be interpreted as the relative importance of the various IVs in predicting the DV. However, one should interpret very large differences as evidence that one predictor is more important than another.

Associated with multiple regression is R^2, the coefficient of multiple determination, which is the percent of variance in the DV explained collectively by all of the IVs.

Regression coefficients generated from sample data will fluctuate above and below the actual value of the population parameter. These sampling fluctuations tend to be more severe in situations involving smaller samples or a large proportion of IVs to subjects. In such situations, the value generated for the coefficient of multiple determination (R^2) tends to be overestimated. To compensate for this situation, an adjustment is made to the value of the R^2 that produces a better estimate of the true population parameter. SPSS output identifies this value as adjusted R^2 in all multiple regression output.

One needs to be alert for suppressor variables. A suppressor variable is a variable that appears to be positively related to the DV but when included in the regression model has a negative regression coefficient. This is due to the fact that an IV (the suppressor variable) is highly related to another IV and any variability that is explained in the DV by the suppressor variable is explained by the other IV. Conger (1974) provides the following definition of a suppressor variable: "...a variable which increases the predictive validity of another variable (or set of variables) by its inclusion in a regression equation" (pp. 36-37).

SPSS supports several regression methods (Norusis, 2011):

- The standard model is the SPSS default method of conducting multiple regression is the standard model (labeled Enter by SPSS). In the standard model all predictors enter into the regression equation at once and each one is evaluated as if it had entered the regression after all other predictors had entered. Each predictor is evaluated in terms of what it adds to prediction of the DV that is different from the predictability afforded by all the other predictors.

- In the sequential or hierarchical model, predictors enter the equation in an order specified by the researcher. Each predictor (or set of predictors) is evaluated in terms of what it adds to the equation at its own point of entry. The researcher normally assigns order of entry of predictors according to theoretical considerations. Using SPSS, the sequential model is implemented using sequential blocks to enter predictors or sets of predictors in a given order.

- The statistical model can be implemented using forward selection, backwards elimination, or stepwise regression. This model adds or removes variables one-at-a-time until some stopping rule is satisfied.

  - Forward selection starts with an empty model. The variable that would have the smallest p-value if it were the only predictor in the regression is placed in the model first. Each subsequent step adds the variable that has the smallest p-value in the presence of the predictors already in the equation.

  - Backward elimination starts with all of the predictors in the model. The variable that is least significant, that is, the one with the largest p-value, is removed first. Each subsequent step removes the least significant variable in the model until all remaining variables have individual p-values smaller than the à priori significance level.

- Stepwise regression is similar to forward selection except that variables are removed from the model if they become nonsignificant after other predictors are added.

The researcher can request residuals be saved as variables with the following names for subsequent analysis:

- The *unstandardized residual* (*RES*) is the difference between the observed value of the DV and the predicted value. The residual and its plot are useful for checking how well the regression line fits the data and, in particular, if there is any systematic lack of fit.

- The *standardized residual* (*ZRE*) is a residual divided by the standard error of the estimate. Standardized residuals should behave like a sample from a normal distribution with a mean of 0 and a standard deviation of 1. The standardized residual can be viewed as a *z*-score. So any observation with a standardized residual greater than I2I would be viewed as an outlier or an extreme observation.

- The *studentized residual* (*SRE*) is a type of standardized residual. It recognizes that the error associated with predicting values far from the mean of x is larger than the error associated with predicting values closer to the mean of x. The studentized residual increases the size of residuals for points distant from the mean of x.

SPSS will also allow saving of *predicted* (*PRE*) values. Predicted values, also called fitted values, are the values of each case based on using the regression equation for all cases in the analysis.

Effect size. The coefficient of multiple correlation (R) and the adjusted coefficient of multiple determination (R^2) are appropriate effect size statistics for regression analysis.

Key Assumptions & Requirements

Random selection of samples (probability samples) to allow for generalization of results to a target population.

Gauss-Markov assumptions (Berry & Feldman, 1985):

All variables are at least interval scale and are measured without error (one can use dummy variables for ordinal or nominal scale predictors). Measurement errors in the DV do not lead to estimation bias in the correlation coefficients, but they do lead to an increase in the standard error of the estimate, thereby weakening the test of statistical significance. Additionally, measurement errors in the IVs may lead to either an upward or a downward bias in the regression coefficients (Pedhazur, 1997).

- Mean value of the error term is zero.

- The variance of the error term is constant.

- Error terms are uncorrelated.

- Each predictor is uncorrelated with the error term.

- No extreme multicollinearity or between pairs of predictor variables.

Note: When Gauss-Markov assumptions are met,

the least squares estimators of regression parameters are unbiased and efficient... The Gauss-Markov theorem holds only when the assumptions of the regression model are met. (Berry & Feldman, 1985, p. 15)

Variables. Data range is not truncated (i.e., unrestricted variance).

Normality. Residuals (predicted minus observed values) are distributed normally.

Outliers. Absence of extreme outliers.

Linearity. If the relationship between IVs and the criterion variable is not linear, the results of the regression analysis will under-estimate the true relationship. This under-estimation carries an increased chance of a Type II error.

Proper specification of the model. If relevant variables are omitted from the model, the common variance they share with included variables may be wrongly attributed to those variables, and the error term is inflated. If causally irrelevant variables are included in the model, the common variance they share with included variables may be wrongly attributed to the irrelevant variables. The more the correlation of the irrelevant variable(s) with other independents, the greater the standard errors of the regression coefficients for these independents. Omission and irrelevancy can both affect substantially the size of the b and beta coefficients. The specification problem in regression is similar to the problem of spuriousness in correlation, where a given bivariate correlation may be inflated because one has not yet introduced control variables into the model by way of partial correlation.

When the omitted variable has a suppressing effect, coefficients in the model may underestimate rather than overestimate the effect of those variables on the dependent. Suppression occurs when the omitted variable has a positive causal influence on the included independent and a negative influence on the included dependent (or vice versa), thereby masking the impact the independent would have on the dependent if the third variable did not exist.

Sample size. Various rules of thumb have been suggested regarding sample size, but much depends on the amount of noise in the data and the nature of the phenomena being investigated. Tabachnick and Fidell (2007) suggest researchers have 104 events plus the number of independent variables if they wish to test regression coefficients. Stevens (2002) suggests regression analysis must include at least 15 events per predictor variable.

Example Research Question

Can sense of classroom community, intrinsic motivation, and extrinsic motivation predict grade point average?

Example Null Hypothesis

H_0: Sense of classroom community, intrinsic motivation, and extrinsic motivation cannot predict grade point average, $\beta_1 = \beta_2 = \beta_k = 0$

Note: The beta (β) weights are the regression coefficients for standardized data. Beta is the average amount the DV increases when the IV increases one standard deviation and other IVs are held constant. Don't confuse beta weight with beta (Type II) error.

SPSS Procedure

SPSS > Analyze > Regression > Linear

SPSS Output & Analysis

SPSS output varies based on options selected by the user.

Multiple linear regression using the standard (Enter) model was conducted for this analysis.

Descriptive Statistics (mean, standard deviation, *N*).

Correlations.

Correlations

		GPA	Classroom Community	Intrinsic Motivation	Extrinsic Motivation
Pearson Correlation	GPA	1.000	.358	.172	-.141
	Classroom Community	.358	1.000	.143	.031
	Intrinsic Motivation	.172	.143	1.000	.587
	Extrinsic Motivation	-.141	.031	.587	1.000
Sig. (1-tailed)	GPA	.	.000	.013	.034
	Classroom Community	.000	.	.032	.346
	Intrinsic Motivation	.013	.032	.	.000
	Extrinsic Motivation	.034	.346	.000	.
N	GPA	168	168	168	168
	Classroom Community	168	168	168	168
	Intrinsic Motivation	168	168	168	168
	Extrinsic Motivation	168	168	168	168

The above SPSS output displays all bivariate correlations. Classroom community and extrinsic motivation are not significantly related. All other bivariate relationships are significant. The low to moderate strengths of relationship suggest multicollinearity is not an issue in this model.

Model Summary.

- *R* is the coefficient of multiple correlation. It reflects the relationship between the DV and the multiple IVs. When there is only one IV, this statistic is the same as Pearson r.

- *R* square is the coefficient of multiple determination. It identifies the portion of variance in the DV explained by variance in the IVs.

- Adjusted *R* square is a downward adjustment to *R* square because *R* square becomes artificially high simply because of the addition of more IVs. At the extreme, when there are as many IVs as cases in the sample, *R* square equals 1.0.

- The standard error of the estimate is the standard deviation of the prediction errors. Approximately 68% of actual scores will fall between ±1 standard error of their predicted values.

- Change statistics show how the sequential entry of each IV influenced the model. In the standard (*Enter*) model, all IVs are entered in one step.

- The Durbin-Watson statistic is used to detect the presence of autocorrelation of residuals. Generally, a Durbin-Watson statistic in the range of 1.5 to 2.5 means that one may assume independence of observations.

Model Summary[b]

Model	R	R Square	Adjusted R Square	Std. Error of the Estimate	Change Statistics					Durbin-Watson
					R Square Change	F Change	df1	df2	Sig. F Change	
1	.468[a]	.219	.205	.54112	.219	15.362	3	164	.000	.446

a. Predictors: (Constant), Extrinsic Motivation, Classroom Community, Intrinsic Motivation

b. Dependent Variable: GPA

The above SPSS output summarizes the standard regression model. This model is significant, $F(3,164) = 15.36$, $p < .001$, and the set of IVs accounts for 20.5% (adjusted R square) of the variance of grade point average. The Durbin-Watson statistic of .45 suggests the presence of autocorrelation and a possible violation of the assumption of independence of observations.

ANOVA.

- The *ANOVA* table tests the overall significance of the model (that is, of the regression equation).

- Sum of squares (*SS*) is the sum of the squared deviations of the predicted variable about its mean.

- Mean square (*MS*) is an estimate of variance across groups. *MS* equals *SS* divided by its appropriate degrees of freedom.

ANOVA[a]

Model		Sum of Squares	df	Mean Square	F	Sig.
1	Regression	13.494	3	4.498	15.362	.000[b]
	Residual	48.021	164	.293		
	Total	61.515	167			

a. Dependent Variable: GPA

b. Predictors: (Constant), Extrinsic Motivation, Classroom Community, Intrinsic Motivation

The above SPSS output shows that the regression model with all three IVs is statistically significant, $F(3,164) = 15.36$, $p < .001$. These results are the same as those presented in the "Model Summary" table since the standard (*Enter*) model was used in this analysis.

Coefficients.

- The unstandardized regression coefficient, *b* (reported as *B* by SPSS), is the average amount the DV increases when the IV increases one unit and other IVs are held constant. Put another way, this coefficient is the slope of the regression line: the larger the value, the steeper the slope, the more the dependent changes for each unit change in the independent. The *b* coefficients and the constant term are used to create the unstandardized prediction (regression) equation.

- Beta is the average amount the DV increases when the IV increases one standard deviation and other IVs are held constant.

- There are two possible reasons why a predictor might not be contributing to a multiple regression model: (a) the variable is not correlated with the criterion or (b) the predictor is correlated with the criterion, but is collinear with one or more other predictors and has no independent contribution to the multiple regression model.

- A significant *t*-test is evidence that the coefficient is significantly different from zero.

- Zero-order correlation is the relationship between two variables, while ignoring the influence of other variables.

- Partial correlation is the relationship between two variables after removing the overlap of a third or more other variables from both variables.

- Part correlation is the relationship between two variables after removing a third variable from just the IV.

- If the tolerance value is less than some cutoff value, usually .20, the independent should be dropped from the analysis due to multicollinearity.

- The variance inflation factor (VIF) has a range 1 to infinity. When VIF is high there is high multicollinearity and instability of the b and beta coefficients. A common cutoff threshold is a VIF value of 10, which corresponds to a tolerance value of .10.

Coefficients[a]

		Unstandardized Coefficients		Standardized Coefficients			Correlations			Collinearity Statistics	
Model		B	Std. Error	Beta	t	Sig.	Zero-order	Partial	Part	Tolerance	VIF
1	(Constant)	2.687	.267		10.051	.000					
	Classroom Community	.031	.007	.321	4.597	.000	.358	.338	.317	.975	1.026
	Intrinsic Motivation	.013	.003	.327	3.793	.000	.172	.284	.262	.640	1.563
	Extrinsic Motivation	-.015	.004	-.343	-4.012	.000	-.14	-.299	-.28	.653	1.532

a. Dependent Variable: GPA

The above SPSS output shows each IV is significant, $p < .001$, and provides the standardized and unstandardized prediction equation coefficients. Because the Beta coefficients express coefficients in terms of the same standard deviation units, they are useful in comparing the relative importance of each IV to the regression model. However, since no Beta value is substantially larger than others in this model, one cannot identify the most important predictor.

The resultant unstandardized prediction equation is

$$Y' = .03x_1 - .02x_2 + .01x_3 + 2.69$$

where x_1 = classroom community, x_2 = extrinsic motivation, and x_3 = intrinsic motivation.

Casewise Diagnostics (case number, standard residual, observed value, predicted value, residual).

Collinearity Diagnostics.

- Eigenvalues close to 0 indicate dimensions that explain little variance. Multiple eigenvalues close to 0 indicate an ill-conditioned crossproduct matrix, meaning there may be a problem with multicollinearity and the condition indices should be examined as described below.

- Condition indices over 15 indicate possible multicollinearity problems and over 30 indicate serious multicollinearity problems. If a dimension has a high condition index, one looks in the variance proportions columns to see if that dimension accounts for a sizable proportion of variance in two or more variables (that is, if two or more variables are most heavily loaded on that dimension). If this is the case, these variables have high linear dependence and multicollinearity is a problem, with the effect that small data changes may translate into very large changes or errors in the regression analysis.

- Coefficients that have high variance proportions for a same condition index are largely responsible for the amount of multicollinearity identified by the condition index. A value of .50 is commonly used as a cut-off threshold.

Collinearity Diagnostics[a]

Model	Dimension	Eigenvalue	Condition Index	(Constant)	Classroom Community	Intrinsic Motivation	Extrinsic Motivation
1	1	3.898	1.000	.00	.00	.00	.00
	2	.059	8.154	.03	.35	.24	.08
	3	.028	11.891	.12	.17	.67	.41
	4	.016	15.769	.85	.48	.08	.51

a. Dependent Variable: GPA

Residuals Statistics.

P-P Plot of Regression Standardized Residuals.

- Used to assess normality of residuals and to identify outliers.

Discriminant Analysis

Purpose

Discriminant analysis (sometimes called discriminant function analysis) is a parametric procedure that describes or predicts membership in two or more mutually exclusive groups from a set of predictors. It is very similar to multiple regression with the major difference being that in discriminant analysis the DV is categorical rather than continuous.

Discriminant analysis is the mathematical reversal of a one-way multivariate analysis of variance (*MANOVA*):

- *MANOVA* asks, "Does being a member of a group influence scores on a set of continuous DVs?"

- Discriminant analysis asks, "Can I predict group membership on the basis of a set of continuous predictors?"

The levels of the IV for *MANOVA* become the categories of the DV for discriminant analysis, and the DVs of the *MANOVA* become the predictors for discriminant analysis. In *MANOVA* one asks whether group membership produces reliable differences on a combination of DVs. If the answer to that question is yes, then that combination of variables can be used to predict group membership.

There are two generic types of discriminant analysis: descriptive discriminant analysis and predictive discriminant analysis. The goal of descriptive discriminant analysis is to identify the IVs that have a strong relationship to group membership in the categories of the DV. The goal of predictive discriminant analysis is to use the relationships to build a predictive model. Discriminant analysis can generate functions from a sample of cases for which group membership is known. The functions can then be applied to new cases with measurements for the predictor variables but unknown group membership. Discriminant analysis creates an equation that minimizes the possibility of misclassifying cases into their respective groups or categories. Below is the generic prediction equation for a discriminant analysis function

$$D = v_1 X_1 + v_2 X_2 + ... v_i X_i + c$$

where D = discriminate function, v = the discriminant coefficient, X = respondent's score for that variable, c = constant, and i = the number of predictor variables.

In a two-group discriminant analysis, predicted membership is calculated by first producing a score for D for each case using the discriminate function. The group centroid is the mean value of the discriminant score for a given category of the DV. There are as many centroids as there are categories. The cut-off is the mean of the two centroids. Cases with D values smaller than the cut-off value are classified as belonging to one category while those with values larger are classified into the other category.

There is one discriminant function for a two-group discriminant analysis. However, for higher order discriminant analysis, the number of functions is the lesser of $(g - 1)$, where g is the number of groups, or the number of IVs. Each discriminant function is orthogonal to the others. A dimension in multiple discriminant analysis is simply one of the discriminant functions when there are more than one.

Discriminant analysis has two steps:

1. Wilks' lambda is used to test if the discriminant model as a whole is significant.

2. If Wilks' lambda is significant, the individual IVs are assessed to determine which differ significantly in mean by group.

Key Assumptions & Requirements

Random selection of samples (probability samples) to allow for generalization of results to a target population.

Variables. IVs (predictors): continuous variables, interval/ratio scale. The maximum number of IVs is $N - 2$, where N is the sample size. No IV has a zero standard deviation in one or more of the groups formed by the DV. DV (criterion variable): one categorical variable.

Measurement without error.

Multivariate normality. Each IV has a normal distribution about fixed values of all the other IVs.

Outliers. Absence of extreme outliers. Discriminant analysis is highly sensitive to outliers, which can produce either Type I or Type II errors.

Independence. Independence of observations. Residuals are randomly distributed.

Linearity. If the relationship between IVs and the criterion variable is not linear, the results of the regression analysis will under-estimate the true relationship. This under-estimation carries an increased chance of a Type II error.

Multicollinearity. Absence of high multicollinearity. Multicollinearity between IVs indicates the presence of redundant IVs, which decreases statistical efficiency.

Homogeneity of variance-covariance matrices. If sample sizes are equal, the robustness of discriminant analysis is expected and the results of Box's *M* test can be disregarded (Tabachnick & Fidell, 2007). However, if sample sizes are unequal and Box's *M* test is significant at p < .001, then robustness is not guaranteed.

Sample size. Tabachnick and Fidell (2007) state that "the sample size of the smallest group should exceed the number of predictor variables" (p. 381).

Example Research Question

Can one reliably predict whether a university student is an online or on campus student based on classroom community spirit and classroom community trust?

Example Null Hypothesis

H_0: One cannot predict whether a university student is an online or on campus student based on classroom community spirit and classroom community trust.

SPSS Procedure

SPSS > Analyze > Classify > Discriminant

SPSS Output & Analysis

SPSS output varies based on options selected by the user.

Group Statistics.

- This table provides group descriptive statistics (i.e., mean, standard deviation, and *N*).

Tests of Equality of Group Means.

- Wilks' lambda is used to test the null hypothesis that the populations have identical means on *D*. The smaller the Wilks' lambda, the more important is the IV is to the discriminant function. If the test is significant, the two groups differ on the tested dimension (i.e., discriminant function).

- One would consider dropping from the model any IV that is not significant.

Tests of Equality of Group Means

	Wilks' Lambda	F	df1	df2	Sig.
Spirit Posttest	.755	38.215	1	118	.000
Trust Posttest	.788	31.681	1	118	.000

The above SPSS output shows that both IVs are significant, $p < .001$, and are thus important to the model.

Pooled Within-groups Matrices.

- This matrix lists all bivariate correlations. It can be used to identify multicollinearity problems if any correlation coefficients are very high (i.e., $r > .80$).

Covariance Matrices.

Box's Test of Equality of Covariance Matrices (log determinants, Box's *M*, *F*, degrees of freedom, significance level).

- Log determinants should be equal if the assumption of homogeneity of variance-covariance matrices is tenable.

- Box's *M* is sensitive to meeting the assumption of multivariate normality.

Log Determinants

Favor Online	Rank	Log Determinant
No	2	3.153
Yes	2	6.046
Pooled within-groups	2	5.813

The ranks and natural logarithms of determinants printed are those of the group covariance matrices.

The above SPSS output shows log determinants are not equal. Consequently, the assumption of homogeneity of variance-covariance matrices will be an issue in this analysis. The log determinant for students responding with a "No" to favoring online courses is low, suggesting the analysis of this group is problematic.

Test Results

Box's M		24.517
F	Approx.	7.834
	df1	3
	df2	13266.550
	Sig.	.000

Tests null hypothesis of equal population covariance matrices.

The above SPSS output confirms that the assumption of homogeneity of variance-covariance matrices is not tenable, $F(3,13266.50) = 7.83$, $p < .001$. Since Box's M test was significant, one can ask SPSS to run discriminant analysis using the "separate covariances'"option (under Classify) and compare the results.

Eigenvalues.

- The number of discriminant functions calculated is equal to the lesser of $g - 1$ (where g is the number of dependent groups) or the number of IVs.

- Eigenvalues show how much of the variance in the DV is accounted for by each of the functions. To attach meaning to the functions (like factors in factor analysis) one uses the discriminant analysis structure matrix.

- The canonical correlation, R_c, is a measure of the association between the groups formed by the DV and the given discriminant function. When R_c is zero, there is no relation between the groups and the function. When the canonical correlation is large, there is a high correlation between the discriminant functions and the groups. R_c is used to tell how much each function is useful in determining group differences. Squared canonical correlation, R_c^2, is the percent of variation in the DV discriminated by the set of IVs and is a measure of effect size.

Eigenvalues

Function	Eigenvalue	% of Variance	Cumulative %	Canonical Correlation
1	.345[a]	100.0	100.0	.507

a. First 1 canonical discriminant functions were used in the analysis.

The above SPSS output shows that one discriminant function was calculated. This is expected since the DV, type course, has two groups.

Wilks' Lambda.

- Wilks' lambda tests the significance of each discriminant function.

Wilks' Lambda

Test of Function(s)	Wilks' Lambda	Chi-square	df	Sig.
1	.743	34.692	2	.000

Standardized Canonical Discriminant Function Coefficients.

- The standardized discriminant function coefficients serve the same purpose as beta weights in multiple regression. They indicate the relative importance of the IVs in predicting the DV.

Standardized Canonical Discriminant Function Coefficients

	Function 1
Spirit Posttest	.698
Trust Posttest	.368

The above SPSS output shows that classroom community spirit is more important than classroom community trust in predicting the DV.

Structure Matrix.

- The structure matrix table shows the correlations of each variable with each discriminant function. The Pearson correlations are similar to factor loadings in factor analysis. Similar to factor loadings, loadings above .6 are usually considered high and those below .4 are low.

Structure Matrix

	Function
	1
Spirit Posttest	.969
Trust Posttest	.882

Pooled within-groups correlations between discriminating variables and standardized canonical discriminant functions
 Variables ordered by absolute size of correlation within function.

Canonical Discriminant Function Coefficients.

Canonical Discriminant Function Coefficients

	Function
	1
Spirit Posttest	.130
Trust Posttest	.073
(Constant)	-5.390

Unstandardized coefficients

The above SPSS output provides the unstandardized discriminant function coefficients and the constant value in order to produce the prediction equation, similar to multiple regression. The prediction equation is

$$D = .13x_1 + .07x_2 - 5.39$$

where x_1 = classroom community spirit and x_2 = classroom community trust.

Functions at Group Centroids.

- Functions at group centroids are the mean values of each group of the DV for each function. The group centroid is the mean value for the discriminant scores for a given group (category of the dependent). Two-group discriminant analysis has two centroids, one for each group. This information is used to establish the cutting points for classifying cases.

- The cutting points set ranges of the discriminant score to classify cases into each category of the DV. If the discriminant score of the function is less than or equal to the cutoff, the case is classed as 0, or if above it is classed as 1. When group sizes are equal, the cutoff is the mean of the two centroids (for two-group discriminant analysis). If the groups are unequal, the cutoff is the weighted mean.

Functions at Group Centroids

Favor Online	Function 1
No	1.343
Yes	-.253

Unstandardized canonical discriminant functions evaluated at group means

The above SPSS output provides information to establish a cutoff score so that cases can be classified as to group membership. Since group sample sizes differ in this analysis, a weighted average is used to calculate the cutoff score. Cutoff score = $((19/120)(1.34) + (101/120)(-.25))/2 = .0022$. Consequently, cases with $D \le .0022$ are classified as not favoring online courses and cases with $D > .0022$ are classified as favoring online courses. (No was coded as 0 and Yes was coded as 1 in the SPSS dataset.)

Classification Results.

Classification Results[a]

		Favor Online	Predicted Group Membership		Total
			No	Yes	
Original	Count	No	4	15	19
		Yes	4	97	101
	%	No	21.1	78.9	100.0
		Yes	4.0	96.0	100.0

a. 84.2% of original grouped cases correctly classified.

The above SPSS output assess how well the discriminant function works. Here it correctly classifies 84.2% of the cases. The model correctly classifies 96% of the students who favor online courses. However, it misclassifies 78.9% of the students who do not favor online courses. Consequently, the model is not satisfactory. It would be better to analyze a sample that is balanced in terms of numbers of students in each group.

Plots (combined-groups, separate groups, territorial map).

- Combined-groups plot: The histogram (if two groups) or scatterplot (if more than two groups) includes all groups in a single plot.

- Separate-groups plot: This plot creates as many plots as there are groups and displays one group on each plot.

- Territorial map: This map shows centroids and boundaries in a graphic format; it is appropriate only if there are three or more levels of the DV.

Principal Components and Factor Analysis

Purpose

Principal components and factor analysis is a parametric procedure used to analyze interrelationships among a large number of variables and to explain these variables in terms of their common underlying dimensions (i.e., factors or components). Factor analysis (*FA*) is a generic term that includes principal components analysis (*PCA*). While the two techniques are very similar and are used for the same general purpose (data reduction and summarization), they are different in the underlying theory.

Mathematically, the difference between *PCA* and *FA* is in the variance that is analyzed. In *PCA*, all the variance in the observed variables is analyzed. In *FA*, only shared variance is analyzed (i.e., variance in common); attempts are made to estimate and eliminate variance due to error and variance that is unique to each variable (Jackson, 2003; Tabachnick & Fidell, 2007).

The selection of one procedure over the other is based upon the following criteria.

- In *FA*, a small number of factors are extracted to account for the intercorrelations among the observed variables and to identify the latent dimensions that explain why the variables are correlated to each other. The purpose of *FA* is to find the underlying structure among variables by data reduction. A typical use of factor analysis is in survey research, where a researcher wishes to represent a number of items with a smaller number of factors.

- In *PCA*, the objective is to account for the maximum portion of the variance present in the original set of variables with a minimum number of composite variables called principal components. The purpose of *PCA* is to combine variables into composites that have larger variance than single variables (or simple means)

Principal components and factor analysis addresses two types of variables:

- observed variables
- latent variables (i.e., factors or components that are relatively independent of one another)

If the observed variables are measured relatively error free, (for example, age), or if it is assumed that the error and specific variance represent a small portion of the total variance in the original set of the variables, then *PCA* is appropriate. But if the observed variables are only indicators of the latent constructs to be measured (such as test scores or responses to attitude scales), or if the error (unique) variance represents a significant portion of the total variance, then the appropriate technique to select is *FA* (Tabachnick & Fidell, 2007).

The issue of whether factor structures should be theory-based or data-based depends on whether the analysis is confirmatory or exploratory.

- *Exploratory factor analysis* (*EFA*) seeks to uncover the underlying structure of a relatively large set of variables. The researcher's *à priori* assumption is that any indicator may be associated with any factor. This is the most common form of factor analysis. There is no prior theory and one uses factor loadings to discern the factor structure of the data.

- *Confirmatory factor analysis* (*CFA*) seeks to determine if the number of factors and the loadings of observed variables on them conform to what is expected on the basis of pre-established theory. A minimum requirement of *CFA* is that one hypothesize beforehand the number of factors in the model, but usually also expectations about which variables will load on which factors (Kim & Mueller, 1978). The researcher seeks to determine if measures created to represent a latent variable really belong together.

In *PCA* and *FA* the initial factor pattern matrix is unrotated. The original, unrotated solution maximizes the sum of squared factor loadings, creating a set of factors or components that explain as much of the variance in the original variables as possible. The amount explained is reflected in the sum of the eigenvalues of all factors. However, unrotated solutions are hard to interpret because variables tend to load on multiple factors. Consequently, several different methods of rotation are available to make interpretation easier. Bryant and Yarnold (1995) define rotation as

a procedure in which the eigenvectors (factors) are rotated in order to achieve simple structure. (p. 132)

Simple structure refers to unambiguous loadings of observed variables onto extracted factors or components (i.e., the latent variables).

There are two main classes of rotation: orthogonal and oblique. In all cases, interpretation is easiest if simple structure is achieved. If this is the case, one can more easily label factors for the observed variables highly correlated with them.

Orthogonal rotation assumes that the factors are at right angles to each other; in other words, the factors are not correlated.

- Varimax rotation is an orthogonal rotation of the factor axes to maximize the variance of the squared loadings of a factor (column) on all the variables (rows) in a factor matrix. A Varimax solution yields results that make it as easy as possible to identify each variable with a single factor. This is the most common orthogonal rotation option.

- Quartimax rotation is an orthogonal alternative which minimizes the number of factors needed to explain each variable.

- Equimax rotation is a compromise between Varimax and Quartimax criteria.

Oblique rotation allows for correlations between the factors. It often simplifies the factor solution since many attitudinal dimensions are, in fact, likely to be correlated. Unlike orthogonal rotation, the pattern matrix and the structure matrix are not equal after oblique rotation. However, only the pattern matrix need be examined since it allows for the easiest interpretation of factors. An oblique rotation will likely produce correlated factors with less-than-obvious meaning, that is, with many cross-loadings.

- Direct oblimin rotation is the standard method when one wishes to use a non-orthogonal, oblique rotation.

- Promax rotation is an alternative non-orthogonal rotation method.

SPSS offers several methods of factor extraction (Norusis, 2011):

- Principal Components – PCA seeks a linear combination of variables such that the maximum variance is extracted from the variables. It then removes this variance and seeks a second linear combination that explains the maximum proportion of the remaining variance, and so on.

- Unweighted Least Squares – this is a factor extraction method that minimizes the sum of the squared differences between the observed and reproduced correlation matrices ignoring the diagonals.

- Generalized Least Squares – this is a factor extraction method that minimizes the sum of the squared differences between the observed and reproduced correlation matrices. Correlations are weighted by the inverse of their uniqueness, so that variables with high uniqueness are given less weight than those with low uniqueness.

- Maximum Likelihood – this method of extraction allows computation of assorted indices of goodness-of-fit (of data to the model) and the testing of the significance of loadings and correlations between factors, but requires the assumption of multivariate normality. Correlations are weighted by the inverse of the uniqueness of the variables, and an iterative algorithm is employed.

- Principal Axis Factoring – this is the most common method of *FA*. It is a method of extracting factors from the original correlation matrix with squared multiple correlation coefficients placed in the diagonal as initial estimates of the communalities. These factor loadings are used to estimate new communalities that replace the old communality estimates in the diagonal. Iterations continue until the changes in the communalities from one iteration to the next satisfy the convergence criterion for extraction.

- Alpha Factoring – a factor extraction method that considers the variables in the analysis to be a sample from the universe of potential variables. It maximizes the alpha reliability of the factors.

- Image Factoring – a factor analysis method based on image theory. The common part of the variable, called the partial image, is defined as its linear regression on remaining variables, rather than a function of hypothetical factors.

Determining the optimal number of factors to extract is not entirely a statistical issue. In practice, most researchers seldom use a single criterion to decide on the number of factors to extract. Some of the most commonly used guidelines are as follows (Dunteman, 1989):

- Scree plot – the scree plot plots the factors/components as the *x*-axis and the corresponding *eigenvalues* as the *y*-axis. Eigenvalues are the variances of the factors. As one moves to the right, the eigenvalues drop. When the drop ceases and the curve makes an elbow toward less steep decline, the scree plot suggests that all further factors/ components after the one starting the elbow be dropped.

- Kaiser-Guttman rule – the number of factors to be extracted should be equal to the number of factors having an eigenvalue (variance) greater than 1.0. The rationale for choosing this particular value is that a factor must have variance at least as large as that of a single standardized original variable.

- Variance Explained Criterion. Keep enough factors to account for 90% (sometimes 80%) of the variation.

- Interpretability. Factor solutions should be evaluated not only according to empirical criteria but also according to the criterion of theoretical meaningfulness.

Factor loadings (component loadings in *PCA*) are the Pearson correlation coefficients between the variables and factors (components). Factor loadings are the basis for labeling the different factors. Loadings above .6 are usually considered high and those below .4 are low. Tabachnick and Fidell (2007) identify .32 or larger as the usual criterion. However, Comrey and Lee (1992) suggest that loadings in excess of .71 (50% overlapping variance) are excellent while loadings of .63 (40% overlapping variance) are very good, .55 (30% overlapping variance) are good, .45 (20% overlapping variance) are fair, and .32 (10% overlapping variance) are poor.

Oblique rotations – e.g., direct oblimin – produce both factor pattern and factor structure matrices that display factor loadings. For orthogonal rotations – e.g., varimax – the factor structure and the factor pattern matrices are the same. The factor structure matrix represents the correlations between the variables and the factors. The factor pattern matrix represents the linear combination of the variables.

Key Assumptions & Requirements

Variables. Interval/ratio data are assumed.

Measurement without error.

Multivariate normality. Multivariate normality of data is required for related significance tests if maximum likelihood is used as the extraction method.

Outliers. Absence of extreme outliers.

Homoscedasticity. The variability in scores for one variable is roughly the same at all values of a second variable.

Linearity.

Sphericity. The variance of the difference between all pairs of means is constant across all combinations of related groups.

Independence. Independence of observations.

Proper specification of the model. No selection bias/proper specification. The exclusion of relevant variables and the inclusion of irrelevant variables in the correlation matrix being factored will influence the factors that are uncovered.

Sample size. A few rules of thumb from the professional literature: A large number of cases is required. Hutcheson and Sofroniou (1999) recommend at least 150 to 300 cases. There should be at least 200 cases (Gorsuch, 1983). There should be at least 20 cases per item (Tabachnick & Fidell, 2007).

Example Research Question

How many reliable and interpretable factors are represented in a proposed sense of community scale?

Note: This is a exploratory factor analysis question. A confirmatory question would specify the number of factors.

Example Null Hypothesis

H_0: The proposed sense of community scale is unidimensional.

SPSS Procedure

SPSS > Analyze > Dimension Reduction > Factor

SPSS Output & Analysis

SPSS output varies based on options selected by the user.

Exploratory factor analysis with maximum likelihood extraction and oblique rotation (direct oblimin) was conducted.

Descriptive Statistics (mean, standard deviation, *N*).

Correlation Matrix.

- The correlation matrix shows the simple correlations, *r*, between all possible pairs of variables included in the analysis.

KMO and Bartlett's Test.

- The Kaiser-Meyer-Olkin (*KMO*) measure of sampling adequacy predicts if data are likely to factor well. *KMO* varies from 0 to 1.0. Criteria: test statistic > .9 is excellent, test statistic > .8 is meritorious, test statistic > .7 is middling, test statistic > .6 is mediocre, test statistic >.5 is miserable, and test statistic < .5 is unacceptable. *KMO* overall should be .60 or higher to proceed with factor analysis. If it is not, drop the indicator variables with the lowest individual *KMO* statistic values, until *KMO* overall rises above .60. (Jackson, 2003; Kaiser, 1970).

- The Bartlett test of sphericity tests whether the correlation matrix is an identity matrix (factor analysis is meaningless with an identity matrix). A significant *p*-value supports the assumption of sphericity.

KMO and Bartlett's Test

Kaiser–Meyer–Olkin Measure of Sampling Adequacy.		.935
Bartlett's Test of Sphericity	Approx. Chi-Square	3883.847
	df	190
	Sig.	.000

The above SPSS output shows that the data will factor well (the Kaiser-Meyer-Olkin measure is > .9) and Bartlett's test results, *p* < .05, supports the assumption of sphericity.

Communalities.

- The communalities (h^2) measure the percent of variance in a given variable explained by all the factors. The extracted communalities are the percent of variance in a given variable explained by the factors that are extracted.

• Extraction is the process by which the factors are determined from a large set of variables. The values in the extraction column show the proportion of each variable's variance that can be explained by the retained factors.

Communalities

	Initial	Extraction
q01	.566	.594
q02	.463	.422
q03	.661	.687
q04	.525	.462
q05	.623	.640
q06	.392	.298
q07	.569	.559
q08	.404	.502
q09	.582	.580
q10	.489	.724
q11	.593	.579
q12	.500	.530
q13	.575	.575
q14	.506	.470
q15	.417	.396
q16	.577	.610
q17	.504	.489
q18	.495	.513
q19	.461	.443
q20	.529	.560

Extraction Method: Maximum Likelihood.

The above SPSS output shows that 72% of the variance in question 10 is explained by the three factors that were extracted, while only 30% of the variance in question 6 is explained by the extracted factors. What one desires are values close to 1.00 for each question. This would indicate that the model explains most of the variation for those variables (questions or items on the instrument). In this case, the model does better for some variables than it does for others.

Total Variance Explained.

- This table shows the eigenvalues, which are the proportion of total variance in all the variables that is accounted for by the identified factor/component.

- % of variance is the percentage of the total variance attributed to each factor.

- The cumulative % column displays the cumulative percentage of variance accounted for by the current and all preceding factors.

Total Variance Explained

Factor	Initial Eigenvalues			Extraction Sums of Squared Loadings			Rotation Sums of Squared Loadings [a]
	Total	% of Variance	Cumulative %	Total	% of Variance	Cumulative %	Total
1	8.563	42.813	42.813	8.099	40.496	40.496	7.031
2	2.248	11.239	54.052	1.766	8.828	49.324	6.045
3	1.163	5.815	59.866	.768	3.842	53.167	3.855
4	.996	4.978	64.845				
5	.736	3.680	68.524				
6	.651	3.257	71.781				
7	.590	2.948	74.729				
8	.528	2.641	77.370				
9	.513	2.563	79.933				
10	.503	2.514	82.447				
11	.477	2.386	84.832				
12	.461	2.304	87.136				
13	.406	2.030	89.166				
14	.374	1.869	91.035				
15	.366	1.831	92.867				
16	.337	1.687	94.553				
17	.309	1.545	96.098				
18	.277	1.387	97.485				
19	.260	1.300	98.785				
20	.243	1.215	100.000				

Extraction Method: Maximum Likelihood.

a. When factors are correlated, sums of squared loadings cannot be added to obtain a total variance.

The above SPSS output shows that the three extracted factors altogether account for 53% of the total variance (the first factor accounts for 40%, the second factor adds another 9%, and the third factor adds 4%).

Scree Plot.

- The scree plot is a plot of the eigenvalues against the number of factors in order of extraction. As one moves to the right, toward additional factors, the eigenvalues drop. When the drop ceases and the curve makes an elbow toward less steep decline, the scree plot suggests that one to drop all further factors after the one starting the elbow.

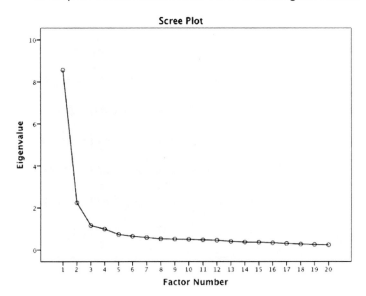

The above scree plot supports a three factor solution. However, ultimate determination of the optimum number of factors to be extracted should be based on theoretical meaningfulness in addition statistical evidence.

Factor Matrix.

- The factor matrix shows the unrotated factor loadings. Factor loading is interpreted as the Pearson correlation between the variable and the factor.

Factor Matrix[a]

	Factor		
	1	2	3
q01	.645	-.420	.027
q02	.624	.151	.102
q03	.774	-.294	.030
q04	.611	.294	.039
q05	.756	-.257	.046
q06	.422	.314	.147
q07	.739	-.117	-.002
q08	.478	.213	-.478
q09	.755	-.096	-.040
q10	.582	.304	-.541
q11	.665	-.370	-.016
q12	.603	.382	.141
q13	.696	-.281	.107
q14	.519	.362	.263
q15	.580	-.224	-.100
q16	.632	.417	.191
q17	.665	-.216	-.022
q18	.594	.379	.129
q19	.647	-.156	-.004
q20	.615	.369	.211

Extraction Method: Maximum
Likelihood.

a. 3 factors extracted. 6 iterations
required.

Goodness-of-fit Test.

- This test assesses whether the data adequately fits the model. The null hypothesis is that the factor model adequately describes the data.

Goodness-of-fit Test

Chi-Square	df	Sig.
334.508	133	.000

The above SPSS output provides evidence that the data analyzed do not adequately fit the model. One concludes that the relationships among the variables are not adequately described by the three factor model. There are potential issues, such as the possibility of nonlinearity, that preclude a good-fitting factor model. One may be able to drop observed variable(s) from the dataset to obtain a better fitting model. Alternatively, one can increase the number of factors until an adequate fit is achieved.

Pattern Matrix.

- The pattern matrix and the structure matrix are equal after orthogonal rotation.

- The pattern matrix and the structure matrix are not equal after oblique rotation. However, only the pattern matrix need be examined since it allows for the easiest interpretation of factors.

Pattern Matrix[a]

	Factor		
	1	2	3
q01	.856	-.120	.071
q02	.257	.453	-.034
q03	.808	.046	.011
q04	.093	.529	-.153
q05	.760	.086	.020
q06	-.037	.562	-.006
q07	.598	.169	-.080
q08	.030	-.009	-.699
q09	.582	.163	-.134
q10	-.004	.062	-.819
q11	.811	-.101	.001
q12	.008	.687	-.065
q13	.753	.091	.107
q14	-.011	.735	.095
q15	.595	-.067	-.131
q16	-.004	.771	-.024
q17	.651	.035	-.058
q18	.003	.672	-.076
q19	.579	.097	-.055
q20	.037	.737	.017

Extraction Method: Maximum Likelihood.
Rotation Method: Oblimin with Kaiser Normalization.

a. Rotation converged in 6 iterations.

The above SPSS output displays the pattern matrix. The model presented looks good because simple structure is achieved as each variable loads unambiguously onto one and only one factor using .30 as a cutoff. Cross-loadings are relatively small. This provides for a clean, simple interpretation of the data.

An examination of the observed variables that load onto each factor allows the researcher to label the factors and view them as subscales (dimensions) of the instrument. In the case of the tested instrument, "Factor 1" can be labelled as social community, "Factor 2" can be labelled learning community, and "Factor 3" can be labelled acommunity (i.e., inability or unwillingness to participate in a normal community environment).

Dropping observed variables *q08* and *q10* may produce a better fitting factor model.

Component Matrix/Structure Matrix.

- The structure matrix can be ignored when oblique rotation is used.

Factor Correlation Matrix.

- Very high correlations between factors suggest such factors should be combined into a single factor.

Canonical Correlation Analysis

Purpose

Canonical correlation analysis (*CCA*) is a parametric procedure for assessing the relationship between two sets of continuous variables. One set is sometimes called the dependent set and the other is the independent set, but this distinction is not necessary. It is one of the most general multivariate forms; multiple regression and correlation, discriminate analysis, and *MANOVA* are all special cases of *CCA* (Grimm & Yarnold, 2000).

CCA requires multivariate data on both sides of the equation. The basic *CCA* data model is

$$B_1Y_1 + B_2Y_2 + ... B_nY_n = A_0 + A_1X_1 + A_2X_2 + ... A_nX_n$$

More precisely, canonical correlation is the correlation of two canonical variables, one representing the set of IVs, the other representing the set of DVs. Each set may be considered a latent variable based on the measured indicator variables in its set. The canonical correlation is optimized such that the linear correlation between the two latent variables is maximized.

Whereas multiple regression and correlation is used for many-to-one relationships, canonical correlation is used for many-to-many relationships. There may be more than one such linear correlation relating the two sets of variables, with each correlation representing a different dimension by which the independent set of variables is related to the dependent set. The purpose of CCA is to explain the relation of the two sets of variables, not to model the individual variables. For each canonical variate one can also assess how strongly it is related to measured variables in its own set, or the set for the other canonical variate. Wilks' lambda is commonly used to test the significance of canonical correlation.

Analogous with ordinary correlation, canonical correlation squared is the percent of variance in the dependent set explained by the independent set of variables along a given dimension (there may be more than one dimension).

In addition to asking how strong the relationship is between two latent variables, canonical correlation is useful in determining how many canonical functions or dimensions are needed to account for that relationship. The number of canonical dimensions is equal to the number of variables in the smaller set. However, not all dimensions may be significant.

Effect size. Effect size is evaluated by squaring the loadings. In particular, squaring a loading indicates the percent of the variance in a specific dimension that can be explained by that variable.

Key Assumptions & Requirements

Random selection of samples (probability samples) to allow for generalization of results to a target population.

Variables. Two sets of continuous variables with a minimum of two variables in each set. Data range is not truncated (i.e., unrestricted variance).

Measurement without error.

Multivariate normality. Multivariate normal distribution assumptions are required for both sets of variables. This assumption is violated when dichotomous, dummy, and other discrete variables are used.

Outliers. Absence of extreme outliers.

Linearity. Linearity is an important assumption of *CCA*; this technique finds linear relationships between variables within a set and between canonical variate pairs between sets. Nonlinear components are not recognized.

Homoscedasticity. The variability in scores for one variable is roughly the same at all values of other variables.

Independence. Independence of observations.

Multicollinearity. Lack of high multicollinearity. It is important that the variables in each set and across sets are not highly correlated with each other.

Proper specification of the model.

Sample size. If there are strong canonical correlations in the data (e.g., > .7), then even relatively small samples (e.g., N = 50) will detect them most of the time (Stevens, 2002). However, in order to arrive at reliable estimates of the canonical factor loadings (for interpretation), Stevens (2002) recommends that there should be at least 20 times as many cases as variables in the analysis, if one wants to interpret the most significant canonical root only. To arrive at reliable estimates for two canonical roots, Barcikowski and Stevens (1975) recommend including 40 to 60 times as many cases as variables. Enough cases must be included in the analysis to control Type II error.

Example Research Question

How is a set of three alienation subscales (social isolation, powerlessness, and normlessness) related to a set of two classroom community subscales (social community and learning community)?

A journal article (Rovai & Wighting, 2005; http://www.sciencedirect.com/science/article/pii/S109675160500014X)

that responds to this research question is available on the Science Direct online database.

Example Null Hypothesis

H_0: There is no relationship between a set of three alienation subscales (social isolation, powerlessness, and normlessness) and a set of two classroom community subscales (social community and earning community).

SPSS Procedure

SPSS has no menu item to conduct CCA. Instead, the researcher must use the canonical correlation macro provided by SPSS. The SPSS syntax to access this macro is as follows:

INCLUDE '[installdir]/Samples/English/Canonical correlation.sps'.

CANCORR SET1=variable1 variable 2 /

SET2=variable3 variable 4 /.

Note: The two variable lists must be separated with a slash. [installdir] is the installation directory on the computer hard drive. The path should reflect the actual location of the macro file.

Alternatively, researchers can call on the *MANOVA* procedure with the following SPSS syntax:

manova variable 1 variable2 with variable3 variable4

/ discrim all alpha(1)

/ print=sig(eigen dim) .

Note: This procedure will produce a minimal analysis.

SPSS Output & Analysis

The SPSS canonical correlation macro was used in this procedure.

Correlations for Set 1, Correlations for Set 2, Correlations Between Set 1 and Set 2.

Correlations for Set-1		
	social community	learning community
social community	1.0000	0.5768
learning community	0.5768	1.0000

Correlations for Set-2			
	social isolation	powerlessness	normlessness
social isolation	1.0000	0.3801	0.0562
powerlessness	0.3801	1.0000	0.3385
normlessness	0.0562	0.3385	1.0000

Correlations Between Set-1 and Set-2			
	social isolation	powerlessness	normlessness
social community	-0.4889	-0.2547	0.0070
learning community	-0.3239	-0.1875	-0.3778

The above SPSS output displays three tables that report the inter-item correlations for all five variables in this model (2 variables in set 1 and 3 variables in set 2). By drawing from these tables one can produce a 5 x 5 correlation matrix. Note that the canonical correlation function does not report a p-value related to these correlations. One needs to conduct bivariate correlations to determine statistical significance (SPSS Analyze > Correlate > Bivariate).

Canonical Correlations and Test that Remaining Correlations are Zero.

Canonical Correlations	
1	0.500
2	0.486

Test that remaining correlations are zero:				
	Wilk's	Chi-SQ	DF	Sig.
1	0.573	62.937	6.000	0.000
2	0.764	30.485	2.000	0.000

The above SPSS output (first table) reports on the two canonical dimensions that were created (1 & 2) and the responding correlations with each dimension. The first pair of variates, a linear combination of the alienation measurements and a linear combination of the classroom community measurements, has a correlation coefficient of 0.50. The second pair has a correlation coefficient of 0.49.

In the second table, Wilks' lambda, χ^2, and the statistical significance are reported for each canonical dimension. This table shows that both of the canonical dimensions are statistically significant at the .05 level. For this data set, one finds a significant relationship for each canonical dimension: $\chi^2(6) = 62.94$, $p < .001$ and $\chi^2(2) = 30.49$, $p < .001$.

Standardized and Raw Canonical Coefficients for Set 1 and Set 2.

- SPSS reports both the standardized and the raw (unstandardized) coefficients. The tables are arranged according to variable sets and coefficients are reported by canonical dimensions (columns 1 & 2).

- Canonical coefficients are used to assess the relative importance of individual variables' contributions to a given canonical correlation. The canonical coefficients are the weights in the linear equation of variables that create the canonical variables. As such they are analogous to b and beta weights in regression analysis.

Standardized Canonical Coefficients for Set-1		
	1	2
social community	-1.153	-0.411
learning community	0.329	1.179

Raw Canonical Coefficients for Set-1		
	1	2
social community	-0.178	-0.064
learning community	0.073	0.261

Standardized Canonical Coefficients for Set-2		
	1	2
social isolation	0.828	-0.412
powerlessness	0.288	0.250
normlessness	-0.409	-0.983

Raw Canonical Coefficients for Set-2		
	1	2
social isolation	0.167	-0.083
powerlessness	0.058	0.051
normlessness	-0.122	-0.293

The above SPSS output shows that social community and social isolation are the most important variables in the first dimension while learning community and normlessness are the most important variables in the second dimension.

Canonical Loadings and Cross Loadings for Set 1 and Set 2.

- SPSS also reports loadings (structure coefficients) and cross-loadings for sets 1 and 2. These should be interpreted in much the same way factor loadings are interpreted in factor analysis. The reason these loadings are of particular interest is they can detect if a given variable was given a low standardized coefficient because it truly has no effect on the canonical dimension, or if the variable is essentially measuring the same thing as another variable.

- Effect size is evaluated by squaring the loadings. In particular, squaring a loading indicates the percent of the variance in a specific dimension that can be explained by that variable. Squared loadings can also assist in determining which variable is the best predictor in each variable set for the variables in the other set.

- Also using a cutoff structure coefficient of 0.30, social isolation and normlessness in the alienation set were related to the alienation variate in the second dimension, while learning community in the classroom community set was related to the classroom community variate. Social isolation and normlessness were 14% and 85% useful, respectively in explaining variance in the alienation variate, and learning community was 88% useful in the classroom community variate. Thus, the second pair of canonical variates that comprise the second dimension suggests that participants with stronger feelings of both social isolation and normlessness were also more likely to have weaker feelings of learning community.

- SPSS also produces the cross loadings, that is how each variable correlates with the opposite set of variables. Cross loadings offers an alternative interpretative method to canonical loadings. For the first dimension of the classroom community variate, one sees that social community has a significant cross loading (> 0.30) and learning community does not. For the first dimension of the alienation variate, one sees a significant cross-loading for social isolation (> .30) but not for normlessness or powerlessness. Hence, the researcher could conclude that social community correlated negatively (note the negative sign in the cross loading) with social isolation.

- The canonical communality coefficient (h^2) is the sum of the squared loadings (structure coefficients) for a given variable. The canonical communality coefficient measures how much of a given original variable's variance is reproducible from the canonical variables.

Canonical Loadings for Set-1		
	1	2
social community	-0.963	0.269
learning community	-0.336	0.942

Cross Loadings for Set-1		
	1	2
social community	-0.481	0.131
learning community	-0.168	0.458

Canonical Loadings for Set-2		
	1	2
social isolation	0.915	-0.372
normlessness	0.464	-0.239
powerlessness	-0.265	-0.922

Cross Loadings for Set-2		
	1	2
social isolation	0.457	-0.181
normlessness	0.232	-0.116
powerlessness	-0.133	-0.448

The above SPSS output shows that using a cutoff loading of 0.30, in the classroom community set, both social community and learning community are correlated with the classroom community variate in the first dimension. In the alienation set, social isolation and normlessness are the only variables that are correlated with the alienation variate in the first dimension.

Social isolation is 85% useful and powerlessness is 21% useful in explaining variance in the alienation variate, whereas social community is 92% useful and learning community is 12% useful in explaining variance in the classroom community variate. Thus, the first pair of canonical variates that comprise the first canonical function suggests that participants with both stronger feelings of social isolation and powerlessness were also more likely to have both weaker feelings of social community and learning community.

Once the loadings are squared for both dimensions, the canonical communality coefficient can be computed by obtaining the sum of the two squared structure coefficients (for powerlessness: 0.21 + 0.06 = 0.27). The relatively low communality coefficient for powerlessness (in relation to scores above 0.90 for all other variables) indicates that the other variables have relatively little to do with scores on the powerlessness scale.

Proportion of Variance of Set 1 and Set 2 Explained by Its Own Canonical Variate; Proportion of Variance of Set 1 and Set 2 Explained by Opposite Canonical Variate.

- SPSS also reports the adequacy and redundancy coefficients although they are not labeled as such. "Proportion of Variance of Set-n Explained by Its Own Can. Var." identifies the adequacy coefficients and "Proportion of Variance of Set-n Explained by Opposite Can. Var." provides the redundancy coefficients.

- The adequacy coefficient indicates, on average, how much of the variables included in the set are reproduced by the canonical dimension.

- Redundancy coefficients are used to determine predictability of a dimension.

Proportion of Variance of Set-1 Explained by Its Own Van. Var.	
	Prop. Var.
CV1-1	0.520
CV1-2	0.480

Proportion of Variance of Set-1 Explained by Opposite Can. Var.	
	Prop Var
CV1-1	0.130
CV1-2	0.113

Proportion of Variance of Set-2 Explained by its Own Can. Var.	
	Prop Var
CV2-1	0.374
CV2-2	0.349

Proportion of Variance of Set-2 Explained by Opposite Can. Var.	
	Prop Var
CV2-1	0.093
CV2-2	0.082

For set 1, adequacy coefficients show 52% of the variance is reproduced in the first canonical dimension and 48% is reproduced in the second canonical dimension. Looking at set 1 redundancy coefficients, one sees limited predictability for either dimension (dimension 1 = 13% and dimension 2 = 11%). Grimm and Yarnold (2004) urge not trying to interpret redundancy coefficients for various theoretical reasons.

Two-Step Cluster Analysis

Purpose

Two-step cluster analysis is an exploratory, descriptive tool designed to identify natural groupings within a dataset. It is able to create clusters using both categorical and continuous variables. Ordinal variables are handled as either categorical or continuous variables (researcher's choice). Continuous variables are z-standardized by default.

The procedure does not involve hypothesis testing and the calculation of significance levels. Cluster analysis is used to find homogeneous subsets based on the variables examined, where the similarity between cases of the same group is high and the similarity between cases of different groups is low.

The researcher selects the following options:

- Identify the number of clusters to extract or allow the procedure to select the optimum number of clusters.

- Select one of two distance measures: log-likelihood (default) is used for categorical and continuous variables while Euclidean distance is only used when all variables are continuous. Log-likelihood distance is a probability-based distance. Euclidean distance is the straight line distance between two clusters.

- Select the clustering (i.e., goodness of fit) criterion: Schwarz's Bayesian Criterion (*BIC*; default) or Akaike's Information Criterion (*AIC*). *AIC* is less conservative than *BIC* and generally results in more clusters.

Key Assumptions & Requirements

Variables. Variables are categorical and/or continuous. Categorical variables have a multinomial distribution. (A multinomial distribution deals with events that have multiple discrete outcomes, in contrast to a binomial distribution, which has two discrete outcomes.)

Independence. Independence of observations and independence of variables. Cases should be listed in the SPSS data view in random order.

Normality. For best results, variables should be normally distributed.

Example Research Question

Do statistically different clusters exist for age, intrinsic motivation, extrinsic motivation, and self-esteem among university graduate students?

Example Null Hypothesis

Two-step cluster analysis involves no hypothesis testing. Therefore, there is no null hypothesis to test.

SPSS Procedure

SPSS > Analyze > Classify > TwoStep cluster

SPSS Output & Analysis

The following model was used: distance measure: log-likelihood; number of clusters: determine automatically, maximum 15; clustering criterion: Schwarz's Bayesian Criterion (BIC).

Model Summary.

Model Summary

Algorithm	TwoStep
Inputs	4
Clusters	4

The above SPSS output shows that four clusters were created.

Cluster Sizes.

Size of Smallest Cluster	24 (14.4%)
Size of Largest Cluster	65 (38.9%)
Ratio of Sizes: Largest Cluster to Smallest Cluster	2.71

Clusters.

- The size of each cluster is a percentage of the overall sample.

- The individual inputs (predictors) are sorted by overall importance (indicated by the color of the cell background shading; the most important feature is darkest and the least important feature is unshaded).

Clusters

Input (Predictor) Importance
▨ 1.0 ▨ 0.8 ▢ 0.6 ▢ 0.4 ▢ 0.2 ▢ 0.0

Cluster	4	2	3	1
Label				
Description				
Size	38.9% (65)	31.1% (52)	15.6% (26)	14.4% (24)
Inputs	Age 21-30 (100.0%)	Age 31-40 (100.0%)	Age 41-50 (73.1%)	Age 18-20 (100.0%)
	Extrinsic Motivation 63.83	Extrinsic Motivation 59.02	Extrinsic Motivation 62.50	Extrinsic Motivation 67.75
	Intrinsic Motivation 56.37	Intrinsic Motivation 53.56	Intrinsic Motivation 59.96	Intrinsic Motivation 51.33
	Self-Esteem 24.77	Self-Esteem 24.54	Self-Esteem 25.92	Self-Esteem 24.17

The above SPSS output displays four clusters. The most important predictor is age category. The youngest age category (18-20) is grouped with the highest level of extrinsic motivation and the lowest levels of intrinsic motivation and self-esteem. The oldest age category (41-50) is grouped with the highest levels of intrinsic motivation and self-esteem.

9.4: Chapter 9 Review

The answer key is at the end of this section.

1. What correlation coefficient reflects the strongest relationship?

   A.   0.45

   B.   0.78

   C.   -0.90

   D.   -0.35

2. What is the possible range of the Pearson *r* correlation coefficient?

   A.   0 to +1

   B.   -1 to 0

   C.   -1 to +1

3. In factor analysis, what does one call the correlations between an individual variable and an underlying dimension?

   A.   Communalities

   B.   Extractions

   C.   Eigenvalues

   D.   Factor loadings

4. In factor analysis, what does one call the percent of variance in a given variable explained by the factors that are extracted?

   A.   Communalities

   B.   Extractions

   C.   Eigenvalues

   D.   Factor loadings

5. When is a positive correlation present?

   A.   As one variable goes up, the other goes down

    B.   As one variable goes down the other variable goes down

    C.   When there is an inverse relationship between variables

    D.   None of the above

6.   Below is an extract from SPSS Pearson product-moment correlation test output. What is the correct finding?

		Classroom Community	Alienation
Classroom Community	Pearson Correlation	1	-.200**
	Sig. (2-tailed)		.009
	N	169	169
Alienation	Pearson Correlation	-.200**	1
	Sig. (2-tailed)	.009	
	N	169	169

    A. $r(169) = -.20$, $p = .009$

    B. $r(166) = -.20$, $p = .009$

    C. $r(166) = -.20$, $p = .00$

    D. $r(167) = -.20$, $p = .009$

7.   What is the name of the relationship between two variables after removing the overlap of a third variable from both variables?

    A.   Part correlation

    B.   Zero order correlation

    C.   Semi-partial correlation

    D.   Partial correlation

8.   What is NOT an assumption of the Spearman rank order correlation test?

    A.   Random selection of sample

    B.   Two ordinal variables

    C.   Normality

    D.   Absence of restricted range

9. You conduct the Pearson product moment correlation test and produce the following results: $r(28) = .40, p = .09$. What can you NOT conclude?

   A. There exists a low relationship between the two variables

   B. The sample consists of 30 pairs of scores

   C. The significance level is .09

   D. The confidence level is .91

10. You want to predict membership in two mutually exclusive groups from a set of predictors that include both continuous and categorical variables. What is the best test to use?

   A. Multiple regression and correlation

   B. Discriminant analysis

   C. Binomial logistic regression

   D. Bivariate regression

11. Which of the following tests is a parametric test?

   A. Spearman rank order correlation

   B. Cramér's V

   C. Binomial logistic regression

   D. Partial correlation

12. Which of the following models does NOT address internal consistency reliability?

   A. Split-half

   B. Cronbach's alpha

   C. Test-retest

   D. Kuder-Richardson

13. What is the best correlation test involving two collapsed ordinal variables?

   A. Spearman rank order correlation

   B. Kendall's tau-b

  C. Pearson chi-square contingency table analysis

  D. Cramér's *V*

14. What is the best correlation test involving two nominal variables while controlling for a third nominal variable?

  A. Spearman rank order correlation

  B. Kendall's tau-b

  C. Pearson chi-square contingency table analysis

  D. Cramér's *V*

15. What is the best correlation test to determine total relationship (linear and nonlinear)?

  A. Eta correlation coefficient

  B. Spearman rank order correlation

  C. Phi

  D. Cramér's *V*

16. What is the best test to determine effect size of a 2 x 2 contingency table?

  A. Eta correlation coefficient

  B. Spearman rank order correlation

  C. Phi

  D. Cramér's *V*

17. What is the best test to determine effect size of a contingency table larger than 2 x 2?

  A. Eta correlation coefficient

  B. Spearman rank order correlation

  C. Phi

  D. Cramér's *V*

18. What is the correct interpretation when a multiple regression null hypothesis is rejected?

  A. All IVs have a slope of zero

  B. There is a linear relationship between y and all IVs

C. There is curvilinear relationship between y and at least one of the IVs

D. There is a linear relationship between y and at least one of the IVs

19. In a multiple regression what can you conclude if F is significant, but none of the t-ratios are significant?

A. There is a multicollinearity problem

B. The DV is not normally distributed

C. The regression is valid

D. The relationship is curvilinear

20. How many dummy variables will be included in a multiple regression analysis to address socioeconomic status (low, medium, high) as an IV?

A. One

B. Two

C. Three

D. Four

21. Below is an extract from SPSS bivariate regression output. What is the correct prediction equation?

	Unstandardized Coefficients		Standardized Coefficients
	B	Std. Error	Beta
(Constant)	25.570	1.792	
Intrinsic Motivation	.058	.031	.143

A. Y' = 25.57 + .058x

B. Y' = 25.57 + .143x

C. Y' = 1.792 + .058x

D. Y' = 25.57 + .031x

22. What is a zero-order correlation?

A. The relationship between two variables after removing the overlap of a third or more other variables from both variables

B. The relationship between two variables after removing a third variable from just the IV

C. The relationship between two variables, while ignoring the influence of other variables

23. Which of the following measures is asymmetric?

A. Eta correlation coefficient

B. Phi

C. Kendall's Tau-*b*

D. Cramér's *V*

24. What is the most appropriate test if one has multiple IVs and multiple DVs?

A. Multiple regression and correlation

B. Canonical correlation

C. Discriminant analysis

D. Factor analysis

25. You have two variables, each consisting of percentile ranks. What is the best measure of bivariate correlation?

A. Pearson product-moment correlation

B. Pearson chi-square

C. Spearman rank-order correlation

D. Eta correlation coefficient

Chapter 9 Answers

1C, 2C, 3D, 4A, 5B, 6B, 7D, 8C, 9A, 10C, 11D, 12C, 13B, 14C, 15A, 16C, 17D, 18D, 19A, 20B, 21A, 22C, 23D, 24B, 25C

Glossary

5% Trimmed Mean

The 5% trimmed mean is the mean that would be obtained if the lower and upper 2.5% of values of the variable were deleted. If the value of the 5% trimmed mean is substantially different from the mean, it is reasonable to conclude the presence of outliers in the original dataset.

A-B Design

The A-B design is a single-case design that begins with baseline observations (A) before the introduction of an intervention (B).

A-B-A Design

The A-B-A design is a single-case design that begins with baseline observations (A) before the introduction of an intervention (B). After repeated observations are made on the participant during the intervention period, the intervention is withdrawn and more observations are made (A).

Acquiescence Bias

Acquiescence bias is a type of response style bias that results in the tendency to respond positively to survey items.

Action Research

Action research is a type of self-reflective investigation that professional practitioners undertake for the purpose of improving the rationality and justice of their work (Gall, Gall, & Borg, 2007, p. 500).

Analysis of Covariance

Analysis of covariance (*ANCOVA*) is a parametric procedure that assesses whether the means of multiple groups are statistically different from each other after controlling for the effects of one or more control variables (potentially confounding variables). This procedure is similar to *ANOVA* with the exception of the inclusion of additional variables (known as covariates) into the model that may be influencing scores on the *DV*.

Analysis of Variance

Analysis of variance (*ANOVA*) is a parametric procedure that assesses whether the means of multiple groups are statistically different from each other.

Anonymity

Anonymity is a research privacy measure in which either the study does not collect identifying information of individual participants (e.g., name, e-mail address, etc.), or the study cannot link individual responses with participants' identities.

Asymptotic Distribution

An asymptotic distribution is a sample distribution that approximates the true distribution of a random variable for large samples, but not necessarily for small samples.

Asymptotic Significance

Asymptotic significance means that the asymptotic method was used to calculate the significance level. This method is considered to be accurate for large samples, but less so for smaller samples. In both large and small samples the exact test is the most accurate method of calculating statistical significance.

Autocorrelation

Autocorrelation (also called serial correlation) refers to the correlation of numbers in a series of numbers. It is present when observations are not independent of each other. The Wald-Wolfowitz runs test is a test for the presence of autocorrelation in a dataset.

Bar Chart

A bar chart is made up of columns positioned over a label that represents a categorical variable. The height of the column represents the size of the group defined by the column label.

Behavioral Measurement

Behavioral measurement is the measurement of behaviors through observation; e.g. recording reaction times, reading speed, disruptive behavior, etc.

Between Subjects Design

Between-subjects designs are quantitative research designs in which the researcher is comparing different groups of research participants who experience different interventions.

Binomial Distribution

Binomial distributions model discrete random variables. A binomial random variable represents the number of successes in a series of trials in which the outcome is either success or failure.

Binomial Logistic Regression

Binomial logistic regression is a nonparametric procedure that describes or predicts membership in two mutually exclusive groups from a set of predictors. It is very similar to multiple regression with the major difference being that in logistic regression the DV is categorical rather than continuous. It is also very similar to discriminant analysis with the major difference being that in logistic regression the IVs may be continuous variables, categorical variables, or both.

Binomial Test

The binomial test is a nonparametric procedure that determines if the proportion of individuals in one of two categories is different from a specified test proportion, e.g., different from .5. If no test proportion is entered, SPSS assumes $P = .5$.

Bivariate Regression

Bivariate regression is a parametric procedure that predicts individual scores on a continuous DV based on the scores of one continuous IV.

Blind Study

A blind study, also known as a single blind study, is a common standard used by researchers to protect against bias in experimental research. In blind studies, the investigators or observers are unaware of the nature of the treatment the participants are receiving; e.g., whether participants are in a treatment or control group.

Bonferroni Correction

The Bonferroni correction is a procedure for controlling familywise Type I error for multiple pairwise comparisons by dividing the p-value to be achieved for significance by the number of paired comparisons to be made.

Box's *M* Test

Box's *M* test evaluates the equality of the covariance matrices for each level of the criterion variable. This is a test of multivariate normality.

Boxplot

A boxplot is a graphical way depicting a univariate dataset of an interval or ratio scale variable. It identifies the following values:

- High outliers
- Largest case not an outlier
- Upper quartile (Q3)
- Median (Q2)
- lower quartile (Q1)
- Smallest case not an outlier
- Low outliers

Canonical Communality Coefficient

The canonical communality coefficient (h2) is the sum of the squared structure coefficients (loadings) for a given variable. It measures how much of a given original variable's variance is reproducible from the canonical variables and reflects how much variance in measured variables is reproduced by the latent factors in a model. The coefficient is used in principal components and factor analysis as well as in canonical correlation analysis.

Canonical Correlation Analysis

Canonical correlation analysis (*CCA*) is a parametric procedure for assessing the relationship between two sets of continuous variables.

Canonical Variate

A canonical variate, also called a canonical variable, is a linear combination of a set of original variables in which the within-set correlation has been controlled (that is, the variance of each variable accounted for by other variables in the set has been removed). There are two canonical variates (sets of variables) per canonical correlation.

Case

A case represents one unit of analysis in a research study. Cases can be research participants or subjects, classes of students, countries, states, provinces, etc. One case represents one row in SPSS data view.

Categorical Variable

A categorical variable, also called a discrete or qualitative variable, has values that differ from each other in terms of quality or category (e.g., gender, political party affiliation, etc.).

Causal-Comparative Study

Causal-comparative studies (also called ex post facto studies) employ designs that are non-experimental; i.e., research in which the values of the IVs are not manipulated by the researcher, but occur naturally or were manipulated prior to the research; e.g., smokers and non-smokers, dropouts and non-dropouts, and females and males. Causal-comparative research attempts to explore the possible causes or consequences of differences that already exist between or among groups of individuals.

Cause and Effect

A cause is an explanation for some phenomenon that involves the belief that variation in an IV will be followed by variation in the DV when all other possible explanations are held constant. Social researchers often explore possible causal relationships – e.g., correlation and causal-comparative studies – or attempt to generate evidence to support a specific causal relationship, as in experimental studies in which specific hypotheses are tested. One must address several factors to obtain evidence of a cause and effect relationship:

- temporal precedence of the cause over the effect

- covariation of the cause and effect
- no plausible alternative explanations for the effect
- theoretical basis for the cause and effect relationship

Ceiling Effect

A ceiling effect is a type of range effect that causes the clustering of scores at the high end of a measurement scale.

Central Limit Theorem

According to the central limit theorem, the sampling distribution of any statistic will be normal or nearly normal, if the sample size is large enough. The central limit theorem is useful to inferential statistics. Assuming a large sample, it allows one to use hypothesis tests that assume normality, even if the data appear non-normal. This is because the tests use the sample mean, which the central limit theorem posits is approximately normally distributed.

Chi-Square Goodness of Fit Test

The chi-square ($\chi2$) goodness of fit test is a nonparametric procedure that determines if a sample of data for one categorical variable comes from a population with a specific distribution. The researcher compares observed values with theoretical or expected values.

Cluster Analysis

Cluster analysis is an exploratory, descriptive tool designed to identify natural groupings within a dataset.

Cluster Random Sample

A cluster random sample is a probability sample in which existing clusters or groups are randomly selected and then each member of the cluster is used in the research. For example, if classes of students are selected at random and then the students in each class become participants in the research study, the classes are the clusters.

Cochran's *Q* Test

Cochran's *Q* test is a nonparametric procedure for related samples that tests for differences between three or more matched sets of frequencies or proportions. The DV can be any dichotomy, such as pass-fail, presence-absence, hit-miss, etc. It is an extension of the McNemar test.

Coefficient of Determination

The coefficient of determination is the percentage of the variability among scores on one variable that can be attributed to differences in the scores on the other variable (or multiple variables in multiple regression). To compute the coefficient of determination one simply squares the correlation coefficient. For example, if the bivariate correlation is $r = .7$ (a high relationship), $r^2 = .7 * .7 = .49$. Therefore, 49% of the variation in the criterion variable is related to the predictor variable. In other words, the IV is said to explain 49% of the variance in the DV.

Coefficient of Multiple Correlation

R is the coefficient of multiple correlation. It reflects the relationship between one DV and multiple IVs. When there is only one IV, this statistic is the same as Pearson r.

Coefficient of Multiple Determination

The coefficient of multiple determination (R^2) is the percent of variance in the DV (criterion variable) explained collectively by multiple IVs (predictor variables).

Coefficient of Nondetermination

The coefficient of nondetermination is the proportion of total variance in one variable that is not predictable by another variable. It is calculated by subtracting the coefficient of determination from 1.

Cognitive Psychology

Cognitive psychology is the study of the structures and processes involved in mental activity, and of how these structures and processes are learned or how they develop with maturation (Gall, Gall, & Borg, 2007).

Cohen's Kappa Measure of Agreement

The Kappa (κ) measure of agreement is a nonparametric procedure that tests for inter-rater agreement between two raters who use the same categorical rating scale. It produces a κ coefficient. This statistic compares the observed agreement to the expected agreement if the ratings were independent.

Cohort Study

A cohort study is a type of longitudinal study that follows a specific subpopulation repeatedly over time, but not the same people. Different samples are drawn over time of the same population of interest; e.g., university alumni who graduated in 1998.

Collapsed Ordinal Data

Collapsed ordinal data are ordinal data displayed as categories.

Compensatory Equalization of Treatments Threat

Compensatory equalization of treatments is a threat to internal validity that occurs when one treatment condition seems more desirable to those who are responsible for administering the experiment. As a consequence, there may be a tendency to compensate in the other treatment condition.

Compensatory Rivalry Threat

Compensatory rivalry is a threat to internal validity that occurs when it is common knowledge among participants that one of the treatment groups is expected to perform better than the control group. Consequently, a competitive environment may result in which the control group uses extraordinary means not to be beaten (Gall, Gall, & Borg, 2007).

Concurrent Validity

Concurrent validity is the effectiveness of an instrument to predict present behavior by comparing it to the results of a different instrument that has been shown to predict the behavior.

Condition Index

Condition indices are used to flag excessive collinearity in the data. Values over 15 indicate possible multicollinearity problems and over 30 indicate serious multicollinearity problems. If a dimension has a high condition index, one looks in the variance proportions to see if that factor accounts for a sizable proportion of variance in two or more variables (that is, if two or more variables are most heavily loaded on that dimension). If this is the case, these variables have high linear dependence and multicollinearity is a problem, with the effect that small data changes may translate into very large changes or errors in the regression analysis.

Confidence Interval

A confidence interval is an estimated range of values that is likely to include an unknown population parameter. Confidence intervals are constructed at a confidence level, such as 95%, selected by the statistician. It means that if a population is sampled repeatedly and interval estimates are made on each occasion, the resulting intervals would reflect the true population parameter in approximately 95% of the cases. This example corresponds to hypothesis testing with $p = .05$.

Confidence Level

The confidence level is the probability that a true null hypothesis (H_0) is not rejected ($1 - \alpha$).

Confidentiality

Confidentiality is a research study privacy measure in which only the investigator(s) or individuals of the research team can identify the responses of individual research participants.

Confirmatory Factor Analysis

Confirmatory factor analysis (CFA) seeks to determine if the number of factors and the loadings of observed variables on them conform to what is expected on the basis of pre-established theory. A minimum requirement of CFA is that one hypothesize beforehand the number of factors in the model, but usually also expectations about which variables will load on which factors (Kim & Mueller, 1978).

Confounding Variable

A confounding variable, also called a lurking variable, is an extraneous variable relevant to a research study that the researcher fails to control, thereby adversely affecting the internal validity of a study.

Constitutive Definition

A constitutive definition is a dictionary-like definition using terms commonly understood within the discipline. Constitutive definitions provide a general understanding of the characteristics or concepts that are going to be studied, but these definitions must be changed into operational definitions before the study can actually be implemented. For example, Howard Gardner's constitutive definition of intelligence is an ability to solve a problem or fashion a product which is valued in one or more cultural settings.

Construct

A construct is a concept for a set of related behaviors or characteristics of an individual that cannot be directly observed or measured (Gall, Gall, & Borg, 2007).

Construct Validity

Construct validity refers to whether an instrument actually reflects the true theoretical meaning of a construct, to include the instrument's dimensionality (i.e., existence of subscales). Construct validity also refers to the degree to which inferences can be made from the operationalizations in a study to the theoretical constructs on which these operationalizations are based. Construct validity includes convergent and discriminant validity.

Content Validity

Content validity is based on the extent to which a measurement reflects the specific intended domain of content based on the professional expertise of experts in the field (Anastasi, 1988).

Contingency Coefficient

The contingency coefficient (C) is a chi-square-based measure of the relationship between two categorical variables. It determines whether the rows and columns of a two-way contingency table are independent (i.e., row and column variables are not associated).

Contingency Table Analysis

Contingency table analysis is a chi-square nonparametric procedure that determines the association between two categorical variables. It is a test of independence that compares the frequencies of one nominal variable variable to those of a second nominal variable. The dataset produces a R x C table, where R is the number of rows (categories of one variable) and C is the number of columns (categories of the second variable).

Continuous Variable

A continuous variable is a type of random variable that can take on any value between two specified values.

Contrast

A contrast is a linear combination of means. Usually such a combination takes the form of a difference between two means, or a difference between averages of two sets of means.

Control

Control is a characteristic of a true experiment. Campbell and Stanley (1963) observed that obtaining scientific evidence requires at least one comparison. Control groups are used for this purpose.

Control Group

Control group refers to the participants who do not receive the experimental intervention and their performance on the DV serves as a basis for evaluating the performance of the experimental group (the group who received the experimental intervention) on the same DV.

Convenience Sample

A convenience sample is a non-probability sample where the researcher relies on readily available participants. While this is the most convenient method, a major risk will be to generalize the results to a known target population.

Convergent Validity

Convergent validity is the degree to which scores on one test correlate with scores on other tests that are designed to measure the same construct.

Cook's Distance

Cook's distance (D_i) is a measure for identifying multivariate outliers, which are operationally defined as cases that have a Cook's distance greater than some cutoff (some use a cutoff of 1; some use $4/(n - p)$, where p is the number of parameters in the model; some use $4/(n - k - 1)$, where n is the number of cases and k is the number of independents).

Correlation

Correlation is a statistical technique that measures and describes the strength and direction of relationship (i.e., association, correlation) between two or more variables.

Correlation Study

A correlation study is a type of quantitative, non-experimental study that examines relationships (i.e., correlation, association, co-variation) between two or more existing, non-manipulated variables drawing from a single group of research participants.

Count Coding System

A count coding system is used in behavioral measurement to count the number of instances and/or duration of all instances of each key behavior.

Counterbalanced Design

A counterbalanced design (also known as a Latin square) is a quasi-experiment in which all groups are exposed to all treatments, but in a different order. The design can consist of posttests only, but variations of this design to include pretests are possible.

Coverage Error

Coverage or frame error is a type of non-sampling error that occurs when the sampling frame is a biased representation of the target population.

Cramér's *V*

The Cramér's *V* test is a nonparametric procedure used to determine if there is an association between columns and rows in contingency tables. It is a measure of nominal by nominal association based on the chi square statistic. Cramér's *V* can be used for tables larger than 2 x 2. The test is symmetric, so it will produce the same value regardless of how the variables are designated IV and DV. Cramér's *V* is frequently used to calculate effect size in conjunction with contingency table analysis.

Criterion Validity

Criterion validity relates to how adequately a test score can be used to infer an individual's most probable standing on an accepted criterion (Hopkins, 1998). Criterion validity includes predictive validity and concurrent validity.

Criterion Variable

Criterion variable (or response variable) is another name for the DV in regression analysis.

Criterion-Referenced Test

A criterion-referenced test defines the performance of each test taker without regard to the performance of others. The success is being able to perform a specific task or set of competencies at a certain predetermined level or criterion.

Cronbach's Alpha

Cronbach's alpha is a model of internal consistency reliability based on the average inter-item correlation of an instrument.

Cross Validation

Cross validation is a procedure to ascertain how much shrinkage occurs in a regression solution when the regression equation is applied to a new sample.

Cross-Sectional Study

A cross-sectional study is a type of descriptive study used to collect data that reflect current attitudes, opinions, or beliefs. The defining feature of a cross-sectional study is that it collects data on and compares different population groups at a single snapshot in time.

Crosstabulation

Crosstabulation is a procedure that cross-tabulates two categorical variables in order to determine their relationship. It represents the number of cases in a category of one variable divided into the categories of another variable. From a crosstabulation, a number of statistics can be calculated, such as Pearson chi-square, phi, Cramér's V, and the contingency coefficient.

Cultural Studies and Critical-Theory Research

Cultural studies and critical-theory research is the study of contestation of oppressive power relationships in a culture (Gall, Gall, & Borg, 2007, p. 491).

Data Mining

Data mining is an approach designed to analyze large datasets and find meaningful patterns through computer-based analysis.

Decile

A decile (D) divides the data into ten equal parts based on their statistical ranks and position from the bottom, where $D_1 = P_{10}$ and $D_5 = P_{50} = Q_2$.

Deductive Reasoning

Deductive reasoning moves from general principles to specific conclusions. Quantitative research employs deductive reasoning.

Degrees of Freedom

Degrees of freedom (df) represent the number of independent pieces of information that go into the estimate of a parameter. The higher the degrees of freedom, the more representative the sample is of the population.

Delimitation

A delimitation addresses how a study is narrowed in scope; i.e., how it is bounded.

Density Curve

A density curve is a smooth curve (rather than a frequency curve as one sees in the histogram of a small sample) that is on or above the x-axis and displays the overall shape of a distribution. The area under any density curve sums to 1. Since the density curve represents the entire distribution, the area under the curve on any interval represents the proportion of observations in that interval. Since a density curve represents the distribution of a specific dataset, it can take on different shapes. The normal distribution is an example of a density curve.

Dependent *t*-test

The dependent *t*-test (also called a paired-samples *t*-test) is a parametric procedure that compares mean scores obtained from two dependent (related) samples. Dependent or related data are obtained by:

- Measuring participants from the same sample on two different occasions (i.e., using repeated-measures or within subjects design).

- Using a matching procedure by pairing research participants and dividing them so one member of the pair is assigned to each group.

Dependent Variable

Dependent variables (DVs) are outcome variables or those that one expects to be affected by IVs. They are measured variables in a research study.

Descriptive Statistics

Descriptive statistics are used to describe what the data shows regarding a dataset. They summarize datasets and are used to detect patterns in the data in order to convey their essence to others and/or to allow for further analysis using inferential statistics.

Descriptive Study

A descriptive study (sometimes called observational study or survey research) is meant to generate an accurate record of what is happening in a specific situation with a given population. The researcher does not attempt to exert control over the phenomena of interest. Instead, phenomena are observed (measured) as they occur in a situation or at a given point or points in time.

Detrended Q-Q Plot

A detrended Q-Q plot provides information that is similar to that provided by the Q-Q plot. The *y*-axis represents standard deviations from the 45-degree line seen in the non-detrended Q-Q plot and the *x*-axis represents values. The plot shows the difference between an observation's expected *z*-score under normality and its actual *z*-score.

Dichotomous Variable

A dichotomous variable is a nominal variable that has two categories or levels; e.g., gender (male, female).

Difficulty Index

The difficulty index is a measure of the difficulty level of test items. For items with one correct answer worth a single point, the item difficulty index is the number of correct answers divided by the number of respondents. The higher the difficulty factor, the easier the question is. A value of 1 means all test takers got the question correct. When an item is worth other than a single point, or when there is more than one correct choice per item, the item difficulty is the average score on that item divided by the highest number of points for any one alternative.

Discrete Variable

A discrete variable, also known as a categorical or qualitative variable, is one that cannot take on all values within the limits of the variable. For example, consider responses to a five-point rating scale that can only take on the values of 1, 2, 3, 4, and 5. The variable cannot have the value of 2.5. Therefore, data generated by this rating scale represent a discrete variable.

Discriminant Analysis

Discriminant analysis (sometimes called discriminant function analysis) is a parametric procedure that describes or predicts membership in two or more mutually exclusive groups from a set of predictors, when there is no natural ordering on the groups. It is very similar to multiple regression with the major difference being that in discriminant analysis the DV is categorical rather than continuous.

Discriminant Validity

Discriminant validity is the degree to which scores on one test do not correlate with scores on other tests that are not designed to assess the same construct. For example, one would not expect scores on a trait anxiety test to correlate with scores on a state anxiety test.

Discrimination Index

The discrimination index is used to determine if each item on a test adequately discriminates between upper and lower achieving examinees.

Distribution

The distribution of a variable refers to the set of observed or theoretical values of a variable to include associated frequencies of occurrence or probabilities.

Double Blind Study

The double blind study ensures that both investigators and participants are unaware of the nature of the treatment the participants are receiving.

Dummy Variable

A dummy variable is one that takes the values 0 or 1 to indicate the absence or presence of some categorical effect. It is used as a numeric stand-in for a categorical IV in regression analysis.

Durbin-Watson Test

The Durbin–Watson test is used to detect the presence of autocorrelation. Generally, a Durbin-Watson statistic in the range of 1.5 to 2.5 means that one may assume independence of observations.

Ecological Validity

Ecological validity is a type of external validity that looks at the testing environment and determines how much it influences behavior. Methods, materials, and setting of the study must approximate the real-life situation that is under investigation (Brewer, 2000). The focus is on the extent to which the results of a research study can be generalized from the set of environmental conditions created by the researcher to the environmental conditions characteristic of the target population.

Effect Size

Effect size is a measure of the magnitude of a treatment effect. It is the degree to which H_0 is false and is indexed by the discrepancy between the null hypothesis and the alternate hypothesis. It is frequently used to assess the practical significance of an effect.

Eigenvalue

An eigenvalue is used "to indicate how much of the variation in the original group of variables is accounted for by a particular factor" (Vogt, 2005, pp. 103–104). Eigenvalues close to 0 indicate dimensions that explain little variance.

Equivalent Posttest-Only Control Group Design

The equivalent posttest-only control group design is the most powerful true experiment when properly executed with random assignment (Campbell & Stanley, 1963). When the two groups (treatment and control) are not equivalent, the study becomes a very weak pre-experiment.

Equivalent Pretest-Posttest Control Group Design

The equivalent pretest-posttest control group design is very common true experimental design (Campbell & Stanley, 1963). Additional groups are often introduced in this design.The design is used when it is necessary to measure groups on pretest measures, despite the fact that the groups are equivalent. Random assignment does not guarantee equivalency, particularly with small sample sizes.

Estimation

Estimation is a way to estimate a population parameter based on measuring a sample. It can be expressed in two ways:

- A point estimate of a population parameter is a single value of a statistic.

- An interval estimate is defined by two numbers, between which a population parameter is said to lie.

Eta (η) Correlation Coefficient

The eta (η) correlation coefficient (nominal by interval/ratio data) is a measure that provides the strength and direction of the total linear and nonlinear relationship between two variables. For linear relationships, eta equals the Pearson r correlation coefficient.

Ethnographic Content Analysis

Ethnographic content analysis is the examination of the content of documents found in field settings as reflections of social interactions in the culture (Gall, Gall, & Borg, 2007, p. 520).

Ethnography

Ethnography is the intensive study of the features of a given culture and the patterns in those features (Gall, Gall, & Borg, 2007, p. 500).

Ethnography of Communication

Ethnography of communication is the study of how members of a cultural group use speech in their social life (Gall, Gall, & Borg, 2007, p. 520).

Ethnomethodology

Ethnomethodology is the study of the techniques that individuals use to make sense of everyday social environments and to accomplish the tasks of communicating, making decisions, and reasoning within them (Gall, Gall, & Borg, 2007, p. 518).

Evaluation

According to Posavac and Carey (2002), evaluation is a collection of methods, skills, and sensitivities necessary to determine whether a human service is needed and likely to be used, whether it is conducted as planned, and whether the human service actually does help people.

Evaluation Research

Evaluation research is a type of research closely related to traditional social research and utilizes many of its tools and methodologies. However, unlike traditional research, evaluation research takes place within an organizational context that requires consideration of the needs of multiple program stakeholders. Evaluation research is typically used to evaluate programs.

Ex Post Facto Study

An ex post facto study is a non-experimental study that examines outcomes that occur after the fact (i.e., after manipulation of the IV) in situations where the researcher was not able to manipulate the IV. The term is often used to describe a causal-comparative study.

Experimental Mortality Threat

The experimental mortality threat to internal validity occurs when there is a differential loss of participants by group from the study through attrition. The result is that group equivalence formed at the start of the study may be destroyed (Campbell & Stanley, 1963).

Experimental Study

An experimental research study is a type of quantitative study in which the researcher tests relationships between variables by controlling or manipulating research participants and/or conditions. There are four types of experimental studies: true experiments, quasi-experiments, pre-experiments, and single-case (single organism) studies.

Experimental Treatment Diffusion Threat

The experimental treatment diffusion threat to internal validity (also known as contamination) occurs when experimental and control groups become aware of both treatments and treatments are diffused throughout participants and groups (Gall, Gall, & Borg, 2007). This threat occurs when there is communication about the treatment between groups of participants.

Experimentally Accessible Population

The experimentally accessible population are all those in the target population accessible to be studied or included in the sample.

Exploratory Factor Analysis

Exploratory factor analysis seeks to uncover the underlying structure of a relatively large set of variables. The researcher's à priori assumption is that any indicator may be associated with any factor. This is the most common form of factor analysis.

There is no prior theory and one uses factor loadings to discern the factor structure of the data.

External Validity

External validity is the generalizability of study findings to the target population (i.e., can the experiment be replicated with the same results?; Campbell & Stanley, 1963). It is the ability to generalize across categories or classes of individuals and across settings within the same target population. It includes population validity and ecological validity.

Extraneous Variable

An extraneous variable is an additional variable relevant to a research study that the researcher needs to control. An extraneous variable becomes a confounding variable when the researcher cannot or does not control for it, thereby adversely affecting the internal validity of a study by increasing error.

Extrapolation

Extrapolation occurs when one uses a regression equation to predict values outside the range of values used to produce the equation. Since a relationship between two variables can be approximately linear over a certain range, then change, one should be very cautious about predictions beyond the range of observed data that produced a regression equation.

Extreme and Central Tendency Bias

Extreme and central tendency bias is a type of response style bias that results in the tendency to respond to self-reports using only certain portions of the measurement scale.

Extreme Outlier

Extreme outliers are extreme values that are greater than 3 x *IQR* either above the top hinge or below the bottom hinge of a boxplot and are identified by an asterisk and a case number in SPSS-produced boxplots.

Face Validity

Face validity is an evaluation of the degree to which an instrument appears to measure what it purports to measure.

Factor

A factor is a categorical variable with two or more values, referred to as levels; e.g., gender (male, female). For example, IVs in the two-way *ANOVA* procedure are often referred to as factors.

Factor Loadings

Factor or component loadings in principal components and factor analysis are the correlation coefficients between the variables and factors (components). Factor loadings are the basis for labeling the different factors. Loadings above .6 are usually considered high and those below .4 are low.

Factorial Design

Intervention studies with two or more categorical explanatory variables (IVs) that influence a DV are referred to as factorial designs.

Floor Effect

A floor effect is a type of range effect that causes the clustering of scores at the low end of a measurement scale.

Focus Group

A focus group is a method of group interviewing in which the interactions between the moderator and the group and between group members produce a level of insight that is usually not obtained from observation, surveys, and less interactional interviews.

Forced-Choice Scale

A forced-choice scale is a measurement scale missing the middle or neutral option, thereby forcing the participant to take a position.

Formative Evaluation

Formative evaluation is a type of program evaluation that is meant to strengthen or improve the program being evaluated – they help form it by examining the delivery of the program, the quality of its implementation, and the assessment of the organizational context, personnel, procedures, inputs, and so on (Fitzpatrick, Sanders, & Worthen, 2004).

Friedman Test

The Friedman test is a nonparametric procedure that compares medians between multiple dependent groups when the DV is either ordinal or interval/ratio. It is an extension of the Wilcoxon signed ranks test. The test uses the ranks of the data rather than their raw values to calculate the statistic. If there are only two groups for this test, it is equivalent to the related samples sign test.

Gamma (γ)

Gamma (γ) is a nonparametric symmetric procedure that determines the monotonic strength and direction of association between two categorical ordinal variables (or with dichotomous nominal variables).

Gaussian Distribution

The Gaussian distribution is the normal distribution.

General Linear Model

The general linear model (GLM) is the underlying mathematical model for relational parametric tests covering the range of procedures used to analyze one continuous DV and one or more IVs (continuous or categorical).

Geometric Distribution

Geometric distributions model discrete random variables. A geometric random variable typically represents the number of trials required to obtain the first failure.

Guttman Scale

The Guttman scale is a cumulative design approach to scaling. The purpose is to establish a one-dimensional continuum for a concept one wishes to measure. Essentially, the items are ordered so that if a respondent agrees with any specific item in the list, he or she will also agree with all previous items.

Halo Effect

The halo effect is a threat to internal validity that occurs as a result of the tendency for an irrelevant feature of a unit of analysis to influence the relevant feature (Rosenzweig, 2007).

Typically, a strong initial positive or negative impression of a person, group, or event tends to influence ratings on all subsequent observations.

Hawthorne Effect

Hawthorne effect is a threat to external validity that refers to the tendency of some people to work harder and perform better when they are being observed. Therefore, it represents the increase in efficiency/achievement/productivity due to awareness that one is a participant in a research study.

Hermeneutics

Hermeneutics is the study of the process by which individuals arrive at the meaning of any text (Gall, Gall, & Borg, 2007, p. 520).

Histogram

A histogram is a graphical representation of a univariate dataset of a variable measured on the interval or ratio scales. It is constructed by dividing the range of data into equal-sized bins (classes or groups) and plotting each bin on a chart.

History Threat

The history threat to internal validity consists of specific events external to the treatment occurring between observations (measurements) that affect the DV.

Holm's Sequential Bonferroni Correction

The Holm's sequential Bonferroni correction is a less conservative variant of the Bonferroni correction for controlling familywise Type I error when there are multiple comparisons.

Homogeneity of Regressions

Homogeneity of regressions is the absence of an interaction between the covariate and main effect IV in an ANCOVA procedure. In other words, the regression lines have a common slope.

Homogeneity of Variance

Homogeneity of variance (or error variance) is the assumption that two or more groups have equal or similar variances. The assumption is that the variability in the DV is expected to be about the same at all levels of the IV.

Homogeneity of Variance-Covariance Matrices

Homogeneity of variance-covariance matrices is the multivariate equivalent of homogeneity of variance and is an assumption of multivariate analysis of variance (MANOVA). It assumes that the variance/covariance matrix in each cell of the design is sampled from the same population so they can be reasonably pooled together to make an error term.

Homoscedasticity

The assumption of homoscedasticity is that the variability in scores for one variable is roughly the same at all values of a second variable.

Hypothesis Testing

Hypothesis testing is the use of statistics to determine the probability that a given hypothesis is true.

Implementation Threat

The implementation threat to internal validity occurs when the treatment and/or control conditions are not implemented objectively and consistently across all groups (Wallen & Fraenkel, 2001). In particular, the treatment group might be treated in unintended ways that are not part of the intervention but give one group an advantage (or disadvantage) over other groups.

Inductive Reasoning

Inductive reasoning begins with specifics and then works toward broader generalizations. Qualitative research employs inductive reasoning

Independence of Observations

Independence of observations means that multiple observations are not acted on by an outside influence common to the observations. It would be violated, for example, if one participant's response to a measurement item was influenced by another's response. Generally, implementation of a survey questionnaire excludes any possibility of dependence among the observations provided the researcher implements controls to prevent respondents for discussing their responses prior to completing the survey.

Independent *t*-Test

The independent *t*-test is a parametric procedure that assesses whether the means of two independent groups are statistically different from each other. This analysis is appropriate whenever one wants to compare the means of two independent groups.

Independent Variable

Independent variables (IVs) are the predictor variables that one expects to influence other variables. In an experiment, the researcher manipulates the IV(s), which typically involve an intervention of some type.

Inferential Statistics

Inferential statistics are used to reach conclusions that extend beyond the sample measured to a target population. It is divided into estimation and hypothesis testing.

Information Visualization

Information visualization refers to

techniques used for creating images, diagrams, or animations to communicate, understand, and improve the results of big data analyses. (Manyika et al., 2011, p. 31)

Informed Consent

Informed consent means that research participants need to know what they are being asked to participate in before deciding whether to engage in the study.

Instrumentation Threat

The instrumentation threat to internal validity consists of changes in calibration of the measuring instrument or use of an unreliable instrument.

Institutional Review Board

Institutional Review Boards (IRBs) serve to provide an institutional and governmental required evaluation of certain proposed projects and investigations to ensure their compliance with ethical standards for the protection of human research subjects by treating them humanely, maintaining their dignity, and preserving their rights.

Inter-Rater Reliability

Inter-rater or inter-observer reliability (rater agreement) is used to assess the degree to which different raters/observers give consistent estimates of the same phenomenon.

Interaction Effect

According to Keppel (2004), an interaction effect is present when the effects of one IV on behavior change at different levels of a second IV.

Internal Consistency Reliability

Internal consistency reliability addresses how consistently individuals respond to the items within a scale that are measuring the same construct or dimension.

Internal Validity

Internal validity is the extent to which one can accurately state that the IV produced the observed effect (Campbell & Stanley, 1963). It reflects the extent of control over confounding variables (possible rival hypotheses) in a research study.

Interquartile Range

The interquartile range (*IQR*) is used with continuous variables and reflects the distance between the 75th percentile and the 25th percentile. In other words, the *IQR* is the range of the middle 50% of the data.

Interval Estimate

An interval estimate is defined by two numbers, between which a population parameter is said to lie.

Interval Scale

Interval scale intervals, like ratio scale intervals, are equal to each other. However, unlike ratio scale variables, interval scales have an arbitrary zero (i.e., negative values are permissible).

Intra-Rater Reliability

Intra-rater or intra-observer reliability is used to assess the degree to which the same raters/observers give consistent estimates of the same phenomenon over time.

Intraclass Correlation Coefficient

The intraclass correlation coefficient (ICC) is a nonparametric correlation procedure used to measure correlations within a class. A class is defined as variables that share a metric (scale) and variance. The procedure is used to assess reliability, to include inter-rater and test-retest reliability.

Item Analysis

Item analysis is the process used to evaluate the effectiveness of items in a test by exploring the examinees' responses to each item.

John Henry Effect

The John Henry Effect, which comes from the story of John Henry trying to lay railroad track faster than a machine, is another name for the compensatory rivalry threat to internal validity.

Kaiser-Guttman Rule

The Kaiser-Guttman rule is a method of extracting factors or components in principal components and factor analysis. The number of factors to be extracted should be equal to the number of factors having an eigenvalue greater than 1.0. The rationale for choosing this particular value is that a factor must have variance at least as large as that of a single standardized original variable.

Kaiser-Meyer-Olkin Measure of Sampling Adequacy

The Kaiser-Meyer-Olkin (*KMO*) measure of sampling adequacy is used in conjunction with principal components and factor analysis and predicts if data are likely to factor well, based on correlation and partial correlation. *KMO* varies from 0 to 1.0. Criteria: test statistic > .9 is excellent, test statistic > .8 is meritorious, test statistic > .7 is middling, test statistic > .6 is mediocre, test statistic >.5 is miserable, and test statistic < .5 is unacceptable. *KMO* overall should be .60 or higher to proceed with factor analysis.

Kendall's Tau-b

Kendall's tau-b (τ_b) test is a nonparametric symmetric procedure that determines the strength and direction of association between two ordinal variables. It is often used with but not limited to 2 x 2 tables. This test is appropriate for collapsed ordinal-level variables where the number of rows and number of columns are equal.

Kendall's Tau-c

Kendall's tau-c (τ_c) (also called Stuart's tau-c) is a nonparametric variant of tau-b for determining strength and direction of association between two ordinal variables for large tables. It is used when the number of rows and number of columns are not equal.

Kolmogorov-Smirnov Test

The one-sample Kolmogorov-Smirnov test is a nonparametric procedure that determines whether a sample of data comes from a specific distribution. The test can evaluate goodness-of-fit against many theoretical distributions, to include the normal distribution.

Kruskal-Wallis *H* Test

The Kruskal-Wallis *H* test is a nonparametric procedure that compares medians between multiple independent groups when the DV is either ordinal or interval/ratio. It is an extension of the Mann-Whitney *U* test.

Kurtosis

Kurtosis measures heavy-tailedness or light-tailedness relative to the normal distribution. A heavy-tailed distribution has more values in the tails (away from the center of the distribution) than the normal distribution, and will have negative kurtosis.

- Platykurtic = flat shape, kurtosis statistic below 0, large SD.

- Mesokurtic = normal shape, between extremes, normal shape, kurtosis statistic around 0.

- Leptokurtic = peaked shape, kurtosis statistic above 0, small SD.

Lambda

Lambda (λ) is nonparametric asymmetric procedure used to determine if there is an association between two nominal (or a nominal and ordinal) variables. The values of lambda can range from 0 to 1. A value of 0 means no improvement in prediction. A value of 1 indicates that the prediction can be made without error.

Latent Variable

A latent variable is a variable that is not directly observed but rather is inferred from other variables that are observed. Factors or components in principal components and factor analysis are examples of latent variables.

Latin Square

Latin square is another name for a counterbalanced research design.

Levene's Test

Levene's test of equality of variances is a parametric procedure that tests the assumption that each group has the same variance (σ^2) on an interval/ratio scale DV. If the Levene statistic is significant at the .05 level, the researcher rejects H_0 and concludes the groups have unequal variances.

Leverage

Leverage values reflect the relative influence of each observation on the model's fit. It is also a measure of multivariate outliers.

Life History Research

Life history research is the study of the life experience of individuals from the perspective of how these individuals interpret and understand the world around them and might be called a biography, a life story, an oral history, a case study, a testimonial, or a portrait or if the researcher writes about him or herself might be called an autobiography or a memoir (Gall, Gall, & Borg, 2007, p. 498).

Likert Scale

The Likert scale is a unidimensional, summative design approach to scaling. It consists of responses to a series of statements, based on the attitudes/opinions to be assessed, that are typically expressed in terms of a five- or seven-point scale. For example, the choices of a five-point Likert scale might be strongly disagree, somewhat disagree, neither agree nor disagree, somewhat agree, and strongly agree.

Limitation

A limitation is a potential weakness of a research study (i.e., threats to validity that were not adequately controlled).

Line Chart

A line chart allows one to visually examine the mean (or other statistic) of a continuous variable across the various levels of a categorical variable. Line charts are ideally suited to show trends for data over time in longitudinal studies.

Linearity

Linearity means that the amount of change, or rate of change, between scores on two variables are constant for the entire range of scores for the two variables. The graph representing a linear relationship is a straight line.

Logistic Regression

See binomial logistic regression.

Logit

Logits are the natural logs of odds ratios. They contain exactly the same information as odds ratios, but because they are symmetrical, they can be compared more easily. For example, in logistic regression, a positive logit means the IV (predictor) has the effect of increasing the odds that the DV (criterion) equals a given value. A negative logit means the IV has the effect of decreasing the odds that the DV equals the given value.

Longitudinal Study

A longitudinal or time-series study is a type of descriptive study used to study individuals over time. The defining feature of a longitudinal study is that researchers conduct several observations of the same research participants over a period of time, sometimes lasting years.

Mahalanobis Distance

Mahalanobis distance (D^2) is a measure for identifying multivariate outliers. It measures the distance of a case from the centroid (multidimensional mean) of a distribution, given the covariance (multidimensional variance) of the distribution. A case is a multivariate outlier if the probability associated with its D^2 is 0.001 or less.

Manipulation

Manipulation is a characteristic of a true experiment in which the researcher manipulates the IV by administering it to some research participants and withholding it from other participants. In other words, the researcher varies the IV and observes the effect that the manipulation has on the DV.

Mann-Whitney *U* Test

The Mann-Whitney *U* test is a nonparametric procedure that compares medians between two independent groups when the DV is either ordinal or interval/ratio.

Matched Pairs Design

A matched pairs design is achieved when participants are matched on known extraneous variable(s) and then one member of each matched pair is randomly assigned to each group. The researcher is thus assured that the groups are initially equivalent on the variables used in the matching procedure.

Maturation Threat

The maturation threat to internal validity is a threat produced by internal (physical or psychological) changes in subjects not related to the IV. It consists of the processes within participants that act as a function of time – e.g. if the project lasts a few years – such that participants may improve their performance regardless of treatment.

McNemar Test

The McNemar test is a nonparametric chi-square procedure that compares proportions obtained from a 2 x 2 contingency table where the row variable (A) is the DV and the column variable (B) is the IV. The McNemar test can be used to test if there is a statistically significant difference between the probability of a (0,1) pair and the probability of a (1,0) pair.

Mean

The mean or arithmetic average is a statistic such that the sum of deviations from it is zero. That is, it is based on the sum of the deviation scores raised to the first power, or what is known as the first moment of the distribution, and captures the central location of the distribution.

Mean Square (*MS*)

The mean square (*MS*) is an estimate of variance across groups. *MS* is used in analysis of variance and regression analysis. It equals sum of squares divided by its appropriate degrees of freedom.

Measure of Central Tendency

A measure of central tendency is a descriptive statistic that tells one where the middle of a distribution lies. Researchers typically report the best measures of central tendency and dispersion for each variable in research reports.

Measure of Dispersion

A measure of dispersion is a descriptive statistic that indicates the variability of a distribution. Researchers typically report the best measures of central tendency and dispersion for each variable in research reports.

Measure of Relative Position

A measure of relative position is a descriptive statistic that indicates where a score is in relation to all other scores in a distribution.

Measurement

Measurement is the process of representing a construct with numbers in order to depict the amount of a phenomenon that is present at a given point in time. The purpose of this process is to differentiate between people, objects, or events that possess varying degrees of the phenomenon of interest.

Measurement Error

Measurement error is a type of non-sampling error that occurs when data collection is not reliable. Instrument reliability as well as inter- and intra-rater reliability are ways to help protect against measurement error. Measurement Error = True Score − Observed Score.

Measurement Validity

Measurement validity refers the relative correctness of a measurement. In other words, it evaluates how well an instrument measures a construct and refers to the degree to which evidence and theory support the interpretations of test scores.

Measurement Without Error

The assumption of measurement without error refers to the need for error-free measurement when using the general linear model.

Median

The median divides the distribution into two equal halves. It is the midpoint of a distribution when the distribution has an odd number of scores. It is the number halfway between the two middle scores when the distribution has an even number of scores.

Median Test

The median test is a nonparametric procedure that compares medians between two or more independent groups when the DV is either ordinal or interval/ratio. The test counts the number of cases in each group that are above and below the combined median, and then performs a chi-square test.

Mediating Variable

A given variable may be said to function as a mediator to the extent that it accounts for the relationship between the predictor and the criterion.

Meta-Analysis

A meta-analysis is often characterized as a type of descriptive study in which the units of analysis are individual studies. It incorporates a systematic review of the research literature to determine effect size. The aim of the study is to obtain the magnitude of an effect with adequate precision based on numerous research studies that addressed the phenomenon of interest. More weight is given to studies with more precise estimates.

Mild Outlier

Mild outliers are extreme values of a distribution that fall between 1.5 x *IQR* and 3 x *IQR* either above the top hinge or below the bottom hinge of a boxplot and are identified by a circle and a SPSS case number (i.e., dataset row number).

Mixed Methods Research

Mixed methods research is a methodology for conducting research that involves collecting, analyzing, and integrating quantitative and qualitative research in a single study. The basis for this form of research is that both qualitative and quantitative research, in combination, provide a better understanding of a research problem or issue than either research approach alone.

Mode

The mode is the most frequently occurring score(s) in a distribution.

Moderating Variable

A moderator is a qualitative or quantitative variable that affects the direction and/or strength of the relationship between an independent or predictor variable and a dependent or criterion variable.

Monotonicity

A monotonic relationship is one where the value of one variable increases as the value of the other variable increases or the value of one variable increases as the value of the other variable decreases, but not necessarily in a linear fashion.

Multicollinearity

Multicollinearity is the high intercorrelation of IVs. Very high correlations violate the assumption of no multicollinearity by increasing the standard error of the beta coefficients.

Multinomial Distribution

A multinomial distribution deals with events that have multiple discrete outcomes, in contrast to a binomial distribution, which has two discrete outcomes.

Multiple Regression and Correlation

Multiple regression and correlation is a parametric procedure that determines the relationship between a DV and multiple IVs (multiple correlation) or to predict individual scores on a DV based on scores of multiple IVs (multiple regression).

Multiple Time Series Design

The multiple time series design is a quasi-experiment that adds a control group to the the simple time series design.

Multiple Treatment Interference Threat

Multiple treatment interference is a threat to external validity. Effects of previous treatments are not usually erasable. Consequently, the research findings may be generalized only to persons who experience the same sequence of treatments.

Multivariate Analysis of Variance

Multivariate analysis of variance (*MANOVA*) is a parametric procedure used to determine if multiple DVs are changed by manipulation of the IV(s). *MANOVA* is an extension of *ANOVA* in which main effects and interactions are assessed on a combination of DVs. *MANOVA* uses one or more categorical independents as factors, like *ANOVA*, but unlike *ANOVA*, there are multiple DVs.

Multivariate Normality

Multivariate normality is achieved when all variables and all combinations of variables are normally distributed. When this condition is met, the residuals are normally distributed and independent, the differences between predicted and obtained scores (the errors or residuals) are symmetrically distributed around a mean of zero, and there is no pattern to the errors.

Multivariate Outlier

Multivariate outliers are cases that have an unusually high or low combination of values for a number of variables. The value for individual variables may not be univariate outliers, but in combination with other variables, the case is an outlier.

Narrative Analysis

A narrative analysis is the study of organized representations and explanations of human experience (Gall, Gall, & Borg, 2007, p. 491).

Negative Affectivity Bias

Negative affectivity bias is a type of response style bias that is a manifestation of neuroticism and can affect self-reports regarding health matters, life events, etc.

Network Analysis

Network analysis is "A set of techniques used to characterize relationships among discrete nodes in a graph or a network" (Manyika et al., 2011, p. 29). In social research, network analysis can be used to find connections between individuals, communities, or organizations.

Nominal Scale

Nominal scale variables are unordered categories. Also called categorical or discrete variables, they allow for only qualitative classification. That is, they can be measured only in terms of whether individual units of analysis belong to some distinctively different categories, but one cannot rank order those categories.

Non-Experimental Study

A non-experimental research study is a type of quantitative study that is meant to identify the characteristics of a phenomenon and describe the variable(s) under study. The researcher tests relationships between variables without controlling or manipulating research participants and/or conditions. In other words, the researcher studies what naturally occurs or has already occurred. The following three classifications of non-experimental designs encompass the major types of non-experimental research: descriptive studies, to include survey research; correlation studies, and causal-comparative (ex post facto) studies.

Non-Probability Sampling

Non-probability sampling (purposeful or theoretical sampling) is a type of sampling that does not involve the use of randomization to select research participants. Consequently, research participants are not selected according to probability or mathematical rules, but by other means (e.g., convenience or access). It occurs when random sampling is too costly, where nonrandom sampling is the only feasible alternative, or when the sampling frame is not known.

Non-Sampling Error

Non-sampling error is an error caused by human error that effects a specific statistical analysis. These errors can include data entry errors and biased questions.

Noncentrality Parameter

The noncentrality parameter is used by SPSS as a value when calculating the power level of the F-test in SPSS general linear model procedures and reflects the extent to which the null hypothesis is false.

Nonequivalent Pretest-Posttest Control Group Design

The nonequivalent pretest-posttest control group design is a very popular quasi experimental design. It is very similar to the true experimental version of this design with the exception that non-equivalent groups are used. Like the true experiment, this design can also include more than two groups.

Nonparametric Test

A nonparametric test does not make any assumptions regarding the distribution or scales of measurement. Consequently, a nonparametric test is considered a distribution-free method because it does not rely on any underlying mathematical distribution. Nonparametric tests do, however, have various assumptions that must be met and are less powerful than parametric tests.

Nonreactive Measure

A measurement is nonreactive when it does not change that which is being measured. It is a passive or unobtrusive measure of behavior and does not introduce stimulus factors to which the research participant might otherwise react.

Nonresponse Bias

Nonresponse bias occurs when some individuals selected for the sample are unwilling or unable to participate in the study. It results when respondents differ in meaningful ways from nonrespondents.

Nonresponse Error

Nonresponse error is a type of non-sampling error that occurs when some members of the sample don't respond. A high response rate is essential to reliable statistical inference.

Norm

A norm is a standard average performance on a particular characteristic by a specific population with a given background or age. It can also refer to normative data that are standards of comparison based on the results of a test administered to a specific population.

Norm-Referenced Test

A norm-referenced test defines the performance of test-takers in relation to one another.

Normal Curve Equivalent Score

NCE-scores are normalized standard scores with a mean of 50 and a standard deviation of 21.06. The standard deviation of 21.06 was chosen so that *NCE* scores of 1 and 99 are equivalent to the 1st (P_1) and 99th (P_{99}) percentiles.

Normal Distribution

The normal or Gaussian distribution is a special type of density curve. It is shaped like a bell curve. Its importance flows from the fact that any sum of normally distributed variables is itself a normally distributed variable. Sums of variables that, individually, are not normally distributed tend to become normally distributed.

Normality

Normality refers to the shape of a variable's distribution. The variable of interest is distributed normally, which means it is symmetrical and shaped like a bell-curve.

Novelty Effect

The novelty effect occurs when responses or performance of study participants are different from what they would have been otherwise as a result of the awareness by participants that they are involved in a study. The effectiveness of a new treatment may also increases because the treatment is new or different.

Null Hypothesis

The null hypothesis, denoted by H_0, is the hypothesis of no difference or no relationship.

Oblique Rotation

Oblique rotation in principal components and factor analysis allows for correlations between factors.

Odds Ratio

Odds are defined as the ratio of the probability that an event will occur divided by the probability that an event will not occur. In other words, odds are described by the ratio of the probability that something is true divided by the probability that it is not true.

One-Group Pretest-Posttest Design

A one-group pretest-posttest design is a pre-experiment.

One-Sample *t*-Test

The one-sample *t*-test is a parametric procedure that compares a calculated sample mean to a known population mean or a previously reported value in order to determine if the difference is statistically significant.

One-Shot Case Study

A one-shot case study is a pre-experiment. It consists of one sample that receives a treatment followed by a posttest.

One-Tailed Hypothesis

A one-tailed hypothesis is directional (i.e., the direction of difference or association is predicted); e.g., H_0: $\mu_1 \gtreqless \mu_2$, H_a: $\mu_1 > \mu_2$. For example, sense of classroom community in graduate students is higher in face-to-face courses than online courses. Here the DV is sense of classroom community and the IV is type course (face-to-face, online).

Operational Definition

An operational definition of a construct is a procedure for measuring and defining a construct and provides an indirect method of measuring something that cannot be measured directly.

Order Effect

The order effect occurs when responses to a series of questions or items depend on the order in which the questions or items are presented.

Ordinal Scale

Ordinal scale variables allow one to rank order the items one measures in terms of which has less and which has more of the quality represented by the variable, but they do not provide information regarding much more. In other words, the values simply express an order of magnitude.

Orthogonal Rotation

Orthogonal rotation in principal components and factor analysis assumes that the factors are at right angles to each other; in other words, the factors are not correlated.

Outlier

Outliers are extreme values. There are regular or mild outliers and extreme outliers. Extreme outliers are any data values that lie more than 3.0 times the IQR below Q_1 or above Q_3. Mild outliers are any data values that lie between 1.5 times and 3.0 times the IQR below Q_1 or above Q_3.

Panel Study

A panel study is a type of longitudinal study that examines the same people from a specific population repeatedly over time.

The sample is called a panel. Panel studies can involve replacement of panel members as they leave the study because they no longer meet certain criteria, such as age or informed consent.

Parallel Design

Parallel design is a type of mixed methods research in which quantitative and qualitative methods are used at the same time.

Parallel Forms Reliability

Parallel-forms reliability is used to measure consistency over two forms of an instrument. Parallel or alternate forms of an instrument are two forms that have similar kinds of items so that they can be interchanged.

Parametric Test

A parametric test is a statistical test that assumes that the data come from a probability distribution and makes inferences about the parameters of the distribution. It also assumes the data are normally distributed and the DV(s) are measured on the interval or ratio scales.

Part (Semi-Partial) Correlation

Part (semi-partial) correlation is the relationship between two variables after removing a third variable from just the IV.

Partial Correlation

Partial correlation is the relationship between two variables after removing the overlap of a third or more other variables from both variables.

Pearson Product-Moment Correlation Test

The Pearson product-moment correlation test (Pearson r) is a parametric procedure that determines the strength and direction of the linear relationship between two continuous variables. Pearson r is symmetric, with the same coefficient value obtained regardless of which variable is the IV and which is the DV.

Percentile

A percentile is a measure that tells one the percent of the total frequency that scored below that measure.

Percentile Rank

A percentile rank is a number between 0 and 100 that shows the percent of cases falling at or below that score.

Phenomenographic Research

Phenomenographic research is a specialized method for describing the different ways in which people conceptualize the world around them (Gall, Gall, & Borg, 2007, p. 497).

Phenomenology

Phenomenology is the study of the world as it appears to individuals when they lay aside the prevailing understandings of those phenomena and revisit their immediate experience of the phenomena (i.e., how individuals construct reality; Gall, Gall, & Borg, 2007, p. 495).

Phi Coefficient

The phi (Φ) test is a nonparametric procedure used to determine if there is an association between columns and rows in 2 x 2 contingency tables. It measures nominal by nominal association based on the chi square statistic. The coefficient is symmetric, so it will produce the same value regardless of how the variables are designated IV and DV. Phi is frequently used to calculate effect size in conjunction with contingency table analysis.

Physiological Measurement

Physiological measurement deals with measurements pertaining to the body. An apparatus can be used to take measurements; e.g., a scale to measure weight, a tape measure to measure height, a device to measure heart rate, or a galvanic skin response sensor to measure anxiety.

Placebo Effect

The placebo effect is a measurable improvement caused by the expectations of participants rather than by any provided intervention.

Point Estimate

A point estimate of a population parameter is a single value of a statistic.

Point-Biserial Correlation

The point-biserial correlation is the special case of the Pearson product moment correlation applied to a dichotomous and a continuous variable. The correlation coefficients produced by the SPSS correlations procedure are point-biserial correlations when these types of variables are used.

Poisson Distribution

Poisson distributions model discrete random variables. A Poisson random variable typically is the count of the number of events that occur in a given time period when the events occur at a constant average rate.

Population Validity

Population validity is a type of external validity that describes how well the sample used is representative of the target population. The focus is on the extent to which the results of a study can be generalized from the specific sample to a larger population.

Post Hoc Multiple Comparison Tests

Post hoc (or follow-up) multiple comparison tests are used following a significant test involving over two groups in order to determine which groups differ from each other. For example, a significant *ANOVA* only provides evidence to the researcher that the groups differ, not where the groups differ. In a three group test the researcher does not know if group A differs significantly from group B and group C or if group B differs significantly from group C. Hence there is a need to conduct post hoc multiple comparison tests to determine where the pairwise differences lie.

Poststructuralism

Poststructuralism is a postmodern approach to the study of systems, especially language as a system, that denies the possibility of finding any inherent meaning in them (Gall, Gall, & Borg, 2007, p. 524).

Practical Significance

Researchers frequently refer to effect size as practical significance in contrast to statistical significance (α). There is no practical significance without statistical significance. While statistical significance is concerned with whether a statistical result is due to chance, practical significance is concerned with whether the result is useful in the real world.

Pre-Experiment

A pre-experimental research design is one that utilizes one of three designs (one-shot case study, one group pretest-posttest, and posttest-only nonequivalent control group) that are universally regarded as very weak and crude.

Predictive Analytics

Predictive analytics use statistical and mathematical techniques to relate a variety of variables and create models used to predict future behavior or outcomes.

Predictive Validity

Predictive validity is the effectiveness of an instrument to predict the outcome of future behavior. Examples of predictor measures related to academic success in college include the Scholastic Aptitude Test (SAT) scores, the Graduate Record Exam (GRE) scores, and high school grade point average (GPA).

Predictor Variable

Predictor variable (or explanatory variable) is another name for the IV in regression analysis.

Principal Components and Factor Analysis

Principal components and factor analysis is a parametric procedure used to analyze interrelationships among a large number of variables and to explain these variables in terms of their common underlying dimensions (i.e., factors or components).

Probability

Probability is the chance that something random will occur. The basic rules of probability are:

- Any probability of any event, $p(E)$, is a number between 0 and 1.

- The probability that all possible outcomes can occur is 1.

- If there are k possible outcomes for a phenomenon and each is equally likely, then each individual outcome has probability 1/k.

- The chance of any (one or more) of two or more events occurring is the union of the events. The probability of the union of events is the sum of their individual probabilities.

- The probability that any event E does not occur is $1 - p(E)$.

- If two events E_1 and E_2 are independent, then the probability of both events is the product of the probabilities for each event, $p(E_1 \text{ and } E_2) = p(E_1)p(E_2)$.

Probability Distribution

A probability distribution is a function that describes the probability of a random variable taking on certain values.

Probability Sampling

Probability sampling uses some form of random selection of research participants from the experimentally accessible population. Only random samples permit true statistical inference and foster external validity.

Probability-Probability Plot

A Probability-Probability (P-P) plot is very similar to a Q-Q plot. The P-P plot plots two cumulative distribution functions against each other. They are used with interval or ratio level data. If the data points do not all fall on the diagonal line, then one can use this plot to visually determine where the data do and do not follow the distribution.

Processing Error

Processing error is a type of non-sampling error that occurs as a result of editing errors, coding errors, data entry errors, programming errors, etc. during data analysis.

Program

A program is a collection of organizational resources that is geared to accomplish a certain major goal or set of goals (Fitzpatrick, Sanders, & Worthen, 2004).

Program Evaluation

Program evaluation is the process of making a judgment concerning the quality of a social program (i.e., regarding merit, worth, and value). Rossi, Lipsey, and Freeman (2004) refine this definition by suggesting program evaluation is the use of social research procedures to systematically investigate the effectiveness of social intervention programs.

Proportional Reduction in Error

Proportional reduction in error (PRE) is a statistical procedure that measures the improvement, expressed as a percentage, in predicting a DV based on knowledge of the IV. Lambda is an example of a PRE measure.

Purposive Sample

A purposive sample is a non-probability sample selected on the basis of the researcher's knowledge of the target population. The researcher then chooses research participants who are similar to this population in attributes of interest.

Qualitative Research

Qualitative research involves the study things in their natural settings, attempting to make sense of or interpret phenomenon in terms of the meanings people bring to them Creswell, 2012). Strauss and Corbin (1998) defined qualitative research as follows:

> Any type of research that produces findings not arrived at by statistical procedures or other means of quantification.... [Q]ualitative analysis [is] a non-mathematical process of interpretation. (pp. 10-11)

Qualitative Variable

A qualitative variable, also known as categorical variable or discrete variable, have values that differs from each other in terms of quality or category (e.g., gender, political party affiliation, etc.).

Quantile-Quantile Plot

The Quantile-Quantile (Q-Q) plot displays the quantiles of a variable's distribution against the quantiles of a normal distribution (or other specified distribution). If the two sets come from a population with the same distribution, the points should fall approximately along the reference line depicted on the plot.

Quantitative Research

A quantitative approach to research is one in which the investigator uses scientific inquiry. It involves the analysis of numerical data using statistical procedures in order to test a hypothesis.

Quantitative Variable

Quantitative variables have values that differ from each other by amount or quantity (e.g., test scores). Ratio and interval scale variable are quantitative variables.

Quartile

A quartile is one of the four divisions of observations that have been grouped into four equal-sized sets based on their statistical rank. $Q_1 = P_{25}$, $Q_2 = P_{50} = Mdn$, $Q_3 = P_{75}$.

Quartile Deviation

Quartile deviation (or semi-interquartile range) is half the IQR. It is sometimes preferred over the range as a measure of dispersion because it is not affected by extreme scores.

Quasi-Experiment

Quasi-experimental research designs lack one or more of the design elements of a true experiment (i.e., manipulation, control, randomization). Quasi-experimental designs were developed to explore causality in situations where one cannot use a true experiment.

Quota Sample

A quota sample is a stratified, non-probability convenience sampling strategy. The sample is formed by selecting research participants that reflect the proportions of the target population on key attributes; e.g., gender, race, socioeconomic status, education level, etc.

Random Assignment

Random assignment is the random allocation of research participants from the sample to groups; e.g., treatment group and control group.

Random Error

Random error is caused by any factors that randomly affect measurement of the variable across the sample. For example, in a particular testing situation, some individuals may be tired while others are alert. If mood affects their performance on a measure, it may artificially inflate the observed scores for some individuals and artificially weaken them for others. Random error does not have consistent effects across the entire sample.

Random Selection

Random selection means that research participants are randomly selected from a designated target population to participate in the study. Random selection refers to how the research sample is formed. Random selection enhances external validity.

Random Variable

A random variable is a variable whose value is determined by chance. For example, if a coin is tossed 30 times, the random variable X is the number of tails that come up. There are two types of random variables: discrete and continuous.

Randomization

Randomization is the random assignment of research participants to groups.

Randomized Block Design

In a randomized block design (matched pairs design), the researcher divides research participants into subgroups called blocks. Then, participants within each block are randomly assigned to treatment conditions.

Range

The range of a distribution is a measure of dispersion calculated by subtracting the minimum score from the maximum score.

Range Effect

Range effects are typically a consequence of using a measure that is inappropriate for a specific group (i.e., too easy, too difficult, not age appropriate, etc.).

Ratio Scale

Ratio scale variables allow one to quantify and compare the sizes of differences between individual values. They also feature an identifiable absolute zero, thus they allow for statements such as x is two times more than y.

Reactive Measure

A measurement is reactive whenever the participant is directly involved in a study and he or she is reacting to the measurement process itself.

Regression

Regression analysis consists of techniques for modeling and analyzing multiple variables for the purpose of prediction and forecasting.

Related Samples Sign Test

The related samples sign test is a nonparametric procedure that compares the signs (plus, minus, or tied) of the differences between data pairs of dependent data (e.g., pretest-posttest observations) or median differences of independent paired observations where the DV is either ordinal or nominal. It does not measure magnitude of differences. It tests for a median difference of zero. The sign test may be used with interval data, but the Wilcoxon signed ranks test is preferred.

Relative Risk

Relative risk, also called the risk ratio, is nonparametric procedure used to determine the relative risk between two dichotomous variables (2 x 2 frequency table). It addresses the question of how much more likely is one condition if the person has a risk factor than if the person does not have the risk factor.

Reliability

Reliability refers to the consistency of measurement. For example, instrument reliability is the extent to which an item, scale, or instrument will yield the same score when administered at different times, locations, or populations, assuming the two administrations do not differ on relevant variables.

Research Design

A research design is a logical blueprint for research that focuses on the logical structure of the research and identifies how research participants are grouped and when data are to be collected.

Research Hypothesis

The research or alternative hypothesis, denoted by H_1 or H_a or H_A, is the hypothesis that sample observations are influenced by a nonrandom cause; i.e., the intervention.

Research Question

A research question is a question that seeks an answer to a researchable problem using quantitative or qualitative research methodologies. A good research question is concise, identifies relevant variables or phenomena, implies a research design and, in the case of quantitative designs, also implies a research hypothesis and statistical procedure. Additionally, a good research question is grounded in current theory and knowledge.

Resentful Demoralization Threat

The resentful demoralization threat to internal validity occurs when there is demoralization and/or resentment that influences the outcome of the research when participants in one group feel that they are receiving less benefit than are those in another group (Gall, Gall, & Borg, 2007).

Residual

A residual is the difference between a predicted and observed value.

Response Bias

Response bias occurs when some individuals selected for the sample are unwilling or unable to respond in a truthful manner to questions or items on a survey.

Response Set Bias

Response-set bias reflects a conscious or subconscious attempt by the respondent to create a certain impression; e.g., social desirability bias.

Response Style Bias

Response style bias implies bias in a certain direction; e.g., acquiescence, extreme and central tendency responding, and negative affectivity bias.

Retrospective Self-Report

A retrospective self-report is a self-report in which a person is asked to look back in time and remember details of a behavior or experience.

Rosenthal Effect

The Rosenthal effect occurs when the researcher unintentionally modifies the behavior of research participants through verbal or nonverbal cues. It is a threat to external validity.

Sample

A sample consists of a individuals drawn from the experimentally accessible population who participate in a research study.

Sampling

Sampling involves the collection, analysis, and interpretation of data gathered from random samples of a population under study. It is concerned with the selection of a subset of individuals from a population to participate in a research study whose results can be generalized to the population.

Sampling Distribution

A sampling distribution is the resultant probability distribution of a statistic created by drawing all possible samples of size N from a given population and computing a statistic – e.g., mean – for each sample.

Sampling Error

Sampling error is an error because the researcher is working with sample data rather than population data. When one takes a sample from a population, as opposed to collecting information from the entire population, there is a probability that one's sample will not precisely reflect the characteristics of the population because of chance error.

Sampling Frame

The sampling frame is the list of ultimate sampling entities, which may be people, organizations, or other units of analysis, from the experimentally accessible population. The list of registered students may be the sampling frame for a survey of the student body at a university. Problems can arise in sampling frame bias. Telephone directories are often used as sampling frames, for example, but tend to under-represent the poor (who have no phones) and the wealthy (who may have unlisted numbers).

Scale of Measurement

The scale of measurement categorizes variables according to the amount of information they convey. The four scales of measurement commonly used in statistical analysis are nominal, ordinal, interval, and ratio scales.

Scaling

Scaling is the branch of measurement that involves the construction of an instrument. Three unidimensional scaling methods frequently used in social science measurement are Likert, Guttman, and Thurstone scalings.

Scatterplot

Scatterplots (also called scattergrams) show the relationship between two variables. For each case, scatterplots depict the value of the IV on the *x*-axis and the value of the DV on the *y*-axis. Each dot on a scatterplot is a case. The dot is placed at the intersection of each case's scores on *x* and *y*. Scatterplots are often used to evaluate linearity between two continuous variables as well as to display strength of relationship.

Scree Plot

The scree plot displays factors/components as the *x*-axis and the corresponding eigenvalues as the *y*-axis in principal components and factor analysis. As one moves to the right, the eigenvalues drop. When the drop ceases and the curve makes an elbow toward a less steep decline, the scree plot suggests that all further factors/components after the one starting the elbow be dropped.

Selection Threat

The selection threat to internal validity results from differential selection of participants to groups (i.e., use of non-equivalent or intact groups; Campbell & Stanley, 1963). Biases are introduced as the result of the differential selection. Self-selection of participants to groups is an example of this threat. These group differences become alternative explanations for any differences observed between groups at the end of the study

Selection-Maturation Interaction Threat

The selection-maturation interaction threat to internal validity comes about if one group matures at a faster rate than the other group, even though groups might be identical at the pretest (Campbell & Stanley, 1963).

Self-Report Measurement

Self-report measurement is a type of measurement in which the researcher asks participants to describe their behavior, to express their opinions, or to engage in interviews or focus groups in order to express their views. Alternatively, study participants can be asked to complete a survey, either face-to-face or online using the Internet. The self-report is the least accurate and most unreliable of the three types of measurements.

Semantic Differential Scale

A semantic differential scale (a type of Likert scale) asks a person to rate a statement based upon a rating scale anchored at each end by opposites. For example,

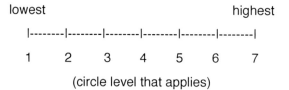

```
        lowest                              highest

        |--------|--------|--------|--------|--------|--------|
         1        2        3        4        5        6        7
```

(circle level that applies)

Semi-Interquartile Range

The semi-interquartile range is half the *IQR*. It is sometimes preferred over the range as a measure of dispersion because it is not affected by extreme scores.

Semi-Structured Interviews

Semi-structured interviews use some pre-formulated questions, but there is no strict adherence to them. New questions might emerge during the interview process.

Semiotics

Semiotics is the study of sign systems, in particular, the study of how objects (e.g., letters of the alphabet) come to convey meaning and how sign systems relate to human behavior (Gall, Gall, & Borg, 2007, p. 522).

Sequential Design

Sequential design is a type of mixed methods research in which quantitative and qualitative methods are used sequentially.

Shapiro-Wilk Test

The one-sample Shapiro-Wilk test is a nonparametric procedure that determines if a sample of data comes from a normal distribution. It is more appropriate for small sample sizes (< 50) but can also handle larger sample sizes, although the Kolmogorov-Smirnov test is preferred in this situation.

Significance Level

The significance level (also called statistical significance level) is the probability of making a Type I error. The criterion for any hypothesis test is established by the researcher. Normally set at .05 for social science research (.10 is sometimes used for exploratory research and .01 or .001 is sometimes used when greater confidence in the results is required). The significance level is set prior to analyzing data.

Simple Random Sample

A simple random sample is a probability sample that is selected from a population in such a manner that all members of the population have an equal and independent chance of being selected.

Single Case Study

A single-case study is a type of experimental study that focuses on a single participant or organism, rather than a group or groups of participants. It is a form of intervention research.

Researchers observe a participant under one condition, then they change conditions and further observe the participant. (The number of conditions introduced depends on the levels of the IV and the specific design.) Evidence that the IV may influence the dependent measure occurs when a participant reacts differently to the different conditions.

Singularity

Singularity refers to perfect correlation where the correlation coefficient equals 1 or -1. It represents an extreme case of multicollinearity.

Skewness

Skewness is a measure of the lack of symmetry. A distribution, or dataset, is symmetric if it is the same to the left and right of the center point. If the data are not distributed symmetrically, the distribution is said to be skewed.

Social Desirability Bias

Social desirability bias occurs during testing or observation when individuals respond or behave in a way they believe is socially acceptable and desirable as opposed to being truthful. It can manifest itself in a number of ways, including being political correct.

Solomon Four-Group Design

The Solomon four-group design is a true experimental design meant to deal with a potential testing threat (Campbell & Stanley, 1963). A testing threat to internal validity occurs when the act of taking a test affects how people score on a retest or posttest. Two of the four groups receive the treatment and two do not. Furthermore, two of the groups receive a pretest and two do not.

Somer's *d*

Somers' *d* is a nonparametric asymmetric procedure that determines the monotonic strength and direction of association between two categorical ordinal variables.

Spearman Rank Order Correlation Test

The Spearman rank order correlation test is a nonparametric procedure that determines the strength and direction of the linear relationship between two variables. It can be used for any type of data, except categories that cannot be ordered. It can be used instead of Pearson r if the parametric assumptions cannot be met. The symbol for the correlation coefficient is r_s (formerly Spearman rho).

Spearman-Brown Prophecy Formula

The Spearman-Brown prophecy formula is used in the split-half reliability procedure. The split-half procedure splits the scale into two parts and examines the correlation between the parts. The correlation obtained, however, represents the reliability coefficient of only half the test, and since reliability is related to the length of the test, the Spearman-Brown prophecy formula is used to make this correction.

Specification Error

Specification error is non-sampling error that occurs when the measurement instrument is not properly aligned with the construct that is measured. In other words, the construct validity of the instrument is weak.

Sphericity

Sphericity is an assumption in repeated measures *ANOVA/ MANOVA* designs. In a repeated measures design, the univariate *ANOVA* tables will not be interpreted properly unless the variance/covariance matrix of the DVs is circular in form. In other words, sphericity means that the variance of the difference between all pairs of means is constant across all combinations of related groups.

Split-Half Reliability

Split-half is a model of internal consistency reliability that splits the scale into two parts and examines the correlation between the two parts.

Spurious Relationship

A spurious relationship exists between two variables that are significantly related to each other when there is no direct causal connection due to the presence of a third (or more) variable, often referred to as a confounding or lurking variable, which is related to each of the original variables. The spurious relationship between the original two variables becomes evident when the original relationship becomes insignificant after controlling (i.e., removing) the effects of the third (or more) variable.

Standard Deviation

Standard deviation (*SD*) is a measure of variability or dispersion of a set of data. It is calculated from the deviations between each data value and the sample mean. It is also the square root of the variance.

Standard Error of Measurement

The standard error of measurement (SE_m) is used to determine the range of certainty around an individual's reported score. If one SE_m is added to an observed score and one SE_m is subtracted from it, one can be 68% sure that the true score falls within the created range.

Standard Error of the Estimate

The standard error of the estimate is the standard deviation of the prediction errors. Approximately 68% of actual scores will fall between ±1 standard error of their predicted values.

Standard Error of the Mean

The standard error of the mean is the standard deviation of the sampling distribution of the mean.

Standard Normal Distribution

The standard normal distribution is a normal distribution that has a mean of 0 and a standard deviation of 1. *Z*-scores are used to represent the standard normal distribution.

Standard Score

A standard score is a general term referring to a score that has been transformed for reasons of convenience, comparability, etc. The basic type of standard score, known as a *z*-score, is an expression of the deviation of a score from the mean score of the group in relation to the standard deviation of the scores of the group.

Standardized Residual

A standardized residual (*ZRE*) is a residual divided by the standard error of the estimate. Standardized residuals should behave like a sample from a normal distribution with a mean of 0 and a standard deviation of 1. The standardized residual is essentially a z-score. So any observation with a standardized residual greater than |2| would be viewed as an outlier or an extreme observation. Standardized residuals are useful in detecting anomalous observations or outliers.

Stanine Score

Stanine scores are groups of percentile ranks consisting of nine specific bands, with the 5th stanine centered on the mean, the first stanine being the lowest, and the ninth stanine being the highest. Each stanine is one-half standard deviation wide.

Static Group Comparison Design

A static group comparison design is a pre-experiment representing a nonequivalent posttest only design.

Statistical Power

Statistical power or observed power of a statistical test is the probability that a false H_0 is rejected. It is equal to 1 minus the probability of accepting a false H_0 $(1 - \beta)$.

Statistical Regression Threat

The statistical regression threat to internal validity can occur when selecting participants on the basis of extremely low (or high) score on some test, giving them some intervention, and then retesting them (Campbell & Stanley, 1963). If scores have gone up (or down) significantly, a false conclusion can be drawn that this is due to the intervention. It is actually a statistical artifact known as regression to the mean. Extreme scores tend to move toward the center of the distribution the next time they are measured.

Stem-and-Leaf Plot

A stem and leaf plot is a type of graph that is similar to a histogram. The purpose is to allow one to identify exact scores in the plot and also get a sense of the shape of the distribution. It depicts the shape of a set of data in a sideway orientation and provides detail regarding individual values. The digits in the largest place are the stems and the digits in the smallest place are the leaves. The leaves are displayed to the right of the stem.

Stratified Random Sample

A stratified random sample is a probability sample in which the accessible population is first divided into subsets or strata; e.g., a population of college students can first be divided into freshman, sophomores, juniors, and seniors, and then individuals are selected at random from each stratum.

Structuralism

Structuralism focuses on the systemic properties of phenomena, including relationships among elements of a system (Gall, Gall, & Borg, 2007, p. 523).

Structured Interviews

Structured interviews use pre-formulated questions and regulate the order of the questions and time available.

Studentized Residual

A studentized residual (SRE) is a type of standardized residual that recognizes the error associated with predicting values far from the mean of x is larger than the error associated with predicting values closer to the mean of x. The studentized residual boosts the size of residuals for points distant from the mean of x.

Sum of Squares

Sum of squares (*SS*) is the sum of squared differences from the mean. Type III *SS* used by SPSS adjusts *SS* of a given effect for all other effects in the model statement, regardless of whether they contain the given effect or not. For example, the main effects will be adjusted for the interaction effect.

Summative Evaluation

Summative evaluations examine the effects or outcomes of a program – they summarize it by describing what happens subsequent to delivery of the program, assessing whether the program can be said to have caused the outcome, determining the overall impact of the causal factor beyond only the immediate target outcomes, and estimating the relative costs associated with the program.

Suppressor Variable

A suppressor variable is a variable that appears to be positively related to the DV but when included in the regression model has a negative regression coefficient. This is due to the fact that an IV (the suppressor variable) is highly related to another IV and any variability that is explained in the DV by the suppressor variable is explained by the other IV. Conger (1974) provides the following definition of a suppressor variable: "...a variable which increases the predictive validity of another variable (or set of variables) by its inclusion in a regression equation" (pp. 36-37).

Symbolic Interactionism

Symbolic interactionism is the study of how individuals engage in social transactions and how these transactions contribute to the creation and maintenance of social structures and the individual's self-identity (Gall, Gall, & Borg, 2007, p. 500).

Systematic Error

Systematic error is caused by any factors that systematically affect measurement of the variable across the entire sample.

T-Score

A *T*-score is standard score with a mean of 50 and a standard deviation of 10.

Target Population

The target population refers to the group of individuals or objects to which researchers are interested in generalizing research study conclusions.

Test Analysis

Test analysis examines how the test items perform as a set.

Test-Retest Reliability

Test-retest reliability is a method of estimating the stability of scores generated by a measurement instrument over time. It involves administering the same instrument to the same individuals at two different times. The test-retest method should only be used when the variables being measured are considered to be stable over the test-retest period.

Testing Threat

The testing threat to internal validity consists of the effects of taking a pretest upon scores of a posttest.

Thurstone Scale

The Thurstone scale consists of a series of items. Respondents rate each item on a 1- to-11 scale in terms of how much each statement elicits a favorable attitude representing the entire range of attitudes from extremely favorable to extremely unfavorable. A middle rating is for items in which participants hold neither a favorable nor unfavorable opinion.

Time Series Design

A time-series design is a quasi-experiment that involves repeated measurements or observations of the same group over time, both before and after treatment (Campbell & Stanley, 1963). The interval between observations is held constant throughout the entire range of observations, to include the interval between the last pretest and the first posttest. The number of pretest and posttest observations can vary.

Tolerance

Tolerance is "the proportion of the variability in one independent variable not explained by the other independent variables" (Vogt, 2005, p. 325). It is mathematically defined as 1 − R^2, where R^2 is the multiple correlation of a given independent regressed on all other independent variables. If the tolerance value is less than some cutoff value, usually .20, the independent should be dropped from the analysis due to multicollinearity. This is better than just using simple $r > .90$ since tolerance looks at the IV in relation to all other independents and thus takes interaction effects into account in addition to simple correlations.

Total Design Method

Total Design Method (TDM) is a methodology developed by D. A. Dillman to obtain high response rates from survey research.

Trend Study

A trend study is a type of longitudinal study that involves identifying a population and examining changes within that population repeatedly over time; e.g., university faculty. Typically, trend studies are not composed of the same people at different time periods.

Triangulation

Triangulation is the use of more than one measurement technique to measure a single construct in order to enhance the confidence in and reliability of research findings.

True Experiment

True experiments are the model for research conducted in the natural and social sciences. Characteristics of true experiments include manipulation of the IV, use of control groups, and random assignment of research participants to groups.

Two-Tailed Hypothesis

A two-tailed hypothesis is non-directional (i.e., the direction of difference or association is not predicted); e.g., H_0: $\mu_1 = \mu_2$, H_a: $\mu_1 \neq \mu_2$. For example, a two-tailed test determines whether or not the mean of the sample group is either less than or greater than the mean of the control group.

Type I Error

Type I error (α) is the probability of deciding that a significant effect is present when it is not. That is, it is the probability of rejecting a true null hypothesis.

Type II Error

Type II error (β) is the probability of not detecting a significant effect when one exists. That is, it is the probability of not rejecting a false null hypothesis.

Uniform Distribution

Uniform distributions model both continuous random variables and discrete random variables. The values of a uniform random variable are uniformly distributed over an interval.

Unstandardized Residual

An unstandardized residual (*RES*) is the difference between the observed value of the DV and the predicted value. The residual and its plot are useful for checking how well the regression line fits the data and, in particular if there is any systematic lack of fit.

Unstructured Interview

An unstructured interview has few if any pre-formulated questions. The interviewees are free to say whatever they desire.

Variable

A variable is anything that is measured – e.g., characteristic, attitude, behavior, weight, height, etc. – that possesses a value that changes within the scope of a given research study. Variables appear as columns in SPSS data view.

Variance

Variance is a measure of variability derived from the sum of the deviation scores from the mean raised to the second power (i.e., the second moment of the distribution). It is the square of the standard deviation.

Variance Inflation Factor

The variance inflation factor (VIF; reciprocal of tolerance) quantifies how much the variance is inflated and reflects the presence or absence of multicollinearity. The VIF has a range 1 to infinity. When VIF is high there is high multicollinearity and instability of the *b* and beta coefficients. VIF and tolerance are found in the SPSS output section on collinearity statistics. A common cutoff threshold is a VIF value of 10, which corresponds to a tolerance value of .10.

Variance Proportion

Variance proportions represent the proportion of variance for each regression coefficient (and its associated variable) attributable to each condition index. Coefficients that have high proportions for the same condition index are largely responsible for the amount of multicollinearity identified by the condition index. A value of .50 is commonly used as a cut-off threshold.

Varimax Rotation

Varimax rotation is an orthogonal rotation of the factor axes to maximize the variance of the squared loadings of a factor (column) on all the variables (rows) in a factor matrix. A Varimax solution yields results that make it as easy as possible to identify each variable with a single factor. This is the most common rotation option.

Volunteer Bias

Volunteer bias occurs when sample members are self-selected. Volunteers tend to overrepresent individuals who have strong opinions.

Wald-Wolfowitz Runs Test

The Wald-Wolfowitz runs test is a nonparametric procedure that tests for the randomness of a distribution. A run is any sequence of cases having the same value. The total number of runs in a sample is a measure of randomness in the order of the cases in the sample. Too many or too few runs can suggest a nonrandom ordering.

Wilcoxon Signed Ranks Test

The Wilcoxon signed-ranks test is a nonparametric procedure that compares median scores obtained from two dependent (related) samples. The test factors in the size as well as the sign of the paired differences. It assesses the null hypothesis that the medians of two samples do not differ, or that the median of one sample does not differ from a known value. The Wilcoxon test is more powerful than the related samples sign test.

Within Subjects Design

Within-subjects or repeated measures designs are quantitative research designs in which the researcher is comparing the same participants repeatedly over time.

Z-Score

A *z*-score distribution is the standard normal distribution, $N(0,1)$, with mean = 0 and standard deviation = 1.

Zero Order Correlation

Zero-order correlation is the relationship between two variables, while ignoring the influence of other variables.

References

American Psychological Association. (2010). *Publication manual of the American Psychological Association* (6th ed.). Washington, DC: Author.

Anastasi, A. (1988). *Psychological testing.* New York, NY: Macmillan.

Audi, R. (2011). *Epistemology: A contemporary introduction to the theory of knowledge* (3rd ed). New York, NY: Routledge.

Barcikowski, R., & Stevens, J. P. (1975). A Monte Carlo study of the stability of canonical correlations, canonical weights, and canonical variate-variable correlations. *Multivariate Behavioral Research, 10*, 353-364.

Baron, R. M., & Kenny, D. A. (1986). The moderator-mediator variable distinction in social psychological research: Conceptual, strategic, and statistical considerations. *Journal of Personality and Social Psychology, 51*, 1173-1182.

Bartos, R. B. (1992). *Educational research.* Shippensburg, PA: Shippensburg University.

Bauer, H. H. (1994). *Scientific literacy and the myth of the scientific method.* Urbana, IL: University of Illinois Press.

Berry, W. D., & Feldman, S. (1985). *Multiple regression in practice.* Newbury Park, CA: Sage.

Biemer, P. P., & Lyberg, L. E. (2003). *Introduction to survey quality: Wiley series in survey methodology.* Hoboken, NJ: Wiley.

Bishop, Y. M., Feinberg, S. E., & Holland, P. W. (1975). *Discrete multivariate analysis: Theory and practice.* Cambridge, MA: MIT Press.

Bogdan, R. C., & Biklen, S. K. (1998). *Qualitative research for education: An introduction to theory and methods.* Boston, MA: Allyn and Bacon.

Bracht, G. H., & Glass, G. V. (1968). The external validity of experiments. *American Education Research Journal, 5*, 437-474.

Bradley, J. (1968). *Distribution-free statistical tests.* Englewood Cliffs, NJ: Prentice-Hall.

Brewer, M. (2000). Research design and issues of validity. In H. Reis & C. Judd (Eds), *Handbook of research methods in social and personality psychology.* Cambridge:Cambridge University Press.

Brooks, P., & Baumeister, A. (1977). A plea for consideration of ecological validity in the experimental analysis of psychology of mental retardation: A guest editorial. American *Journal of Mental Retardation, 81*, 407-416.

Brown, M. B., & Forsythe, A. B. (1974). Robust tests for the equality of variances. *Journal of the American Statistical Association, 69*, 364-367.

Bryant, F. B., & Yarnold, P. R. (1995). Principal-components analysis and confirmatory factor analysis. In L. G. Grimm & P. R. Yarnold (Eds.), *Reading and understanding multivariate statistics* (pp. 99-136). Washington, DC: American Psychological Association.

Bryman, A. (2007). Barriers to integrating quantitative and qualitative research. *Journal of Mixed Methods Research, 1*, 8-22.

Campbell, D. T., & Stanley, J. C. (1963). Experimental and quasi-experimental designs for research on teaching. In N. L. Gage (Ed.), *Handbook of research on teaching.* Chicago, IL: Rand McNally.

Chakravarti, I. M., Laha, R. G., & Roy, J. (1967). *Handbook of methods of applied statistics, Volume I.* New York: John Wiley & Sons.

Chatterjee, S., & Hadi, A. S. (1988). *Sensitivity analysis in linear regression.* New York, NY: John Wiley & Sons.

Cohen. J. (1988). *Statistical power analysis for the behavioral sciences* (2nd ed.). Hillsdale, NJ: Lawrence-Erlbaum.

Cohen, J., & Cohen, P. (1983). *Multiple regression/correlation for the behavioral sciences* (2nd ed.). Hillsdale, NJ: Erlbaum.

Comrey, A. L., & Lee, H. B. (1992). *A first course in factor analysis*. Hillsdale, NJ: Erlbaum.

Conger, A. J. (1974). A revised definition for suppressor variables: A guide to their identification and interpretation. *Educational and Psychological Measurement, 34*, 35-46.

Cook, T. D., & Campbell, D. T. (1979). *Quasi-experimentation: Design and analysis issues for field settings*. Boston, MA: Houghton Mifflin.

Creswell, J. W. (2007). *Qualitative inquiry and research design: Choosing among five approaches* (2nd ed.). Thousand Oaks, CA: Sage.

Creswell, J. W. (2012). *Educational research: Planning, conducting, and evaluating quantitative and qualitative research* (4th ed.). Boston, MA: Pearson.

Cronbach, L. J., & Furby, L. (1970) How should we measure change – or should we? *Psychological Bulletin 74*, 68.

Denzin, N. K. (2008). *Qualitative inquiry under fire: Toward a new paradigm dialogue*. Walnut Creek, CA: Left Coast Press.

Denzin, N. K., & Lincoln, Y. (2000). Introduction: The discipline and practice of qualitative research. In N. K. Denzin & Y. Lincoln (Eds.), *Handbook of qualitative research* (2nd ed., pp.1-17). Thousand Oaks, CA: Sage.

Diekhoff, G. (1992). *Statistics for the social and behavioral sciences: Univariate, bivariate, multivariate*. Dubuque, IA: Wm. C. Brown.

Dillman, D. A. (1978). *Mail and telephone surveys: The total design method*. New York, NY: Wiley.

Dunteman, G. H. (1989). *Principal components analysis. Quantitative applications in the social sciences series, No. 69*. Thousand Oaks, CA: Sage.

Ebel, R. L., & Frisbie, D. A. (1986). *Essentials of educational measurement*. Englewood Cliffs, NJ: Prentice-Hall.

Fetterman, D. M. (1998). *Ethnography: Step by step* (2nd ed.). Thousand Oaks, CA: Sage.

Fink, A. (Ed.). (1995). *How to measure survey reliability and validity*, Vol. 7. Thousand Oaks, CA: Sage.

Fish, L. J. (1988). Methods, plainly speaking: Why multivariate methods are usually vital. *Measurement and Evaluation in Counseling and Development, 21*, 130-137.

Fitzpatrick, J. L., Sanders, J. R., & Worthen, B. R. (2004). *Program evaluation: Alternative approaches and practical guidelines* (3rd ed.). New York, NY: Allyn & Bacon.

Flaherty, T. B., Honeycutt, E. D., Jr., & Powers, D. (1998). Exploring text-based electronic mail surveys as means of primary data collection. *The 1998 Academy of Marketing Science National Conference Proceedings*, 260-264.

Flinders, D. J. (1992). In search of ethical guidance: constructing a basis for dialogue. *Qualitative Studies in Education, 5*(2), 101-115.

Gall, M. D., Gall, J. P., & Borg, W. R. (2007). *Educational research: An introduction* (8th ed.). White Plains, NY: Longman.

Gay, L. R. (1987). *Educational research: Competencies for analysis and application* (3rd ed.). Columbus, OH: Merrill.

Glass, G. V. (1976). Primary, secondary, and meta analysis of research. *The Educational Researcher, 10*, 3-8.

Glesne, C., & Peshkin, A. (1992). *Becoming qualitative researchers: An introduction*. White Plains, NY: Longman.

Gorsuch, R. L. (1983). *Factor analysis*. Hillsdale, NJ: Lawrence Erlbaum.

Green, S. B., & Salkind, N. J. (2008). *Using SPSS for Windows and Macintosh* (5th ed.). Upper Saddle River, NJ: Pearson,

Grimm, Y. G., & Yarnold, P. R. (2000). *Reading and understanding more multivariate statistics*. Washington, DC: American Psychological Association.

Grissom, R. J., & Kim, J. J. (2012). *Effect sizes for research: Univariate and multivariate applications* (2nd ed.). New York, NY: Taylor & Francis.

Gulliksen, H. (1987). *Theory of mental tests*. Hillsdale, NJ: Erlbaum.

Henrysson, S. (1971). Gathering, analyzing, and using data on test items. In R. L. Thorndike (Ed.), *Educational measurement* (2nd ed., pp. 130-159). Washington, DC: American Council on Education.

Heppner, P. P., Kivlighan, D. M., Jr., & Wampold, B. E. (1999). *Research design in counseling* (2nd ed.). Belmont, CA: Wadsworth.

Hinkle, D. E., Wiersma, W., & Jurs, S. G. (1998). *Applied statistics for the behavioral sciences* (4th ed.). Chicago, IL: Rand McNally College Publishing.

Holm, S. (1979). A simple sequentially rejective multiple test procedure. *Scandinavian Journal of Statistics, 6*, 65-70.

Hopkins, J. D. (1998). *Educational and psychological measurement and evaluation*. Needham Heights, MA: Allyn & Bacon.

Hosmer, D., & Lemeshow, S. (2000). *Applied logistic regression* (2nd. ed.). New York, NY: John Wiley & Sons, Inc.

Hutcheson, G., & Sofroniou, N. (1999). *The multivariate social scientist: Introductory statistics using generalized linear models*. Thousand Oaks, CA: Sage.

Huxley, E. (1959). *The flame trees of Thika*. London: Chatto and Windus.

Isaac, S., & Michael, W. B. (1990). *Handbook in research and evaluation for education and the behavioral sciences* (2d ed.). San Diego, CA: EdITS.

Jackson, J. E. (2003). *A user's guide to principal components*. New York, NY: John Wiley & Sons.

Jacob, E. (1987). Qualitative research traditions: A review. *Review of Educational Research, 57*(1), 1-50.

Johnson, R. B. (1997). Examining the validity structure of qualitative research. *Education, 118*(2), 282-292.

Johnson, C. E., Wood, R., & Blinkhorn, S. F. (1988). Spriouser and spriouser: The use of ipsative personality tests. *Journal of Occupational Psychology, 61*, 153-162.

Kaiser, H. F. (1970). A second generation little jiffy. *Psychometrika, 35*, 401- 415.

Kalton, G., & Schuman, H. (1982), The effect of the question on survey responses: A review. *Journal of the Royal Statistical Society, 145*, Part 1, 42-73

Kelle, U. (Ed). (1995). *Computer-aided qualitative data analysis theory, methods and practice.* Newbury Park, CA: Sage.

Keppel, G. (2004). *Design and analysis: A researcher's handbook* (4th ed.). Upper Saddle River, NJ: Prentice-Hall.

Kerlinger, F. N. (1973). *Foundations of behavioral research* (2nd ed.). New York, NY: Holt, Rinehart & Winston.

Kim, J., & Mueller, C. W. (1978). Factor analysis: Statistical methods and practical issues. *Quantitative Applications in the Social Sciences Series, No. 14.* Thousand Oaks, CA: Sage.

Kline, R. B. (2004). *Beyond significance testing.* Washington, DC: American Psychological Association.

Krueger, R. A. (1994). *Focus groups* (2nd ed.). Thousand Oaks, CA: Sage.

Lanyon, R. I. & Goodstein, L. D. (1997). *Personality assessment* (3rd ed.). New York, NY: Wiley.

Leech, N. L., & Onwuegbuzie, A. J. (2002). A call for greater use of nonparametric statistics. *Paper presented at the Annual Meeting of the Mid-South Educational Research Association,* Chattanooga, TN, November 6-8.

Lord, F. M. (1952). The relationship of the reliability of multiple-choice test to the distribution of item difficulties. *Psychometrika, 18*, 181-194.

Manyika, J., Chui, M., Brown, B., Bughin, J., Dobbs, R., Roxburgh, C., & Byers, A. H. (2011, May). B*ig data: The next* *frontier for innovation, competition, and productivity.* Retrieved from McKinsey Global Institute website: http://www.mckinsey.com/~/media/McKinsey/dotcom/Insights%20and%20pubs/MGI/Research/Technology%20and%20Innovation/Big%20Data/MGI_big_data_full_report.ashx

McGraw, K. O., & Wong, S. P. (1996). Forming inferences about some intraclass correlation coefficients. *Psychological Methods, Vol. 1, 1,* 30-46

McMillan, J. H., & Schumacher, S. S. (1997). *Research in education: A conceptual introduction.* New York, NY: Longman.

Merriam, S. B. (1988). *Case study research in education: A qualitative approach.* San Francisco, CA: Jossey-Bass.

Miles, M .B., & Huberman, A. M. (1980). *Qualitative data analysis: An expanded sourcebook* (2nd ed.). Newbury Park, CA: Sage.

Miller, R., Jr. (1986). *Beyond ANOVA, basics of applied statistics.* New York, NY: John Wiley & Sons.

Morgan, D., & Krueger, R. (1993). When to use focus groups and why. In D. Morgan (Ed.), *Successful focus groups: Advancing the state of the art* (pp. 3-20). Newbury Park, CA: Sage.

Moore, D. S., & McCabe, G. P. (1999). *Introduction to the practice of statistics* (3rd ed.). New York, NY: Freeman.

Nardi, P. M. (2006). *Doing survey research: A guide to quantitative methods* (2nd ed.). Boston, MA: Pearson.

Neuman, W. L. (2011). *Social research methods: qualitative and quantitative approaches* (7th ed.). Boston, MA: Allyn & Bacon.

Newman, I., & Benz, C. R. (1998). *Qualitative-quantitative research methodology: Exploring the interactive continuum.* Carbondale, IL: University of Illinois Press.

Norusis, M. (2011). *IBM SPSS Statistics 19 advanced statistical procedures companion.* Boston, MA: Addison Wesley.

Nunnally, J. C. (1975). *Introduction to statistics for psychology and education.* New York, NY: McGraw Hill.

Nunnally, J. C., & Bernstein, I. H. (1994). *Psychometric theory* (3rd ed.). New York, NY: McGraw-Hill.

Olson, C. L. (1976). On choosing a test statistic in multivariate analyses of variance. *Psychological Bulletin, 83*, 579-586.

Onwuegbuzie, A. J. (2000, November). Effect sizes in qualitative research. *Paper presented at the Annual Meeting of the Association for the Advancement of Educational Research*, Ponte Vedra, FL. Retrieved from the ERIC website: http://www.eric.ed.gov/PDFS/ED448206.pdf

Patton, M. Q. (2002). *Qualitative research & evaluation methods* (3rd ed.). Thousand Oaks, CA: Sage.

Peat, J. (2001). *Health science research: A handbook of quantitative methods*. Sydney, Australia: Allen and Unwin.

Pedhazur, E. J., (1997). *Multiple regression in behavioral research* (3rd ed.). Orlando, FL: Harcourt Brace.

Pedhazur, E. J., & Schmelkin, L. P. (1991). *Measurement, design, and analysis*. Hillsdale, NJ: Lawrence Erlbaum.

Posavac, E. J., & Carey, R. G. (2002). *Program evaluation: methods and case studies* (6th ed.). Englewood Cliffs, NJ: Prentice-Hall.

Protection of Human Subjects, 45 C.F.R. § 46.102 (2009).

Rea, L. M., & Parker, R. A. (2005). *Designing and conducting survey research* (3rd ed.). San Francisco, CA: Jossey-Bass.

Reichardt, C. S., & Cook, T. D. (1979). Beyond qualitative versus quantitative methods. In T. D. Cook & C. S. Reichardt (Eds.), *Qualitative and quantitative methods in evaluation research* (pp. 7-32). Beverly Hills, CA: Sage.

Rosenzweig, P. (2007). *The halo effect*. New York, NY: Free Press.

Rosenthal, R., & Rosnow, R. L. (1975). *The volunteer subject*. New York, NY: Wiley.

Rossi, P. H., Lipsey, M. W., & Freeman, H. E. (2004). *Evaluation: A systematic approach* (6th ed.). Thousand Oaks, CA: Sage.

Rosnow, R. L., & Rosenthal, R. (1996). Computing contrasts, effect sizes, and counternulls on other people's published data: General procedures for research consumers. *Psychological Methods, 1*, 331-340.

Rosnow, R. L., & Rosenthal, R. (2003). Effect sizes for experimenting psychologists. *Canadian Journal of Experimental Psychology, 57*, 221-237.

Rovai, A. P. (2002). Development of an instrument to measure classroom community. *Internet & Higher Education, 5*(3), 197-211. (ERIC Document Reproduction Service No. EJ663068)

Rovai, A. P. (2003). A practical framework for evaluating online distance education programs. *Internet & Higher Education, 6*(2), 109-124. (ERIC Document Reproduction Service No. EJ668373)

Rovai, A. P., & Wighting, M. J. (2005). Feelings of alienation and community among higher education students in a virtual classroom. *Internet & Higher Education, 8*(2), 97-110. (ERIC Document Reproduction Service No. EJ803728)

Schwandt, T. A. (1994). Constructivism, interpretivist approaches to human inquiry. In N. K. Denzin & Y. S. Lincoln (Eds.), *Handbook of qualitative research* (pp. 118-137). Thousand Oaks, CA: Sage.

Scriven, M. (1967). The methodology of evaluation. In R. E. Stake (Ed.). *Perspectives of curriculum evaluation* (Vol. 1, pp. 39-55). Chicago, IL: Rand McNally.

Shadish, W. R., Cook, T. D., & Campbell, D. T. (2002). *Experimental and quasi-experimental design for generalized causal inference*. Boston, MA: Houghton-Mifflin.

Shapiro, S. S., & Wilk, M. B. (1965). An analysis of variance test for normality (complete samples). *Biometrika 52*(3-4): 591–611.

Shrout, P. E., & Fleiss, J. L. (1979). Intraclass correlations: Uses in assessing rater reliability. *Psychological Bulletin, 2*, 420-428.

Silverman, D. (1993). The logic of qualitative methodology. In D. Silverman (Ed.), *Interpreting qualitative data* (pp. 20-29). London, England: Sage.

Smith, M. F. (1989). *Evaluability assessment: A practical approach.* Clemson, SC: Kluwer Academic.

Snedecor, G. W., & Cochran, W. G. (1989). *Statistical methods* (8th ed.). Ames, IA: Iowa State University Press.

Stake, R. E. (1978, February). The case study method in social inquiry. *Educational Researcher, 7*(2), 5-8.

Stevens, J. (2002). *Applied multivariate statistics for the social sciences* (4th ed.). Mahwah, NJ: Lawrence Erlbaum.

Strauss, A., & Corbin, J. (1998). *Basics of qualitative research: Techniques and procedures for developing grounded theory* (2nd ed.). Thousand Oaks, CA: Sage.

Stufflebeam, D. L. (2000). The CIPP model for evaluation. In D. L. Stufflebeam, G. F. Madaus, & T. Kellaghan, (Eds.), *Evaluation models* (2nd ed.). (Chapter 16). Boston, MA: Kluwer Academic Publishers.

Tabachnick, B., & Fidell, L. (2007). *Using multivariate statistics* (5th ed.). Needham Heights, MA: Allyn & Bacon.

Thompson, B., & Levitov, J. E. (1985). Using microcomputers to score and evaluate test items. *Collegiate Microcomputer, 3*, 163-168.

Tiku, M. L. (1971). Power function of the F-test under non-normal situations. *Journal of the American Statistical Association, 66*, 913-915.

Trochim, W. M. (2006a). Deduction & induction. In W. M. Trochim (Ed.), *The research methods knowledge base* (2nd ed.). Retrieved from http://www.socialresearchmethods.net/kb/dedind.php

Trochim, W. M. (2006b). Introduction to evaluation. In W. M. Trochim (Ed.), *The research methods knowledge base* (2nd ed.). Retrieved from http://www.socialresearchmethods.net/kb/intreval.php

Trochim, W., & Land, D. (1982). Designing designs for research. *The Researcher, 1*(1), 1-6.

Vogt, P. (2005). *Dictionary of statistics and methodology* (3rd ed.). London, England: Sage.

Wallen, N., & Fraenkel, J. (2001). *Educational research: A guide to the process*. Mahwah, NJ: Lawrence Erlbaum.

Wholey, J. S. (1979). *Evaluation: Promise and performance*. Washington, DC: The Urban Institute.

Wholey, J. S. (1994). Assessing the feasibility and likely usefulness of evaluation. In K. E. Newcomer, H. P. Hatry, & J. S. Wholey (Eds.), *Handbook of practical program evaluation* (pp. 15-39). San Francisco, CA: Josey-Bass.

Wiersma, W., & Jurs, S. G. (1990). *Educational measurement and testing* (2nd ed.). Boston, MA: Allyn and Bacon.

Worthen, B. R., Sanders, J. R., & Fitzpatrick, J. L. (1997). *Program evaluation: alternative approaches and practical guidelines* (2nd ed.). New York, NY: Longman.

Yin, R. K. (1989). *Case study research: Design and methods* (Revised Edition). London, England: Sage.

About the Authors

Alfred P. (Fred) Rovai

Fred, a native of San Jose, California, received a BA degree (mathematics) from San Jose State University, an MA degree (public administration) from the University of Northern Colorado, and an MS degree (education) and PhD degree (academic leadership) from Old Dominion University. He also completed postgraduate work in systems management at the University of Southern California and possesses a postgraduate professional license in mathematics from the Commonwealth of Virginia. Following his retirement from the U.S. Army he served as a faculty member at Old Dominion University and then at Regent University and retired in December 2011 as Associate Vice President for Academic Affairs, Regent University. During his career in academe he authored or co-authored three books and more than 50 articles in scholarly journals and served on four editorial review boards. He presently writes, consults, and serves as an adjunct professor teaching research and statistics courses online.

aprovai@mac.com

Jason D. Baker

Jason is a professor of education at Regent University where he serves as the distance education advisor in a blended EdD program. He earned his BS degree in electrical engineering from Bucknell University, MA degree in education from The George Washington University, and PhD in communication from Regent University. Jason has authored or edited Internet-related books, numerous publications and presentations related to online learning, and currently serves on four editorial review boards for academic journals interested in education and technology. Additionally, he has consulted with various organizations regarding the effective use of educational technology and the development and management of online learning programs. Prior to joining the Regent University faculty, he served as an educational consultant and senior systems engineer at Loyola College in Maryland and associate engineer (communications) at IBM Federal Systems Company.

jbaker@regent.edu

Michael K. Ponton

Michael holds an EdD degree in higher education administration and a MS degree in engineering, both from The George Washington University, and a BS degree in physics from Old Dominion University. He presently serves as professor of education at Regent University, teaching primarily research related courses in EdD and PhD programs. He has published extensively in the field of self-directed learning, where his research interests include adult learning, personal initiative, autonomous learning, and social cognitive theory. He serves on the editorial boards for the International Journal of Self-Directed Learning and New Horizons in Adult Education and Human Resource Development. Before coming to Regent University, he was associate professor of higher education at the University of Mississippi. Prior to entering academe full-time, he was an aerospace engineer for the National Aeronautics and Space Administration at the Langley Research Center.

michpon@regent.edu

Index

CPSIA information can be obtained at www.ICGtesting.com
Printed in the USA
BVOW042332150812

297923BV00006B/122/P